History of the American Greyhound Derby

By James J. Smith

With David Jeswald

History of the American Greyhound Derby
Copyright © 2011 by Big Jackpot Betting

ISBN 978-1467945561

Table of Contents

Preface 5

Past Derby Champions List 6

Introduction 7

The Taunton Years 9

The Raynham Years 79

The Lincoln Years 91

The Mardi Gras Years 153

History of
The American Greyhound Derby

Joseph M. Linsey

Founder of the

American Greyhound Derby

Greyhound World Awaits American Derby

Preface

This book is comprised from almost 100 percent of material supplied from the private collection of David Jeswald. The compilation of greyhound memorabilia assembled by Mr. Jeswald is most likely the most extensive archive of United States Greyhound Racing history that exists today. With a personal history as a greyhound fan that spans almost forty years it is safe to say that Mr Jeswald is indeed a greyhound racing aficionado. It is through the foresight and generously of Mr Jeswald that the History of the American Greyhound Derby has been preserved in the pages of this book. Fans of greyhound racing everywhere are fortunate that Mr Jeswald opened up his collection for all of us to enjoy and for that we owe him our gratitude.

Derby Finalist Rastro Ricky owned by David Jeswald

Past American Greyhound Derby Champions

Oklahoman	*1949*	Texas Brass	*1979*
Real Huntsman	*1950*	Position	*1980*
Real Huntsman	*1951*	Devon Unocopy	*1981*
On The Line	*1952*	Mr Wizard	*1982*
However	*1953*	Anxious Wait	*1983*
MelloJean	*1954*	Dutch Bahama	*1984*
Koliga	*1955*	Dutch Bahama	*1985*
Go Rock	*1956*	Prince Proper	*1986*
Clydesdale	*1957*	Fuel's Stargazer	*1987*
Feldcrest	*1958*	Ico Evan	*1988*
Go Super	*1959*	Winterfest	*1989*
Serape	*1960*	Swedish Episode	*1990*
Velvet Sis	*1961*	Pro's Hi Gear	*1991*
Cactus Noel	*1962*	Boligee Champ	*1992*
Thermel	*1963*	Wiki Wiki Peka	*1993*
Canadian Hi There	*1964*	TM's Rescue Me	*1994*
Nitrana	*1965*	Pat C Anguish	*1995*
Golden In	*1966*	Tricia's Anchor	*1996*
Xandra	*1967*	Phoebe Ann	*1997*
LG's Ada	*1968*	Granny	*1998*
Lucky Bannon	*1969*	Deuce's Wild	*1999*
Rising Queen	*1970*	NR's Fast Eddie	*2000*
SS Jeno	*`1971*	Redmoon Clyde	*2001*
Twilight Belle	*1972*	Kiowa Sweet Joe	*2002*
June's Tuffy	*1973*	Sale N Pelletier	*2003*
Abella	*1974*	No Race Run	*2004*
No Race Run	*1975*	Inspecta Deck	*2005*
P.L. Greer	*1976*	Will Ferrell	*2006*
Downing	*1977*	BNS Jimbo Di	*2007*
Blazing Red	*1978*	Magic Penny Ante	*2008*

Introduction

On May 14 ,1949 the **American Greyhound Derby** was born at the old **Taunton Dog Track**. This race was conceived by the Managing Director of the Taunton Dog Track, Mr. Joseph M. Linsey and he was the driving force behind this great event for many years. After the sensational series of match races between *Lucky Pilot* and *Flashy Sir,* that took place in the late 1940's, Mr. Linsey saw the need for a national championship event for greyhound racing and he devised the **American Derby** to be just that. With an unheard of purse, for the time, of $25,000 the Derby was a resounding success right from the very beginning. From its inception foreign entries to the Derby were common which provided the Derby its International appeal.

The American Derby was dubbed *"The Run for Orchids"* and its prestige and pageantry were cemented into place from its earliest days. The "**Greatest Greyhound in the World",** in the early 1950's was generally recognized to be the Randle Kennels' *Real Huntsman.* After winning both the 1950 and 1951 events, *Real Huntsman* was able to secure his spot in the Greyhound Hall of Fame and also establish the standard for excellence in the Derby. *Real Huntsman's* record of back to back wins in the **American Derby** stood unchallenged until *Dutch Bahama* was able to duplicate that feat by winning in 1984 and 1985. As of today these are the only two greyhounds to record this remarkable achievement.

The list of past champions is a who's who of greyhound racing history including the great past champions of *Real Huntsman, Dutch Bahama, Feldcrest, Downing, On The Line, Lucky Bannon, Prince Proper* and *Blazing Red.* The list of superstar greyhounds that competed for the Derby and came up a bit short is just as impressive and includes names like *Unruly, Rastro Ricky, RB's Bounty, Miss Whirl* and *Bang Bang Billy*.

Introduction

The beautiful **Taunton Dog Track** in Taunton, Massachusetts was the host track for the Derby from 1949 to 1981. In 1982 the Derby moved down the street to the **Raynham Dog Track** where it stayed through the 1985 running. Beginning in 1986 the **American Derby** was moved to the **Lincoln Greyhound Park** in Lincoln, Rhode Island and was hosted by the Lincoln track until the last running of the Derby in 2008.

The American Greyhound Derby has been suspended for the last three years but now the **Mardi Gras Racetrack i**n Hallandale, Florida has agreed to host this fabulous event during their 2012 winter meet. **The American Derby** will travel some 1500 miles to its new Florida home and with it will go all of the prestige and traditions of this great greyhound race including the Joseph M. Linsey Trophy. Mr. Linsey's *"Run for the Orchids"* will once again serve as the measuring stick of who is "**The Greatest Greyhound in the World.**"

Taunton Dog Track First Home of Derby

Mardi Gras Racetrack New Home Of Derby

The Taunton Years
(1949-1981)

Oklahoman-1949

Oklahoman-1949

TENTH RACE

The American Greyhound Derby

Race No. 150 PURSE $25,000.00 **Dighton Course—525 Yards**

P.P.	Ind.	Date	Dis.	TC	Ti.	Wt	PP	Off	1-8	St	Fin	Odds	FW	Comment	Order of Finish

Red 1 — RURAL STREAK
Richard H. Stevenson, owner — N. D. Taylor, trainer — Starts 2, 1st 1, 2nd 1, 3rd 0
66 Red Brindle D., November 1946. Rural Rube—Glenbawn Lass, Imp.

129	5-12	DC	F	30.4	65	6	2	1^3	1^3	1^1	13.80	—	Gamely	Frank'sGirl, H.Again, ChenYu
097	5- 9	DC	F	30.3	65	1	2	1^2	1^1	2^5	2.60	$1\frac{1}{2}$	Outgamed in stretch	Mannix, Bri.Boru, Promptness
290s	5- 6	DC	F	30.4	$65\frac{1}{2}$	5	3	$1\frac{1}{2}$	2	1^{hd}	.....	—	Gamely	FawnDough, D.Streak, Sewanee
279s	5- 3	DC	F	30.2	$66\frac{1}{2}$	1	4	1^1	2	2^1	.....	6	Good effort	J.Thatcher, Gal'rette, WarrenA.
264s	4-28	DC	F	31.1	66	1	4	3	3	$5^{1\frac{1}{2}}$	.....	$6\frac{1}{2}$	Factor early	Y.Timer, Oklahoman, H.Rube
188s	4-25	DC	F	30.4	$65\frac{1}{2}$	1	4	$1^{1\frac{1}{2}}$	1^{nk}	2^{hd}	.....	1	Met interf. ent. str.	Promptness, S.Clown, DoraJay[7]

Blue 2 — HELLO AGAIN
H. E. Alderson, owner — H. E. Alderson, trainer — Starts 2, 1st 1, 2nd 0, 3rd 1
$62\frac{1}{2}$ Red Brindle D., December 1946. Never Roll—Ruby Sue.

129	5-12	DC	F	30.4	62	7	5	4	2	$3^{2\frac{1}{2}}$	1.20	1	Gained much	Rur.Streak, Fran.Girl, ChenYu
100	5- 9	DC	F	30.2	$61\frac{1}{2}$	1	3	$1^{2\frac{1}{2}}$	1^5	$1^{5\frac{1}{2}}$	.80	—	Much best	W.Rememb'd, Suel'n, J.Th'cher
287s	5- 5	DC	F	30.1	62	7	2	1^1	1^3	1^4	.....	—	Drawing away	R.Cola, H.Hollenbeck, F.Steam
273s	5- 2	DC	F	31.1	$62\frac{1}{2}$	4	3	3	3	1^{nk}	.....	—	Finished on rail	A.B'mer, OB'sCal'w'y, Y.Timer[7]

White 3 — NEVER RISK
H. E. Alderson, owner — H. E. Alderson, trainer — Starts 2, 1st 1, 2nd 0, 3rd 0
$73\frac{1}{2}$ Brindle D., September 1946. Never Happy—Lady Lin.

130	5-12	DC	F	30.4	$72\frac{1}{2}$	5	8	7	5	4^1	3.70	$1\frac{1}{2}$	From far back	Transp't'n, Okla'm'n, OB'sCal'y
108	5-10	DC	F	30.2	72	7	5	2	2	$1\frac{1}{2}$	2.30	—	Gamely	D.Roll, Forevermor, R.Sp'dster
286s	5- 5	DC	F	30.2	73	3	4	3	1^1	1^1	.....	—	Gamely	Oklah'm'n, M.L.Lad, J.Th'ch'r[7]
273s	5- 2	DC	F	31.1	74	1	7	6	5	5^4	.....	5	Off slowly	H.Again, A.B'mer, OB'sCal'w'y[7]

Green 4 — CHEN YU
L. H. Nave, owner — Jack Mooney, trainer — Starts 4, 1st 2, 2nd 1, 3rd 0
59 Black B., March 1944. Never Roll—Shasta.

129	5-12	DC	F	30.4	59	2	3	2	5	4^{hd}	14.50	$3\frac{1}{2}$	Held on well	Rur.Streak, Fran.Girl, H.Again
099	5- 9	DC	F	30.2	$58\frac{1}{2}$	3	3	3	2	2^{hd}	4.50	$5\frac{1}{2}$	Good effort	Frank'sGirl, F.Dough, R.Roll[6]
048	5- 3	DC	F	31	$58\frac{1}{2}$	4	4	4	3	1^{nk}	2.40	—	In closing strides	JovialJohn, Rea.Jack, Dan.John
016	4-29	DC	F	31	$58\frac{1}{2}$	4	1	$1^{1\frac{1}{2}}$	1^3	1^5	5.50	—	Much best	Baseball, Trinidad, Republic
226s	4-26	DC	F	31.1	59	6	2	7	5	3^{nk}	.....	$4\frac{1}{2}$	Gained much	BigJive, Rock.Lad, GrayGable[7]
168s	4-23	DC	F	31	$58\frac{1}{2}$	1	5	5	4	3^2	.....	$3\frac{1}{2}$	Gained some	Ra.Bolby, Br.Boru, Han.Rube[6]

Black 5 — OB'S CALOWAY
Oswald Bros. Kennels, owner — Jack Herold, trainer — Starts 2, 1st 0, 2nd 1, 3rd 1
68 Red Fawn D., April 1946. Lucky Sir—Anna Cole.

130	5-12	DC	F	30.4	$67\frac{1}{2}$	8	1	1^2	1^2	$3^{\frac{1}{2}}$	19.80	1	Held on gamely	Transp't'n, Oklahoman, N.Risk
110	5-10	DC	F	30.3	$67\frac{1}{2}$	7	3	1^3	1^1	$2^{1\frac{1}{2}}$	1.50	$1\frac{1}{2}$	Held on well	M.LuckyLad, B.Town, B.Jive[6]
289s	5- 6	DC	F	30.1	$67\frac{1}{2}$	5	5	4	4	4no	.....	11	Crowded first turn	R.Sp'dster, N.Sunny, A.Boomer
283s	5- 4	DC	F	30.4	$67\frac{1}{2}$	4	3	2	2	2^4	.....	$2\frac{1}{2}$	Forward factor	Frank.Girl, S.Relic, Skipastep[6]
273s	5- 2	DC	F	31.1	68	7	4	2	2	$3^{2\frac{1}{2}}$	.....	2	Forward factor	H.Again, A.Boomer, Y.Timer[7]

Yellow 6 — FRANK'S GIRL
H. E. Heaton, owner — H. E. Heaton, trainer — Starts 2, 1st 1, 2nd 1, 3rd 0
65 Black & White B., May 1946. Steppin' Frank—Air Maiden.

129	5-12	DC	F	30.4	64	4	1	5	3	2no	3.10	1	Closing fastest	RuralStreak, H.Again, ChenYu
099	5- 9	DC	F	30.2	64	7	1	2	1^1	$1^{5\frac{1}{2}}$	1.70	—	Drawing away	ChenYu, FawnDough, Ro.Roll[6]
283s	5- 4	DC	F	30.4	$65\frac{1}{2}$	8	1	1^2	1^1	$1^{2\frac{1}{2}}$	.....	—	All the way	OB'sCalow'y, S.Relic, Skipast'p[6]
133s	4-22	DC	F	31	$65\frac{1}{2}$	5	7	4	3	2^1	.....	3	Made up ground	Mannix, Rumack, Stepp.Clown
078s	4-20	DC	F	31	$65\frac{1}{2}$	4	5	5	5	$5^{2\frac{1}{2}}$	.....	7	Even effort	R.Allbrass, J.Rawdon, Hap.Sis[6]
019s	4-18	DC	F	31.1	$65\frac{1}{2}$	8	3	3	1^1	$1^{2\frac{1}{2}}$	.....	—	Drawing away	Hap.Sis, Step.Clown, Hap.Son[7]

Green &Whi. 7 — TRANSPORTATION
E. L. Beckner, owner — E. L. Beckner, trainer — Starts 5, 1st 3, 2nd 0, 3rd 0
63 Brindle D., May 1946. Never Roll—Twinkle's Girl.

130	5-12	DC	F	30.4	$62\frac{1}{2}$	2	6	6	3	1^{nk}	8.70	—	From far back	Okla'man, OB'sCal'w'y, N.Risk
109	5-10	DC	F	30.3	62	5	4	6	3	1^1	3.60	—	Rush in stretch	Q.Beauty, ClipClop, Styl.King
079s	5- 6	DC	F	30.4	$62\frac{1}{2}$	1	6	6	5	5^2	3.70	$3\frac{1}{2}$	Good effort	JoeRawdon, Wes.Glow, R.Pass
049	5- 3	DC	F	31.1	$62\frac{1}{2}$	8	2	2	1^{nk}	$1\frac{1}{2}$	5.00	—	Gamely	JoeRawdon, Wes.Glow, B.Boru
019	4-29	DC	F	30.3	62	7	2	2	3	5^2	9.80	4	Good effort	DennisRoll, Mannix, J.Rawdon
200s	4-25	5-16	F	32.4	63	7	5	5	1^1	1^2	.....	—	Drawing away	JackPark, Roc.Roll, G.Leader[7]

Yellow &Black 8 — OKLAHOMAN
Earl L. Williams, owner — Tommy Lee, trainer — Starts 2, 1st 1, 2nd 1, 3rd 0
71 Brindle D., September 1946. Scatter Brain—Real Pansy.

130	5-12	DC	F	30.4	71	4	3	2	2	2^{hd}	2.30	nk	Strong bid	Transp't'n, OB'sCal'w'y, N.Risk
107	5-10	DC	F	30.3	71	1	3	1^3	1^4	$1^{6\frac{1}{2}}$	.70	—	Much best	Earmarked, Train.Bud, Trump
286s	5- 5	DC	F	30.2	$70\frac{1}{2}$	8	1	2	2	$2^{3\frac{1}{2}}$	.....	1	Game bid	Nev.Risk, M.L.Lad, J.Thatcher[7]
270s	5- 2	DC	F	30.3	$71\frac{1}{2}$	2	5	$1\frac{1}{2}$	1^2	1^3	.....	—	Easy victor	K.Nester, H.Rube, B.Whiteth'n
264s	4-28	DC	F	31.1	70	6	2	2	2	$2^{3\frac{1}{2}}$	.....	nk	Catching winner	YoungTimer, Han.Rube, R.Cola

Handicapper's Selections—Never Risk, Frank's Girl, Hello Again

Real Huntsman-1950

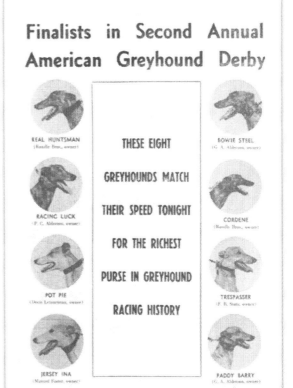

REAL HUNTSMAN and the Randle Brothers kennel are looking for a repeat victory in tonight's third annual renewal of the $25,000 American Greyhound Derby. In the above picture, Gene Randle is seen accepting the $15,000 check, winner's purse which Real Huntsman won last season. Left to right are Managing Director Jos. M. Linsey; Thomas Beedem, chairman of the Massachusetts racing commission; leadout boy Robert Byrne; Randle and J. Barry Welsh, director of racing at America's Blue Ribbon Track. In front of Real Huntsman is the handsome American Derby trophy which goes to the winner along with the big purse.

Real Huntsman-1950

TENTH RACE

The American Greyhound Derby

Race No. 390 — PURSE $25,000.00 — Bristol Course—675 Yards

P.P. | Ind. Date Dis. TC Ti. Wt PP Off 1-8 St Fin Odds FW Comment Order of Finish

Red 1 — RACING LUCK

P. C. Alderson, owner
Eddy Alderson, trainer

Starts 12, 1st 4, 2nd 5, 3rd 1

71 Brindle D., July 1948. Black Rustler—Happy Dora

Ind.	Date	Dis.	TC	Ti.	Wt	PP	Off	1-8	St	Fin	Odds	FW	Comment	Order of Finish
359	8-9	BC	F	38.4	69½	4	1	1^{1}	1^{4}	$1^{4\frac{1}{2}}$	5.90	—	*Never threatened*	Cordene, Pad.Barry, Trespasser
320	8-4	BC	F	39.1	70½	5	2	1^{1}	$1^{1\frac{1}{2}}$	1^{1}	1.90	—	*Gamely*	JerseyIna, MySonia, Rapid
280	7-31	BC	F	39	70½	4	3	3	2	$2^{3\frac{1}{2}}$	4.80	9	*Good effort*	Bo.Steel, B.Trigger, Gamester^{7}
259	7-28	5-16	F	31.1	70½	3	5	1^{nk}	1^{nk}	2^{1}	4.70	2½	*Saved inside*	Bow.Steel, A.Judge, O.B.Dream
239	7-26	5-16	F	31.2	70½	3	2	3	1^{1}	1^{hd}	4.20	—	*Gamely*	Slattery, BowieSteel, Blush
209	7-22	5-16	F	31.3	70½	8	7	3	3	$2^{1\frac{1}{2}}$	3.60	hd	*Catching winner*	Blush, AskaJudge, JerseyIna

Blue 2 — TRESPASSER

F. B. Stutz, owner
Willard Futrell, trainer

Starts 12, 1st 2, 2nd 2, 3rd 1

70 Red Fawn D., November 1947. Razor's Edge—Brownie Girl

Ind.	Date	Dis.	TC	Ti.	Wt	PP	Off	1-8	St	Fin	Odds	FW	Comment	Order of Finish
359	8-9	BC	F	38.4	68	8	6	8	5	4^{1}	11.80	6½	*Gained at end*	Rac.Luck, Cordene, PaddyBarry
329	8-5	BC	F	38.2	68½	7	4	7	5	$4^{2\frac{1}{2}}$	6.70	13	*Shuffled back turn*	R.Huntsm'n, P.Barry, Q.Beauty^{7}
290	8-1	BC	F	39.1	68½	7	6	4	$1^{2\frac{1}{2}}$	$1^{7\frac{1}{2}}$	2.40	—	*Much best*	O.B.P'rlin, Q.Beauty, J.Rawdon
270	7-29	EC	F	45.1	69	6	5	6	7	7^{7}	7.30	6½	*Shuffled back turn*	Trinidad, N.Trumpet, Fan.Kitty
*197**	*7-21*	*5-16*	*F*	*31.1*	*69½*	*1*	*4*	1^{1}	$1^{2\frac{1}{2}}$	$1^{2\frac{1}{2}}$	*2.60*	—	*Never threatened*	*Rim.Repeat, HicksG., B.Trigger*
*177**	*7-19*	*5-16*	*F*	*31.2*	*69½*	*5*	*4*	*7*	*4*	3^{hd}	*5.50*	4½	*Gained much*	*O.B.Dream, La.Debby, K.Quick*

White 3 — REAL HUNTSMAN

Randle Bros. owner
Duane Randle, trainer

Starts 6, 1st 6, 2nd 0, 3rd 0

68 Brindle D., February 1948. Never Roll—Medora

Ind.	Date	Dis.	TC	Ti.	Wt	PP	Off	1-8	St	Fin	Odds	FW	Comment	Order of Finish
360	8-9	BC	F	38.2	68	1	1	1^{4}	1^{5}	1^{4}	.30	—	*Never in doubt*	BowieSteel, PotPie, JerseyIna
329	8-5	BC	F	38.2	68	5	3	1^{4}	1^{8}	$1^{8\frac{1}{2}}$	.30	—	*Much best*	P.Barry, Q.Beauty, Trespasser^{7}
288	8-1	BC	F	39.1	68	3	2	2	1^{5}	$1^{8\frac{1}{2}}$	.30	—	*Much best*	Raven, BrendaLee, Shapiro^{7}
157s	7-27	5-16	F	30.3	67½	2	4	2	1^{2}	1^{5}	.....	—	*Drawing away*	MySonia, Cordene, TrimTrick^{7}
147s	7-20	5-16	F	31	68½	8	5	1^{nk}	1^{6}	1^{8}	.....	—	*Much best*	Froz.Fire, Qu.Beauty, Dis.Lady^{6}
150	7-15	5-16	F	31.2	68	4	6	6	2	1^{1}	.60	—	*Much best*	Blush, PaddyBarry, NeverUp

Green 4 — BOWIE STEEL

G. A. Alderson, owner
Frank Hall, trainer

Starts 12, 1st 7, 2nd 1, 3rd 1

72 Brindle D., March 1948. Never Roll—Fawn Beau

Ind.	Date	Dis.	TC	Ti.	Wt	PP	Off	1-8	St	Fin	Odds	FW	Comment	Order of Finish
360	8-9	BC	F	38.2	70½	5	8	3	2	$2^{4\frac{1}{2}}$	2.90	4	*Steady gain*	R.Huntsman, PotPie, JerseyIna
319	8-4	BC	F	38.4	71	6	3	1^{3}	1^{7}	1^{7}	.40	—	*Much best*	Cordene, Tarlton, YutaLin
280	7-31	BC	F	39	70½	3	1	1^{6}	1^{10}	1^{9}	.30	—	*Much best*	Rac.Luck, B.Trigger, Gamester^{7}
259	7-28	5-16	F	31.1	71	7	8	6	3	$1^{2\frac{1}{2}}$	1.00	—	*From far back*	Rac.Luck, A.Judge, O.B.Dream
239	7-26	5-16	F	31.2	71½	4	6	6	5	3^{2}	1.30	1	*Blocked far turn*	RacingLuck, Slattery, Blush
210	7-22	BC	F	39	70½	3	3	2	1^{5}	1^{6}	1.40	—	*Much best*	Raven, PaddyBarry, Mahomet

Black 5 — JERSEY INA

Manuel Foster, owner
Manuel Foster, trainer

Starts 11, 1st 1, 2nd 4, 3rd 2

58 Fawn & White B., February 1947. Knockroe Dasher, Imp.—Big Tilly

Ind.	Date	Dis.	TC	Ti.	Wt	PP	Off	1-8	St	Fin	Odds	FW	Comment	Order of Finish
360	8-9	BC	F	38.2	57	8	3	2	3	4^{1}	37.30	9	*Tired in stretch*	R.Huntsman, Bow.Steel, PotPie
320	8-4	BC	F	39.1	57½	8	4	2	2	$2^{2\frac{1}{2}}$	9.30	1	*Strong contender*	RacingLuck, MySonia, Rapid
279	7-31	BC	F	39.3	57	8	5	4	2	3^{2}	3.50	3	*Good effort*	YutaLin, Cordene, WhiskeySour
238	7-26	5-16	F	31.2	58	2	2	3	3	2no	8.40	1½	*Strong stretch drive*	O.B.Dream, Pa.Barry, NeverUp
209	7-22	5-16	F	31.3	57½	5	1	5	4	$4^{1\frac{1}{2}}$	8.80	3	*Good effort*	Blush, RacingLuck, AskaJudge
179	7-19	5-16	F	31	57½	8	2	3	4	3no	15.90	11	*Good effort*	BowieSteel, Blush, PaddyBarry

Yellow 6 — CORDENE

Randle Bros. owner
Duane Randle, trainer

Starts 6, 1st 0, 2nd 4, 3rd 0

54 Brindle B., March 1948. Rural Rube—Princess Pak

Ind.	Date	Dis.	TC	Ti.	Wt	PP	Off	1-8	St	Fin	Odds	FW	Comment	Order of Finish
359	8-9	BC	F	38.4	53½	2	4	5	3	2^{1}	4.10	4½	*Gained at end*	Rac.Luck, P.Barry, Trespasser
319	8-4	BC	F	38.4	53½	2	2	3	2	$2^{3\frac{1}{2}}$	7.70	7	*Raced forwardly*	BowieSteel, Tarlton, YutaLin
279	7-31	BC	F	39.3	53½	7	4	5	4	2^{2}	1.50	1	*Belated stretch rush*	YutaLin, JerseyIna, Whisk.Sour
157s	7-27	5-16	F	30.3	53½	1	2	3	3	3^{4}	.....	6	*Good effort*	R.Huntsman, M.Sonia, T.Trick^{7}
150	7-15	5-16	F	31.2	53½	8	4	8	8	8	12.70	7½	*Forced wide turn*	RealHuntsman, Blush, Pa.Barry
119	7-12	5-16	F	31.2	52½	4	4	6	4	$4^{2\frac{1}{2}}$	4.20	4	*Good effort*	Pad.Barry, Shapiro. O.B.Dream

Green & Whi. 7 — POT PIE

Doris Letourneau, owner
R. C. Letourneau, trainer

Starts 12, 1st 1, 2nd 1, 3rd 6

67 Red Fawn D., May 1947. Waltzing Paddy, Imp.—Rough Babe

Ind.	Date	Dis.	TC	Ti.	Wt	PP	Off	1-8	St	Fin	Odds	FW	Comment	Order of Finish
360	8-9	BC	F	38.2	65½	4	6	4	4	3^{nk}	49.80	8½	*Good effort*	R.Huntsman, Bow.Steel, Jer.Ina
330	8-5	BC	F	39	65½	1	1	5	4	3^{1}	6.10	11½	*Knocked back ent. tn*	Gree.Tanist, Trinidad, Tr.Trick
287	8-1	BC	F	39.3	66½	8	5	2	2	$1^{2\frac{1}{2}}$	10.90	—	*Drawing away*	G.Tanist, Trinidad, Thoughtl's^{7}
270	7-29	EC	F	45.1	66	7	1	3	3	$4^{1\frac{1}{2}}$	10.40	8	*Factor thruout*	Trinidad, N.Trumpet, Fan.Kitty
*208**	*7-22*	*5-16*	*F*	*31.2*	*66*	*6*	*7*	*6*	*5*	5^{hd}	*5.10*	8½	*Close quarters early*	*Shapiro, O.B.Orphan, Fran.Girl*
*178**	*7-19*	*5-16*	*F*	*31.2*	*66*	*5*	*8*	*6*	*4*	$3^{\frac{1}{2}}$	*8.30*	4½	*From far back*	*RandyRoll, N.Trumpet, So.Guy*

Yellow & Black 8 — PADDY BARRY

G. A. Alderson, owner
Frank Hall, trainer

Starts 12, 1st 4, 2nd 1, 3rd 4

70 Brindle D., March 1948. Never Roll—Fawn Beau

Ind.	Date	Dis.	TC	Ti.	Wt	PP	Off	1-8	St	Fin	Odds	FW	Comment	Order of Finish
359	8-9	BC	F	38.4	69	6	7	4	4	3^{1}	4.30	5½	*Gained at end*	Rac.Luck, Cordene, Trespasser
329	8-5	BC	F	38.2	68½	4	5	4	2	$2^{2\frac{1}{2}}$	8.50	8½	*Good effort*	R.Huntsm'n, Q.B'uty, Tresp's'r^{7}
289	8-1	BC	F	39.1	69	8	4	1^{2}	1^{3}	$1^{1\frac{1}{2}}$	1.40	—	*Handily*	TrimTrick, JackPark, Slattery^{7}
259	7-28	5-16	F	31.1	69	5	7	8	6	$5^{2\frac{1}{2}}$	9.10	6½	*Late gain*	BowieSteel, Rac.Luck, A.Judge
238	7-26	5-16	F	31.2	70	8	8	6	5	3no	1.30	1½	*From far back*	O.B.Dream, JerseyIna, NeverUp
210	7-22	BC	F	39	69	1	1	1^{2}	3	3^{2}	4.40	11	*Faded late stages*	BowieSteel, Raven, Mahomet

*—Performance shown not in proper sequence but is last race of dog at distance shown. †—Indicates dead heat.

Handicapper's Selections—Real Huntsman, Bowie Steel, Cordene

Real Huntsman-1951

Real Huntsman-1951

THE AMERICAN GREYHOUND DERBY

TENTH RACE
No. 390—Grade s

Purse $25,000

Bristol Course—675 Yards
Track-World's Record Real Huntsman 38.2

P.P.	Ind.	Date	Dis.	TC	Ti.	Wt	PP	Off 1-8	St	Fin	Odds	FW	Comment	Grade	Order of Finish

Red 1 — REAL HUNTSMAN 68
Randle Bros, owner — Duane Randle, trainer — Starts 3, 1st 2, 2nd 1, 3rd 0
Brindle D., February 1948. Never Roll—Medora

360	6-6	BC	F	38.4	67¼	8	3	3	1hd	2¼	.10	no	Held determinedly	s	Raven, Mahomet, PaddyBarry
330	6-2	BC	F	38.2	67	8	2	1⁴	1¹⁰	1¹¹½	.20	—	Much best	s	M.S.Foot, C.Comrade, Bla.Jane
295	5-30	BC	F	38.4	66½	4	3	3	1²	1⁵	.10	—	Much best	s	ICanDo, O.B.Orphan, Sw.Tune
244s	5-21	5-16	F	30.4	68½	8	2	2	1³	1⁷	.....	—	Drawing away		B.Foggy, Mau.Twin. M.Corsair⁶
234s	5-18	5-16	F	30.4	69	7	1	1²	1⁴	1⁶	.....	—	Much best		L.Easter, M.Twin, O.B.A.Act's⁶
227s	5-14	5-16	F	30.4	69	7	1	1⁴	1⁶	1¹⁰	.....	—	Much best		SuperSonic, BusterB., Bla.Jane

Blue 2 — CAMELYN 55
Jack Roche, owner — Ken Perkins, trainer — Starts 12, 1st 6, 2nd 1, 3rd 0
Brindle B., April 1949. Cameron—Jane Evelyn

359	6-6	BC	F	38.4	54	5	1	1³	1³	1³½	.30	—	Much best	s	Pope.Bobby, LaGrace, YutaLin
329	6-2	BC	F	38.3	54	2	6	4	1¹	1⁵	.40	—	Much best	s	Q.O.N.Y., GayScamp, LaGrace
296	5-30	BC	F	38.4	54½	8	1	7	1¹	1⁷½	.60	—	Much best	s	Maud.Twin, L.Topper, RollFlag
270	5-26	EC	F	44.4	53½	7	1	2	1²	1³½	.90	—	Drew out at end	s	FancyKitty, Mahomet, Raven
237	5-23	5-16	F	31.1	55	1	5	6	7	7³½	4.50	3½	Blocked far turn	1	Qu.OfN.Y., Celestial, M.S.Foot
210	5-19	BC	F	38.4	54½	7	4	5	1½	1²	3.30	—	Drawing away	s	Raven, FancyKitty, HeavyDate

White 3 — CITY EDGE 53
Thomas Makin, owner — Forbe Spencer, trainer — Starts 11, 1st 3, 2nd 1, 3rd 1
Black B., September 1949. Razor's Edge—Don Marie

357	6-6	BC	F	38.4	52½	5	3	6	3	3⁵½	5.00	1	Belated str. drive	s	TexieBoy, KeyRing, R.F.Texas
324	6-2	BC	F	39	53	1	4	2	1⁴	1⁸½	1.40	—	Much best	s	O.B.A.Actr's, PotPie, B.Pepper⁷
293	5-30	BC	F	39	53	1	5	3	2	1¹	3.40	—	In closing strides	s	Sta.Boy, G.Carlson, JoanMary⁷
270	5-26	EC	F	44.4	52½	4	3	5	5	6²	38.40	10½	Never prominent	s	Camelyn, FancyKitty, Mahomet
239	5-23	5-16	F	31.2	53	6	4	5	6	6¹²	13.50	15	Never prominent	1	KeyRing, Shapiro, ClassTells
209	5-19	BC	F	39.1	53	1	1	1½	1½	2²½	5.50	2	Outfinished in str.	s	Mahomet, Deeptone, Bl.Pepper

Green 4 — STRUTTING BILL 63½
C. D. McCarthy, owner — C. D. McCarthy, trainer — Starts 5, 1st 0, 2nd 3, 3rd 2
Brindle D., February 1949. Buzzie Roll—Lady Jester

358	6-6	BC	F	38.3	62	1	1	1¹	2	2hd	2.70	6	Held determinedly	s	BowieSteel, Deauville, He.Date
327	6-2	BC	F	38.4	62½	8	4	2	2½	1¹	11.80	3	Forward factor	s	KeyRing, Bo.Steel, O.B.Orphan
298	5-30	BC	F	38.3	62½	1	3	1²	2	2½	24.10	4	Outfinished at end	s	BowieSteel, Mahomet, Raven
256	5-25	5-16	F	31.1	62½	5	2	1½	2	3⁵½	5.30	½	Outfinished at end	3	O.B.Orphan, C.Herman, Drotha
226	5-22	5-16	F	31.1	63	8	5	3	3	3²½	8.60	½	Good effort	3	Hon.Rube, Sing.Edge, Ton.Step
234s	5-18	5-16	F	30.4	63½	5	2	6	6	6	.....	16	Outrun early		R.Huntsm'n, L.Easter, M.Twin⁶

Black 5 — SLOW TIME 71
C. D. McCarthy, owner — C. D. McCarthy, trainer — Starts 5, 1st 3, 2nd 0, 3rd 0
Red Fawn D., October 1949. Time Bomb—Princess Lorna

356	6-6	BC	F	38.3	69½	2	1	1³	1³	1⁴	2.20	—	Never threatened	s	G.Carlson, Indicator, Rich.Moss
328	6-2	BC	F	38.3	70	6	1	1⁵	1¹	1no	9.20	—	Just lasted	s	TexieBoy, Deauville, Mas.Mind
297	5-30	BC	F	39	70½	8	1	1⁵	15	1⁴½	24.00	—	Never in doubt	s	R.F.Texas, Deauv'le, H.M.Tight
255	5-25	5-16	F	31.2	70	3	6	7	4	4¹½	6.50	4	Gaining at end	3	W.Airways, SingleEdge, Evasive
222	5-22	5-16	F	31.2	70	4	7	8	8	7¹	5.50	10½	Never a factor	3	S.Sp'klite, A.B.A.Act's, Luxuria
234s	5-18	5-16	F	30.4	71	8	6	4	5	5¹	.....	15	Never a factor		R.Huntsm'n, L.Easter, M.Twin⁶

Yellow 6 — PADDY BARRY 70
G. A. Alderson, owner — Frank Hall, trainer — Starts 10, 1st 3, 2nd 0, 3rd 3
Brindle D., March 1948. Never Roll—Fawn Beau

360	6-6	BC	F	38.4	68½	2	4	4	4	4³½	5.40	3½	Made up ground	s	Raven, R.Huntsman, Mahomet
326	6-2	BC	F	38.4	69	8	3	1⁵	1⁴	1³	2.40	—	Much best	s	Whis.Sour, Fan.Kitty, Mariella
299	5-30	BC	F	39	69	6	1	1⁴	1²½	1½	2.00	—	All the way	s	O.Bobbie, Pop.Bobby, Mariella
260	5-25	BC	F	38.4	69	3	3	2	1⁵	1⁵½	1.50	—	Much best	2	F.Williams, Jo.Mary, Capricorn
229	5-22	5-16	F	31.2	69½	5	7	7	7	7⁶	4.00	8½	Never prominent	1	Fu.Time, Mia-O-Shan, Sw.Tune
199	5-18	5-16	F	31.3	69½	2	6	7	7	7²½	6.50	5	Wide, collided	1	Fu.Time, YutaLin, Gunn.Mate

Green & Whi. 7 — BOWIE STEEL 72
G. A. Alderson, owner — Frank Hall, trainer — Starts 9, 1st 4, 2nd 0, 3rd 1
Brindle D., March 1948. Never Roll—Fawn Beau

358	6-6	BC	F	38.3	70½	5	3	3	1⁴	1⁶	.50	—	Much best	s	Strut.Bill, Deauville, Heav.Date
327	6-2	BC	F	38.4	70½	3	3	6	3	3⁴½	.40	3½	Close quarters early	s	KeyRing, Stru.Bill, O.B.Orphan
298	5-30	BC	F	38.3	70	4	1	3	1¹	1⁴	1.20	—	Drawing away	s	StruttingBill, Mahomet, Raven
246s	5-23	5-16	F	31.2	72	7	5	3	2	1³	.....	—	Bumped turn, best		Mau.Twin, Pl.Reply, R.Rocket⁶
199	5-18	5-16	F	31.3	70½	3	5	6	6	5½	.60	3	Collided ent. turn	1	Fu.Time, YutaLin, Gunn.Mate
169	5-15	5-16	F	31.2	70½	5	6	6	6	6⁴	1.00	11	Collided ent. turn	1	Mahomet, Fut.Time, M.Su.Foot

Yellow & Black 8 — TEXIE BOY 72
Collier Bros., owner — R. M. Collier, trainer — Starts 3, 1st 1, 2nd 1, 3rd 0
Brindle D., July 1948. Texas Comrade—Trudy May

357	6-6	BC	F	38.4	72	1	1	3	2	1½	.70	—	In closing strides	s	KeyRing, CityEdge, R.Fr.Texas
328	6-2	BC	F	38.3	72	1	2	2	2	2⁴	.80	no	Catching winner	s	SlowTime, Deauville, Mas.Mind
294	5-30	BC	F	39	72	2	7	7	5	4³	.40	10½	Shuffled back brk	s	Fan.Kitty, Indicator, Rich.Moss
251s	5-25	5-16	F	30.4	72	5	2	1⁴	1⁵	1⁶	.....	—	Much best		Mariella, H.M.Tight, G.Scamp⁷
245s	5-22	5-16	F	31	72	3	7	2	1⁵	1⁶½	.....	—	Much best		GayScamp, Mariella, H.M.Tight

*—Performance shown not in proper sequence but is last race of dog at distance shown.   †—Indicates dead heat.

Handicapper's Selections — Real Huntsman, Camelyn, City Edge

On The Line-1952

SATURDAY NIGHT — SEPTEMBER 27, 1952

Taunton News

SECOND BEST EIGHT GREYHOUNDS IN WORLD COMPETE MONDAY NITE

TAUNTON Greyhound Association, Inc.

Arnault B. Edgerly .... *President*
Benjamin Fishman .... *Comptroller*
Kenneth Dorn .... *Director*

JOS. M. LINSEY
Managing Director

J. BARRY WELSH
Director of Racing

Presiding Judge .... Harry L. Cheney
Associate Judge .... Francis J. O'Boy
Associate Judge .... William J. Cleary
Paddock Judge .... E. J. L'Italien
Racing Secretary .... Andrew Leddy
Clerk of Scales .... A. J. Burnside
Timer .... Gilbert Millar
Starter .... A. J. Schillinger
Lure Operator .... John A. Morgan
Patrol Judge .... Colin Chisholm
Kennel Master .... Peter Edgerly
Chart Writer .... Thomas Benner
Mutuels Manager .... L. W. Skaggs
Veterinary Surgeon ... Dr. James H. O'Brien
Track Physician .... Dr. C. A. Pattajo
Publicity Director .... John A. Needs
Announcer .... Edward Litchfield
Promotional Manager ...... Robert Goldman
Track Superintendent ...... John A. Morgan

Mass. Racing Commission Officials

Chairman .... Thomas Beedem
Commissioner .... Allan M. Macleod
Commissioner .... Ira Hamilburg
Secretary .... Lawrence J. Lane
Chief Inspector .... Frank Mullen
Chief Accountant .... George Donahue
Asso. Com. Judge ... Harrison C. P. Humphrey
Asso. Com. Judge .... Earl Leary

CLUB HOUSE Daily Double tickets are sold at windows on the main line and may be cashed at any $2.00 straight cashier's window.

Another stellar attraction is on the ten-race program for Monday night here at the Taunton Dog Track where the second eight outstanding greyhounds in the world compete for top honors in the Consolation Derby, the tenth race over the long 675-yard Bristol Course.

Monday's greyhounds in the tenth race and the eight participants in tonight's fourth American Greyhound Derby make up the 16 best greyhounds in the world. Although not quite fortunate to earn enough points to qualify for the "Race of Champions" on tonight's program, the eight greyhound field in Monday's feature race gave the Derby finalists plenty of trouble before being eliminated from the $25,000 event.

The Consolation Derby will renew an old but friendly rivalry between the Taunton Dog Track and Wonderland Park in the days of Flashy Sir and Lucky Pilot when the Taunton entry collected 27 points to edge out the Revere entry by a single point in the American Challenge Cup six-race series.

As in the 1946 inter-track series, four Taunton and four Revere entries are listed to run in the Consolation Derby. Taunton is represented by a grand total of 62 points while Wonderland is represented by Neat Tax, Cumon Irene, Fiery Dawn and Lady Sailor for a total of 53½ points.

The Consolation entries, points and owners follow:

Entry and Points	Owner
DOIT EASY (17)	H. E. Heaton
HANDY EDGE (16)	Randle Brothers
NEAT TAX (15½)	Oscar Evers
WEE JESSIE (15)	Mrs. Iva Pollock
CUMON IRENE (14)	James J. Ryan (Estate)
LADY SAILOR (14)	Ray E. Holmes
SUMMER QUEEN (14)	C. C. Wilson
FIERY DAWN (14)	Fleet Wing Kennel

On The Line-1952

AMERICAN GREYHOUND DERBY

Purse $25,000

TENTH RACE

No. 270—Grade s

Bristol Course—675 Yards
Track-World's Record Real Huntsman 38.2

◄ Please call for Dog by Number

P.P.	Ind.	Date	Dis.	TC	Ti.	Wt	PP	Off	1-8	St	Fin	Odds	FW	Comment	Grade	Order of Finish

Red 1 — CLAREMORE
Earl L. Williams, owner — L. H. Henneke, trainer — Starts 3, 1st 0, 2nd 2, 3rd 1
74 — Brindle D., March 1950. Oklahoman—Gracie M.

239	9-24	BC	F	38.4	73	3	5	5	4	3¹	13.10	6	Moved up at end	s	G.Mouse, Mel.-Jean, S.Colleen
206	9-20	BC	F	39.1	73	4	2	8	5	2¹	3.90	1½	Pinched back turn	s	KindWords, Sc.Poppy, NeatTax
173	9-17	BC	F	39	72½	2	2	3	3	2ⁿᵒ	15.80	2	Raced forwardly	s	NeatTax, Pico, Fool'sChance
291s	9-15	5-16	F	31.1	73½	3	3	5	5	4¹½	.....	10	Blocked far turn		Graded, MelviaJo, RipRowan⁷
287s	9-12	5-16	F	31.1	74	3	6	5	4	4²½	.....	7½	Good effort		March.Mike, Janella, AJewel⁷
280s	9-10	5-16	F	31.2	75	6	7	8	7	7²⁰	.....	11½	Never a factor		Vik.Lady, Rel.Frosty, N.Matron

Blue 2 — MELLO-JEAN
John Prevatt, owner — John Prevatt, trainer — Starts 8, 1st 2, 2nd 5, 3rd 0
60 — Brindle B., January 1951. Transportation—Fatty Jean

239	9-24	BC	F	38.4	60½	5	2	2	2	2⁵	2.30	1	Gaining on winner	s	G.Mouse, Claremore, S.Colleen
205	9-20	BC	F	38.4	60¾	7	5	4	1¹	1⁶	1.60	—	Drawing away	s	WeeJessie, Gunn.Mate, Tireless
179	9-17	BC	F	39.1	60¼	1	6	4	4	2¹	2.40	4	L'ked rac. rm early	s	Cobra, Tex.Brenda, Swallowtail
150	9-13	5-16	F	31.1	60	1	3	4	2	2³¾	3.10	2½	Steady gain	s	Har.Pride, BraveIris, P.Report
119	9-10	5-16	F	31.2	60½	6	7	6	4	4¹	3.10	9	Good effort	s	Har.Pride, Sw.Song, M.Stories
078	9-5	5-16	F	31.2	60½	5	5	3	2	2¹	3.90	3	Bumped offstr. str.	s	Har.Pride, P.Report, M.Stories

White 3 — KIND WORDS
Jack B. Herold, owner — Jack B. Herold, trainer — Starts 7, 1st 2, 2nd 2, 3rd 1
61 — Red Brindle B., June 1950. O.B.'s Caloway—She's Telling Me

238	9-24	BC	F	39	60	7	3	2	2	2³	19.30	1½	Contender thruout	s	Cobra, Sum.Queen, LadySailor
206	9-20	BC	F	39.1	60	2	5	4	1²	1¹½	3.00	—	Lead early backstr.	s	Claremore, Sca.Poppy, NeatTax
180	9-17	BC	F	39	60	6	8	6	3	3²	16.90	7½	Made up ground	s	Gyp.Mouse, O.T.Line, V.Ginger
139	9-12	5-16	F	31.4	60	1	4	3	2	1ⁿᵏ	5.50	—	Steady gain	1	RoyalIris, Fu.Time, BlucPepper
109	9-9	5-16	F	31.3	60	7	8	6	6	5ʰᵈ	4.80	10	Offstrided ent. turn	1	MasterAll, RoyalIris, J-H.Harry
077	9-5	5-16	F	31.4	59¾	1	8	8	7	7ʰᵈ	3.90	15	Never a factor	1	BirthMark, RoyalIris, DoitEasy

Green 4 — HOLY BROTHER
G. A. Alderson, owner — Lee Wells, trainer — Starts 4, 1st 2, 2nd 0, 3rd 2
70 — Black D., September 1950. Cameron—Twilight Charm

240	9-24	BC	F	38.3	70	8	3	2	3	3ⁿᵒ	.90	7	Raced forwardly	s	OnTheLine, Raymalea, H.Edge
208	9-20	BC	F	38.4	70	8	1	1⁵	1⁷	1⁷	.50	—	Much best	s	W.J.Cr'km're, S.Queen, T.Des'n
177	9-17	BC	F	39	70	8	1	1⁵	1⁶	1⁶	1.70	—	Much best	s	La.Sailor, Tireless, Sum.Queen
147	9-13	5-16	F	31.2	69¾	7	3	5	4	3¹½	1.40	2	Gained steadily	1	Ear.Seven, S.Catcher, Gun.Mate
281s	9-10	5-16	F	31.1	70	7	4	1²¾	1⁵	1⁶	.....	—	Much best		LadySailor, Pico, Midget⁷
276s	9-8	5-16	F	31.1	70	6	2	2	2	2⁶	.....	hd	Contender thruout		Mar.Mike, Han.Edge, B.Finest

Black 5 — COBRA
Fleet Wing Kennel, owner — C. W. Montieth, trainer — Starts 3, 1st 2, 2nd 0, 3rd 1
73 — Black D., February 1950. Jack O' Johno, Imp.—Light Hearted

238	9-24	BC	F	39	73	4	7	5	1½	1¹½	1.20	—	Drew away at end	s	KindWords, S.Queen, La.Sailor
210	9-20	BC	F	38.4	73½	2	8	7	3	3⁴	1.70	5	Off poorly, gained	s	Gy.Mouse, S.Colleen, Mar.Mike
179	9-17	BC	F	39.1	73	2	7	3	1³	1⁴	.90	—	Drawing away	s	M.-Jean, T.Brenda, Swallowtail
290s	9-12	5-16	F	31.1	73½	6	6	5	3	3⁵	.....	3	Wide first turn		M.Lu.Rose, O.T.Line, Cu.Irene⁶
277s	9-8	5-16	F	31	73	3	5	1¹	1²½	1²	.....	—	Command first turn		OnTheLine, L.Rance, G.Mouse⁷
270s	9-5	5-16	F	30.4	73	5	4	1⁵	1⁸	1¹⁰	.....	—	Much best		CapeCod, AJewel, Qui.Thought

Yellow 6 — GYPSY MOUSE
L. M. Baltes, owner — W. R. Millsap, trainer — Starts 3, 1st 3, 2nd 0, 3rd 0
59½ — Brindle B., July 1949. Roanoke Rambler—Stepping G.

239	9-24	BC	F	38.4	59½	4	3	1³	1²	1¹	.60	—	Lead rounding turn	s	Mel.-Jean, Claremore, S.Colleen
210	9-20	BC	F	38.4	59½	1	2	1¹	1²	1³½	.70	—	Never threatened	s	SweetColleen, Cobra, Mar.Mike
180	9-17	BC	F	39	59½	3	2	1¹	1⁵	1⁶½	2.00	—	Drawing away	s	O.TheLine, K.Words, V.Ginger
289s	9-12	5-16	F	31.1	59½	2	6	2	2	1¹	.....	—	Strong str. drive		Fool.Chance, N.Matron, L.Sailor
282s	9-10	5-16	F	31	59½	3	1	1³	1³	1⁶	.....	—	Much best		Car.Ace, Bos.Finest, F.Chance⁷
277s	9-8	5-16	F	31	60½	4	1	4	4	4³	.....	7	Good effort		Cobra, OnTheLine, La.Rance⁷

Green & Whi. 7 — ON THE LINE
Chappell Kennel, owner — A. W. Kulchinsky, trainer — Starts 3, 1st 2, 2nd 1, 3rd 0
71½ — Red Brindle D., January 1950. Creekmore—Handy Judy

240	9-24	BC	F	38.3	69½	3	6	4	1³	1⁷	1.00	—	Much best	s	Raymalea, H.Brother, Han.Edge
209	9-20	BC	F	38.4	70½	6	8	5	1¹	1⁴	.40	—	Much best	s	Han.Edge, Raymalea, Co.Chute
180	9-17	BC	F	39	71	7	7	7	2	2¹	.50	6½	Rough trip	s	Gyp.Mouse, K.Words, V.Ginger
290s	9-12	5-16	F	31.1	72	2	3	2	2	2²	.....	1	Contender thruout		M.Luc.Rose, Cobra, Cum.Irene⁶
277s	9-8	5-16	F	31	71¾	3	3	2	2	2⁵	.....	2	Contender thruout		Cobra, LadyRance, Gyp.Mouse⁷

Yellow & Black 8 — SWEET COLLEEN
P. C. Alderson, owner — Richard Helvy, trainer — Starts 8, 1st 3, 2nd 1, 3rd 1
60 — Dark Brindle B., July 1950. Happy Harvest—Miss Darky

239	9-24	BC	F	38.4	60	2	4	4	3	4³¾	6.00	7	Good effort	s	G.Mouse, Mel.-Jean, Claremore
210	9-20	BC	F	38.4	60	6	3	3	2	2¹½	19.10	3½	Raced forwardly	s	GypsyMouse, Cobra, Mar.Mike
178	9-17	BC	F	39.2	60½	1	1	1⁵	1³	1²	3.20	—	Never in doubt	s	Bos.Finest, Fic.Dawn, Vik.Lady
150	9-13	5-16	F	31.1	60	3	4	8	8	8	6.60	13½	Wide ent. first turn	s	Har.Pride, Mello-Jean, Bra.Iris
118	9-10	5-16	F	31.3	60	2	1	2	2	4¹½	2.50	2	Outfinished in str.	s	BraveIris, P.Report, RouteFive
088	9-6	5-16	F	31.1	59½	5	2	1⁴	1²½	1²	4.50	—	Early command	s	Sw.Song, R.Raisin, Swallowtail

Handicapper's Selections—On The Line, Gypsy Mouse, Mello-Jean

17

However-1953

THIRTY-EIGHTH NIGHT

Taunton News

Consolation Derby Field Lists
Second Best Eight Greyhounds

TAUNTON Greyhound Association, Inc.

Arnault B. Edgerly .... *President*
David Yaffe .... *Vice President*
Benjamin Fishman .... *Comptroller*
Kenneth Dorn .... *Director*

JOS. M. LINSEY
Managing Director

J. BARRY WELSH
Director of Racing

Presiding Judge .... Harry L. Cheney
Associate Judge .... Richard Maliff
Associate Judge .... William J. Cleary
Paddock Judge .... Peter Edgerly
Racing Secretary .... Andrew Leddy
Clerk of Scales .... A. J. Burnside
Timer .... Gilbert Millar
Starter .... A. J. Schillinger
Lure Operator .... John A. Morgan
Patrol Judge .... Deverde Jackson
Kennel Master .... Colin Chisholm
Chart Writer .... E. J. L'Italien
Mutuels Manager .... L. W. Skaggs
Veterinary Surgeon .. Dr. James H. O'Brien
Track Physician .... Dr. John A. Kenney
Publicity Director .... John A. Needs
Announcer .... Edward Litchfield
Promotional Manager ..... Robert Goldman
Track Superintendent ..... John A. Morgan

Mass. Racing Commission Officials

Chairman .... Allan M. Macleod
Commissioner .... Thomas Beedem
Commissioner .... John E. Lawrence
Secretary .... Lawrence J. Lane
Chief Inspector .... Frank Mullen
Chief Accountant .... George Donahue
Asso. Com. Judge .... Harrison C. P. Humphrey
Asso. Com. Judge .... Frank P. Feeney
State Veterinarian .... Dr. Thomas J. O'Brien

The second best eight greyhounds in the world will be featured in the main attraction of a ten-card program here Monday night when the Taunton Dog Track stages its fifth annual Consolation Derby over the long 675-yard Bristol Course.

Greyhounds in the consolation just missed the Derby field on Saturday night, especially Jerry George, Satin Sis, Milam Light and May She. The quartet collected 16 points each and were in the drawing with Cobra, the Fleet Wing Kennel nominee for the $25,000 added purse in the fifth running of the American Greyhound Derby.

With five greyhounds listed to take over the eighth spot in the richest stake in greyhound racing, a drawing was necessary to decide which of the stellar performers would be eligible for the Derby. Cobra won the draw and advanced to the "Race of Champions" event while the remaining four greyhounds were automatic qualifiers for the Consolation Derby and the added purse event.

Cool Rocket, representing Mile High Kennel Club of Denver, Colorado, was the fifth entry for the Consolation with 15 points. Five greyhounds were tied for the other three positions in the Consolation Derby with each boasting 14 points. In the drawing for the remaining berths in Monday's feature attraction, Jenny Jo, Dancing Maid and Flyin' Sis won over Bright Sepal and Southern Lassie.

The Consolation Derby entries, points and owners follow:

Entry and Points	Owner
JERRY GEORGE (16)	Herbert Wulf
MAY SHE (16)	L. M. Kirkpatrick
MILAM LIGHT (16)	A. L. Sparks
SATIN SIS (16)	H. E. Heaton
COOL ROCKET (15)	Cen-Tex Kennel
DANCING MAID (14)	Myron A. Haughn
FLYIN' SIS (14)	Jack B. Herold
JENNY JO (14)	W. C. Grove

However-1953

American Greyhound Derby — Purse $25,000 Added

No. 450— Grade s

TENTH RACE

Bristol Course—675 Yards
Track-World's Record Real Huntsman 38:2

◀ Please call for Dog by Number

P.P.	Ind.	Date	Dis.	TC	Ti.	Wt	PP	Off	1-8	St	Fin	Odds	FW	Comment	Grade	Order of Finish

Red 1 — TRANSPAT

John Prevatt, owner / I. C. Scott, trainer — Starts 14, 1st 6, 2nd 6, 3rd 1

54 — Black and White B., January 1951. Transportation—Patty Jean

Ind.	Date	Dis.	TC	Ti.	Wt	PP	Off	1-8	St	Fin	Odds	FW	Comment	Grade	Order of Finish
416	10-14	BC	F	38.4	53½	3	5	1¹	1²	2ⁿᵒ	1.60	1	Led to wire	s	MayShe, CoolRocket, BigZip
389	10-10	BC	F	39.1	53½	8	2	1²	1³	1ⁿᵒ	1.40	—	Won stretch duel	s	Tumb.Sis, H.Brother, R.Samoa⁷
359	10-7	BC	F	39.1	53½	5	7	7	6	4½	1.50	4½	Late gain	s	However, HolyBrother, Peir
329	10-3	5-16	F	31	54½	3	1	3	2	1¹½	1.40	—	Lead entering str.	1	O.B.Gunner, H.Pride, J.Leonard
298	9-30	5-16	F	31.1	54	1	4	3	3	3¹	1.00	½	Raced evenly	1	Har.Pride, O.B.Gunner, Peg.Pat
269	9-26	5-16	F	30.4	54	1	1	2	2	2³	.60	1	Forward factor	1	Har.Pride, J.Leonard, S.Colleen

Blue 2 — GYPSY MOUSE

H. G. Weigar, owner / W. R. Millsap, trainer — Starts 5, 1st 3, 2nd 1, 3rd 0

60 — Brindle B., July 1949. Roanoke Rambler—Stepping G.

Ind.	Date	Dis.	TC	Ti.	Wt	PP	Off	1-8	St	Fin	Odds	FW	Comment	Grade	Order of Finish
418	10-14	BC	F	38.3	59	8	1	1¹½	1²	1¹	2.50	—	All the way	s	Mellojean, J.George, RatherRed
386	10-10	BC	F	38.4	59	6	2	2	2	2²	.90	½	Chased winner	s	She'sAPilot, SatinSis, FlyIt
360	10-7	BC	F	39	58½	3	1	1³	1³	1³	2.60	—	Never headed	s	Danc.Maid, Nobility, So.Lassie
339	10-5	5-16	F	31	59	3	2	1²	1²	1⁶	1.70	—	Drawing away	1	Nug, CoalChute, Trust
309	10-1	5-16	F	31.1	58½	6	2	8	8	8	6.50	12½	Collided first turn	1	Mellojean, Nug, JustLooking
301s	9-28	5-16	F	30.4	59½	1	4	2	2	2²½	.....	4	Raced forwardly		Janella, SlipStitch, N.Current⁷

White 3 — MELLOJEAN

John Prevatt, owner / I. C. Scott, trainer — Starts 13, 1st 5, 2nd 4, 3rd 2

61 — Brindle B., January, 1951. Transportation—Patty Jean

Ind.	Date	Dis.	TC	Ti.	Wt	PP	Off	1-8	St	Fin	Odds	FW	Comment	Grade	Order of Finish
418	10-14	BC	F	38.3	60½	2	2	2	2	2⁴	1.60	1	Forward factor	s	G.Mouse, J.George, RatherRed
388	10-10	BC	F	39	60	5	5	8	6	4¹	2.00	2½	Good late bid	s	South.Lassie, RatherRed, Cobra
358	10-7	BC	F	39.2	60	8	3	3	2	1ʰᵈ	.60	—	Up at wire	s	Ornamental, J.George, B.Bonnie
309	10-1	5-16	F	31.1	60½	1	8	3	3	1½	2.20	—	Belated str. drive	1	Nug, JustLooking, MilamLight
280	9-28	BC	F	38.4	60½	6	2	2	1²	1ʰᵈ	3.20	—	Held determinedly	1	Mil.Light, J.Looking, H.Brother
249	9-24	5-16	F	31	61	7	1	3	2	2ⁿᵒ	3.70	1	Forward factor	1	H.Brother, Ornamental, M.Light

Green 4 — HOWEVER

C. H. Lovely, owner / C. H. Lovely, trainer — Starts 3, 1st 3, 2nd 0, 3rd 0

56 — Red Brindle B., January 1951. Oklahoman—Gay Glitter

Ind.	Date	Dis.	TC	Ti.	Wt	PP	Off	1-8	St	Fin	Odds	FW	Comment	Grade	Order of Finish
419	10-14	BC	F	38.3	55	6	1	1²	1²	1⁸½	.40	—	Drew away	s	MilamLight, Peir, DustyJerry
387	10-10	BC	F	38.3	55½	8	2	1³	1⁵	1⁶	.80	—	Unopposed	s	Fl.Light, B.Hunter, Claremore⁷
359	10-7	BC	F	39.1	56	3	5	5	4	1½	.80	—	Strong str. drive	s	HolyBrother, Peir, Transpat
302s	10-2	5-16	F	30.4	57½	2	3	1ⁿᵏ	1³	1⁴	.....	—	Inside first turn		Janella, Ro.Samoa, Su.Holiday⁶
299s	9-28	5-16	F	30.4	57	6	1	1¹½	1⁵	1⁷	.....	—	Much best		Ri.Marker, V.Ginger, R.Samoa⁷

Black 5 — JANELLA

E. J. Boyle, owner / E. J. Boyle, trainer — Starts 3, 1st 2, 2nd 1, 3rd 0

55½ — Black Brindle B., February 1951. Lucky Pilot—Telephone Girl

Ind.	Date	Dis.	TC	Ti.	Wt	PP	Off	1-8	St	Fin	Odds	FW	Comment	Grade	Order of Finish
417	10-14	BC	F	38.3	55½	4	4	3	2	2⁵	1.30	1	Moved up	s	Nobility, Flyin'Sis, Sum.Queen
390	10-10	BC	F	39	55½	8	3	2	1³	1³½	4.30	—	Handily	s	Bri.Sepal, Dan.Maid, SlipStitch
355	10-7	BC	F	39.2	55½	6	5	3	1²	1¹	.90	—	Held determinedly	s	SatinSis, Bri.Sepal, RubySocks
302s	10-2	5-16	F	30.4	55½	5	2	3	2	2⁴	.....	4	Factor thruout		However, Ro.Samoa, S.Holiday⁶
301s	9-28	5-16	F	30.4	55½	6	2	1³	1⁴	1⁴	.....	—	Never threatened		G.Mouse, Sl.Stitch, N.Current⁷
291s	9-25	5-16	F	30.3	55	6	3	1½	1³	1⁵	.....	—	Drawing away		Dan.Maid, G.Mouse, So.Lassie⁷

Yellow 6 — HOLY BROTHER

G. A. Alderson, owner / Lee Wells, trainer — Starts 6, 1st 2, 2nd 1, 3rd 1

72 — Black D., September 1950. Cameron—Twilight Charm

Ind.	Date	Dis.	TC	Ti.	Wt	PP	Off	1-8	St	Fin	Odds	FW	Comment	Grade	Order of Finish
420	10-14	BC	F	39	72	8	1	2	2	1ⁿᵒ	4.80	—	Up at wire	s	JohnnyLeonard, SatinSis, Cobra
389	10-10	BC	F	39.1	72	4	1	4	5	3²½	2.80	11	Rough trip	s	Transpat, Tumb.Sis, R.Samoa⁷
359	10-7	BC	F	39.1	72	7	4	4	1½	2²½	5.10	½	Outfin. at wire	s	However, Peir, Transpat
309	10-1	5-16	F	31.1	71½	7	3	6	6	5¹	1.20	4½	Collided first turn	1	Mellojean, Nug, JustLooking
280	9-28	BC	F	38.4	71	3	1	1²½	3	4ⁿᵏ	1.90	4	Led to far turn	1	Mellojean, Mi.Light, J.Looking
249	9-24	5-16	F	31	71	1	5	1¹	1ʰᵈ	1¹	.80	—	Saved on inside	1	Mellojean, Ornamental, M.Light

Green & Whi. 7 — NOBILITY

Orville Moses, owner / A. B. Kershaw, trainer — Starts 11, 1st 1, 2nd 6, 3rd 3

62 — Fawn B., July 1951. Pageant—Flashy Sara

Ind.	Date	Dis.	TC	Ti.	Wt	PP	Off	1-8	St	Fin	Odds	FW	Comment	Grade	Order of Finish
417	10-14	BC	F	38.3	62½	1	1	1¹	1¹	1¹	4.10	—	Held gamely	s	Janella, Flyin'Sis, Summ'rQueen
384	10-10	BC	F	38.3	62½	2	1	2	2	2¹½	3.30	3½	Contender thruout	s	RubySocks, Flyin'Sis, Mil.Light
360	10-7	BC	F	39	62	8	4	2	2	3²	12.50	5½	Early factor	s	Gyp.Mouse, Da.Maid, So.Lassie
328	10-3	5-16	F	31.1	62½	4	3	2	2	2³	1.90	2½	Contender thruout	1	JennyJo, TumbleSis, Fre.Ready
289	9-29	5-16	F	31.2	62	7	4	3	3	2ʰᵈ	2.40	1	Offstr. str. turn	1	Tescot, MorningNip, Sp.Control
259	9-25	5-16	F	31	62	6	5	3	2	2⁴	11.20	1	Gaining on winner	1	JustLooking, Tescot, TumbleSis

Yellow & Black 8 — COBRA

Fleet Wing Kennel, owner / J. B. Cohen, trainer — Starts 3, 1st 1, 2nd 0, 3rd 1

73½ — Black D., February 1950. Jack O'Johno, Imp.—Light Hearted

Ind.	Date	Dis.	TC	Ti.	Wt	PP	Off	1-8	St	Fin	Odds	FW	Comment	Grade	Order of Finish
420	10-14	BC	F	39	73½	7	7	3	3	4ⁿˢ	4.60	3	Moved up, wide	s	HolyBrother, J.Leonard, Satinis
388	10-10	BC	F	39	73	8	8	6	5	3½	2.00	2	Closing on outside	s	So.Lassie, RatherRed, Mellojean
357	10-7	BC	F	39.1	73½	4	7	4	2	1²	2.70	—	Wide, driving	s	JennyJo, FlyIt, ForeverFaye
303s	10-2	5-16	F	31	73½	8	6	3	1¹	1²	.....	—	Wide thruout		BigZip, Claremore, RubySocks⁶
300s	9-28	5-16	F	31.1	73½	7	8	3	4	4¹	.....	1½	Off slowly, gained		Sou.Lassie, Bri.Sepal, C.Rocket
291s	9-25	5-16	F	30.3	74½	3	7	7	5	5²	.....	16	Never a factor		Janella, Dan.Maid, Gyp.Mouse⁷

Handicapper's Selections—However, Gypsy Mouse, Transpat

Mellojean-1954

As her owner Charley Lovely sits by, however, voted both outstanding female and greyhound of 1953 by the Greyhound Writers of America at annual party given them by American Track Operators Association at El Comodoro Hotel in Miami Sunday, Feb. 7, gazes appreciatively at the Joseph M. Linsey Trophy won by her when she became American Greyhound Derby Champion last fall.

American Derby Champion Wins Two Awards

SATURDAY NIGHT, OCTOBER 16, 1954   Post Time 7:47 P.M.

Taunton News

Eight Top Greyhounds Race In $25,000 Added Purse Derby

The owner of the winning greyhound in the sixth running of the $25,000 American Greyhound Derby will receive $15,000 and the handsome Jos. M. Linsey Trophy, symbolic of the World Championship, while the victorious speedster will be adorned with a floral blanket of orchids tonight, after the big race, 11th on the program, over the Bristol Course.

The 11th race includes:

Greyhound	Owner
THIN INK WON $10,000 VETERANS STAKE AT RAYNHAM PARK IN 1954	A. Lee Sparks Columbus, Kansas
MILAM STAR WON 1954 GOLD COLLAR CHAMPIONSHIP AT TAUNTON, PURCHASED AS PUP FOR $5,000	A. Lee Sparks Columbus, Kansas
MILAM LIGHT CONSISTENT CAMPAIGNER AT TAUNTON	A. Lee Sparks Columbus, Kansas
MELLOJEAN WINNER 1954 RAYNHAM DERBY, SECOND TO HOWEVER IN 1953 AMERICAN GREYHOUND DERBY, WON INAUGURAL AT MIAMI BEACH, SECOND IN MIAMI BEACH DERBY.	John Prevatt Jacksonville, Florida
DANCING MAID WONDERLAND PARK, REVERE, STANDOUT, WON TWO QUALIFYING ROUNDS AT TAUNTON	Myron A. Haughn St. Petersburg, Florida
FRAYDY'S LADY HAS BEEN RUNNING WITH THE HOT-BOX STARTERS AT WONDERLAND PARK, REVERE	Fleet Wing Kennel North Andover, Mass.
JANELLA ANOTHER WONDERLAND PARK, REVERE, SPEEDSTER	Edward J. Boyle St. Petersburg, Florida
HOLY BROTHER MILE HIGH KENNEL CLUB, DENVER, COLORADO, REPRESENTATIVE IN THE	George A. Alderson St. Petersburg, Florida

Mellojean-1954

The American Greyhound Derby

PURSE $25,000 ADDED — **ELEVENTH RACE** — **Bristol Course**—675 Yards

Please Call for Dog by Number

Track-World's Record Real Huntsman 38.2

Red 1 — HOLY BROTHER 72

G. A. Alderson, owner; Lee Wells, trainer — Starts 3, 1st 1, 2nd 1, 3rd 0

Black D., September 1950. Cameron—Twilight Charm

Date	Dis.	TC	Ti.	Wt	PP	Off	1-8	St	Fin	Odds	FW	Comment	Grade	Order of Finish
10-13^{8}	BC	F	39.2	71½	6	7	7	4	6^{hd}	14.10	7	*Never prominent*	①	BillHunter, Flyin'Sis, MilamStar
10-9^{5}	BC	F	39.2	72	4	1	1^{2}	1^{2}	1^{nk}	3.30	—	*Immediate lead*	①	Twirler, H.ClassMate, Tra.Melba
10-6^{7}	BC	F	39.4	71	2	2	2	2	2^{hd}	2.10	2½	*Contender thru't*	①	Middleboro, Ran.Ross, H.Cl.Mate
10-1s	5-16	F	30.3	71½	8	5	4	3	3^{1}	.....	8	*Good effort*		Janella, DancingMaid, Beechwood
9-27s	5-16	F	31	70½	8	5	6	5	5^{4}	.....	7½	*Never prominent*		Janella, CircusDoll, N.Snowdrop^{7}

Blue 2 — MILAM STAR 58

A. L. Sparks, owner; Robert Wyman, trainer — Starts 11, 1st 5, 2nd 3, 3rd 2

Black B., August 1952. Colfax—Inky Ina

Date	Dis.	TC	Ti.	Wt	PP	Off	1-8	St	Fin	Odds	FW	Comment	Grade	Order of Finish
10-13^{8}	BC	F	39.2	57½	8	8	5	7	3^{hd}	.60	6	*Offstr. ctn turn*	①	BillHunter, Flyin'Sis, Frayd.Lady
10-9^{8}	BC	F	38.4	57½	2	4	2	1^{2}	1^{2½}	.40	—	*Lead far turn*	①	Mellojean, MorningNip, GayJag
10-6^{11}	BC	F	39	57	8	4	1^{5}	1^{4}	1^{3½}	2.30	—	*Much best*	①	SatinSis, NoCurrent, Privacy
10-2^{10}	5-16	F	30.4	57½	4	2	4	3	3^{3½}	1.40	2½	*Moved up steadily*	1	Remarque, O.B.Gunner, J.Looking
9-29^{9}	5-16	F	31	57½	3	5	4	3	2^{2}	3.10	3	*Steady gain*	1	PilotLights, PlayGun, Mir.Power
9-25^{10}	5-16	F	31	57½	1	3	4	3	1^{nk}	2.40	—	*Moved up on rail*	1	MiraclePower, Fala, PilotLights

White 3 — THIN INK 62

A. L. Sparks, owner; Robert Wyman, trainer — Starts 10, 1st 4, 2nd 4, 3rd 1

Black B., August 1952. Colfax—Inky Ina

Date	Dis.	TC	Ti.	Wt	PP	Off	1-8	St	Fin	Odds	FW	Comment	Grade	Order of Finish
10-13^{9}	BC	F	39	62	2	8	6	4	2^{hd}	.70	2½	*Much late speed*	①	Remarque, NoCurrent, BestWay
10-9^{7}	BC	F	39.1	62	1	3	6	1^{3}	1^{6½}	.50	—	*Much best*	①	SatinSis, FreddyReady, Tenteen
10-6^{4}	BC	F	39.1	61½	8	8	5	2	1^{3}	.40	—	*Moved thru rap'ly*	①	Fala, Tenteen, SilverButterfly
10-1^{11}	BC	F	39	61½	6	8	5	3	1^{2}	2.90	—	*From far back*	1	Mo.Butterfly, Mellojean, Twirler
9-28^{9}	5-16	F	31.1	61½	2	7	7	5	4no	2.60	1½	*Much late speed*	1	EasyCoin, Mellojean, BlueFax
9-24^{9}	5-16	F	31.1	61½	4	7	8	5	2^{1}	2.30	1	*From far back*	1	EasyCoin, Manifest, Swam.Poodle

Green 4 — FRAYDY'S LADY 57

Fleet Wing Kennel, owner; J. B. Cohen, trainer — Starts 4, 1st 2, 2nd 1, 3rd 0

Brindle B., May 1952. Mixed Harmony—Miss Nocturne

Date	Dis.	TC	Ti.	Wt	PP	Off	1-8	St	Fin	Odds	FW	Comment	Grade	Order of Finish
10-13^{8}	BC	F	39.2	56	3	6	6	6	4^{nk}	2.70	6	*Closed fast*	①	BillHunter, Flyin'Sis, MilamStar
10-9^{6}	BC	F	39	57	1	1	1^{2½}	1^{3}	1^{6}	.70	—	*Much best*	①	Mr.Ram, Tran'sBlaze, RubySocks
10-6^{9}	BC	F	39.2	55½	8	6	2	2	2^{1½}	2.40	5	*Forward factor*	①	M.Butterfly, M.Str'cher, O.B.Idea
10-2^{9}	5-16	F	30.4	55½	2	3	2	2	1^{1½}	13.00	—	*Strong str. drive*	1	MiraclePower, BlueFax, BestWay
9-29s	5-16	F	31.1	56	7	6	4	3	3^{2}	.....	4	*Made up ground*		M.Stretcher, Rans.Ross, Privacy^{6}
9-27s	5-16	F	31	56½	4	1	4	4	3^{nk}	.....	5½	*Wide ent. 1st turn*		FayeWomack, Let'sBuz, Mr.Ram^{7}

Black 5 — MILAM LIGHT 56

A. L. Sparks, owner; Robert Wyman, trainer — Starts 9, 1st 2, 2nd 2, 3rd 4

Brindle B., July 1951. Colfax—Dauntsey Spotlight, Imp.

Date	Dis.	TC	Ti.	Wt	PP	Off	1-8	St	Fin	Odds	FW	Comment	Grade	Order of Finish
10-13^{7}	BC	F	39.2	56	1	5	4	1^{1}	1^{4}	1.00	—	*Drawing away*	①	WarPlane, RubySocks, Tran.Blaze
10-9^{9}	BC	F	39.1	56	4	3	2	1½	3^{5}	4.60	½	*Outfin. in str.*	①	However, Beechwood, O.B.'sIdea^{7}
10-6^{10}	BC	F	38.4	55½	3	7	6	4	2½	2.90	6	*Steady gain*	①	Danc.Maid, However, PilotLights
9-30^{9}	5-16	F	31.1	55½	8	7	4	2	2^{4}	2.10	no	*Moved up rapidly*	1	WarPlane, BankWalker, Tenteen
9-27^{10}	5-16	F	31	55½	2	8	5	4	3½	7.00	2½	*From far back*	1	M.Butterfly, Speedwell, W.Plane
9-22^{10}	5-16	F	31.2	55	4	6	5	6	3^{nk}	9.20	2	*Belated str. drive*	1	Mir.Power, MilamStar, BestWay

Yellow 6 — MELLOJEAN 61

John Prevatt, owner; I. C. Scott, trainer — Starts 11, 1st 4, 2nd 4, 3rd 2

Brindle B., January 1951. Transportation—Patty Jean

Date	Dis.	TC	Ti.	Wt	PP	Off	1-8	St	Fin	Odds	FW	Comment	Grade	Order of Finish
10-13^{10}	BC	F	38.4	60½	3	3	3	2	1^{1½}	2.60	—	*Moved up rapidly*	①	M.Butterfly, JennyJo, MissOakey
10-9^{8}	BC	F	38.4	60½	7	5	6	3	2^{3½}	3.10	2½	*Steady gain*	①	MilamStar, MorningNip, GayJag
10-6^{8}	BC	F	39.3	60½	3	5	5	1^{hd}	1^{1}	.60	—	*Moved up steadily*	①	Noc.Snowdrop, Flyin'Sis, Twirler
10-1^{11}	BC	F	39	61	7	6	7	4	3½	3.10	2½	*Steady gain*	1	ThinInk, Mon.Butterfly, Twirler
9-28^{9}	5-16	F	31.1	61	5	3	4	3	2^{1}	2.30	½	*Moved up steadily*	1	EasyCoin, BlueFax, ThinInk
9-24^{10}	5-16	F	31.2	60½	8	6	4	1½	3^{3}	.70	½	*Outfinished in str.*	1	MissOakey, Comstock, Gr.Fonder

Green & Whi. 7 — DANCING MAID 60

M. A. Haughn, owner; R. B. Marshall, trainer — Starts 3, 1st 2, 2nd 1, 3rd 0

Brindle B., October, 1951. No Refund—Wilful Maid

Date	Dis.	TC	Ti.	Wt	PP	Off	1-8	St	Fin	Odds	FW	Comment	Grade	Order of Finish
10-13^{11}	BC	F	39	59	2	2	4	4	2^{1}	.80	2	*Much late speed*	①	Janella, Twirler, Agreeable
10-9^{10}	BC	F	38.4	59	3	6	5	1½	1^{3½}	.30	—	*Moved up rapidly*	①	Agreeable, Remarque, CircusDoll
10-6^{10}	BC	F	38.4	59½	8	8	4	1^{3}	1^{6}	1.30	—	*Much best*	①	MilamLight, However, Pil.Lights
10-1s	5-16	F	30.3	60	6	7	6	2	2^{5}	.....	3	*Gained backstr.*		Janella, HolyBrother, Beechwood
9-27s	5-16	F	31	59½	7	5	7	5	5^{1}	.....	6	*Bmpd ent. 1st turn*		Fa.Womack, Let.Buz, Fray.Lady^{7}

Yellow & Black 8 — JANELLA 56

E. J. Boyle, owner; J. P. Boyle, trainer — Starts 3, 1st 2, 2nd 0, 3rd 0

Black Brindle B., February 1951. Lucky Pilot—Telephone Girl

Date	Dis.	TC	Ti.	Wt	PP	Off	1-8	St	Fin	Odds	FW	Comment	Grade	Order of Finish
10-13^{11}	BC	F	39	56	8	1	1^{5}	1^{4}	1^{2}	1.90	—	*Never in doubt*	①	DancingMaid, Twirler, Agreeable
10-9^{4}	BC	F	38.4	56½	1	3	2	1^{5}	1^{7}	2.40	—	*Command ctn tn*	①	MoneyStretcher, Fala, BillHunter
10-6^{9}	BC	F	39.2	56	4	2	4	6	7^{4½}	1.60	8½	*W'kened late stgs*	①	M.Butterfly, Fra.Lady, M.Str'cher
10-1s	5-16	F	30.3	56	7	1	1^{3}	1^{4}	1^{3}	.....	—	*Instant command*		Dan.Maid, H.Brother, Beechwood
9-27s	5-16	F	31	56	6	2	1^{1}	1^{3}	1^{2}	.....	—	*Muzzle hanging*		Cir.Doll, N.Snowdrop, N.Current^{7}

①—Numeral in circle in grade column denotes Stake or Special race.

†—Indicates Dead Heat.

Handicapper's Selections—Mellojean, Milam Star, Dancing Maid

Koliga-1955

$25,000 American Greyhound DERBY

Tenth Race · · Tonight

OFFICIAL PROGRAM 15¢

TAUNTON DOG TRACK

America's Blue Ribbon Track

SATURDAY, OCT. 15, 1955

RIB LOCK

I am here tonight to avenge a defeat of my pappy in the year 1950. He finished second in the American Greyhound Derby. He was defeated by none other than the champ, Real Huntsman, whom you all remember well as he also won the Derby in 1951. Then he broke the track and world record for the Bristol Course, 675 yards, in the fast time of 38.2. My pappy's name was Racing Luck, and the last part of his name is what I need and with that you will see me down with Mr. Linsey in the winner's circle getting all the awards that go to the winner of the Derby.

HONEY'S FOX

This is one race I hope I can win with a bit of racing luck. I know I can do it. I am sure that I will live like a king. Perhaps I can talk my boss into getting me a nice feather bed, for after all, with that kind of money I rate it.

AMORE

You might think me a bit selfish after reading this but I just can't help it. I fully realize $15,000 goes to the winner of this race and the Jos. M. Linsey Trophy also. But the reason I want to win this race is to have the blanket of orchids draped over me. Just think of the pretty ladies that will wait around to look at me and will I feel proud!

CENSOR

Boy, oh, boy, would I be happy to win this one. Have been looking at the Jos. M. Linsey Trophy since the meeting started and when I get old and can't run any more and retire, my owner will look at that trophy which will always make him think of me and say to himself, "She sure was a great champion."

WAUKEAZY

Just think of how I would fit with my boss when he collects that $15,000 for winning this race. I sure will do my best for me and my boss and all my kennel mates. We sure will have a great party, nothing but the best for all of us. Should I win this big race it will be the second time for my kennel as Mellojean won last year.

GULF FISHERMAN

Everybody feels as though I am stepping up in fast company because I am under two years of age and here I am running for the biggest honor and the richest stake in greyhound racing. So far, I have done pretty good and I am proud of myself. The oldsters in the race better do some running when the starting box opens for I will sure show them some speed and they will have to catch me. They sure will hang their heads in shame when I step into the winner's circle—but I won't have a swelled head—believe me.

KOLIGA

This is the seventh running of this Derby and I am about sick and tired of the Taunton dogs winning this event. As you know, I did all my racing during the season at Wonderland Park in Revere, and this year I am out to break the streak of the Taunton dogs winning this big race. I am representing Wonderland Park. Yes, I know that in the six Derby races that were run four Taunton dogs won this event and two from Revere. I am in great shape for this race. If I don't win it, I will be afraid to go back to Wonderland Park.

TRAN'S CHOICE

This race is the most important event in my life. You perhaps would like to know the reason. I am in kind of a rough spot. Do you know why? Well, I will tell you. In the first American Greyhound Derby, my daddy was in the race. His name was Transportation and he finished second to Oklahoman, and if I don't win this race I will be afraid to go back home, for he whispered advice to me and schooled me very well as to how to run and come home a winner.

Koliga-1955

The American Greyhound Derby

📢 Please Call for Dog by Number

TENTH RACE

Bristol Course—675 Yards
Track-World's Record Real Huntsman 38.2

P.P.	Date	Dis. TC Ti.	Wt	PP	Off 1-8	St	Fin	Odds	FW	Comment	Grade	Order of Finish

Red 1 — RIB LOCK
G. A. Alderson, owner
Clement Zwack, trainer
Starts 5 | 1st 3 | 2nd 2 | 3rd 0
72 — Red Brindle D., October 1952. Rural Speedster—Sea Flower

Date	Dis. TC Ti.	Wt	PP	Off 1-8	St	Fin	Odds	FW	Comment	Grade	Order of Finish
10-12¹⁰	BC F 38.4	70	4	2	3	2	2¹	1.10	3	Forward factor	①	GulfFisherman, Perico, PestPest
10-8⁹	BC F 38.4	70	2	1	2	1²	1²¹	1.10	—	Lead far turn	①	Amore, RagtimeRastus, Str.Force
10-5¹⁰	BC F 39	70¹	5	1	1¹¹	1¹	1ⁿᵒ	1.80	—	Just lasted	①	Koliga, Sherm, Fraydy'sLady
9-29¹⁰	BC F 39	71	1	2	2	2	2¹	1.50	1¹	Factor thruout	1	Waukeazy, Sh.Salty, G.Fisherman
9-24⁹	5-16 S 31.1	71	5	7	2	2	1³	2.00	—	Moved thru ctn tn	1	PilotLights, Waukeazy, Da.Mades
9-22¹s	5-16 F 31	71¹	3	4	1²	1³	1⁵	.....	—	Drawing away		Amore, StrongForce, HonestStyle⁷

Blue 2 — HONEY'S FOX
John Prevatt, owner
Ivel C. Scott, trainer
Starts 12 | 1st 4 | 2nd 3 | 3rd 0
63 — Dark Brindle D., September 1952. Rural Streak—Rebelette

Date	Dis. TC Ti.	Wt	PP	Off 1-8	St	Fin	Odds	FW	Comment	Grade	Order of Finish
10-12¹⁰	BC F 38.4	63	5	4	4	5	5²	9.00	7	Good effort	①	GulfFisherman, RibLock, Perico
10-8⁷	BC F 38.4	63¹	2	1	1³	1¹¹	2²	5.20	ⁿᵒ	Outfin. in str.	①	Censor, EasterGift, ThinInk
10-5³	BC F 39	63	5	2	2	1¹	1¹¹	2.50	—	Lead far turn	①	PestPest, CloudyBoy, SilverTray
10-1⁹	5-16 F 31	63	4	5	6	8	8	9.80	5¹	Never prominent	1	PilotLights, Fray.Lady, TransBud
9-28⁸	5-16 F 31	62¹	4	6	8	8	8	5.80	10	Never a factor	1	T.V.Review, Sherm, TransBud
9-24¹⁰	BC S 39.2	63	8	6	3	1³	1⁴	6.40	—	Lead far turn	1	TransBud, But.Bounce, Ferdinand

White 3 — AMORE
R. L. Block, owner
Hugh Ross, trainer
Starts 3 | 1st 1 | 2nd 2 | 3rd 0
57 — Black B., April 1953. Texas Comrade—Paree

Date	Dis. TC Ti.	Wt	PP	Off 1-8	St	Fin	Odds	FW	Comment	Grade	Order of Finish
10-12⁷	BC F 39	56¹	7	4	4	3	1¹	1.20	—	Strong str. drive	①	Censor, Fraydy'sLady, Stro.Force
10-8⁹	BC F 38.4	56¹	7	5	4	4	2¹	1.80	2¹	Belated str. drive	①	RibLock, Ragti.Rastus, Str.Force
10-5⁸	BC F 38.4	56¹	5	3	3	2	2⁷¹	1.00	3	Held on well	①	G.Fisherman, MilamLight, Censor
9-26¹s	5-16 F 30.3	57¹	2	2	2	2	2⁴	.....	2	Forward factor		B.T.B.Better, Str.Force, Jud.Doll⁷
9-22¹s	5-16 F 31	58	4	1	4	3	2ⁿᵈ	.....	5	Moved up steadily		RibLock, StrongForce, Hon.Style⁷

Green 4 — CENSOR
Orville Moses, owner
Orville Moses, trainer
Starts 11 | 1st 2 | 2nd 3 | 3rd 3
63 — Brindle B., September 1953. Texie Boy—Lovalon

Date	Dis. TC Ti.	Wt	PP	Off 1-8	St	Fin	Odds	FW	Comment	Grade	Order of Finish
10-12⁷	BC F 39	62¹	1	1	1²	1¹	2²	2.40	¹	C'ght nearing wire	①	Amore, Fraydy'sLady, Stro.Force
10-8⁷	BC F 38.4	62¹	3	2	2	2	1ⁿᵒ	7.90	—	In closing stride	①	Honey'sFox, EasterGift, ThinInk
10-5⁸	BC F 38.4	62¹	3	2	5	4	4ⁿᵒ	4.10	10¹	Crowded early	①	G.Fisherman, Amore, MilamLight
10-1⁸	5-16 F 31	63	4	7	3	1¹	1¹	4.70	—	Lead far turn	1	Ragti.Rastus, LostDollar, Inviting
9-28⁷	5-16 F 31	62¹	6	8	7	3	2²	2.50	1	Moved up rapidly	1	Ferdinand, Mir.Power, O.B.Spots
9-24¹⁰	BC S 39.2	63	6	8	7	6	6⁶	4.60	8	Never a factor	1	Honey.Fox, Tra.Bud, But.Bounce

Black 5 — WAUKEAZY
John Prevatt, owner
Ivel C. Scott, trainer
Starts 10 | 1st 3 | 2nd 1 | 3rd 3
68 — Dark Brindle D., July 1953. Rural Speedster—Up Late

Date	Dis. TC Ti.	Wt	PP	Off 1-8	St	Fin	Odds	FW	Comment	Grade	Order of Finish
10-12⁹	BC F 39.1	68¹	8	4	3	3	3¹¹	4.60	2¹	Never far back	①	Sherm, Cap'sHope, ThinInk
10-8¹	BC F 39.1	69	7	3	1¹¹	2	1ⁿᵒ	1.60	—	Came again in str.	①	FreddyReady, Sherm, TransBud
10-5⁴	BC F 38.4	68¹	7	5	4	3	2¹	1.00	3¹	Moved up st'dily	①	EasterGift, Nike, ForeverTempest
9-29¹⁰	BC F 39	68¹	4	1	1²	1¹¹	1¹¹	9.30	—	Never threatened	1	RibLock, She.Salty, G.Fisherman
9-24⁹	5-16 S 31.1	68¹	4	8	3	3	3⁸¹	18.80	4	Good effort	1	RibLock, PilotLights, DaveMades
9-21¹⁰	BC F 39.2	68	1	1	1⁴	1³	1³	2.10	—	Never in doubt	2	TransTopper, MilamLight, Prude

Yellow 6 — GULF FISHERMAN
Knotty Pine Kennel, owner
Barney Mullin, trainer
Starts 10 | 1st 6 | 2nd 2 | 3rd 1
67½ — Brindle D., March 1954. Mixed Harmony—Merry Catch

Date	Dis. TC Ti.	Wt	PP	Off 1-8	St	Fin	Odds	FW	Comment	Grade	Order of Finish
10-12¹⁰	BC F 38.4	66¹	8	6	5	1¹	1³	3.60	—	Thru inside str. tn	①	RibLock, Perico, PestPest
10-8¹⁰	BC F 38.4	67	2	1	1²	1¹	2⁷	1.10	ⁿᵏ	Outfinished in str.	①	She'sSalty, GayJag, Baby'sSon⁷
10-5⁸	BC F 38.4	66¹	2	1	1²	1²	1³	3.80	—	Held safe lead	①	Amore, MilamLight, Censor
9-29¹⁰	BC F 39	66¹	8	5	5	3	4²¹	7.00	2¹	Made up ground	1	Waukeazy, RibLock, She'sSalty
9-24⁷	5-16 S 31.4	66¹	2	4	4	1¹	1¹	2.70	—	Lead far turn	2	Rool.Streak, Mr.Tab, MilamLight
9-20⁷	5-16 F 31.3	66	2	5	5	5	3ⁿᵏ	1.50	2	Strong str. drive	2	AmpleTime, Cloud.Boy, Congoer⁷

Green & Whi. 7 — KOLIGA
R. L. Block, owner
Hugh Ross, trainer
Starts 3 | 1st 1 | 2nd 1 | 3rd 0
68 — Black D., April 1953. Texas Comrade—Paree

Date	Dis. TC Ti.	Wt	PP	Off 1-8	St	Fin	Odds	FW	Comment	Grade	Order of Finish
10-12⁹	BC F 39.1	68	5	7	7	7	5¹	.50	5	Bpd offstr. far tn	①	Sherm, Cap'sHope, Waukeazy
10-8⁸	BC F 38.2	67¹	4	4	3	1⁴	1⁷	.60	—	Lead mid-bkstr.	①	MilamLight, RoolingStreak, Peir
10-5¹⁰	BC F 39	67	2	8	7	3	2¹	3.70	ⁿ⁹	Overtak'g winner	①	RibLock, Sherm, Fraydy'sLady
9-26¹s	5-16 F 30.3	68¹	7	7	7	7	6²	.....	11	Never a factor		B.T.B.Better, Amore, StrongForce
9-22¹s	5-16 F 31	69	6	2	5	5	5³	.....	7	Never prominent		RibLock, Amore, StrongForce⁷

Yellow & Black 8 — TRANS CHOICE
E. L. Beckner, owner
N. D. Taylor, trainer
Starts 12 | 1st 5 | 2nd 1 | 3rd 0
58 — Brindle & White B., January 1953. Transportation—Eudora

Date	Dis. TC Ti.	Wt	PP	Off 1-8	St	Fin	Odds	FW	Comment	Grade	Order of Finish
10-12⁸	BC F 39.1	57¹	2	8	8	5	1¹¹	3.90	—	Belated str. drive	①	V.Panther, Rool.Streak, Mil.Light
10-8⁶	BC F 39.1	58	2	8	8	4	1¹	4.10	—	Belated str. drive	①	Cap'sHope, Fraydy'sLady, Perico
10-5⁵	BC F 39.1	58	5	7	5	3	1ⁿᵒ	3.30	—	Up at wire	②	Middleboro, Headway, BeBest
10-1¹⁰	EC F 44	57	5	8	8	1¹	1³¹	1.40	—	From far back	③	Mil.Light, MoonBaby, Nor.Morn
9-28¹⁰	BC F 39.1	57¹	7	8	8	3	2¹	2.00	1	From far back	⑤	Nor.Morn, Primitive, MilamLight
9-26¹⁰	BC F 39.2	58	2	8	7	5	4ʰᵈ	3.10	4¹	Shuf. back crtn tn	2	Manifest, Remo, ColPie

① —Numeral in circle in grade column denotes Stake or Special race.   †—Indicates dead heat.

Handicapper's Selections—Gulf Fisherman, Tran's Choice, Koliga

Go Rock-1956

Greyhound Racing World Loses Top Champion

Real Huntsman

Gone from the familiar greyhound haunts is the greatest speedster in the world of the popular Sport of Queens!

Real Huntsman is with us no more . . .

The only greyhound in the universe to win the American Greyhound Derby championship two times, since the richest stake in greyhound racing was introduced to the Sport of Queens by Managing Director Jos. M. Linsey in 1949, met a tragic death two weeks ago Thursday in a fire that broke out in a trailer in which Real Huntsman was one of 19 greyhounds being transported from Daytona Beach to Miami.

According to Duane Randle, who is in charge of the Wheat State Kennel racing here at the Taunton Dog Track, the catastrophe to brother Gene Randle's Real Huntsman occurred at the halfway point between Daytona Beach and Miami on Route 1 as Billy Walsh, trainer, was transporting the kennel at the end of the Daytona meet to the Randle Farm at Ojus, Fla.

While driving, Walsh noticed sparks coming out of the trailer. Billy stopped immediately to investigate. He pulled out the greyhounds as fast as he could but Real Huntsman was one of the speedsters burnt to death.

When asked, "How is it that The Huntsman was on the trip to Daytona since the great speedster was used only for stud not racing?", Duane replied, "Gene liked The Huntsman so much he took him to every track where he raced greyhounds." Duane added, "Real Huntsman was the best Gene ever had!" Duane thought a passing motorists might have accidently thrown a cigarette that landed inside the trailer and finally started the disastrous fire. In the last report six greyhounds were dead and the others, although given a chance to recover, may or may not be able to race again.

Real Huntsman gained world renown at Taunton Dog Track by winning the 1950 and 1951 running of the American Greyhound Derby. The Huntsman also won the 1950 Gold Collar Stake and the 1950 Blue Ribbon Stake here at the Blue Ribbon Track of America. Up until Sept. 29, 1956 when Splendored posted 38 seconds flat, The Huntsman held the 675-yard distance track-world record with 38.2, chalking up the fast time in 1951.

The great son of Never Roll—Medora earned $63,000 odd in purses, not counting the stud fees collected by Randle Farm. Fans all over the world, especially here at Taunton, regret the passing of the great champion. The Huntsman also, among other tracks, will be missed by followers at Daytona Beach, West Flagler and Hollywood.

At one stretch, The Huntsman won 27 consecutive races, certainly a remarkable feat.

$25,000 American Greyhound DERBY

KOLIGA

Tenth Race – Tonight

OFFICIAL PROGRAM 25c

TAUNTON DOG TRACK

America's Blue Ribbon Track

SATURDAY, OCT. 13, 1956

Go Rock-1956

The American Greyhound Derby

Track-World's Record
Splendored 38

TENTH RACE

BRISTOL COURSE
675 YARDS

P.P. | Date | Dis. TC Ti. | Wt PP Off 1-8 | St | Fin | Odds | FW | Comment | Grade | Order of Finish

Red 1 — SPLENDORED

M. J. Gavan, owner
M. J. Gavan, trainer
Starts 12, 1st 5, 2nd 2, 3rd 3

54 — Brindle B., October 1954. On The Line—Mariella

Date	Dis.	TC	Ti.	Wt	PP	Off	1-8	St	Fin	Odds	FW	Comment	Grade	Order of Finish
10-10^{8}	BC	F	38.3	54	7	3	3	$1^{1\frac{1}{2}}$	1^{6}	.70	—	*Drew out easily*	①	Lit.Tumbler, L.Effort, O.B.Molto
10-6^{9}	BC	F	38	53½	2	1	1^{4}	1^{6}	1^{7}	.60	—	*Equls trk-wld rec.*	①	CutOver, O.B.'sMolto, OleBennie
10-3^{10}	BC	F	38.2	53	2	5	4	2	2^{6}	.70	1½	*Good stretch gain*	①	GoldBelle, KittySilver, S.Answer,
9-29^{9}	BC	F	38	53	5	2	3	1^{3}	1^{8}	1.40	—	*New trk-wld rec.*	1 2	KittySilver, CutOver, Censor
9-26^{8}	5-16	F	31.1	53½	3	7	8	6	5^{nk}	3.50	7½	*Bpd offstr. 1st tn*	1	RealArcher, Lako.Sue, Kit.Silver
9-22^{9}	5-16	F	30.3	54	1	2	5	5	3no	3.10	2	*Rapid stretch drive*	1	RealArcher, KittySilver, Nob.Kid

Blue 2 — GO ROCK

Deep Rock Kennels, owner
L. B. Benedict, trainer
Starts 3, 1st 3, 2nd 0, 3rd 0

65 — Brindle D., June 1954. Rural Streak—Handy Byers

Mile High 22 7 0 0

Date	Dis.	TC	Ti.	Wt	PP	Off	1-8	St	Fin	Odds	FW	Comment	Grade	Order of Finish
10-10^{10}	BC	F	39	64½	4	2	1^{3}	1^{4}	1^{2}	.80	—	*Held safe lead*	①	GoldBelle, G.Fisherman, Fra.Best
10-6^{10}	BC	F	38.2	64½	7	5	3	3	$1^{\frac{1}{2}}$	1.70	—	*Rapid str. drive*	①	Valued, GoldBelle, KittySilver
10-3^{8}	BC	F	38.3	64½	1	3	2	1^{2}	1^{1}	.90	—	*Held safe lead*	①	O.B.Molto, KayJay, Tex.Yel.Rose
9-29^{2}s	5-16	F	30.3	65	6	2	2	2	$2^{1\frac{1}{2}}$	.....	½	*Almost up*		O.Bennie, Pret.Pam, L.Tumbler^{7}
9-24^{4}s	5-16	F	31	65	4	3	3	3	1^{1}	.....	—	*Wide 1st tn, driving*		SuperToy, OleBennie, Rustum
9-21^{5}s	5-16	F	30.3	65	4	1	1^{3}	1^{10}	1^{8}	.....	—	*Equals track-wld rec.*		OleBennie, PansyPot, LittleEffort

White 3 — NOBLE KID

M. C. Rogers, owner
Arthur Bowser, trainer
Starts 11, 1st 3, 2nd 3, 3rd 0

77 — Brindle D., March 1954. Cavalier—Austin's Pride

Date	Dis.	TC	Ti.	Wt	PP	Off	1-8	St	Fin	Odds	FW	Comment	Grade	Order of Finish
10-10^{9}	BC	F	38.2	76	7	8	6	5	$5^{2\frac{1}{2}}$	29.00	11½	*Never prominent*	①	PrettyPam, Valued, HoneyLine
10-6^{4}	BC	F	39	76	5	2	2	1^{1}	1no	1.40	—	*Just lasted*	①	KayJay, PansyPot, CherryRiver^{7}
10-3^{5}	BC	F	38.4	75½	2	2	2	2	$2^{1\frac{1}{2}}$	1.80	2½	*Raced forwardly*	①	HoneyLine, OleBennie, Lit.Effort
9-29^{8}	5-16	F	31	75½	5	6	4	3	$2^{\frac{1}{2}}$	1.20	½	*Catching winner*	1	Tr.Taylor, Sw.Spoken, LakotaSue
9-26^{8}	5-16	F	31.1	75½	7	8	5	5	4^{1}	6.80	6½	*Shuffled first turn*	1	RealArcher, Lako.Sue, Kit.Silver
9-22^{9}	5-16	F	30.3	76	2	6	4	3	4^{1}	6.30	2½	*Good effort*	1	RealArcher, K.Silver, Splendored

Green 4 — FANELIA

Orville Moses, owner
Charles Rink, trainer
Starts 3, 1st 1, 2nd 1, 3rd 0

53 — Brindle B., January 1955. Mixed Harmony—Secrets

Pensacola 8 6 0 1

Date	Dis.	TC	Ti.	Wt	PP	Off	1-8	St	Fin	Odds	FW	Comment	Grade	Order of Finish
10-10^{10}	BC	F	39	52½	5	6	7	7	7^{2}	26.80	8	*Outrun*	①	GoRock, GoldBelle, G.Fisherman
10-6^{6}	BC	F	38.3	52½	2	5	4	2	2^{5}	1.50	2	*Good effort*	①	G.Fisherman, Chitina, Coun.Game
10-3^{6}	BC	F	39	52½	1	3	2	1^{3}	$1^{3\frac{1}{2}}$	5.50	—	*Easily*	①	MarySuzan, StellaC., Valued
9-29^{2}s	5-16	F	30.3	53	2	6	5	5	5^{2}	.....	5½	*Wide first turn*		OleBennie, GoRock, PrettyPam^{7}
9-24^{3}s	5-16	F	31	53	5	8	8	8	8	.....	10	*Outrun early*		HighGloss, CountryGame, Koliga
9-12 Pen	*3-8*	*F*	*39.4*	*51½*	*1*	*5*	*3*	*2*	1^{4}	*1.70*	—	*Easy winner*	S	*Issuance, MaryLine, Rellis*

lack 5 — PRETTY PAM

Harry McKinney, owner
A. R. Talbot, trainer
Starts 3, 1st 3, 2nd 0, 3rd 0

54 — Brindle B., May 1954. Key Ring—Naughty Nell

Daytona Beach 27 13 7 2

Date	Dis.	TC	Ti.	Wt	PP	Off	1-8	St	Fin	Odds	FW	Comment	Grade	Order of Finish
10-10^{9}	BC	F	38.2	53½	2	1	1^{2}	1^{4}	$1^{3\frac{1}{2}}$	.80	—	*Off alertly, easily*	①	Valued, HoneyLine, Clydesdale
10-6^{7}	BC	F	38.1	53½	2	1	1^{4}	1^{3}	$1^{1\frac{1}{2}}$	1.00	—	*Wire to wire*	①	Surprised, MarySuzan, O.B.Motel
10-3^{4}	BC	F	38.2	53	4	2	2	2	1^{3}	1.40	—	*Drawing away*	①	L.Tumbler, G.Fisherman, Chitina
9-29^{2}s	5-16	F	30.3	54½	1	3	4	4	3^{3}	.....	2	*Good effort*		OleBennie, GoRock, Lit.Tumbler^{7}
9-24^{5}s	5-16	F	31.1	54½	4	1	3	3	2^{3}	.....	2	*Good effort*		FrankBest, KayJay, Pennipost
9-10 Day	*BC*	*F*	*40*	*53*	*2*	*3*	*2*	1^{1}	1^{5}	*.30*	—	*Going away*	T	*BluishFlame, EllieMae, RockinJo*

Yellow 6 — SURPRISED

Blackwell Kennels, owner
Dave Greig, trainer
Starts 3, 1st 1, 2nd 1, 3rd 0

71 — Brindle D., December 1954. Earmarked—Ima Blitz

Mile High 19 7 2 3

Date	Dis.	TC	Ti.	Wt	PP	Off	1-8	St	Fin	Odds	FW	Comment	Grade	Order of Finish
10-10^{8}	BC	F	38.3	70½	4	5	6	5	$6^{\frac{1}{2}}$	3.50	9	*Lacked run'ng rm*	①	Splendored, L.Tumbler, L.Effort
10-6^{7}	BC	F	38.1	71	6	5	4	2	2^{5}	2.50	1½	*Good str. effort*	①	Pret.Pam, MarySuzan, O.B.Motel
10-3^{7}	BC	F	38.4	71	4	7	8	3	$1^{\frac{1}{2}}$	2.10	—	*Crd early, drvg fin*	①	GreatValor, Step.Junior, Labeled
9-29^{3}s	BC	F	38.2	71½	8	3	$1^{\frac{1}{2}}$	1^{5}	1^{4}	.....	—	*Equals trck wld rec.*		StellaC., Sw.Answer, Lit.Effort^{7}
9-24^{5}s	5-16	F	31.1	72	6	8	6	6	5^{1}	.....	6½	*Forced out 1st turn*		FrankBest, PrettyPam, KayJay
8-27 MH	*Col*	*F*	*40.05*	*70½*	*7*	*4*	*6*	*6*	*4*	*4.40*	8	*Saved late*	S-A	*GoRock, S.Rock, Ro'g Doll*

Green & Whi. 7 — GOLD BELLE

Benny Frisch, owner
Benny Frisch, trainer
Starts 3, 1st 1, 2nd 1, 3rd 1

58 — Red B., November 1953. Real Huntsman—Sharlee

Sod. 13 1 2 5

Date	Dis.	TC	Ti.	Wt	PP	Off	1-8	St	Fin	Odds	FW	Comment	Grade	Order of Finish
10-10^{10}	BC	F	39	57½	3	5	4	2	2^{2}	2.40	2	*Some stretch gain*	①	GoRock, G.Fisherman, FrankBest
10-6^{10}	BC	F	38.2	57½	3	8	7	4	3^{1}	1.80	1	*Off late, rap. gain*	①	GoRock, Valued, KittySilver
10-3^{10}	BC	F	38.2	57½	6	7	5	1^{3}	$1^{1\frac{1}{2}}$	6.30	—	*Command str. tn*	①	Splendored, Kit.Silver, S.Answer
9-29^{6}s	BC	F	38.3	59	8	5	4	3	$2^{\frac{1}{2}}$	.....	½	*Almost up*		HoneyLine, KayJay, Jerry'sTom^{6}
9-24^{5}s	5-16	F	31.1	58	7	2	5	5	6^{2}	.....	7½	*Steady fade*		FrankBest, PrettyPam, KayJay
9-4 Sod	*3-8*	*F*	*39.33*	*58½*	*8*	*8*	*4*	*3*	*2*	*1.60*	8½	*Crowded 1st turn*	S	*Ltng.Mike, Midboro, JbltSpri.*

Yellow & Black 8 — HONEY LINE

Oscar Evers, owner
Carl J. Peterson, trainer
Starts 3, 1st 2, 2nd 0, 3rd 1

65 — Red Brindle B., October 1954. On The Line—Vivian's Miss

Revere 25 11 1 5

Date	Dis.	TC	Ti.	Wt	PP	Off	1-8	St	Fin	Odds	FW	Comment	Grade	Order of Finish
10-10^{9}	BC	F	38.2	63	8	3	2	2	3^{6}	2.00	5	*Good effort, wide*	①	PrettyPam, Valued, Clydesdale
10-6^{8}	BC	F	38.2	63½	8	3	1^{3}	1^{7}	17	2.90	—	*As she pleased*	①	Perico, StellaC., ThinInk
10-3^{5}	BC	F	38.4	63½	4	1	1^{3}	1^{3}	$1^{2\frac{1}{2}}$	4.20	—	*Wire to wire*	①	NobleKid, OleBennie, Lit.Effort
9-29^{6}s	BC	F	38.3	64½	2	1	1^{3}	1^{3}	$1^{\frac{1}{2}}$	.....	—	*Just lasted, wide*		GoldBelle, KayJay, Jerry'sTom^{6}
9-24^{6}s	BC	F	38.3	65	3	2	2	3	$4^{\frac{1}{2}}$	.....	10½	*Wide both stretches*		SweetAnswer, Jerry.Tom, ClaireL.
9-19^{6}s	5-16	F	31.1	65	2	2	2	1^{1}	2^{2}	.....	1	*Good effort*		SuperToy, Mr.Gibralter, StellaC.^{7}

①—Numeral in circle in grade column denotes Stake or Special race. †—Indicates dead heat.

Handicapper's Selections—Pretty Pam, Splendored, Go Rock

Clydesdale-1957

$25,000 American Greyhound DERBY

GO ROCK
WINNER OF
1956 AMERICAN GREYHOUND DERBY

Tenth Race - Tonight

OFFICIAL PROGRAM 25c

TAUNTON DOG TRACK

America's Blue Ribbon Track

SATURDAY, OCT. 12, 1957

DERBY CHATTER

By Rusty

Taunton Dog Track startled the greyhound racing world in 1949 when it first offered the American Greyhound Derby ... It was the first time in dog racing history that a purse of $25,000 was put up for greyhound to shoot at ... It still remains as the richest dog race in the world ... Credit goes to Joseph M. Linsey, managing director of the Taunton track, for the foresight in scheduling the Derby with the thought of attracting the best dogs .... Oklahoman emerged the winner of the inaugural running in 1949 .... That first Derby, and the qualifying tests leading to the final, were contested over the now-discarded Dighton course of 525 yards .... Determined to make the Derby and its qualifying rounds a true test of speed and stamina between sprinters and routers alike, Linsey, increased the distance in 1950 to the now popular Bristol course of 675 yards .... On May 30, 1951 ten races were staged over the Bristol course, eight of the events over the long distance were made up of Derby dogs and the remaining two of top-flight greyhounds .... That marked another "first" for Taunton for no such attractive card was ever offered at any other track ....

Saturday's renewal of the star-studded Derby will be its ninth running .... The fields have remained intact for all but one of its runnings .... This occurred in 1949 when Never Risk was forced to be scratched .... Also in 1949, the year of the Derby's inaugural, the rabit lure was changed from the outside railing to the inside, from which point it now operates .... Real Huntsman, whose offsprings are now running with success at Taunton, won the Derby twice in succession — 1950 and 1951 .... In 1950 Real Huntsman accounted for the shortest payoff, $2.60, in the history of the race .... That year "The Huntsman" won all three qualifying rounds and went on to annex the Derby final without a defeat.... In June 6, 1951, in the final qualifying round Real Huntsman left the box at the prohibitive odds of .10 cents to a dollar .... But was beaten by C. C. Wilsons Raven finishing second but maintaining enough points to remain in the Derby, Raven paid $54.80 .... Real Huntsman went on to win the '51 running in the record time of :38 2-5 seconds, a mark that since has been equalled by On The Line in 1952, Mellojean in 1954 and Go Rock last year .... Slowest time for the Derby running was chalked up in 1955 by Koliga over a slow race track in :39 1-5 .... In 1953 the speedy greyhound, However, repeated Real Huntsman's 1950 winning all qualifying rounds and the final ....

One of the Derby oddities occurred in 1955 .... That was the year She's Salty was injured in the third qualifying round after winning the first two .... The dog was forced to be withdrawn and Koliga, ninth in the point standings, was moved into a starting position .... Koliga went on to take top honors .... Splendored, who with Fanelia, will be making a second attempt to lift the rich prize on Saturday, holds the track and world records for the Bristol course of :38 .... This does not affect the Derby mark ....

Clydesdale-1957

THE AMERICAN GREYHOUND DERBY

TENTH RACE

Track-World's Record
Splendored 38

PLEASE CALL FOR DOG BY NUMBER

BRISTOL COURSE
675 YARDS

P.P. Red 1 — CLYDESDALE

Orville Moses, owner
Charles Rink, trainer

Starts 11, 1st 4, 2nd 1, 3rd 3

72 — Brindle D., January 1955. Mixed Harmony—Nobility

Date	Dis.	TC	Ti.	Wt	PP	Off	1-8	St	Fin	Odds	FW	Comment	Grade	Order of Finish
10-9^{9}	BC	F	38.3	71½	2	8	6stb	8	8	.70	6½	*Blckd, stb. bkstr.*	①	GetHappy, BabyRing, Vot.Choice
10-5^{8}	BC	F	38.4	71½	7	8	3	1^{5}	$1^{7\frac{1}{2}}$	1.10	—	*Easily*	①	Tr.Eagle, M.Harmony, Blu.Flame
10-2^{6}	BC	F	39	72	1	5	4	2	1^{1}	.60	—	*Driving wide*	①	RebaCrane, O.B.'sMix, Geo.Mark
9-27^{9}	5-16	F	31.2	71	3	6	5	5	$4^{1\frac{1}{2}}$	3.60	4	*Lacked a rally*	1	TeenQueen, Fanelia, EbbTideGal
9-23^{9}	5-16	F	31.1	72	7	7	7	3	†$2^{\frac{1}{2}}$	3.00	3	*Late sp., DH, place*	1	TransTaylor, Issuance, Valued
9-20^{10}	BC	F	38.4	71	7	6	4	2	3^{7}	9.00	½	*Winning effort*	1 2	Membership, Splendored, Valued

P.P. Blue 2 — BABY RING

M. J. Gavan, owner
M. J. Gavan, trainer

Starts 12, 1st 1, 2nd 3, 3rd 2

50 — Brindle B., May 1954. Key Ring—Headstrong

Date	Dis.	TC	Ti.	Wt	PP	Off	1-8	St	Fin	Odds	FW	Comment	Grade	Order of Finish
10-9^{9}	BC	F	38.3	50	5	1	5	4	2^{1}	17.60	no	*Almost up*	②	GetHappy, Vot.Choice, T.Y.Rose
10-5^{5}	BC	F	39	50	8	7	6	2	$2^{7\frac{1}{2}}$	3.20	1½	*Rap. gn up bkstr.*	②	V.O., MacCohen, RealGeorge
10-2^{8}	BC	F	39.1	49½	1	1	3	2	1^{hd}	4.00	—	*Saved, up at wire*	③	TransEagle, V.O., O.B.'sAmalric
9-28^{10}	EC	F	45	49	1	1	8	5	3^{2}	.90	8½	*Pinched bk 1st tn*	③	Staccato, Geo.Mark, EtherBorne
9-25^{9}	BC	F	39.2	49	3	5	5	2	2^{2}	1.10	1	*Close qrts break*	③	Staccato, SteppinEasy, Eth.Borne
9-20^{8}	5-16	F	31.2	49	4	2	8	6	4^{hd}	7.60	5½	*Drpd bk, late speed*	2	AggieLand, Ire.Logan, O.B.Tena

P.P. White 3 — FANELIA

Orville Moses, owner
Charles Rink, trainer

Starts 10, 1st 3, 2nd 4, 3rd 0

53 — Brindle B., January 1955. Mixed Harmony—Secrets

Date	Dis.	TC	Ti.	Wt	PP	Off	1-8	St	Fin	Odds	FW	Comment	Grade	Order of Finish
10-9^{8}	BC	F	38.1	52	2	1	1^{2}	1^{1}	$2^{\frac{1}{2}}$	5.50	4	*Game effort*	①	Splendored, Surprised, V.O.
10-5^{4}	BC	F	39.1	52	4	5	2	1^{2}	$1^{1\frac{1}{2}}$	1.10	—	*Insi. ctn tn handily*	①	WillO'Wisp, GetHappy, Pet.Pink
10-2^{4}	BC	F	39.1	52	4	7	3	2	$1^{\frac{1}{2}}$	1.70	—	*Up in steady drive*	①	Vot.Choice, E.Ti.Gal, LightMack
9-27^{9}	5-16	F	31.2	51½	1	3	2	2	$2^{2\frac{1}{2}}$	4.00	½	*Winning effort*	1	TeenQueen, E.Ti.Gal, Clydesdale
9-24^{10}	BC	F	39	51½	7	6	6	5	2no	3.20	2	*Much late speed*	1 2	EbbTideGal, Pet.Pink, Tr.Eagle^{7}
9-19^{9}	5-16	F	31	51½	2	6	5	6	6^{2}	5.30	8½	*Never prominent*	1	Firelace, WeeSensation, Haigler

P.P. Green 4 — VALUED

F. B. Stutz, owner
Wm. Black, trainer

Starts 6, 1st 2, 2nd 0, 3rd 1

58 — Red Fawn B., October 1954. Mostest—Tireless

Date	Dis.	TC	Ti.	Wt	PP	Off	1-8	St	Fin	Odds	FW	Comment	Grade	Order of Finish
10-9^{10}	BC	F	38.2	58	6	7	6	7	$6^{\frac{1}{2}}$	.80	6	*Close qrts far tn*	①	RebaCrane, E.Dea.Jones, D.Ring
10-5^{6}	BC	F	38.2	58	7	2	1^{5}	1^{13}	1^{13}	.50	—	*All alone*	①	Jerry.Tom, Re.Crane, Geo.Mark^{7}
10-2^{5}	BC	F	38.4	58	6	5	2	1^{6}	1^{8}	.60	—	*Breezing*	①	D.Ring, Knocker, LeapingTiger
9-26^{9}	5-16	F	31.1	58	6	7	4	4	†$3^{2\frac{1}{2}}$	2.50	4½	*Good efft, DH show*	1	Firel'ce, L.Sue, O.B.Arg's, Valued
9-23^{9}	5-16	F	31.1	58	8	6	4	4	$4^{6\frac{1}{2}}$	1.10	3½	*Shut off far turn*	1	TransTaylor, Issuance, Clydesdale
9-20^{10}	BC	F	38.4	58	8	8	6	6	4^{hd}	2.00	7½	*Offstrided ctn tn*	1 2	Memb'ship, Splend'r'd, Clydesd'le

P.P. Black 5 — SPLENDORED

M. J. Gavan, owner
M. J. Gavan, trainer

Starts 12, 1st 4, 2nd 2, 3rd 2

54 — Brindle B., October 1954. On The Line—Mariella

Date	Dis.	TC	Ti.	Wt	PP	Off	1-8	St	Fin	Odds	FW	Comment	Grade	Order of Finish
10-9^{8}	BC	F	38.1	55	1	4	4	2	1^{4}	.50	—	*Drew out easily*	①	Fanelia, Surprised, V.O.
10-5^{9}	BC	F	38.4	54½	7	5	3	1^{7}	$1^{8\frac{1}{2}}$	.40	—	*Easily*	①	Surprised, StellaC., ForestReserve
10-2^{10}	BC	F	39.1	55	6	4	5	3	1^{1}	.80	—	*Driving wide*	②	Membership, Blu.Flame, Mazola
9-28^{6}	5-16	F	31.3	54½	6	3	5	4	$2^{\frac{1}{2}}$	1.10	3	*Forced out 1st turn*	2	M.Margie, H'rthstone, W.O'Wisp
9-25^{6}s	5-16	F	31.2	54	6	8	7	4	3^{hd}	.....	1½	*Much late speed*		O.B.Amalric, Ok.Maid, E.D.Jones
9-24^{8}	5-16	F	31.1	54½	3	7	6	5	3no	1.00	4½	*Muzzle off*	2	DonLarsen, Elevated, SteelPlate

P.P. Yellow 6 — TEXAS YELLOW ROSE

A. L. Sparks, owner
Fred Trevillion, trainer

Starts 3, 1st 1, 2nd 1, 3rd 0
Revere 25, 6, 9, 4

59 — Red B., April 1955. Rocker Mac—Headstrong

Date	Dis.	TC	Ti.	Wt	PP	Off	1-8	St	Fin	Odds	FW	Comment	Grade	Order of Finish
10-9^{9}	BC	F	38.3	58	8	7	8	5	4no	2.40	1½	*Rapid str. drive*	①	GetHappy, BabyRing, Vot.Choice
10-5^{10}	BC	F	39	58½	4	5	7	4	2^{4}	2.30	2	*Much late speed*	①	Membership, NobleKid, Avalon
10-2^{9}	BC	F	39.2	58½	5	6	7	3	$1^{1\frac{1}{2}}$	1.70	—	*Rapid str. drive*	①	Firelace, Haigler, GetHappy
9-27^{7}s	BC	F	39	59	7	5	7	4	3^{1}	.....	3	*Much late speed*		E.Dea.Jones, Li.Mack, Re.George
9-23^{7}s	BC	F	39	59½	6	5	7	5	$2^{1\frac{1}{2}}$	.....	3	*Much late speed*		M.Harmony, Surprised, Step.Jim^{7}
9-18^{7}s	BC	F	38.4	60½	7	7	6	5	$2^{\frac{1}{2}}$	.....	1½	*Much late speed*		Can.Pacific, F.Reserve, Li.Mack^{7}

P.P. Green & Whi. 7 — REBA CRANE

Otto Mamino, owner
Antone Perry Jr., trainer

Starts 11, 1st 4, 2nd 2, 3rd 1

53 — Brindle B., February 1955. Bowie Steel—Fair Time

Date	Dis.	TC	Ti.	Wt	PP	Off	1-8	St	Fin	Odds	FW	Comment	Grade	Order of Finish
10-9^{10}	BC	F	38.2	53½	5	3	1^{4}	1^{3}	$1^{1\frac{1}{2}}$	15.60	—	*Held safe lead*	①	E.De.Jones, D.Ring, Membership
10-5^{6}	BC	F	38.2	53½	5	5	6	3	3^{2}	3.40	13½	*No early speed*	①	Valued, Jerry.Tom, GeorgeMark^{7}
10-2^{6}	BC	F	39	53	6	1	$1^{2\frac{1}{2}}$	$1^{1\frac{1}{2}}$	2^{2}	2.90	1	*Winning effort*	①	Clydesdale, O.B.'sMix, Geo.Mark
9-28^{9}	5-16	F	31.1	53½	3	2	1^{2}	1^{3}	$1^{3\frac{1}{2}}$	5.20	—	*Handily*	1	Membership, Qu.State, Tr.Taylor
9-26^{8}	5-16	F	31.1	53	6	4	2	1^{2}	$1^{4\frac{1}{2}}$	4.40	—	*Easily*	1	Tr.Taylor, Po.Range, W.Sensation
9-21^{8}	5-16	F	30.4	52½	3	2	6	7	7^{1}	4.40	11	*Forced out 1st turn*	1	TeenQueen, Postal, NobleKid

P.P. Yellow & Black 8 — D. RING

O. L. Life, owner
John McLaughlin, trainer

Starts 3, 1st 1, 2nd 1, 3rd 1
Sodrac Park 24, 7, 3, 6

58 — Brindle D., May 1954. Key Ring—Extra Life

Date	Dis.	TC	Ti.	Wt	PP	Off	1-8	St	Fin	Odds	FW	Comment	Grade	Order of Finish
10-9^{10}	BC	F	38.2	58½	2	1	2	3	3^{hd}	7.50	4½	*Forced wide bkstr.*	①	R.Crane, E.D.Jones, Membership
10-5^{3}	BC	F	38.4	59½	8	3	1^{2}	1^{1}	1^{nk}	1.60	—	*Held gamely*	①	E.D.Jones, O.B.Amalric, Labeled^{7}
10-2^{5}	BC	F	38.4	58½	5	2	1^{hd}	2	$2^{3\frac{1}{2}}$	3.80	8	*Raced forwardly*	①	Valued, Knocker, LeapingTiger
9-25^{7}s	BC	F	39	57½	8	7	2	2	1^{3}	.....	—	*Drew out*		V.O., For.Reserve, Rur.Shannon^{7}
9-23^{4}s	5-16	F	31	58	6	1	3	3	2^{hd}	.....	2	*Some wide thruout*		BluishFlame, V.O., Butter^{7}
9-18^{5}s	5-16	F	31	58	3	2	2	2	$2^{2\frac{1}{2}}$	.....	8	*Chased winner*		R.Shannon, RioSancho, W.Pilot^{6}

*—Performance shown not in proper sequence but is last race of dog at distance shown.

†—Indicates dead heat.

Handicapper's Selections—Fanelia, Splendored, Valued

Feldcrest-1958

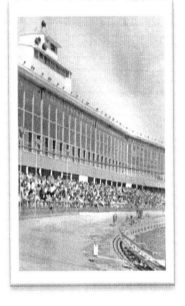

CLYDESDALE
WINNER OF
1957 AMERICAN GREYHOUND DERBY

$25,000 American Greyhound DERBY

Tenth Race – Tonight

OFFICIAL PROGRAM 25c

TAUNTON DOG TRACK

America's Blue Ribbon Track

SATURDAY, OCT. 18, 1958

Feldcrest-1958

The American Greyhound Derby

Track-World's Record Splendored 38 — GRADE S — TENTH RACE — PLEASE CALL FOR DOG BY NUMBER

BRISTOL COURSE 675 YARDS

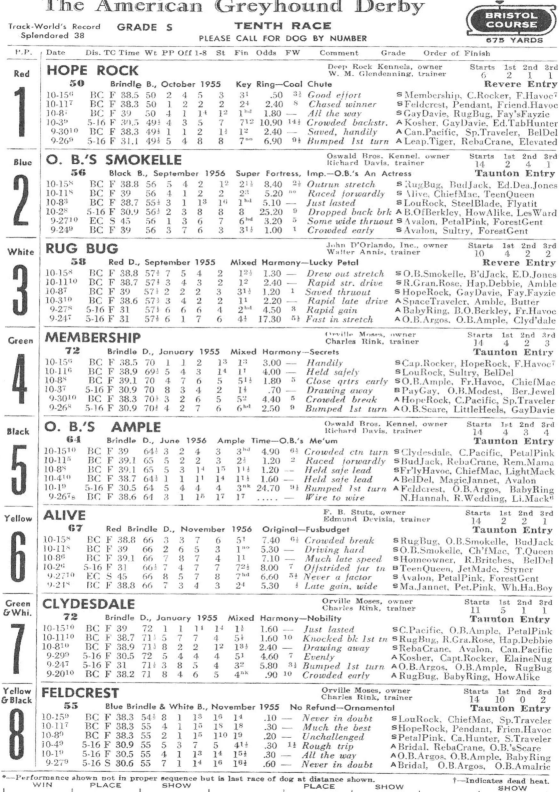

Red 1 — HOPE ROCK

Deep Rock Kennels, owner; W. M. Glendenning, trainer — Starts 6, 1st 2, 2nd 1, 3rd 1

50 Brindle B., October 1955 Key Ring—Coal Chute — **Revere Entry**

Date	Dis.	TC	Time	Wt	PP	Off	1-8	St	Fin	Odds	FW	Comment	Grade	Order of Finish
10-15^{6}	BC	F	38.5	50	2	4	5	3	3^{1}	.50	3½	*Good effort*	S	Membership, C.Rocker, F.Havoc^{7}
10-11^{7}	BC	F	38.3	50	1	2	2	2	2^{4}	2.40	8	*Chased winner*	S	Feldcrest, Pendant, Friend.Havoc
10-8^{7}	BC	F	39	50	4	1	1^{4}	1^{2}	1^{hd}	1.80	—	*All the way*	S	GayDavie, RugBug, Fay'sFayzie
10-3^{9}	5-16	F	30.5	49½	4	3	5	7	7^{12}	10.90	14½	*Crowded backstr.*	A	Kosher, GayDavie, Ed.TabHunter
9-30^{10}	BC	F	38.3	49½	1	1	2	$1^{½}$	1^{2}	2.40	—	*Saved, handily*	A	Can.Pacific, Sp.Traveler, BelDel
9-26^{9}	5-16	F	31.1	49½	5	4	8	8	7no	6.90	9½	*Bumped 1st turn*	A	Leap.Tiger, RebaCrane, Elevated

Blue 2 — O. B.'S SMOKELLE

Oswald Bros. Kennel, owner; Richard Davis, trainer — Starts 14, 1st 2, 2nd 4, 3rd 1

56 Black B., September 1956 Super Fortress, Imp.—O.B.'s An Actress — **Taunton Entry**

Date	Dis.	TC	Time	Wt	PP	Off	1-8	St	Fin	Odds	FW	Comment	Grade	Order of Finish
10-15^{8}	BC	F	38.8	56	5	4	2	1^{2}	$2^{1½}$	8.40	2½	*Outrun stretch*	S	RugBug, BudJack, Ed.Dea.Jones
10-11^{8}	BC	F	39	56	4	1	2	2	2^{3}	5.20	no	*Raced forwardly*	S	Alive, ChiefMac, TeenQueen
10-8^{3}	BC	F	38.7	55½	3	1	1^{3}	1^{6}	1^{hd}	5.10	—	*Just lasted*	S	LouRock, SteelBlade, Flyatit
10-2^{8}	5-16	F	30.9	56½	2	3	8	8	8	25.20	9	*Dropped back brk*	A	B.OfBerkley, HowAlike, LesWard
9-27^{10}	EC	S	45	56	1	3	6	7	6^{hd}	3.20	5	*Some wide thruout*	S	Avalon, PetalPink, ForestGent
9-24^{9}	BC	F	39	56	3	7	6	3	$3^{1½}$	1.00	1	*Crowded early*	S	Avalon, Sultry, ForestGent

White 3 — RUG BUG

John D'Orlando, Inc., owner; Walter Annis, trainer — Starts 10, 1st 4, 2nd 2, 3rd 2

58 Red D., September 1955 Mixed Harmony—Lucky Petal — **Revere Entry**

Date	Dis.	TC	Time	Wt	PP	Off	1-8	St	Fin	Odds	FW	Comment	Grade	Order of Finish
10-15^{8}	BC	F	38.8	57½	7	5	4	2	$1^{2½}$	1.30	—	*Drew out stretch*	S	O.B.Smokelle, B'dJack, E.D.Jones
10-11^{10}	BC	F	38.7	57½	3	4	3	2	1^{2}	2.40	—	*Rapid str. drive*	S	R.Gran.Rose, Hap.Debbie, Amble
10-8^{7}	BC	F	39	57½	2	2	2	3	$3^{1½}$	1.20	1	*Saved thruout*	S	HopeRock, GayDavie, Fay.Fayzie
10-3^{10}	BC	F	38.6	57½	3	4	2	2	1^{1}	2.20	—	*Rapid late drive*	A	SpaceTraveler, Amble, Butter
9-27^{8}	5-16	F	31	57½	6	6	6	4	2^{hd}	4.50	3	*Rapid gain*	A	BabyRing, B.O.Berkley, Fr.Havoc
9-24^{7}	5-16	F	31	57½	6	1	7	6	$4^{½}$	17.30	5½	*Fast in stretch*	A	O.B.Argos, O.B.Ample, Clyd'dale

Green 4 — MEMBERSHIP

Orville Moses, owner; Charles Rink, trainer — Starts 14, 1st 4, 2nd 2, 3rd 3

72 Brindle D., January 1955 Mixed Harmony—Secrets — **Taunton Entry**

Date	Dis.	TC	Time	Wt	PP	Off	1-8	St	Fin	Odds	FW	Comment	Grade	Order of Finish
10-15^{6}	BC	F	38.5	70	1	1	2	1^{3}	1^{3}	3.00	—	*Handily*	S	Cap.Rocker, HopeRock, F.Havoc^{7}
10-11^{6}	BC	F	38.9	69½	5	4	3	1^{4}	1^{1}	4.00	—	*Held safely*	S	LouRock, Sultry, BelDel
10-8^{8}	BC	F	39.1	70	4	7	6	5	$5^{1½}$	1.80	5	*Close qrtrs early*	S	O.B.Ample, Fr.Havoc, ChiefMac
10-3^{7}	5-16	F	30.9	70	8	3	4	2	$1^{½}$	.70	—	*Drawing away*	B	PayGay, O.B.Modest, Ber.Jewel
9-30^{10}	BC	F	38.3	70½	3	2	6	5	5^{2}	4.40	5	*Crowded break*	A	HopeRock, C.Pacific, Sp.Traveler
9-26^{8}	5-16	F	30.9	70½	4	2	7	6	6^{hd}	2.50	9	*Bumped 1st turn*	A	O.B.Scare, LittleHeels, GayDavie

Black 5 — O. B.'S AMPLE

Oswald Bros. Kennel, owner; Richard Davis, trainer — Starts 14, 1st 4, 2nd 3, 3rd 4

64 Brindle D., June 1956 Ample Time—O.B.'s Me'um — **Taunton Entry**

Date	Dis.	TC	Time	Wt	PP	Off	1-8	St	Fin	Odds	FW	Comment	Grade	Order of Finish
10-15^{10}	BC	F	39	64½	3	2	4	3	3^{hd}	4.90	6½	*Crowded ctn turn*	S	Clydesdale, C.Pacific, PetalPink
10-11^{5}	BC	F	39.1	65	5	2	2	3	$2^{½}$	1.20	2	*Raced forwardly*	S	BudJack, RebaCrane, Rem.Mama
10-8^{8}	BC	F	39.1	65	5	3	1^{4}	1^{5}	$1^{1½}$	1.20	—	*Held safe lead*	S	Fr'lyHavoc, ChiefMac, LightMack
10-4^{10}	BC	F	38.7	64½	1	1	1^{1}	1^{4}	$1^{1½}$	1.60	—	*Held safe lead*	A	BelDel, MagicJannet, Avalon
10-1^{9}	5-16	F	30.5	64	5	4	4	4	3^{nk}	24.70	9½	*Bumped 1st turn*	A	Feldcrest, O.B.Argos, BabyRing
9-26^{7}s	BC	F	38.6	64	3	1	1^{5}	1^{7}	1^{7}	.....	—	*Wire to wire*		N.Hannah, R.Wedding, Li.Mack^{6}

Yellow 6 — ALIVE

F. B. Stutz, owner; Edmund Devizia, trainer — Starts 14, 1st 2, 2nd 2, 3rd 1

67 Red Brindle D., November 1956 Original—Fusbudget — **Taunton Entry**

Date	Dis.	TC	Time	Wt	PP	Off	1-8	St	Fin	Odds	FW	Comment	Grade	Order of Finish
10-15^{8}	BC	F	38.8	66	3	3	7	6	5^{1}	7.40	6½	*Crowded break*	S	RugBug, O.B.Smokelle, BudJack
10-11^{8}	BC	F	39	66	2	6	5	3	1no	5.30	—	*Driving hard*	S	O.B.Smokelle, Ch'fMac, T.Queen
10-8^{6}	BC	F	39.1	66	7	8	7	4	1^{1}	7.10	—	*Much late speed*	S	Homeowner, R.Britches, BelDel
10-2^{6}	5-16	F	31	66½	7	4	7	7	$7^{2½}$	8.00	7	*Offstrided far tn*	B	TeenQueen, JetMade, Styner
9-27^{10}	EC	S	45	66	8	5	7	8	7^{hd}	6.60	5½	*Never a factor*	S	Avalon, PetalPink, ForestGent
9-24^{8}	BC	F	38.8	66	7	3	4	3	2^{4}	5.30	½	*Late gain, wide*	S	Ma.Jannet, Pet.Pink, Wh.Ha.Boy

Green & Whi. 7 — CLYDESDALE

Orville Moses, owner; Charles Rink, trainer — Starts 11, 1st 5, 2nd 1, 3rd 1

72 Brindle D., January 1955 Mixed Harmony—Nobility — **Taunton Entry**

Date	Dis.	TC	Time	Wt	PP	Off	1-8	St	Fin	Odds	FW	Comment	Grade	Order of Finish
10-15^{10}	BC	F	39	72	1	1	1^{1}	1^{4}	$1^{½}$	1.60	—	*Just lasted*	S	C.Pacific, O.B.Ample, PetalPink
10-11^{10}	BC	F	38.7	71½	5	7	7	4	$5^{½}$	1.60	10	*Knocked bk 1st tn*	S	RugBug, R.Gra.Rose, Hap.Debbie
10-8^{10}	BC	F	38.9	71½	8	2	2	1^{2}	$1^{3½}$	2.40	—	*Drawing away*	S	RebaCrane, Avalon, Can.Pacific
9-29^{9}	5-16	F	30.5	72	5	4	4	4	5^{1}	4.60	7	*Evenly*	A	Kosher, Capt.Rocker, ElaineNug
9-24^{7}	5-16	F	31	71½	3	8	5	4	3^{2}	5.80	3½	*Bumped 1st turn*	A	O.B.Argos, O.B.Ample, RugBug
9-20^{10}	BC	F	38.2	71	8	4	6	5	4^{nk}	.90	10	*Crowded early*	A	RugBug, BabyRing, HowAlike

Yellow & Black 8 — FELDCREST

Orville Moses, owner; Charles Rink, trainer — Starts 14, 1st 10, 2nd 0, 3rd 2

55 Blue Brindle & White B., November 1955 No Refund—Ornamental — **Taunton Entry**

Date	Dis.	TC	Time	Wt	PP	Off	1-8	St	Fin	Odds	FW	Comment	Grade	Order of Finish
10-15^{9}	BC	F	38.3	54½	8	1	1^{3}	1^{6}	1^{4}	.10	—	*Never in doubt*	S	LouRock, ChiefMac, Sp.Traveler
10-11^{7}	BC	F	38.3	55	4	1	1^{5}	1^{8}	1^{8}	.30	—	*Much the best*	S	HopeRock, Pendant, Frien.Havoc
10-8^{9}	BC	F	38.3	55	2	1	1^{5}	1^{10}	1^{9}	.20	—	*Unchallenged*	S	PetalPink, Ca.Hunter, S.Traveler
10-4^{9}	5-16	F	30.9	55	5	3	7	5	$4^{1½}$	.30	1½	*Rough trip*	A	Bridal, RebaCrane, O.B.'sScare
10-1^{9}	5-16	F	30.5	55	4	1	1^{3}	1^{4}	$1^{5½}$	.30	—	*All the way*	A	O.B.Argos, O.B.Ample, BabyRing
9-27^{9}	5-16	S	30.6	55	7	1	1^{4}	1^{6}	$1^{6½}$	.60	—	*Never in doubt*	A	Bridal, O.B.Argos, O.B.Amalric

*—Performance shown not in proper sequence but is last race of dog at distance shown.

†—Indicates dead heat.

WIN	PLACE	SHOW		PLACE	SHOW		SHOW

Handicapper's Selections—Feldcrest, Hope Rock, Rug Bug

Go Super-1959

GO SUPER
WINNER OF
1959 AMERICAN GREYHOUND DERBY

Go Super-1959

The American Greyhound Derby

Track-World's Record
Splendored 38

ELEVENTH RACE

BRISTOL COURSE
675 YARDS

P.P.	Date	Dis. TC Time Wt PP Off 1-8	St	Fin	Odds	FW	Comment	Grade	Order of Finish

Red 1

WAYSIDE SLOAN

Wayside Kennel, owner
Ralph Boerma, trainer — Starts 3, 1st 2, 2nd 0, 3rd 0

72 Fawn D., December 1957 — Wayside Jerry—Wayside Yukon Gal — DAYTONA 24 14 2 4

Date	Dis. TC Time	Wt	PP	Off	1-8	St	Fin	Odds	FW	Comment	Grade	Order of Finish
10-21[6]	BC F 39.1	71½	2	5	2	2	1³½	.70	—	Drew out in str.	(A)	BettieBess, Ar.Boston, LightMack
10-17[5]	BC F 38.5	71½	8	3	1¹	1²	12½	1.10	—	Handily	(A)	O.B.Medium, A.Boston, T'nAway
10-14[7]	BC F 39	71	6	4	6	5	4no	1.70	5	Crowded early	(A)	R.M'Master, T.Target, Sp.Special
10-9[5]s	BC F 38.7	72	1	6	2	2	2¹	.....	no	Hard try		HappyJoL., Crocadoll, GuyBerry[7]
10-5[4]s	5-16 F 30.8	72	6	5	5	3	3³	.....	6	Gained backstretch		RushingJohn, Bopper, SnowLine[7]
10-2[5]s	5-16 F 30.9	72	3	7	4	5	5½	.....	2½	Blocked far turn		Mr.Tears, Blon.Blazer, Crocadoll[7]

Blue 2

FABLE LAUDATION

Joe Slovick, owner
Joe Slovick, trainer — Starts 3, 1st 1, 2nd 1, 3rd 0

60 Red B., February 1957 — Northam Star, Imp.—Sutters Gold — MULTNOMAH 16 7 4 1

Date	Dis. TC Time	Wt	PP	Off	1-8	St	Fin	Odds	FW	Comment	Grade	Order of Finish
10-21[10]	BC F 39.1	59½	5	3	8	5	4¹½	.60	4½	Knockd bk early	(A)	Crocadoll, M.A.Yours, Ran.Trail
10-17[10]	BC F 38.9	58½	2	8	7	5	2²	.60	no	Crd., hard try	(A)	Ranger.Trail, BudJack, L.Around
10-14[6]	BC F 38.1	58½	6	4	4	2	1³	.90	—	Ard ldrs, dr. out	(A)	SuzyBenny, L.Around, Kub.Khan
10-12[2]s	BC F 38.3	58½	8	4	2	1³	1³	.....	—	Drew out in stretch		L.Around, Peul.Nug, SandyL.P.[4]
10-9[2]s	BC F 39	59½	1	5	5	3	2¹	.....	½	Blocked first turn		T.Y.Rose, F.Laudat'n, S.Comm'd[6]

White 3

RANGER'S TRAIL

Dr. Al M. Bissing, owner
William Green, trainer — Starts 3, 1st 1, 2nd 1, 3rd 1

71 Brindle D., January 1957 — Ample Time—Cactus Trail — DAYTONA 22 8 5 2

Date	Dis. TC Time	Wt	PP	Off	1-8	St	Fin	Odds	FW	Comment	Grade	Order of Finish
10-21[10]	BC F 39.1	70½	1	4	3	3	3³	2.10	1½	Good effort	(A)	Crocadoll, M.A.Yours, F.Laudat'n
10-17[10]	BC F 38.9	70½	5	7	5	3	1no	3.30	—	Crd., just up	(A)	F.Laudation, BudJack, L.Around
10-14[11]	BC F 38.4	70½	7	4	3	2	2³½	4.40	3	Forward factor	(A)	Feldcrest, M.Parkway, R.MacCoy
10-7[3]s	BC F 38.8	71	8	3	1³	1⁵	1³	.....	—	Held safe lead		TurnAway, M.A.Yours, Str.Trail[7]
10-2[3]s	BC F 39.1	71½	3	3	1½	2	1½	.....	—	Up in stretch drive		T.Yel.Rose, CriTears, GuyBerry[4]
9-28[2]s	BC F 39	71	2	1	2	1¹	1⁴	.....	—	Drew out		Strea.Trail, Stockinet, R.Warren[5]

Green 4

GO SUPER

Oscar Block, owner
Earl J. Fitzpatrick, trainer — Starts 3, 1st 3, 2nd 0, 3rd 0

71 Brindle D., November 1956 — Super Fortress, Imp.—Darlin Peggy — SODRAC 22 10 7 2

Date	Dis. TC Time	Wt	PP	Off	1-8	St	Fin	Odds	FW	Comment	Grade	Order of Finish
10-21[9]	BC F 39.1	71½	4	4	4	1hd	1¹½	.80	—	Drew out	(A)	R.M'Master, R.M'Ginty, S.Benny
10-17[9]	BC F 38.7	71½	1	1	1²	1¹½	1hd	1.40	—	Just lasted	(A)	R.M'Ginty, MarDilly, T.Remark[7]
10-14[8]	BC F 38.8	71	6	3	1⁶	1⁶	1⁷	1.00	—	Easily	(A)	MileHigher, Blo.Blazer, Li.Mack
10-7[2]s	BC F 38.5	72	4	1	1³	1¹	2⁶	.....	2	Speed to stretch		MarDilly, BlondBlazer, LouRock
9-30[5]s	5-16 F 31	72	6	4	1²	1⁶	1⁶	.....	—	Easily on rail		PatVinci, Kosher, ElsaG.[6]

Black 5

TOP TARGET

Clement W. Zwack, owner
John J. Ferrell, trainer — Starts 3, 1st 1, 2nd 2, 3rd 0

72 Brindle D., October 1956 — Bell Boy—Shine Up — SODRAC 15 8 2 1

Date	Dis. TC Time	Wt	PP	Off	1-8	St	Fin	Odds	FW	Comment	Grade	Order of Finish
10-21[8]	BC F 39	72½	3	5	4	1hd	2⁴½	4.40	no	Outgmd at wire	(A)	Mr.Tears, Bridal, Geemarie
10-17[6]	BC F 38.8	72½	5	3	3	2	1¹	3.60	—	Despite trouble	(A)	Li.Mack, M.Jannet, Stream.Trail[7]
10-14[7]	BC F 39	72	2	6	2	1²	2¹	1.40	½	Tired in stretch	(A)	R.M'Master, S.Special, Way.Sloan
10-9[1]s	BC F 38.9	72	4	4	4	4	3¹	.....	1	Crowded first turn		BudJack, Sp.Special, SnowLine[6]
10-2[2]s	BC F 38.7	72½	2	2	3	2	1²	.....	—	Won handily		RustyCop, GeraldM., Strea.Trail[5]
9-28[7]s	5-16 F 31.1	71½	1	5	3	2	1hd	.....	—	Up despite trouble		RustyCop, CriTears, ChinaSails[7]

Yellow 6

CROCADOLL

Marlow Kennel, owner
Ted Lippold, trainer — Starts 3, 1st 2, 2nd 1, 3rd 0

61½ White and Brindle B., February 1957 — Royally—Like It — PENSACOLA 12 3 5 2

Date	Dis. TC Time	Wt	PP	Off	1-8	St	Fin	Odds	FW	Comment	Grade	Order of Finish
10-21[10]	BC F 39.1	62	2	8	4	2	1¹	8.10	—	Bnf. early, st. dr.	(A)	M.A.Yours, R.Trail, F.Laudation
10-17[7]	BC F 38.8	61½	6	8	3	2	1½	2.20	—	Driving wide	(A)	Bl'dBlazer, O.B.Ample, M.P'kway
10-14[10]	BC F 38.8	62	5	8	3	2no	8.10	3		Crd., rapid gain	(A)	R.M'Duff, M.Jannet, O.B.Medium
10-9[5]s	BC F 38.7	62	6	3	5	4	3½	.....	1	Very wide		HappyJoL., Way.Sloan, G.Berry[7]
10-7[2]s	BC F 38.5	62	5	6	6	7	5¹	.....	9½	Jammed after break	MarDilly, GoSuper, BlondBlazer
10-5[6]s	5-16 F 31.1	61½	7	6	3	1no	1²	.....	—	Very wide thruout		ElsaG., S.Command, M.A.Yours[7]

Green White 7

MR. TEARS

Oscar Evers, owner
Carl J. Peterson, trainer — Starts 3, 1st 2, 2nd 0, 3rd 0

67 Red Brindle D., May 1957 — On The Line—Viv's Ginger — REVERE 26 12 7 3

Date	Dis. TC Time	Wt	PP	Off	1-8	St	Fin	Odds	FW	Comment	Grade	Order of Finish
10-21[8]	BC F 39	67	6	4	6	3	1no	.40	—	Up at wire	(A)	TopTarget, Bridal, Geemarie
10-17[8]	BC F 38.3	66½	1	1	1½	1³	1⁸	.60	—	Drew out, wide	(A)	BettieBess, R.MacDuff, CriTears[7]
10-14[9]	BC F 38.9	66½	3	2	4	4	4³½	.40	6	Early contender	(A)	TurnAway, PatVinci, T.Yel.Rose
10-9[1]s	BC F 38.5	67	8	3	3	1⁵	1⁴½	.....	—	Drew out wide		PatVinci, N.Hannah, Ch.Matron[6]
10-5[5]s	5-16 F 30.6	67	3	3	2	1⁷	1¹⁵	.....	—	All alone		Na.Hannah, Greg.Lynn, RonaldR.
10-2[5]s	5-16 F 30.9	67	8	6	3	2	1hd	.....	—	Just up		Blon.Blazer, Crocadoll, BudJack[7]

Yellow & Black 8

FELDCREST

Orville Moses, owner
Charles Rink, trainer — Starts 13, 1st 11, 2nd 2, 3rd 0

55 Blue Brindle & White B., November 1955 — No Refund—Ornamental

Date	Dis. TC Time	Wt	PP	Off	1-8	St	Fin	Odds	FW	Comment	Grade	Order of Finish
10-21[11]	BC F 38.9	55	2	3	2	1⁵	1⁷	.20	—	Drew out, easily	(A)	O.B.Melon, T.Yel.Rose, BudJack
10-17[11]	BC F 38.6	55	5	2	2	1³	1²	.30	—	Held safe lead	(A)	O.B.Melon, R.MacCoy, Geemarie
10-14[11]	BC F 38.4	55	2	1	1³	1⁵	1³	.40	—	Held safe lead	(A)	Ran.Trail, M.Parkway, R.MacCoy
10-8[9]	5-16 F 30.7	55½	1	2	1²	1⁴	1⁶½	.40	—	Easily	A	Bridal, PayGay, O.B.'sAmple
10-3[10]	5-16 F 30.7	55	4	2	3	2	2³	.30	1½	Some wide, 1st tn	A	MarDilly, O.B.Melon, Mr.Th.Man
9-28[9]	5-16 F 30.8	55½	8	2	2	2	1⁵	.30	—	Drew out in str.	A	PayGay, O.B.'sSincere, MarDilly

*—Performance shown not in proper sequence but is last race of dog at distance shown. †—Indicates dead heat.

Handicapper's Selections—Feldcrest, Fable Laudation, Mr. Tears

Serape-1960

GO SUPER
WINNER OF
1959 AMERICAN GREYHOUND DERBY

$25,000 American Greyhound DERBY

TONIGHT

OFFICIAL PROGRAM 25c

TAUNTON DOG TRACK

America's Blue Ribbon Track

SATURDAY, OCT. 22, 1960

Serape-1960

BRISTOL COURSE
675 YARDS

12th Annual American Greyhound Derby

ELEVENTH RACE

Track-World's Record
Splendored 38

Red 1 — SERAPE — 61 — Black D., July 1958 — Black Magic, Imp.—Excellence
Orville Moses, owner; Charles Rink, trainer — Starts 14, 1st 2, 2nd 4, 3rd 2

Date	Dis.	TC	Time	Wt	PP	Off	1-8	St	Fin	Odds	FW	Comment	Grade	Order of Finish
10-19^{9}	BC	F	38.5	60½	6	3	4	1^{3}	$1^{3\frac{1}{2}}$	6.20	—	*Despite trouble*	(B)	Selda, MandyGirl, TopHarmony
10-15^{9}	BC	F	39	60½	1	5	3	3	2^{2}	2.00	nk	*Almost up insi.*	(B)	Selda, NobleYet, JustRocker
10-12^{4}	BC	F	39	60½	6	7	6	5	2^{hd}	1.30	no	*Bl'ck'd, late rush*	(B)	M'ndyGirl, IrishCharm, Grac.Ann
10-7^{8}	5-16	F	31.2	60½	6	7	6	5	$4\frac{1}{2}$	2.90	1	*Crowded both tns*	B	Johnny'sBest, Rom.Gossip, Sardo
10-4^{9}	5-16	F	31.1	60½	6	6	6	5	4no	9.10	5	*Wide first turn*	A	Partyman, NewRing, Rush'gJohn
9-30^{9}	5-16	F	31	60½	8	8	6	6	4^{nk}	10.90	7	*Crowded 1st turn*	A	PayGay, Partyman, O.B.Medium

Blue 2 — EVERYBODY WINS — 67 — Light Brindle D., February 1959 — Party Leader—Fraydy's Lady
Fleet Wing Kennel, owner; Donald Hogwood, trainer — Starts 3, 1st 2, 2nd 0, 3rd 0 — WONDERLAND 3 3 0 0

Date	Dis.	TC	Time	Wt	PP	Off	1-8	St	Fin	Odds	FW	Comment	Grade	Order of Finish
10-19^{11}	BC	F	38.7	67	5	2	1^{2}	1^{3}	$1^{2\frac{1}{2}}$	1.10	—	*Handily, wide*	(A)	F.Laudation, L.M'Bee, Solom.Sol
10-15^{11}	BC	F	38.8	67	7	4	$1\frac{1}{2}$	1^{8}	1^{6}	3.00	—	*Easily*	(A)	Gra.Ann, O.B.Med'm, F.Laudat'n
10-12^{11}	BC	F	39	66	8	5	8	8	8	1.00	13½	*Offstr. 1st turn*	(A)	Artistry, SuzyBenny, TrueRemark
10-7^{3}s	BC	F	39	66	4	2	3	3	2^{hd}	.....	1	*Forward factor*		L.MacBee, Pl.Rocker, C'ponAnn^{7}
10-3^{2}s	BC	F	38.5	66½	4	3	4	1^{2}	1^{2}	.....	—	*Despite trouble*		P'chySnow, E.Sil.Putty, Von.Girl^{7}
8-15WON	5-16	F	30.9	67	1	3	1^{4}	1^{6}	1^{9}	.30		*With ease*	S	Locket.Best, Kitch.Aid, Fash.Art

White 3 — MANDY GIRL — 60 — Brindle B., November 1958 — Endless Gossip, Imp.—Mandy Jo
Red Fork Kennel, owner; Ray Gerard, trainer — Starts 10, 1st 2, 2nd 3, 3rd 1

Date	Dis.	TC	Time	Wt	PP	Off	1-8	St	Fin	Odds	FW	Comment	Grade	Order of Finish
10-19^{9}	BC	F	38.5	59	3	1	1^{2}	3	$3^{1\frac{1}{2}}$	9.20	7	*Set pace*	(A)	Serape, Selda, TopHarmony
10-15^{6}	BC	F	38.7	59½	6	1	$1^{1\frac{1}{2}}$	2	2^{2}	3.70	5½	*Forward factor*	(A)	MarDilly, TrueRemark, Clas.Kay
10-12^{4}	BC	F	39	59½	4	1	1^{hd}	2	1no	10.10	—	*Up at wire*	(B)	Serape, IrishCharm, GraciousAnn
10-7^{9}	5-16	F	31.3	60	1	1	5	6	6^{4}	17.30	6½	*Out first turn*	A	Rush'gJohn, O.B.Ample, Artistry
10-4^{9}	5-16	F	31.1	60	1	1	7	8	$7^{1\frac{1}{2}}$	14.60	10½	*Out first turn*	A	Partyman, NewRing, Rush'gJohn
9-30^{11}	BC	F	39.4	60½	8	3	2	2	$1\frac{1}{2}$	1.80	—	*Stretch drive*	B	Way.Perky, Nep.Planet, Clas.Kay

Green 4 — BIG GOSSIP — 71 — Blue Brindle D., November 1958 — Endless Gossip, Imp.—Mandy Jo
Red Fork Kennel, owner; Ray Gerard, trainer — Starts 10, 1st 8, 2nd 1, 3rd 0

Date	Dis.	TC	Time	Wt	PP	Off	1-8	St	Fin	Odds	FW	Comment	Grade	Order of Finish
10-19^{8}	BC	F	38.6	70½	1	1	1^{3}	1^{6}	$1^{7\frac{1}{2}}$	.30	—	*Breezing*	(A)	Grac'sAnn, O.B.Melon, Pl.Rocker
10-15^{8}	BC	F	38.9	71	3	1	$1^{3\frac{1}{2}}$	1^{4}	$1^{2\frac{1}{2}}$	.80	—	*Wire to wire*	(A)	O.B.Melon, Scr.Play, IrishCharm
10-12^{5}	BC	F	39	71	2	2	1^{4}	1^{4}	$1^{2\frac{1}{2}}$	.80	—	*Handily*	(A)	O.B.Melon, L.M'Bee, Nep.Rocker
10-8^{9}	5-16	F	30.9	71	7	1	1^{2}	1^{3}	1^{4}	1.20	—	*Wire to wire*	A	NobleYet, BeHigh, Ro.MacGinty
10-5^{9}	5-16	F	31	71	4	1	1^{1}	1^{2}	1^{1}	2.00	—	*Wire to wire*	A	Featur.Fair, Way.Draw, VelvetSis
9-27^{9}	BC	F	38.9	71	2	1	1^{2}	3	$5\frac{1}{2}$	1.00	5½	*Early leader*	A	VelvetSis, FeaturesFair, Artistry

Black 5 — MAR DILLY — 63 — Red Fawn D., May 1957 — Mar Heat, Imp.—Transpat
W. L. Kirkpatrick, owner; Tony Magnus, trainer — Starts 3, 1st 1, 2nd 2, 3rd 0 — MILE HIGH 18 8 5 2

Date	Dis.	TC	Time	Wt	PP	Off	1-8	St	Fin	Odds	FW	Comment	Grade	Order of Finish
10-19^{10}	BC	F	38.6	63	7	8	5	3	$2\frac{1}{2}$	3.50	1	*Forward factor*	(A)	VelvetSis, NobleYet, Artistry
10-15^{6}	BC	F	38.7	62½	1	2	2	1^{5}	$1^{5\frac{1}{2}}$	.80	—	*Easily inside*	(A)	MandyGirl, Tr.Remark, Clas.Kay
10-12^{6}	BC	F	39.2	62½	5	7	3	1^{2}	2^{6}	.70	½	*Outgamed in str.*	(A)	ScreenPlay, DearAbby, Wa.Perky
10-7^{2}s	BC	F	38.9	63	8	6	4	3	$2\frac{1}{2}$	.....	4	*Crowded, came on*		PeachySnow, DavillaDew, Tonna
10-3^{6}s	5-16	F	30.9	63	6	8	4	2	2^{3}	.....	2	*Forward factor*		Selda, Tonna, IrishCharm
9-30^{3}s	5-16	F	31.2	63½	3	6	5	3	2^{1}	.....	1	*Steady gain*		F.Laudat'n, O.B.S.High, P.Rocker

Yellow 6 — VELVET SIS — 60½ — Brindle B., October 1958 — Endless Gossip, Imp.—Satin Sis
H. E. Heaton, owner; H. E. Heaton, trainer — Starts 13, 1st 8, 2nd 1, 3rd 2

Date	Dis.	TC	Time	Wt	PP	Off	1-8	St	Fin	Odds	FW	Comment	Grade	Order of Finish
10-19^{10}	BC	F	38.6	60	5	6	2	2	1^{1}	1.20	—	*Str. drive inside*	(A)	MarDilly, NobleYet, Artistry
10-15^{10}	BC	F	38.9	60½	7	4	2	$1^{1\frac{1}{2}}$	$1\frac{1}{2}$	1.10	—	*Withst'd ch'l'ges*	(A)	Fea.Fair, O.B.M'gage, E.Sil.Putty
10-12^{8}	BC	F	39	60	2	6	2	$1^{1\frac{1}{2}}$	1^{2}	.60	—	*Handily inside*	(A)	Fe.Fair, O.B.Medium, T.Harmony
10-5^{9}	5-16	F	31	61	3	7	4	4	4^{6}	3.10	3	*Early gain*	A	BigGossip, Feat.Fair, Way.Draw
10-1^{9}	5-16	F	30.9	61	2	4	3	3	3^{5}	1.00	1½	*Good effort inside*	A	NobleYet, Waysi.Draw, R.M'Duff
9-27^{9}	BC	F	38.9	61	6	7	3	1^{2}	$1^{2\frac{1}{2}}$	3.40	—	*Handily*	A	Featu.Fair, Artistry, O.B.Medium

Green & Whi. 7 — ARTISTRY — 56 — Brindle B., March 1958 — Top Agent—Protegee
Orville Moses, owner; Charles Rink, trainer — Starts 13, 1st 4, 2nd 0, 3rd 4

Date	Dis.	TC	Time	Wt	PP	Off	1-8	St	Fin	Odds	FW	Comment	Grade	Order of Finish
10-19^{10}	BC	F	38.6	56½	1	3	8	6	4^{1}	2.70	7	*Crd. both turns*	(A)	VelvetSis, MarDilly, NobleYet
10-15^{7}	BC	F	39	55½	5	3	3	3	$1^{1\frac{1}{2}}$	1.80	—	*Crd early, dr out*	(A)	R.MacGinty, Von.Girl, Su.Benny
10-12^{11}	BC	F	39	56	4	3	3	1^{2}	$1^{6\frac{1}{2}}$	4.10	—	*Drew out easily*	(A)	SuzyBenny, Tr.Remark, Br.Donna
10-7^{9}	5-16	F	31.3	55½	4	8	6	4	3^{1}	4.60	3	*Crowded ctn turn*	A	Rush.John, O.B.Ample, Roc.Pride
10-3^{9}	5-16	F	31.1	55½	5	5	6	5	$3\frac{1}{2}$	11.90	3½	*Blocked far turn*	A	O.B.Ample, W.Sloan, T.Harmony
9-27^{9}	BC	F	38.9	56	8	8	6	4	$3^{1\frac{1}{2}}$	8.70	3½	*Good effort*	A	VelvetSis, Feat.Fair, O.B.Medium

Yellow & Black 8 — SELDA — 51 — Brindle B., May 1958 — Happy Yet—Fleeter
Teddy Meadows, owner; Teddy Meadows, trainer — Starts 3, 1st 2, 2nd 1, 3rd 0 — WONDERLAND 29 9 3 4

Date	Dis.	TC	Time	Wt	PP	Off	1-8	St	Fin	Odds	FW	Comment	Grade	Order of Finish
10-19^{9}	BC	F	38.5	51	4	5	3	2	$2^{3\frac{1}{2}}$	2.50	3½	*Crowded ctn tn*	(A)	Serape, MandyGirl, TopHarmony
10-15^{9}	BC	F	39	51	4	3	2	2	1^{nk}	1.40	—	*Up in stretch*	(A)	Serape, NobleYet, JustRocker
10-12^{7}	BC	F	39	51	3	1	1^{5}	1^{5}	1^{3}	1.90	—	*Wire to wire*	(A)	Vonnie'sGirl, Clas.Kay, Pl.Rocker
10-7^{1}s	BC	F	38.3	50½	2	2	2	2	$2^{1\frac{1}{2}}$	.....	6	*Chased winner*		F.Laudation, E.S.Putty, D.Darkie^{7}
10-3^{6}s	5-16	F	30.9	51	3	2	1^{3}	1^{3}	1^{2}	.....	—	*Handily*		MarDilly, Tonna, IrishCharm
9-3WON	5-16	F	31.3	52	5	7	8	8	8^{7}	8.10		*Collided*	S	TripAndTie, RedTone, MyPaula

WIN PLACE SHOW PLACE SHOW SHOW

Handicapper's Selections—Big Gossip, Velvet Sis, Everybody Wins

Velvet Sis-1961

AMERICAN GREYHOUND DERBY

– $25,000-Added Purse – Thirteenth Renewal –

TONIGHT'S ENTRIES

PP	Greyhound	Pts.	Owner and Track
2	BARNACLE BOB	60	Carl O. Tracy, Portland, Ore.
7	VELVET SIS	60	Howard E. Heaton, Taunton
5	ARTISTRY	54	Orville Moses, Taunton
6	FEATURES FAIR	51	Jack B. Herold, Taunton
4	JOAN JERIS	50	E. J. Boyle, Revere
8	EVERBODY WINS	48	Fleet Wing Kennel, Revere
1	SERAPE	42	Orville Moses, Taunton
3	NEPTUNE'S TRIDENT	40	Julliene J. Goble, Taunton

SERAPE
WINNER OF
1960 AMERICAN GREYHOUND DERBY

$25,000
American
Greyhound
DERBY

TONIGHT

OFFICIAL PROGRAM 25c

TAUNTON
DOG TRACK

Home of The American Greyhound Derby

SATURDAY, OCT. 21, 1961

Velvet Sis-1961

13th Annual American Greyhound Derby

ELEVENTH RACE

Track-World's Record
Splendored 38

PLEASE CALL FOR DOG BY NUMBER

BRISTOL COURSE
675 YARDS

Red 1 — SERAPE

61 Black D., July 1958 Black Magic, Imp.—Excellence

Orville Moses, owner
Charles Rink, trainer

Starts 14 1st 3 2nd 2 3rd 4

Date	Dis.	TC	Time	Wt	PP	Off	1-8	St	Fin	Odds	FW	Comment	Grade	Order of Finish
10-18^{9}	BC	F	38.7	60½	1	2	1^{1}	2	$3^{2\frac{1}{2}}$	1.40	4½	*Set pace*	(A)	Barn.Bob, Nep.Trident, Br.Donna
10-14^{4}	BC	F	39	60½	8	7	2	2	$2^{2\frac{1}{2}}$	.90	2	*Chased winner*	(A)	RuthCruce, Mr.Storm, TrimTim
10-11^{4}	BC	F	38.9	60½	5	5	3	1^{5}	1^{8}	.70	—	*All alone*	(A)	ChiefCash, SkyMint, MacAgain
10-6^{9}	5-16	F	31	61	6	7	8	4	$3^{1\frac{1}{2}}$	4.00	1½	*Lacked early speed*	A	PunkyBoy, SkyBig, NewRing
10-3^{5}	5-16	F	31.3	61	5	8	7	6	6no	2.30	4	*Crowded backstr.*	A	TopekaRose, LadySage, LittleLela
9-28^{10}	5-16	F	30.5	61	4	8	8	7	$6^{1\frac{1}{2}}$	17.90	7½	*Never prominent*	A	VelvetSis, FeaturesFair, NewRing

Blue 2 — BARNACLE BOB

67 White & Brindle D., December 1959 Captain's Rocker—Lady Twist

Carl O. Tracy, owner
Carl O. Tracy, trainer

Starts 3 1st 2 2nd 1 3rd 0
Multnomah 17 13 1 1

Date	Dis.	TC	Time	Wt	PP	Off	1-8	St	Fin	Odds	FW	Comment	Grade	Order of Finish
10-18^{9}	BC	F	38.7	66½	3	3	2	1^{1}	$1^{2\frac{1}{2}}$	1.90	—	*Handily inside*	(A)	Nep.Trident, Serape, Bro.Donna
10-14^{7}	BC	F	39.1	66½	4	7	5	3	$2^{1\frac{1}{2}}$	1.10	1	*Crd. tn, came on*	(A)	Feat.Fair, Cas.Career, Pre.Locket
10-11^{5}	BC	F	38.8	66	1	6	3	2	1^{hd}	1.60	—	*Up near wire*	(A)	Selda, Mr.Storm, O.B.'sMelon
10-9^{7}s	BC	F	38.6	66½	8	5	5	4	$3^{4\frac{1}{2}}$	.....	11½	*Trouble thruout*		R.Cruce, E.Eastman, D.D.Dinah^{7}
10-6MUL	FC	Sl	40.7	67½	2	2	1^{1}	2	2½	.45	½	*Raced wide*	T	Rei.D.Sol, Du.OfLoup, St.Jackson
10-3MUL	FC	F	39.9	67½	8	2	1^{6}	1^{6}	1^{11}	.45	—	*Drew out*	T	AEyes, SirRobinHood, TVSusie

White 3 — NEPTUNE'S TRIDENT

60 Red Brindle B., December 1958 Rocker Mac, Imp.—She's A Pilot

Julliene J. Goble, owner
Amos Goble, trainer

Starts 12 1st 4 2nd 3 3rd 0

Date	Dis.	TC	Time	Wt	PP	Off	1-8	St	Fin	Odds	FW	Comment	Grade	Order of Finish
10-18^{9}	BC	F	38.7	60½	2	1	3	3	2^{2}	8.20	2½	*Late gain*	(A)	Barnac.Bob, Serape, Broad.Donna
10-14^{10}	BC	F	38.9	60½	4	4	7	5	4^{2}	5.40	5½	*Came again*	(A)	Artistry, MacTray, HeroldExpress
10-11^{8}	BC	F	39.5	60½	5	6	7	2	1^{3}	2.60	—	*Crd., drew out*	(A)	W.Pinochle, P.Locket, Amp.Man
10-5^{11}	BC	F	39.1	60½	2	1	7	7	6no	3.60	5½	*Crowded early*	A	Ca.Career, O.B.D.D.T., H.Express
9-30^{10}	EC	F	44.3	60½	3	1	1^{hd}	2	$1^{1\frac{1}{2}}$	1.00	—	*Drew out*	(A)	Nep.Guide, Amp.Man, Sn.Happy
9-27^{9}	BC	F	38.9	60½	8	3	1^{3}	1^{8}	1^{8}	1.50	—	*All alone*	(A)	AmpleMan, PunkyGirl, Saq.Lady

Green 4 — JOAN JERIS

54 Light Brindle B., March 1959 Rocker Mac, Imp.—Handy Peg

E. J. Boyle, owner
Otto Mamino, trainer

Starts 3 1st 2 2nd 0 3rd 0
Wonderland 27 9 6 4

Date	Dis.	TC	Time	Wt	PP	Off	1-8	St	Fin	Odds	FW	Comment	Grade	Order of Finish
10-18^{11}	BC	F	38.8	54	8	3	4	5	$6^{5\frac{1}{2}}$	4.90	4½	*Some early sp.*	(A)	VelvetSis, Everybo.Wins, Artistry
10-14^{9}	BC	F	39.1	54	8	4	4	1^{2}	1^{6}	2.30	—	*Easily*	(A)	Selda, PunkyGirl, TopekaRose
10-11^{7}	BC	F	39.4	53½	2	5	4	1^{2}	$1^{3\frac{1}{2}}$	1.30	—	*Handily inside*	(A)	Her.Express, N.Rocker, MacTray
10-6^{7}s	BC	F	38.9	54	7	2	2	2	2^{2}	.....	3	*Chased winner*		BaySide, SkyNancy, K.Waltzing^{5}
9-27^{1}s	5-16	F	30.7	54	1	3	2	2	$2^{7\frac{1}{2}}$	.....	1½	*Forward factor ins.*		BaySide, MyRedChip, C.P.Bell
9-20^{1}s	5-16	F	30.9	54	5	5	7	6	5^{1}	.....	8	*Crowded 1st turn*		P.P.Pat, O.B.D.D.T., B.M.Money

Black 5 — ARTISTRY

56 Dark Brindle B., March 1958 Top Agent—Protegee

Orville Moses, owner
Charles Rink, trainer

Starts 13 1st 5 2nd 1 3rd 4

Date	Dis.	TC	Time	Wt	PP	Off	1-8	St	Fin	Odds	FW	Comment	Grade	Order of Finish
10-18^{11}	BC	F	38.8	56	2	1	1½	2	3^{1}	2.10	1	*Set pace*	(A)	VelvetSis, Ever.Wins, T.Harmony
10-14^{10}	BC	F	38.9	56	6	7	4	2	1no	.80	—	*Up at wire*	(A)	MacTray, Her.Express, N.Trident
10-11^{6}	BC	F	38.6	56	8	2	3	1^{7}	1^{7}	.60	—	*As she pleased*	(A)	Von.Girl, T.Harmony, Tope.Rose
10-6^{10}	5-16	F	30.7	56	4	5	5	4	$4^{1\frac{1}{2}}$	6.60	3½	*Crowded early*	A	Way.Draw, Ne.Rocker, VelvetSis
10-4^{10}	5-16	F	30.8	56½	2	5	5	4	3^{2}	2.50	1½	*Crowded early*	A	ChiefCash, M.T.Man, Simmering
9-29^{11}	BC	F	38.6	55	7	3	1^{1}	1^{6}	1^{8}	1.80	—	*As she pleased*	A	Nep.Rocker, PunkyBoy, Cadenza

Yellow 6 — FEATURES FAIR

63 White & Brindle B., December 1958 Rocker Mac, Imp.—Mink Coat

Jack B. Herold, owner
Jack B. Herold, trainer

Starts 13 1st 5 2nd 2 3rd 0

Date	Dis.	TC	Time	Wt	PP	Off	1-8	St	Fin	Odds	FW	Comment	Grade	Order of Finish
10-18^{8}	BC	F	38.6	62½	5	2	1^{1}	1^{4}	1^{2}	6.20	—	*Handily*	(A)	MacTray, Nep.Rocker, Mr.Stuff
10-14^{7}	BC	F	39.1	62	8	3	1^{3}	$1^{1\frac{1}{2}}$	1^{1}	3.60	—	*Lasted to win*	(B)	Barna.Bob, Cas.Career, Pr.Locket
10-11^{10}	BC	F	39.3	62	1	1	$1^{2\frac{1}{2}}$	3	$5^{1\frac{1}{2}}$	3.40	2	*Tired on rail*	(A)	CasualCareer, Velv.Sis, Cadenza^{7}
10-6^{10}	5-16	F	30.7	63	2	4	4	7	7½	2.20	9	*Bumped turns*	A	Way.Draw, Ne.Rocker, VelvetSis
10-2^{10}	5-16	F	30.8	62½	3	5	7	6	5^{1}	1.40	5	*Crowded early*	A	VelvetSis, Fathom, O.B.'sD.D.T.
9-28^{10}	5-16	F	30.5	62	3	1	2	2	2^{1}	3.30	3	*Forward factor*	A	VelvetSis, NewRing, Fathom

Green & Whi. 7 — VELVET SIS

61 Dark Brindle B., October 1958 Endless Gossip, Imp.—Satin Sis

H. E. Heaton, owner
H. E. Heaton, trainer

Starts 13 1st 4 2nd 4 3rd 2

Date	Dis.	TC	Time	Wt	PP	Off	1-8	St	Fin	Odds	FW	Comment	Grade	Order of Finish
10-18^{11}	BC	F	38.8	61	7	4	2	1^{2}	1^{1}	1.90	—	*Lasted to win*	(A)	Every.Wins, Artistry, T.Harmony
10-14^{5}	BC	F	38.9	60	6	3	1½	1^{7}	$1^{5\frac{1}{2}}$	.80	—	*Easily*	(A)	Vonnie.Girl, BaySide, MacAgain^{7}
10-11^{10}	BC	F	39.3	60½	4	4	4	2	2^{1}	.70	no	*Jammed early*	(A)	Cas.Career, Cadenza, Bro.Donna^{7}
10-6^{10}	5-16	F	30.7	61	7	6	6	3	3^{1}	1.10	2½	*Trouble thruout*	A	Way.Draw, Nep.Rocker, Artistry
10-2^{10}	5-16	F	30.8	61½	8	6	3	1½	1^{1}	1.40	—	*Stretch drive*	A	Fathom, O.B.'sD.D.T., FriscoWhit
9-28^{10}	5-16	F	30.5	61	2	3	1^{2}	1^{3}	1^{3}	2.70	—	*Handily*	A	FeaturesFair, NewRing, Fathom

Yellow & Black 8 — EVERYBODY WINS

69½ Light Brindle D., February 1959 Party Leader—Fraydy's Lady

Fleet Wing Kennel, owner
Stanley Buturlia, trainer

Starts 3 1st 1 2nd 2 3rd 0
Wonderland 23 11 2 5

Date	Dis.	TC	Time	Wt	PP	Off	1-8	St	Fin	Odds	FW	Comment	Grade	Order of Finish
10-18^{11}	BC	F	38.8	69½	6	7	5	4	2no	2.80	1	*Crd. 1st turn*	(A)	VelvetSis, Artistry, TopHarmony
10-14^{11}	BC	F	39.1	70	1	1	2	1^{6}	1^{9}	.40	—	*All alone*	(A)	MyRedChip, E.Eastman, Defined
10-11^{11}	BC	F	39.2	69½	1	8	5	2	2^{1}	.70	2	*Jammed ctn tn*	(A)	Mr.Stuff, RuthCruce, BlueDuster
10-6^{8}s	BC	F	38.6	69½	5	4	3	1^{4}	1^{7}	.....	—	*Drew out*		MacTray, M.RedChip, Clo.Doll^{6}
9-29^{2}s	5-16	F	30.4	60	4	3	2	2	1^{hd}	.....	—	*Stretch drive*		Mr.Stuff, Selda, CheyenneRose^{6}
9-2WON	RC	F	39.6	70	2	3	5	4	4^{11}	3.10		*Crowded*	A	JoanJeris, BaySide, MacGill

WIN	PLACE	SHOW		PLACE	SHOW		SHOW

Handicapper's Selections—Everybody Wins, Velvet Sis, Barnacle Bob

Cactus Noel-1962

ENTRANCE TO ULTRA MODERN CLUBHOUSE

Cactus Noel-1962

14th Annual American Greyhound Derby

ELEVENTH RACE

TRACK RECORD
Donna Larsen 37.4

PLEASE CALL FOR DOG BY NUMBER

3/8 MILE
1980 FEET

RED 1 — TUXEDO DANCER

John McLaughlin, owner
Antone Perry, trainer

Starts 12, 1st 4, 2nd 1, 3rd 0

60 Dark Red Brindle B., November 1960 Top Agent—Trudie, Imp.

Date	Dis.	TC	Time	Wt	PP	Off	1-8	St	Fin	Odds	FW	Comment	Grade	Order of Finish
10-17^{9}	3-8	F	37.9	59½	4	7	8	8	8	3.10	21½	*Jammed early*	(A)	Nan.Fair, D.Mammy, Longbranch
10-13^{9}	3-8	F	37.9	59½	2	1	$1^{1½}$	1^{4}	$1^{5½}$	2.20	—	*Easily*	(A)	R.FireBall, MacTray, RingRuble
10-10^{8}	3-8	F	37.8	60	3	7	4	$1^{2½}$	1^{4}	12.30	—	*Handily inside*	(B)	Bronica, Mich.Jack, Loveab.Amy
10-6^{1}s	5-16	S	31.3	59½	1	4	4	3	2^{2}	.....	1	*Blocked early*		Upstager, GayEaster, W.Dream^{7}
10-3^{11}	3-8	F	38.2	60	5	5	4	6	5no	6.70	3½	*Crowded crtn turn*	B	FearlessBob, Largesse, Seniority
9-29^{3}s	5-16	F	30.6	60	5	5	7	6	6^{2}	.....	9	*Collided first turn*		Mich.Jack, Di.Mammy, Br.Strupi

BLUE 2 — NANCY'S FAIR

Altino R. Gouveia, owner
James M. Alves, trainer

Starts 12, 1st 5, 2nd 4, 3rd 1

59½ Red Brindle B., November 1960 Metal Jet, Imp.—Loretta's Pick

Date	Dis.	TC	Time	Wt	PP	Off	1-8	St	Fin	Odds	FW	Comment	Grade	Order of Finish
10-17^{9}	3-8	F	37.9	60	8	4	2	1^{4}	1^{4}	3.90	—	*Handily*	(A)	D.Mammy, Longbranch, Protocol
10-13^{7}	3-8	F	38.1	60	6	7	7	2	$1^{½}$	3.60	—	*Up on outside*	(A)	WomanHater, VelvetSis, Silento
10-10^{10}	3-8	F	37.4	60	4	7	5	3	2^{1}	10.10	6½	*Wide front str.*	(A)	D.Larsen, Wo.Hater, E.Eastman^{7}
10-4^{8}	5-16	F	30.7	60	7	2	5	2	1^{1}	6.20	—	*Stretch drive*	B	Wom.Hater,, Wonderon, W.Poker
9-29^{11}	EC	F	44.1	60½	1	3	$1^{1½}$	$1^{2½}$	3^{1}	3.00	1	*Speed to str.*	(B)	Quitclaim, N.S.Lady, Bon.Agent
9-26^{11}	3-8	F	38.4	60½	7	8	7	5	2^{1}	4.60	1	*From far back*	(B)	Ne.SeaLady, Upstager, Fearl.Bob

WHITE 3 — DIANNE'S MAMMY

Teddy Meadows, owner
Mack Dutton, trainer

Starts 3, 1st 0, 2nd 3, 3rd 0
Wonderland 26, 8, 9, 4

63 Fawn B., May 1960 Julius Caesar, Imp.—My Lucky Gertie

Date	Dis.	TC	Time	Wt	PP	Off	1-8	St	Fin	Odds	FW	Comment	Grade	Order of Finish
10-17^{9}	3-8	F	37.9	62	1	2	4	3	$2^{3½}$	1.90	4	*Blocked far turn*	(A)	Nanc.Fair, Longbranch, Protocol
10-13^{5}	3-8	F	37.9	63	5	5	5	2	$2^{½}$	2.40	½	*Crowded early*	(A)	Way.Skin, Bustleton, O.B.Melon^{7}
10-10^{9}	3-8	F	37.7	63	2	6	6	3	$2^{2½}$	3.90	3	*Steady gain ins.*	(A)	CactusNoel, Way.Skin, VelvetSis
10-6^{5}s	3-8	S	38.5	64½	3	8	8	4	3^{2}	.....	8½	*Crowded early*		Do.Larsen, Coronella, R.Fireball
10-1^{7}s	3-8	F	37.5	63	6	7	7	4	2^{1}	.....	7	*Steady gain inside*		D.Larsen, Mich.Jack, H.T.T.Jack
9-29^{3}s	5-16	F	30.6	63	4	7	5	2	2^{5}	.....	2	*Closing inside*		Mich.Jack, Bro.Strupi, Bro.Flash

GREEN 4 — FEARLESS BOB

Otto Mamino, owner
Otto Mamino, trainer

Starts 15, 1st 3, 2nd 3, 3rd 0

64 Black D., April 1960 Membership—Blue Pajamas

Date	Dis.	TC	Time	Wt	PP	Off	1-8	St	Fin	Odds	FW	Comment	Grade	Order of Finish
10-17^{5}	3-8	F	38.3	63½	2	6	8	6	2^{nk}	4.50	hd	*Crd, late rush*	(A)	CliffOrth, Waysi.Skin, Incentive
10-13^{4}	3-8	F	38	63½	7	7	7	7	6^{2}	3.40	8	*Never prom.*	(A)	RestStop, Shan.LaJon, Protocol^{7}
10-10^{6}	3-8	F	37.9	63½	8	8	7	3	$1^{½}$	5.60	—	*Despite trouble*	(A)	E.Warning, Lit.Austie, CliffOrth
10-6^{8}	5-16	S	31.3	63½	7	8	8	8	8	15.90	11	*Outrun*	A	S.Value, Longbranch, O.B.Deacon
10-3^{11}	3-8	F	38.2	63	6	8	7	3	1^{1}	5.60	—	*Up around leaders*	B	Largesse, Seniority, Kelleher
9-29^{11}	EC	F	44.1	64	7	8	8	6	6^{5}	2.50	8	*Crd crtn turn*	(B)	Quitclaim, N.SeaLady, Nanc.Fair

BLACK 5 — CLIFF ORTH

Carl O. Tracy, owner
Larry C. Tracy, trainer

Starts 15, 1st 2, 2nd 4, 3rd 1

62 Red Brindle D., January 1959 Freckels Brown—Mazie Grey

Date	Dis.	TC	Time	Wt	PP	Off	1-8	St	Fin	Odds	FW	Comment	Grade	Order of Finish
10-17^{5}	3-8	F	38.3	61	7	8	5	4	1^{hd}	6.00	—	*Despite trouble*	(A)	FearlessBob, Way.Skin, Incentive
10-13^{6}	3-8	F	38.5	61½	4	7	4	3	2^{1}	7.00	½	*Crd, closing*	(A)	SidiaLeddi, Lovea.Amy, Esk.Roll
10-10^{6}	3-8	F	37.9	61½	6	7	4	4	$4^{1½}$	14.00	4	*Collided crtn tn*	(A)	Fearl.Bob, E.Warning, Lit.Austie
10-5^{9}	5-16	S	31.4	62½	6	6	4	4	$4^{½}$	23.50	5½	*Even effort*	A	O.B.D.D.T., J.Grandson, H.Profit
10-2^{11}	3-8	F	37.8	62	8	8	4	3	2^{1}	14.00	6	*Wide thruout*	A	Protocol, WaysideFaro, Bustleton
9-28^{8}	5-16	F	31	62	2	4	6	6	5no	7.80	8	*Dropped bk early*	A	Sardo, DangerDan, RegettaRed

YELLOW 6 — DONNA LARSEN

H. E. Alderson & Waldo Lentz, own.
C. B. Gabriel, trainer

Starts 3, 1st 3, 2nd 0, 3rd 0
Wonderland 16, 7, 1, 1

62½ Black B., November 1960 Don Larsen—Cindy Lass

Date	Dis.	TC	Time	Wt	PP	Off	1-8	St	Fin	Odds	FW	Comment	Grade	Order of Finish
10-17^{11}	3-8	F	38	61	3	3	4	3	1^{1}	.20	—	*Despite trouble*	(A)	MacTray, Wom.Hater, O.B.Melon
10-13^{11}	3-8	F	37.6	61	6	2	2	1^{hd}	1^{2}	1.00	—	*Handily inside*	(A)	Ca.Noel, Genemaury, H.T.T.Jack
10-10^{10}	3-8	F	37.4	61	2	2	1^{1}	1^{4}	$1^{6½}$	.70	—	*New track rec'd*	(A)	Na.Fair, Wom.Hater, E.Eastman^{7}
10-6^{5}s	3-8	S	38.5	62	6	1	1^{4}	1^{7}	1^{8}	.....	—	*Easily*		Coronella, Di.Mammy, R.Fireball
10-1^{7}s	3-8	F	37.5	62	5	3	2	1^{6}	1^{7}	.....	—	*Easily*		D.Mammy, Mic.Jack, H.T.T.Jack
9-26^{7}s	5-16	F	30.7	62½	7	5	2	1^{3}	$1^{5½}$	.....	—	*Easily*		Bayside, LittleAustie, Magail^{7}

GREEN & WHITE 7 — CACTUS NOEL

Altino R. Gouveia, owner
James M. Alves, trainer

Starts 15, 1st 9, 2nd 3, 3rd 1

70 Dark Brindle D., November 1960 Metal Jet, Imp.—Loretta's Pick

Date	Dis.	TC	Time	Wt	PP	Off	1-8	St	Fin	Odds	FW	Comment	Grade	Order of Finish
10-17^{10}	3-8	F	37.6	70	4	2	2	1^{6}	$1^{5½}$	.30	—	*Easily*	(A)	VelvetSis, Chourico, Ruston
10-13^{11}	3-8	F	37.6	70	3	5	3	2	$2^{3½}$	2.00	2	*Wide ent. str.*	(A)	D.Larsen, Genem'ry, H.T.T.Jack
10-10^{9}	3-8	F	37.7	70	5	1	1^{2}	1^{4}	1^{3}	1.00	—	*Wire to wire*	(A)	Dian.Mammy, Way.Skin, Vel.Sis
10-8^{8}s	5-16	F	30.9	69½	3	2	3	3	3	.....	3	*Good effort*		MacTray, TakeALead^{3}
10-6^{10}	5-16	S	31.3	70	6	7fl	6	6	6^{4}	1.20	27½	*Fell first turn*	A	Her.Express, Tu.Agent, N.Planet
10-3^{9}	5-16	F	30.5	69½	8	3	$1^{½}$	1^{3}	$1^{2½}$	.90	—	*Handily*	A	MacTray, Hammersmith, C.Cash

YELLOW & BLACK 8 — DANGER DAN

L. H. Nave, owner
B. E. Macdonald, trainer

Starts 16, 1st 5, 2nd 1, 3rd 1

65 Black D., July 1960 Black Magic, Imp.—Golden Challice

Date	Dis.	TC	Time	Wt	PP	Off	1-8	St	Fin	Odds	FW	Comment	Grade	Order of Finish
10-17^{8}	3-8	F	38.3	63	4	8	6	4	$4^{1½}$	4.80	3½	*Blocked ctn tn*	(A)	Bustleton, Bronica, H.T.TurnJack
10-13^{8}	3-8	F	38.1	63½	7	5	4	2	1^{1}	8.30	—	*Stretch drive*	(A)	Sug.Guide, Mich.Jack, FawnAnn
10-10^{7}	3-8	F	38	63½	6	7	4	$1^{1½}$	1^{1}	12.60	—	*Despite trouble*	(A)	N.S.Lady, Upstager, Longbranch
10-6^{8}	5-16	S	31.3	64	8	7	7	7	6^{1}	6.60	7	*Never prominent*	A	S.Value, Longbranch, O.B.Deacon
10-2^{11}	3-8	F	37.8	64	2	5	6	5	5^{2}	11.40	8	*Crowded turns*	A	Protocol, CliffOrth, WaysideFaro
9-28^{8}	5-16	F	31	64	5	8	4	2	$2^{1½}$	11.10	½	*Crowded, hard try*	A	Sardo, RegettaRed, RestStop

WIN	PLACE	SHOW	PLACE	SHOW	SHOW

Handicapper's Selections—Donna Larsen, Cactus Noel, Dianne's Mammy

Thermel-1963

Thermel-1963

15th Annual American Greyhound Derby

ELEVENTH RACE

TRACK RECORD
Donna Larsen 37.4

PLEASE CALL FOR DOG BY NUMBER

3/8 MILE
1980 FEET

1 — Red — MICHIGAN JACK

Teddy Meadows, owner
Edward Dolan, trainer
Starts 3, 1st 2, 2nd 1, 3rd 0

72 — Brindle D., May 1960 — Julius Caesar, Imp.—My Lucky Gertie

Date-Race	Dist	TC	Time	Wt	PP	Off	1-8	Str	Fin-FW	Odds	Comment	Grade	Order of Finish
10-16^{10}	3-8	F	38.6	72	4	7	3	1^{2}	1^{1}	1.40	*Lasted to win*	[A]	RocketRoe, Tux.Agent, Tranway's
10-12^{4}	3-8	F	38.6	72½	6	7	6	1^{6}	1^{7½}	.50	*Despite trouble*	[A]	Roar'gDrama, AbeE. Madamoiselle
10-9^{6}	3-8	F	39	72½	5	3	7	2	2^{1}	1.00	*Bumped first turn*	[A]	Rayoner, LankHank, Tranway's
10-4^{8}s	3-8	F	38.9	73	8	3	3	2	2^{1}	.....	*Crowded ent. str.*		MonaRose, AbeE., RoaringDrama^{5}
9-30^{7}s	3-8	F	38.3	73	4	6	2	2	2^{4½}	.....	*Trouble thruout*		D'naLarsen, Young.One, Pr.Section
9-27^{8}s	5-16	F	32	72½	8	4	3	2	1^{2}	.....	*Despite trouble*		LowBell, Sun'sOut, SirCameron^{4}

2 — Blue — NANCY'S FAIR

Altino R. Gouveia, owner
James M. Alves, trainer
Starts 15, 1st 2, 2nd 4, 3rd 3

60 — Red Brindle B., November 1960 — Metal Jet, Imp.—Loretta's Pick

Date-Race	Dist	TC	Time	Wt	PP	Off	1-8	Str	Fin-FW	Odds	Comment	Grade	Order of Finish
10-16^{9}	3-8	F	38.8	60	7	6	5	2	2½	5.20	*Forward factor*	[A]	BeagleBeak, Momento, O.B.'sWalla
10-12^{8}	3-8	F	39	60½	8	4	4	2	1no	4.30	*Up at wire*	[A]	WaysidePedro, Hockman, PacSac
10-9^{8}	3-8	F	39	60	8	4	3	3	3^{1}	2.90	*Wide backstretch*	[A]	RocketRoe, Hypnotique, CreoleJazz
10-4^{11}	3-8	F	39	60	6	7	7	6	5^{5}	4.30	*Crowded turns*	A	BuckSaturn, Rayoner, Rake
10-1^{10}	5-16	F	31.5	60	5	7	8	7	7^{7½}	2.90	*Wide first turn*	A	Bizlar, Lyrical, ChiefCash
9-27^{11}	3-8	F	38.9	60	6	8	4	3	2^{2½}	4.20	*Steady gain*	A	Waysi.Pedro, Dardeen, BuckSaturn

3 — White — CACTUS NOEL

Altino R. Gouveia, owner
James M. Alves, trainer
Starts 10, 1st 6, 2nd 3, 3rd 0

69 — Dark Brindle D., November 1960 — Metal Jet, Imp.—Loretta's Pick

Date-Race	Dist	TC	Time	Wt	PP	Off	1-8	Str	Fin-FW	Odds	Comment	Grade	Order of Finish
10-16^{11}	3-8	F	38.5	69	4	2	2	1^{4}	2^{2}	1.00	*Wide thruout*	[A]	Bustleton, Thermel, Rayoner
10-12^{11}	3-8	F	38.8	68½	8	1	1^{5}	1^{5}	1^{1}	.70	*Wire to wire*	[A]	Dav.Rocker, Bustleton, ElPasoLass
10-9^{11}	3-8	F	38.9	68½	7	1	1^{3}	1^{6}	1^{3½}	.60	*Wide thruout*	[A]	FriendlyFred, ZippOn, Suel'sRose
10-5^{10}	5-16	F	31.9	67½	5	7	8	5	4^{2}	.70	*Bumped early*	A	Bizlar, O.B.'sMcDuff, Hypnotique
10-2^{5}s	5-16	F	31	68	7	2	1^{2}	1^{3}	1^{3}	.....	*Wide late*		E.Thomps'n, Bullephant, B.Donna^{5}
9-14^{10}	5-16	F	31.5	68½	5	5	4	4	2^{2}	.40	*Blocked first turn*	A	Way.Pedro, Frien.Fred, Tux.Agent

4 — Green — BEAGLE BEAK

Manuel Viveiros, owner
Alfred Monteiro, trainer
Starts 14, 1st 5, 2nd 4, 3rd 1

66½ — Red Brindle D., June 1960 — Smoke Kent's—Lady Hill

Date-Race	Dist	TC	Time	Wt	PP	Off	1-8	Str	Fin-FW	Odds	Comment	Grade	Order of Finish
10-16^{9}	3-8	F	38.8	65½	4	2	1^{1½}	1½	1½	9.70	*Lasted to win*	[A]	Nancy'sFair, Momento, O.B.'sWalla
10-12^{5}	3-8	F	38.7	66½	3	3	2	3	4^{5½}	2.40	*Tired late*	[A]	Tuxe.Agent, Suel.Rose, Tranway's^{7}
10-9^{10}	3-8	F	38.9	66	5	1	1^{1}	1^{hd}	2^{1}	10.90	*Set pace*	[A]	Bustleton, Rinaker, LoveableAmy
10-3^{9}	5-16	F	31.6	66	5	3	5	7	8^{12}	5.30	*Collided far turn*	A	B.Holiday, Tux.Danny, Frien.Fred
9-28^{11}	EC	F	45.3	66	2	1	1^{5}	1^{4}	1^{1}	3.60	*Lasted to win*	[A]	Eddystone, LadyFifi, KindlyLight
9-25^{11}	3-8	F	38.9	66	7	1	1^{5}	1^{5}	1^{3}	4.90	*Wire to wire*	[B]	KindlyLight, Hockman, NiniRock

5 — Black — MOMENTO

F. B. Stutz, owner
F. B. Stutz, trainer
Starts 3, 1st 2, 2nd 0, 3rd 1
Flagler Starts *11*, 1st *2*, 2nd *2*, 3rd *3*

58 — Brindle B., December 1960 — Sunmarker, Imp.—Wealthy Widow

Date-Race	Dist	TC	Time	Wt	PP	Off	1-8	Str	Fin-FW	Odds	Comment	Grade	Order of Finish
10-16^{9}	3-8	F	38.8	58	5	4	3	3	3^{7½}	.70	*Collided front str.*	[A]	Beag.Beak, Nancy.Fair, O.B.Walla
10-12^{10}	3-8	F	38.8	58	8	3	2	1^{5}	1½	1.40	*Lasted inside*	[A]	Rinaker, CreoleJazz, Notified
10-9^{4}	3-8	F	38.7	58½	3	3	3	1^{2}	1^{2½}	.60	*Handily inside*	[A]	BuckSaturn, JaneTip, CronyPinkey
10-4^{6}s	3-8	F	38.3	57½	2	2	2	1^{5}	1^{8}	.....	*Collided crtn turn*		ZippOn, Dian.Mammy, Lib.Judge^{6}
9-30^{6}s	3-8	F	37.9	57½	1	1	1^{2}	1^{6}	1^{10}	.....	*All alone*		Di.Mammy, Lib.Judge, MonaRose^{7}
9-16FLG	FC	F	37.4	58	8	6	7	7	5^{15½}	2.90	*Offstrided 1st turn*	A	Groover, Pet'sPride, Happier

6 — Yellow — DAVIE'S ROCKER

L. H. Nave, owner
Robert Barthold, trainer
Starts 14, 1st 3, 2nd 5, 3rd 2

75 — Red D., December 1960 — Dwight David—Wide Rocker

Date-Race	Dist	TC	Time	Wt	PP	Off	1-8	Str	Fin-FW	Odds	Comment	Grade	Order of Finish
10-16^{8}	3-8	F	38.7	74½	6	4	3	2	1^{4}	3.80	*Drew out*	[A]	Frien.Fred, Love.Amy, Mr.TallMan
10-12^{11}	3-8	F	38.8	73½	2	4	2	2	2^{1}	8.00	*Blocked far turn*	[A]	CactusNoel, Bustleton, ElPasoLass
10-9^{5}	3-8	F	38.9	74	3	2	4	1½	1^{5}	2.20	*Drew out easily*	[A]	AliceChalmers, O.B.Walla, Notified
10-4^{9}	5-16	F	31.7	74	2	7	8	7	6^{4½}	7.00	*Offstrided early*	A	BurtKi, O.B.'sWalla, TuxedoMike
10-1^{11}	3-8	F	38.7	74½	1	5	3	3	3^{1½}	2.80	*Wide thruout*	A	BuckSaturn, Rayoner, O.B.'sWalla
9-27^{10}	5-16	F	31.7	74	1	6	6	6	2^{4}	6.90	*Wide, late bid*	A	BurtKi, SleekPonda, LoveableAmy

7 — Green & White — BUSTLETON

Barney Mullin, owner
Maurice Cyr, trainer
Starts 15, 1st 4, 2nd 4, 3rd 3

62 — Black D., January 1961 — Sunmarker, Imp.—Miss Jolie

Date-Race	Dist	TC	Time	Wt	PP	Off	1-8	Str	Fin-FW	Odds	Comment	Grade	Order of Finish
10-16^{11}	3-8	F	38.5	61	7	5	6	2	1^{2}	3.50	*Handily inside*	[A]	CactusNoel, Thermel, Rayoner
10-12^{11}	3-8	F	38.8	61	4	6	6	4	3^{2}	1.80	*Trouble thruout*	[A]	CactusNoel, Da.Rocker, ElPasoLass
10-9^{10}	3-8	F	38.9	61½	8	5	6	2	1^{1}	2.80	*Despite trouble*	[A]	BeagleBeak, Rinaker, Loveab.Amy
10-4^{11}	3-8	F	39	61	7	6	8	5	4^{4}	1.00	*Trouble thruout*	A	BuckSaturn, Rayoner, Rake
10-2^{10}	5-16	F	31.7	61	2	5	6	5	2^{hd}	2.10	*Pinched bk early*	A	O.B.'sMcDuff, Silvray, Bankrate
9-28^{10}	5-16	F	31.7	61	7	2	4	3	2no	3.70	*Crowded, hard try*	A	O.B.McDuff, O.B.Cook, Lare.Larry

8 — Yellow & Black — THERMEL

Manuel Viveiros, owner
Alfred Monteiro, trainer
Starts 15, 1st 5, 2nd 3, 3rd 1

66½ — Red D., June 1961 — Weary Wrinkles—Lady Hill

Date-Race	Dist	TC	Time	Wt	PP	Off	1-8	Str	Fin-FW	Odds	Comment	Grade	Order of Finish
10-16^{11}	3-8	F	38.5	65½	5	6	4	3	3^{2½}	2.60	*Good effort wide*	[A]	Bustleton, CactusNoel, Rayoner
10-12^{7}	3-8	F	38.9	65½	5	1	2	3	1^{2}	1.20	*Handily*	[A]	ZippOn, Friend.Fred, DonnaLarsen
10-9^{7}	3-8	F	38.7	65½	7	2	1^{4}	1^{6}	1^{7}	2.70	*Easily*	[B]	Dian.Mammy, MonaRose, Dardeen
10-7^{3}s	5-16	F	32	66	6	3	3	2	1^{hd}	.....	*Stretch drive*		SoSplendid, Completed, FairWendi
10-5^{8}	5-16	F	31.8	66½	7	6fl	6	6	6^{32}	.90	*Fell first turn*	B	SleekPonda, LankHank, Tranway's
10-2^{10}	5-16	F	31.7	66	4	4	7	7	6^{4}	7.40	*Wide first turn*	A	O.B.'sMcDuff, Bustleton, Silvray

WIN | PLACE | SHOW | PLACE | SHOW | SHOW

Handicapper's Selections—Momento, Michigan Jack, Cactus Noel

Canadian Hi There-1964

$25,000
American
Greyhound
DERBY
TONIGHT
THERMEL
OFFICIAL PROGRAM 25c
TAUNTON
DOG TRACK
Home of The American Greyhound Derby
FRIDAY, OCTOBER 23, 1964

TAUNTON CONVERTS TIMING TO 1/100ths SECONDS

PHOTO FINISH CAMERA ELECTRICALLY TIMES GREYHOUNDS IN 1/100ths SECONDS

Taunton Dog Track has made an important change in its timing system of the greyhounds for the 1964 season. Each greyhound in a race will be clocked electrically in 1/100ths of a second.

Below is a chart which shows a comparison between hundredths of a second and beaten lengths:

1/100ths of a Sec.	Beaten Lengths								
.01	(nose)	.17-.18	2½	.38-.39	5½	.59-.60	8½	.80-.81	11½
.02	(head)	.19-.23	3	.40-.44	6	.61-.65	9	.82-.86	12
.03-.04	½	.24-.25	3½	.45-.46	6½	.66-.67	9½	.87-.88	12½
.05-.09	1	.26-.30	4	.47-.51	7	.68-.72	10	.89-.93	13
.10-.11	1½	.31-.32	4½	.52-.53	7½	.73-.74	10½	.94-.95	13½
.12-.16	2	.33-.37	5	.54-.58	8	.75-.79	11	.96-100	14

NOTE:—Timing of races and greyhounds at tracks not using the 1/100ths of a second system—the following scale may be used to convert time into lengths:

1/5 second equals 3 lengths
1/10 second equals 1½ lengths
4/60 second equals 1 length

16th Running

American Greyhound Derby
Purse $25,000 Added

CANADIAN HI THERE   JOE CEMENT   ORBIT INN   PARTY ROLLER

Canadian Hi There-1964

16th Annual American Greyhound Derby

ELEVENTH RACE

Please Call for Dog by Number

TRACK RECORD
Donna Larsen 37.40

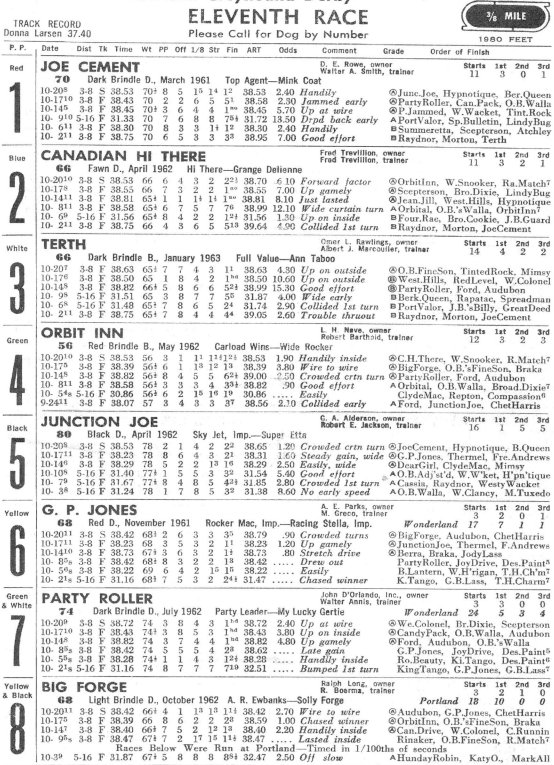

3/8 MILE
1980 FEET

P.P. 1 — Red — JOE CEMENT

D. E. Rowe, owner
Walter A. Smith, trainer

Starts	1st	2nd	3rd
11	3	0	1

70 Dark Brindle D., March 1961 Top Agent—Mink Coat

Date	Dist	Tk	Time	Wt	PP	Off	1/8	Str	Fin	ART	Odds	Comment	Grade	Order of Finish
10-20^{8}	3-8	S	38.53	70½	8	5	1^{5}	1^{4}	1^{2}	38.53	2.40	*Handily*	Ⓐ	Junc.Joe, Hypnotique, Ber.Queen
10-17^{10}	3-8	F	38.43	70	2	2	6	5	5^{1}	38.58	2.30	*Jammed early*	Ⓐ	PartyRoller, Can.Pack, O.B.Walla
10-14^{5}	3-8	F	38.45	70½	3	6	4	4	1no	38.45	5.70	*Up at wire*	Ⓐ	P.Jammed, W.Wacket, Tint.Rock
10- 9^{10}	5-16	F	31.33	70	7	6	8	8	$7^{5½}$	31.72	13.50	*Drpd back early*	A	PortValor, Sp.Bulletin, LindyBug
10- 6^{11}	3-8	F	38.30	70	8	3	3	$1^{½}$	1^{2}	38.30	2.40	*Handily*	B	Summeretta, Scepterson, Atchley
10- 2^{11}	3-8	F	38.75	70	6	5	3	3	3^{3}	38.95	7.00	*Good effort*	B	Raydnor, Morton, Terth

P.P. 2 — Blue — CANADIAN HI THERE

Fred Trevillion, owner
Fred Trevillion, trainer

Starts	1st	2nd	3rd
11	3	2	1

66 Fawn D., April 1962 Hi There—Grange Delienne

Date	Dist	Tk	Time	Wt	PP	Off	1/8	Str	Fin	ART	Odds	Comment	Grade	Order of Finish
10-20^{10}	3-8	S	38.53	66	6	4	3	2	$2^{2½}$	38.70	6.10	*Forward factor*	Ⓐ	OrbitInn, W.Snooker, Ra.Match^{7}
10-17^{8}	3-8	F	38.55	66	7	3	2	2	1no	38.55	7.00	*Up gamely*	Ⓐ	Scepterson, Bro.Dixie, LindyBug
10-14^{11}	3-8	F	38.81	65½	1	1	$1^{½}$	$1^{½}$	1no	38.81	8.10	*Just lasted*	Ⓐ	Jean.Jill, West.Hills, Hypnotique
10- 8^{11}	3-8	F	38.58	65½	6	7	5	7	7^{6}	38.99	12.10	*Wide curtain turn*	A	Orbital, O.B.'sWalla, OrbitInn^{7}
10- 6^{9}	5-16	F	31.56	65½	8	4	2	2	$1^{2½}$	31.56	1.30	*Up on inside*	B	Four.Rae, Bro.Cookie, J.B.Guard
10- 2^{11}	3-8	F	38.75	66	4	3	6	5	5^{13}	39.64	4.90	*Collided 1st turn*	B	Raydnor, Morton, JoeCement

P.P. 3 — White — TERTH

Omer L. Rawlings, owner
Albert J. Marcoullier, trainer

Starts	1st	2nd	3rd
14	4	2	2

66 Dark Brindle B., January 1963 Full Value—Ann Taboo

Date	Dist	Tk	Time	Wt	PP	Off	1/8	Str	Fin	ART	Odds	Comment	Grade	Order of Finish
10-20^{7}	3-8	F	38.63	65½	7	7	4	3	1^{1}	38.63	4.30	*Up on outside*	Ⓐ	O.B.FineSon, TintedRock, Mimsy
10-17^{6}	3-8	F	38.50	65	1	8	4	2	1^{hd}	38.50	10.60	*Up on outside*	Ⓑ	West.Hills, RedLevel, W.Colonel
10-14^{8}	3-8	F	38.82	66½	5	8	6	6	$5^{2½}$	38.99	15.30	*Good effort*	Ⓑ	PartyRoller, Ford, Audubon
10- 9^{8}	5-16	F	31.51	65	3	8	7	7	5^{5}	31.87	4.00	*Wide early*	B	Berk.Queen, Rapatac, Spreadman
10- 6^{8}	5-16	F	31.48	65½	7	8	6	5	2^{4}	31.74	2.90	*Collided 1st turn*	B	PortValor, J.B.'sBilly, GreatDeed
10- 2^{11}	3-8	F	38.75	65½	7	8	4	4	4^{4}	39.05	2.60	*Trouble thruout*	B	Raydnor, Morton, JoeCement

P.P. 4 — Green — ORBIT INN

L. H. Nave, owner
Robert Barthold, trainer

Starts	1st	2nd	3rd
12	3	2	3

56 Red Brindle B., May 1962 Carload Wins—Wide Rocker

Date	Dist	Tk	Time	Wt	PP	Off	1/8	Str	Fin	ART	Odds	Comment	Grade	Order of Finish
10-20^{10}	3-8	S	38.53	56	3	1	1^{1}	$1^{1½}$	$1^{2½}$	38.53	1.90	*Handily inside*	Ⓐ	C.H.There, W.Snooker, R.Match^{7}
10-17^{5}	3-8	F	38.39	56½	6	1	1^{3}	1^{2}	1^{3}	38.39	3.80	*Wire to wire*	Ⓐ	BigForge, O.B.'sFineSon, Braka
10-14^{8}	3-8	F	38.82	56½	8	4	5	5	$6^{2½}$	39.00	2.50	*Crowded crtn turn*	Ⓐ	PartyRoller, Ford, Audubon
10- 8^{11}	3-8	F	38.58	56½	3	3	3	4	$3^{3½}$	38.82	.90	*Good effort*	A	Orbital, O.B.Walla, Broad.Dixie^{7}
10- 5^{4}s	5-16	F	30.86	56½	6	2	1^{5}	1^{6}	1^{9}	30.86	.....	*Easily*		ClydeMac, Repton, Compassion^{6}
9-24^{11}	3-8	F	38.07	57	3	4	3	3	3^{7}	38.56	2.10	*Collided early*	A	Ford, JunctionJoe, ChetHarris

P.P. 5 — Black — JUNCTION JOE

G. A. Alderson, owner
Robert E. Jackson, trainer

Starts	1st	2nd	3rd
16	1	5	5

80 Black D., April 1962 Sky Jet, Imp.—Super Etta

Date	Dist	Tk	Time	Wt	PP	Off	1/8	Str	Fin	ART	Odds	Comment	Grade	Order of Finish
10-20^{8}	3-8	S	38.53	78	2	1	4	2	2^{2}	38.65	1.20	*Crowded crtn turn*	Ⓐ	JoeCement, Hypnotique, B.Queen
10-17^{11}	3-8	F	38.23	78	8	6	4	3	2^{1}	38.31	1.60	*Steady gain, wide*	Ⓐ	G.P.Jones, Thermel, Fre.Andrews
10-14^{6}	3-8	F	38.29	78	5	2	2	1^{3}	1^{6}	38.29	2.50	*Easily, wide*	Ⓐ	DearGirl, ClydeMac, Mimsy
10-10^{8}	5-16	F	31.40	77½	1	5	5	3	3^{2}	31.54	5.40	*Good effort*	A	O.B.Adj'st'd, W.W'ket, H'pn'tique
10- 7^{9}	5-16	F	31.67	77½	8	4	8	5	$4^{2½}$	31.85	2.80	*Crowded 1st turn*	A	Cassia, Raydnor, WestyWacket
10- 3^{8}	5-16	F	31.24	78	1	7	8	5	3^{2}	31.38	8.60	*No early speed*	A	O.B.Walla, W.Clancy, M.Tuxedo

P.P. 6 — Yellow — G. P. JONES

A. E. Parks, owner
M. Greco, trainer

	Starts	1st	2nd	3rd
	3	2	0	1
Wonderland	*17*	*7*	*1*	*1*

68 Red D., November 1961 Rocker Mac, Imp.—Racing Stella, Imp.

Date	Dist	Tk	Time	Wt	PP	Off	1/8	Str	Fin	ART	Odds	Comment	Grade	Order of Finish
10-20^{11}	3-8	S	38.42	68½	2	6	3	3	3^{5}	38.79	.90	*Crowded turns*	Ⓐ	BigForge, Audubon, ChetHarris
10-17^{11}	3-8	F	38.23	68	3	5	3	2	1^{1}	38.23	1.20	*Up gamely*	Ⓐ	JunctionJoe, Thermel, F.Andrews
10-14^{10}	3-8	F	38.73	67½	3	6	3	2	$1^{½}$	38.73	.80	*Stretch drive*	Ⓐ	Berra, Braka, JodyLass
10- 8^{5}s	3-8	F	38.42	68½	8	3	2	2	1^{3}	38.42	.....	*Drew out*		PartyRoller, JoyDrive, Des.Paint^{5}
10- 5^{6}s	3-8	F	38.22	69	6	4	2	1^{5}	1^{5}	38.22	.....	*Easily*		B.Lantern, W.H'rigan, T.H.Ch'm^{7}
10- 2^{1}s	5-16	F	31.16	68½	7	5	3	2	$2^{4½}$	31.47	.....	*Chased winner*		K.Tango, G.B.Lass, T.H.Charm^{7}

P.P. 7 — Green & White — PARTY ROLLER

John D'Orlando, Inc., owner
Walter Annis, trainer

	Starts	1st	2nd	3rd
	3	3	0	0
Wonderland	*24*	*5*	*3*	*4*

74 Dark Brindle D., July 1962 Party Leader—My Lucky Gertie

Date	Dist	Tk	Time	Wt	PP	Off	1/8	Str	Fin	ART	Odds	Comment	Grade	Order of Finish
10-20^{9}	3-8	S	38.72	74	3	8	4	3	1^{hd}	38.72	2.40	*Up at wire*	Ⓐ	We.Colonel, Br.Dixie, Scepterson
10-17^{10}	3-8	F	38.43	74½	3	8	5	3	1^{hd}	38.43	3.80	*Up on inside*	Ⓐ	CandyPack, O.B.Walla, Audubon
10-14^{8}	3-8	F	38.82	74	3	7	4	4	1^{hd}	38.82	4.80	*Up gamely*	Ⓐ	Ford, Audubon, O.B.'sWalla
10- 8^{5}s	3-8	F	38.42	74	5	5	5	4	2^{3}	38.62	.....	*Late gain*		G.P.Jones, JoyDrive, Des.Paint^{5}
10- 5^{5}s	3-8	F	38.28	74½	1	1	4	3	$1^{2½}$	38.28	.....	*Handily inside*		Ro.Beauty, Ki.Tango, Des.Paint^{6}
10- 2^{1}s	5-16	F	31.16	74	8	7	7	7	7^{19}	32.51	.....	*Bumped 1st turn*		KingTango, G.P.Jones, G.B.Lass^{7}

P.P. 8 — Yellow & Black — BIG FORGE

Ralph Long, owner
R. Boerma, trainer

	Starts	1st	2nd	3rd
	3	2	1	0
Portland	*18*	*10*	*0*	*0*

68 Light Brindle D., October 1962 A. R. Ewbanks—Solly Forge

Date	Dist	Tk	Time	Wt	PP	Off	1/8	Str	Fin	ART	Odds	Comment	Grade	Order of Finish
10-20^{11}	3-8	S	38.42	66½	4	1	1^{3}	1^{3}	$1^{1½}$	38.42	2.70	*Wire to wire*	Ⓐ	Audubon, G.P.Jones, ChetHarris
10-17^{5}	3-8	F	38.39	66	8	6	2	2	2^{3}	38.59	1.00	*Chased winner*	Ⓐ	OrbitInn, O.B.'sFineSon, Braka
10-14^{7}	3-8	F	38.40	66½	7	5	2	1^{2}	1^{3}	38.40	2.20	*Handily inside*	Ⓐ	Can.Drive, W.Colonel, C.Runnin
10- 9^{5}s	3-8	F	38.47	67½	7	2	1^{7}	1^{5}	$1^{1½}$	38.47	.....	*Lasted inside*		Rinaker, O.B.FineSon, R.Match^{7}
Races Below Were Run at Portland—Timed in 1/100ths of seconds														
10-3^{9}	5-16	F	31.87	67½	5	8	8	8	$8^{8½}$	32.47	2.50	*Off slow*	A	HundayRobin, KatyO., MarkAll

WIN	PLACE	SHOW	PLACE	SHOW	SHOW

Handicapper's Selections—G. P. Jones, Orbit Inn, Junction Joe

Nitrana-1965

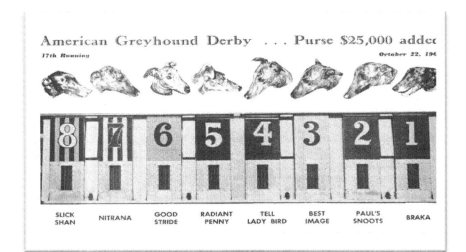

SLICK SHAN — NITRANA — GOOD STRIDE — RADIANT PENNY — TELL LADY BIRD — BEST IMAGE — PAUL'S SNOOTS — BRAKA

Forty-third Night—FRIDAY, OCTOBER 22, 1965

WELCOME TO TONIGHT'S 17th RUNNING OF DERBY

1965 Edition Rates with the Best; Field Most Evenly Matched Ever

ONLY 7 MORE NIGHTS Of Racing At Taunton
FOR THE 1965 SEASON

Taunton Greyhound Association, Inc.
DIGHTON, MASS.
Member of the American Greyhound Track Operators Association
Operating under license issued by the Massachusetts State Racing Commission

JOS. M. LINSEY
President-Treasurer-Managing Director
David Yaffe .... Vice President
C. Grismo .... Vice President
Alfred S. Ross .... Vice President
Stanley Burton .... Comptroller

Mass. State Racing Commission
Chairman .... Dr. Paul F. Walsh
Commissioner .... Amos E. Wasgatt, Jr.
Commissioner .... Grover T. O'Brien
Secretary .... Lawrence J. Lane

Racing Officials
ANDREW LEDDY, Director of Racing
Presiding Judge .... E. J. L'Italien
Judge .... Richard Maliff
Racing Secretary .... Andrew Leddy
Paddock Judge .... Colin Chisholm
Patrol Judge .... Kent N. Lee
Timer .... Peter Edgerly
Clerk of Scales ...... Archibald J. Burnside
Starter .... William F. Harnois
Oper. of Mech. Lure .. William G. Morton, Jr.
Veterinary Surgeon .. Dr. Thomas J. O'Brien
Chart Writer .... Thomas J. Whalen
Mutuel Manager .... L. W. Skaggs

Track Superintendent .... George Jordan
Promotional Manager .... George Lohrie
Publicity .... John A. Needs
Announcer .... Edward Litchfield
Security .... Edward A. Keefe

Mass. Racing Commission Officials
Commission Judge .... Earl J. Leary
Assoc. Comm. Judge .. Edward E. Kammerer
Superv. Rac. Inspector .. James V. Guaragna
Chief Accountant .... James D. Callahan

JOS. M. LINSEY
President, Managing Director

Welcome to tonight's 17th running of the $25,000 added American Greyhound Derby!

We hope you will enjoy the pomp and excitement that go with this annual classic — America's top greyhound attraction. We are sure you will thrill at the Derby race itself, this year one of our finest that rates in color and interest with any of its predecessors.

There have been some great Derby fields and some great greyhounds matching strides over the well-groomed Taunton course every year since this classic was inaugurated in 1949. There have been many all-time greyhound greats that have indelibly written their names into its world-famous history.

There was Oklahoman in 1949; Real Huntsman, both in 1950 and 1951; On The Line, 1952; However, 1953; Mellojean, 1954; Koliga, 1955; Go Rock, 1956; Clydesdale, 1957; Feldcrest, 1958; Go Super, 1959; Serape, 1960; Velvet Six, 1961; Cactus Noel, 1962; Thermel, 1963; and Canadian Hi There in 1964. Remember them?

Tonight, we can safely say and without prejudice, that you will be seeing one of the finest and most evenly-matched fields in the Derby's 17 years of existence. It is a representative group, too. There's Braka, Radiant Penny and Tell Lady Bird from Taunton; Paul's Snoots and Slick Shan, a pair of aces from Multnomah in Portland, Oregon; Good Stride and Best Image from neighboring Wonderland Park in Revere, and Nitrana from the shores of Tampa, Florida.

We salute tonight's Derby starters and we also take our hats off to the greyhounds who have tried ever so hard but just didn't make it—to us at Taunton they are all champions.

**TONIGHT and TOMORROW Night
$10. Twin Double Tickets**
WILL BE SOLD AT THE
$10. DAILY DOUBLE WINDOW
ON THE MEZZANINE FLOOR

Nitrana-1965

17th Annual American Greyhound Derby

TRACK RECORD
Donna Larsen 37.40

TWELFTH RACE
Please Call for Dog by Number

⅜ MILE
1980 FEET

P. P.	Date	Dist	Tk	Time	Wt	PP	Off	1/8	Str	Fin	ART	Odds	Comment	Grade	Order of Finish

Red 1 — BRAKA
Otto Mamino, owner / Otto Mamino, trainer — Starts 15, 1st 7, 2nd 3, 3rd 3

68½ Black D., November 1962 Irish Mix—Leading Dinkie, Imp.

Date	Dist	Tk	Time	Wt	PP	Off	1/8	Str	Fin	ART	Odds	Comment	Grade	Order of Finish
10-19¹⁰	3-8	F	38.41	67½	2	6	3	3	1ʰᵈ	38.41	.40	Despite trouble	Ⓐ	Nob.Clyde, B.Rocker, S.Opinion⁷
10-16¹²	3-8	F	38.36	67	4	1	4	2	1½	38.36	.60	Drew out handily	Ⓐ	Terth, CriForever, WestyColonel
10-13¹¹	3-8	F	38.11	67½	2	1	1²	1⁶	16½	38.11	.60	Wire to wire	Ⓐ	Rad.Penny, ClydeMac, BestImage
10-7⁶	5-16	F	31.29	68	1	8	5	4	3⁴	31.56	3.60	Wide late	A	JustaHabit, Wes.Whizzer, Atmore
10-4¹¹	5-16	F	31.53	68	5	6	5	3	2³	31.73	4.10	Closing	A	WestyWhizzer, Falton, Dr.Wilson
9-29⁶	5-16	F	31.51	68½	6	3	5	5	1½	31.51	1.00	Up on outside	A	Falton, Wa.Harrigan, GenaGreer

Blue 2 — PAUL'S SNOOTS
Harmon & Nasser, owner / Fred Trevillion, trainer — Multnomah: Starts 20, 1st 5, 2nd 5, 3rd 4 / Starts 3, 1st 3, 2nd 0, 3rd 0

57 Fawn B., July, 1962 Sky Jet—Slow Motion

Date	Dist	Tk	Time	Wt	PP	Off	1/8	Str	Fin	ART	Odds	Comment	Grade	Order of Finish
10-19¹¹	3-8	F	38.28	57½	3	1	1²½	1¹	1¹	38.28	1.60	Wire to wire	Ⓐ	Goo. Stride, E.Blackmail, T.Duster
10-16⁶	3-8	F	38.56	57	1	3	2	2	1¹	38.56	.90	Stretch drive	Ⓐ	Dr.Wilson, T.La.Bird, Broa.Doris
10-13⁹	3-8	F	38.58	56½	5	2	1³	1⁶	1³	38.58	4.40	Lasted to win	Ⓐ	Orbital, Broad.Doris, SafetyValve
10-9¹ₛ	3-8	F	38.25	57	1	1	1¹	1½	4⁴	38.56	.....	Some wide		SlickShan, E.Blackmail, Orb.Inn⁵

Races Below Were Run at Multnomah—Timed in 1/100ths of seconds

| 9-28⁸ | 5-16 | F | 31.05 | 57 | 3 | 6 | 7 | 7 | 4 | 31.98 | 2.00 | Collided, esc turn | A | BrownieShan, TripUp, LesDrake |

White 3 — BEST IMAGE
Ryan Kennel, owner / John Ryan, trainer — Starts 11, 1st 4, 2nd 2, 3rd 1

54 Brindle B., August 1963 Cleveland Lad, Imp.—Seemed Best

Date	Dist	Tk	Time	Wt	PP	Off	1/8	Str	Fin	ART	Odds	Comment	Grade	Order of Finish
10-19⁸	3-8	F	38.16	55½	8	4	4	2	1²	38.16	.90	Drew out	Ⓐ	Bratinella, TellFrankie, Urbanna
10-16⁹	3-8	F	38.12	54½	8	6	3	3	1²½	38.12	4.70	Drew out handily	Ⓐ	Ed.Blackmail, B.Rocker, OrbitIn
10-13¹¹	3-8	F	38.11	55	5	5	7	6	4⁹	38.75	9.60	Jammed early	Ⓐ	Braka, RadiantPenny, ClydeMac
10-8¹²	3-8	F	38.66	55	4	3	5	3	1²	38.66	3.20	Drew out	A	Outsi.Jake, Wes.Ripper, Cadenita
10-4¹¹	5-16	F	31.53	54	7	7	8	8	7¹⁰½	32.27	38.70	Crowded 1st turn	A	WestyWhizzer, Braka, Falton
9-30¹²	3-8	F	38.76	54½	1	5	5	5	2³	38.96	5.40	Crowded crtn turn	A	PartyRoller, Tr.Duster, W.Ripper

Green 4 — TELL LADY BIRD
Ivory Tower Kennel, owner / D. W. Bethel, trainer — Starts 16, 1st 4, 2nd 4, 3rd 6

57 Red Fawn B., September 1963 Great Valor—Tell Marcelle

Date	Dist	Tk	Time	Wt	PP	Off	1/8	Str	Fin	ART	Odds	Comment	Grade	Order of Finish
10-19⁶	3-8	F	38.38	57	5	1	3	2	1¹½	38.38	7.40	Drew out	Ⓐ	Mer.Mystery, Terth, Beng.Tigress
10-16⁶	3-8	F	38.56	56½	8	1	4	4	3⁴	38.86	2.60	On inside	Ⓐ	Paul.Snoots, Dr.Wilson, Br.Doris
10-13⁵	3-8	F	38.42	56	2	4	3	2	2²	38.55	1.60	Forward factor	Ⓐ	Gab.Boots, Mag.Away, W.Ripper
10-9¹¹	5-16	F	31.33	56	5	3	3	3	3²	31.46	3.50	Good effort	A	Radia.Penny, Secan, Wes.Colonel
10-6¹²	3-8	F	38.60	56	1	2	2	1½	2¹	38.65	10.10	Good effort	A	Rad.Penny, W.Colonel, RedOnly
10-2¹²	3-8	F	38.96	56	6	5	6	4	3¹	39.03	4.00	Driving wide	A	Broad.Laura, W.Colonel, R.Butch

Black 5 — RADIANT PENNY
H. D. Beckner, owner / Albert J. Marcoulier, trainer — Starts 14, 1st 5, 2nd 6, 3rd 2

61 Brindle & White B., March 1963 Full Value—Penny Bobs

Date	Dist	Tk	Time	Wt	PP	Off	1/8	Str	Fin	ART	Odds	Comment	Grade	Order of Finish
10-19¹²	3-8	F	38.31	60	2	4	4	2	1³	38.31	3.00	Drew out	Ⓐ	Nitrana, Debby'sBest, SlickShan
10-16¹⁰	3-8	F	38.26	60	6	8	3	2	1²	38.26	.90	Handily, wide	Ⓐ	Debby.Best, Gab.Boots, Br.Gwen
10-13¹¹	3-8	F	38.11	60	3	6	6	4	26½	38.57	2.10	Jammed early	Ⓐ	Braka, ClydeMac, BestImage
10-9¹¹	5-16	F	31.33	60	6	4	5	4	1¹	31.33	2.00	From far back	A	Secan, TellLadyBird, We.Colonel
10-6¹²	3-8	F	38.60	59½	6	5	4	2	1¹	38.60	1.80	Driving, wide	A	T.LadyBird, W.Colonel, RedOnly
10-2¹¹	5-16	F	31.41	60	8	4	8	6	3³	31.61	5.20	Good effort	Ⓐ	JustaHabit, Ma.Away, O.B.N.Day

Yellow 6 — GOOD STRIDE
Mike Castellani, Inc., owner / B. J. Castellani, trainer — Starts 12, 1st 3, 2nd 1, 3rd 1

75 Red Fawn D., April 1963 Andale—Kandi Ella

Date	Dist	Tk	Time	Wt	PP	Off	1/8	Str	Fin	ART	Odds	Comment	Grade	Order of Finish
10-19¹¹	3-8	F	38.28	75	5	2	2	2	2¹	38.33	19.30	Saved thruout	Ⓐ	Pa.Snoots, E.Blackmail, T.Duster
10-16¹²	3-8	F	38.36	75	7	7	6	6	5⁵	38.69	56.30	Some gain	Ⓐ	Braka, Terth, CriForever
10-13⁸	3-8	F	38.72	75	3	3	1½	1²	38.72	4.50	Handily	Ⓑ	Jonimora, Melo.Mac, Ben.Tigress
10-9¹²	3-8	F	38.65	75	1	6	4	4	4³	38.85	1.60	Evenly	Ⓑ	Bratinella, ChrisMissin, TellJean
10-5¹²	3-8	F	38.56	74½	8	7	6	7	5⁸	39.11	4.60	Crowded crtn turn	A	BrookGwen, D.Demon, Gab.Boots
9-30¹²	3-8	F	38.76	75½	8	6	6	6	6⁶	39.17	12.30	Crowded crtn turn	A	PartyRoller, Be.Image, Tr.Duster

Green & White 7 — NITRANA
Orville Moses, owner / L. H. Nave, trainer — Tampa: Starts 9, 1st 6, 2nd 1, 3rd 0 / Starts 3, 1st 1, 2nd 2, 3rd 0

54 Red B., February 1963 Clydesdale—Opportunist

Date	Dist	Tk	Time	Wt	PP	Off	1/8	Str	Fin	ART	Odds	Comment	Grade	Order of Finish
10-19¹²	3-8	F	38.31	53½	6	2	1⁶	1⁵	2³	38.50	2.80	Speed to stretch	Ⓐ	Rad.Penny, Debb.Best, SlickShan
10-16⁷	3-8	F	38.16	54	7	4	1⁷	1⁵	1⁴	38.16	2.10	Long early lead	Ⓐ	Sa.Opinion, Bro.Junior, Tr.Duster
10-13⁹	3-8	F	38.58	54	6	8	8	8	8¹¹	39.35	2.70	Offstrided break	Ⓐ	Paul.Snoots, Orbital, Broad.Doris
10-9¹ₛ	3-8	F	38.25	54½	5	3	2	5	5⁸	38.82	.....	Crowded early		SlickShan, E.Blackmail, Orb.Inn⁵

Races Below Were Run at Tampa—Timed in 1/100ths of seconds

| 9-29⁹ | 5-16 | F | 32.02 | 53½ | 7 | 5 | 3 | 3 | 1ⁿᵒ | 32.02 | .80 | Won racing wide | A | HiddenThrne, Mer.Dot, D.L.Mar |

Yellow & Black 8 — SLICK SHAN
J. C. Garber, owner / Donald Garber, trainer — Multnomah: Starts 18, 1st 10, 2nd 3, 3rd 2 / Starts 3, 1st 2, 2nd 0, 3rd 0

82 Black D., March 1963 Rural Shannon—Queen Quality

Date	Dist	Tk	Time	Wt	PP	Off	1/8	Str	Fin	ART	Odds	Comment	Grade	Order of Finish
10-19¹²	3-8	F	38.31	81	8	5	6	5	4⁵½	38.70	1.00	Trouble thruout	Ⓐ	RadiantPenny, Nitrana, Deb.Best
10-16¹¹	3-8	F	38.36	81	4	2	2	2	1¹	38.36	.40	Stretch drive	Ⓐ	Me.Mystery, DeronJ., PartyRoller
10-13¹²	3-8	F	38.26	80½	4	1	1⁴	1⁸	1⁸	38.26	1.50	Easily	Ⓐ	Sam.Opinion, Pa.Roller, C.Missin
10-9¹ₛ	3-8	F	38.25	83	4	4	3	2	1¹½	38.25	.....	Driving thruout		E.Blackmail, OrbitInn, P.Snoots⁵

Races Below Were Run at Multnomah—Timed in 1/100ths of seconds

| 10-4⁵ | 5-16 | W | 31.94 | 82½ | 5 | 2 | 7 | 6 | 5 | 32.52 | 2.00 | Bumped, esc turn | A | Hawker, Paul.Snoots, SophiaLass |

SAVE TIME IN YOUR PAY-OFF LINE BY HANDING OUR CASHIERS CHANGE TO THE NEAREST DOLLAR

Handicapper's Selections—Braka, Paul's Snoots, Radiant Penny

Golden In-1966

$25,000
American
Greyhound
DERBY
TONIGHT

"NITRANA"
WINNER OF
1965 AMERICAN GREYHOUND DERBY

OFFICIAL RACING PROGRAM

TAUNTON DOG TRACK

Home of The American Greyhound Derby

FRIDAY, OCTOBER 21, 1966

Forty-second Night—FRIDAY, OCTOBER 21, 1966   OFFICIAL PROGRAM 24c
SALES TAX 1c   **25c**

Welcome to Tonight's 18th Derby

Taunton Greyhound Association, Inc.
DIGHTON, MASS
Member of the American Greyhound
Track Operators' Association

Operating under license issued by the
Massachusetts State Racing Commission

JOS. M. LINSEY
President-Treasurer-Managing Director

David Yaffe .... *Vice President*
C. Grimmo .... *Vice President*
Alfred S. Ross .... *Vice President*
Kenneth Dorn .... *Vice President*
Stanley Burton .... *Comptroller*

Jos. M. Linsey
President,
Managing Director

Mass. State Racing Commission

Chairman .... Dr. Paul F. Walsh
Commissioner .... Amos E. Wasgatt, Jr.
Commissioner .... Elmer C. Nelson
Secretary .... Lawrence J. Lane

Racing Officials

ALFRED S. ROSS, Director of Racing
Presiding Judge .... Richard Maliff
Judge .... William F. Clemmey
Racing Secretary .... E. J. L'Italien
Paddock Judge .... Colin Chisholm
Patrol Judge .... Kent N. Luz
Timer .... Peter Edgerly
Clerk of Scales........Archibald J. Burnside
Starter .... Thomas F. Cummings
Operator Mech. Lure...William G. Morton, Jr.
Veterinary Surgeon....Dr. Thomas J. O'Brien
Chart Writer .... Thomas J. Whalen
Mutuels Manager .... L. W. Skaggs

Track Superintendent ....George Jordan
Promotional Manager .... George Lobris
Publicity .... John A. Needs
Announcer .... Edward Litchfield
Security .... Warren J. Caples

Mass. Racing Commission Officials

Commission Judge .... Edward E. Kammerer
Associate Comm. Judge ..... Earl J. Leary
Superv. Racing Inspector .. Thomas R. Lynch

NOTICE!
For your own protection DO
NOT cash mutuel tickets for any
person you do not know.

The Management

Welcome to tonight's 18th running of the $25,000 added American Greyhound Derby!

We know that in recent years you have enjoyed the pomp and excitement that go towards making this Taunton classic the best anywhere and we trust that the continuity of our top efforts to make this America's best greyhound attraction will further meet with your approval.

From our first year, 1949, when we inaugurated the American Greyhound Derby and offered the heretofore unheard of purse of $25,000 added, this Derby has been the magnet for the best greyhounds in the country and an invader or two from foreign lands.

It still is THE DERBY!

It goes without saying that Lady Luck is an important unseen factor in this classic, but tonight we all feel that she certainly has waved her magic wand upon us to enable us to present the best candidates—survivors of the three action-packed qualifying rounds.

Not only has this 1966 renewal of the American Greyhound Derby lured the finest champions from practically every track in the nation but it has also become the center of interest of greyhound racing fans everywhere.

We salute tonight's Derby starters and also to the greyhounds who tried but just didn't make it—to us they are all champions.

PAST DERBY WINNERS

1965—NITRANA	1956—GO ROCK
1964—CANADIAN HI THERE	1955—KOLIGA
1963—THERMEL	1954—MELLO-JEAN
1962—CACTUS NOEL	1953—HOWEVER
1961—VELVET SIS	1952—ON THE LINE
1960—SERAPE	1951—REAL HUNTSMAN
1959—GO SUPER	1950—REAL HUNTSMAN
1958—FELDCREST	1949—OKLAHOMAN
1957—CLYDESDALE	

Golden In-1966

18th Annual American Greyhound Derby
TWELFTH RACE
3/8 MILE
1980 FEET

TRACK RECORD
Donna Larsen 37.40

Please Call for Dog by Number

P. P.	Date	Dist	Tk	Time	Wt	PP	Off	1/8	Str	Fin	ART	Odds	Comment	Grade	Order of Finish

Red — 1

ANKEN [DERBY]
H. D. Beckner, owner
Albert Marcoulier, trainer
Starts 15 1st 4 2nd 2 3rd 4

64   Red Brindle D., September 1964   Reveloy—Full Circle

10-18⁸	3-8	F	38.25	62¼	7	6	2	1ʰᵈ2ⁿᵒ	38.26	5.40	Outgamed	(AA)Bratinella, Nept.Lady, MissWhirl
10-15¹⁰	3-8	F	38.00	63	1	6	6	6	5⁴¼	38.32	3.10	Some gain	(AA)GallantCush, Belin.Lou, Co.Coker
10-12⁷	3-8	F	38.24	63½	6	6	4	2	1¹	38.24	4.90	Late speed	(AA)Knock.King, W.Blarney, Hon.Girl
10-7¹²	3-8	F	38.05	62¼	3	8	6	6	4⁵	38.41	3.70	Bumped early	AA Whitewall, Rad.Penny, Bratinella
10-1⁶	5-16	S	31.78	63	7	8	8	5	4⁷	32.27	10.50	Off slowly	AA Wes.Whizzer, Jus.Habit, TanFire
9-28¹²	3-8	F	38.41	63	8	8	4	3	1²	38.41	3.70	Handily inside	AA Way.Blarney, Rad.Penny, C.Susie

Blue — 2

BRATINELLA [DERBY]
Henrietta Furmanik, owner
Matthew Furmanik, trainer
Starts 13 1st 3 2nd 7 3rd 2

59   Brindle B., January 1964   Upstager—Idle One

10-18⁸	3-8	F	38.25	59	8	3	1¹¼2	1ⁿᵒ	38.25	3.40	Up gamely	(AA)Anken, Neptune.Lady, MissWhirl
10-15¹²	3-8	F	37.97	58½	5	2	2	2	2¹¼	38.08	15.20	Chased winner	(AA)MissLouisa, Whitewall, Ra.Penny
10-12⁸	3-8	F	38.00	58½	6	2	2	2	3⁵	38.36	5.30	Wide thruout	(AA)Whitewall, Roy.Topper, I.G.There
10-7¹²	3-8	F	38.05	58	6	4	4	3	3⁵	/38.40	3.20	Wide thruout	AA Whitewall, RadiantPenny, Anken
10-11¹	5-16	S	31.54	58½	4	1	3	2	2²	31.67	4.50	Wide thruout	(AA)GallantCush, MahalaLass, Wyler
9-28⁵	5-16	S	31.29	59	2	2	2	2	2²	31.43	3.40	Very wide	(AA)Maha.Lass, Gal.Cush, I.W.Design

White — 3

GOLDEN IN [DERBY]
L. H. Nave, owner
L. H. Nave, trainer
Starts 3 1st 3 2nd 0 3rd 0
Tampa 1 1st 0 2nd 1 3rd 0

78   Fawn D., June 1963   Carload Wins—Texas Yellow Rose

10-18¹²	3-8	F	37.81	76	5	2	2	1²¼1³¼	37.81	.70	Handily	(AA)Roy.Topper, Belin.Lou, R.Murphy
10-15¹¹	3-8	F	37.72	76½	7	5	2	1⁵ 1⁶¼	37.72	.80	Easily	(AA)BestImage, RoyJ., I'llGetThere⁷
10-12¹²	3-8	F	38.47	76½	3	3	4	2	1¹¼	38.47	1.80	Despite trouble	(AA)T.LadyBird, Silv.Skip, Coco.Susie
10-8¹s	3-8	F	38.52	77	5	4	3	3	1³	38.52	.....	Driving	J'sDacata, Dix.Merry, Prin.Paula⁴

Races Below Were Run at Tampa—Timed in 1/100ths of seconds

| 9-24¹² | 3-8 | F | 37.84 | 76½ | 6 | 5 | 3 | 3 | 2¹ | 37.90 | .90 | Driving at end | A PollToll, MissWhirl, C.Vengeance |

Green — 4

GRANNY'S PICK [DERBY]
D. Q. Williams, owner
D. Q. Williams, trainer
Starts 6 1st 3 2nd 1 3rd 0

53   Red Brindle B., June 1964   Coakfield Hero, Imp.—Betty Barr

10-18⁵	3-8	F	38.07	52	1	1	2	1² 1²¼	38.07	3.60	Handily	(AA)CocosSusie, SaltySteve, SwellEd
10-15⁶	3-8	F	38.19	52	6	1	2	3	†1¹¹	38.19	9.90	Dead heat, win	(A)Rusdale, Bettine, EarlyTimer
10-12¹²	3-8	F	38.47	53	4	1	3	6	6⁸	38.91	21.10	Bumped crtn turn	(A)GoldenIn, Te.LadyBird, Silv.Skip
10-8¹⁰	3-8	F	38.68	52¼	4	1	1¼ 1¹¼ 2¹	38.76	11.20	Outfinished	A WhyJanet, Mirtha, SummerHobo
10-4¹²	3-8	F	37.68	52	4	1	3	4	5¹²	38.54	5.50	Steady fade	A SilverSkip, HondaGirl, W.Paisley
9-28⁸	3-8	F	38.81	52	1	2	1³ 1⁵ 1³	38.81	2.60	Handily	BB CoraCoker, Fribble, RockerSaint

Black — 5

EARLY TIMER [DERBY]
Dock Shockley, owner
Maurice Cyr, trainer
Starts 3 1st 2 2nd 0 3rd 0
Multnomah 16 1st 7 2nd 2 3rd 2

72   Red D., October 1964   Great Valor—Sally Jet

10-18⁶	3-8	F	38.21	70	6	1	2	1¼ 1³	38.21	3.10	Drew out	(AA)Ca.Lonesome, Gal.Cush, Hon.Girl
10-15⁶	3-8	F	38.19	70½	8	5	4	4	4²¼	38.37	2.70	Good effort	(AA)Rusdale, Granny'sPick, Bettine
10-12⁹	3-8	F	38.20	70½	8	3	2	1³ 1⁶	38.20	5.60	Drew out	(AA)W.Colonel, Ad.Jose, C.Lonesome

Races Below Were Run at Multnomah—Timed in 1/100ths of seconds

| 10-5¹¹ | FC | F | 39.83 | 70 | 5 | 2 | 1 | 1 | 1 | 39.83 | 4.70 | Going away | S SkyEmpress, SpringHigh, Fortrel |
| 10-1⁹ | GC | F | 37.49 | 71 | 8 | 6 | 5 | 7 | 7 | 38.25 | 2.35 | On inside | A SallyValor, HappyRick, Antiquia |

Yellow — 6

BELINDA LOU [DERBY]
James E. O'Donnell, Jr., owner
W. H. O'Donnell, trainer
Starts 9 1st 2 2nd 1 3rd 1

61   Brindle B., February 1964   Sam King—Campus Chance

10-18¹²	3-8	F	37.81	60	8	7	6	3⁸¼	38.40	5.20	Steady gain	(AA)GoldenIn, Roy.Topper, R.Murphy
10-15¹⁰	3-8	F	38.00	61	8	3	3	3	2²	38.12	3.40	Crowded on rail	(AA)GallantCush, Co.Coker, Sal.Valor
10-12¹¹	3-8	F	38.22	61	8	4	4	2	1¹¼	38.22	7.60	Handily	(AA)MissWhirl, BestImage, SwellEd
10-5¹²	3-8	F	38.19	61	8	4	8	6	4⁶	38.63	33.30	Bmpd front str.	AA Roy.Topper, W.Melanie, B.Image
9-30¹²	3-8	F	37.90	61	6	8	8	8	6⁷	38.40	11.10	Never prominent	AA Bettine, AdiosJose, RoyJ.
9-27¹²	3-8	F	38.26	61	1	3	6	1³ 1⁶¼	38.26	3.20	Easily	A Mag.Away, Ben.Tigress, Su.Hobo

Green & White — 7

COCOS SUSIE [DERBY]
A. Ray Dupree, Jr., owner
Charles Rink, trainer
Starts 11 1st 3 2nd 1 3rd 1

55   Red B., April 1964   Happy Cotton—Saleslady Mar

10-18⁵	3-8	F	38.07	55	5	2	1ʰᵈ2	2²¼	38.24	2.80	Good effort	(AA)Granny.Pick, SaltySteve, SwellEd
10-15⁹	3-8	F	37.85	55	6	1	1³ 1²¼1³	37.85	2.60	Wire to wire	(AA)BullThru, L.G.Artemis, Contralto
10-12¹²	3-8	F	38.47	54½	6	2	3	4³¼	38.71	10.50	Bumped early	(AA)GoldenIn, Te.LadyBird, Silv.Skip
10-7¹⁰	5-16	F	31.11	54½	3	1	1² 1²¼1³	31.11	18.60	Wire to wire	AA SaltySteve, RedMurphy, TellTom
10-3¹²	3-8	F	38.50	54½	4	4	7	7	8⁹	39.13	26.20	Collided front str.	AA Rusdale, Rad'ntPenny, Whitewall
9-28¹²	3-8	F	38.41	55	3	2	2	2	4⁴	38.67	14.30	Crowded crtn tn	A Anken, Way.Blarney, Rad.Penny

Yellow & Black — 8

MISS LOUISA [DERBY]
W. C. Groves, owner
William M. Maloney, trainer
Starts 3 1st 3 2nd 0 3rd 0

58   Red Brindle B., April 1964   Rostown Genius—Louisa Mac

10-18¹¹	3-8	F	38.16	57½	1	1	1¹ 1¹¼1¹¼	38.16	1.80	Wire to wire	(AA)Rusdale, BullThru, Ways.Blarney
10-15¹²	3-8	F	37.97	57	1	1	1¹ 1¹¼1¹¼	37.97	2.00	Wire to wire	(AA)Bratinella, Whitewall, Rad.Penny
10-12⁵	3-8	F	38.32	57	8	1	1²¼1⁵ 1²	38.32	.90	Wire to wire	(AA)WhyJanet, CoraCoker, Bon.Terri
10-7¹s	5-16	F	31.09	57¼	4	4	2	1²¼ 1⁴	31.09	.....	Drew out	Ma.McCoy, PineKing, I.G.There⁶
10-4⁶s	5-16	F	30.90	58	1	1	1³ 1⁵ 1⁶¼	30.90	.....	Wire to wire	I.W.Rivera, Ken'ngton, S.Chance⁵

WIN   PLACE   SHOW   PLACE   SHOW   SHOW

Handicapper's Selections—Golden In, Miss Louisa, Early Timer

Xandra-1967

XANDRA — 1967 CHAMPION . . . Xandra, winner of the 1967 renewal of the American Greyhound Derby, poses proudly in front of winner's platform as owner E.J. Alderson, second from left, smiles happily. Jos. M. Linsey, Taunton managing director, center, Frank Winchell, secretary of the AGTOA, second from right, and Irving Epstein, left, join in hailing the four-length triumph.

Xandra-1967

19th Annual American Greyhound Derby

TRACK RECORD
Donna Larsen 37.40

TWELFTH RACE

3/8 MILE
1980 FEET

1 (Red) CLARLESS

D. Q. Williams, owner
D. Q. Williams, trainer

Starts 15 · 1st 4 · 2nd 3 · 3rd 2

58 Dark Brindle B., September 1965 Rinaker—Soquel

Date	Dist	Tk	Time	Wt	PP	Off	1/8	Str	Fin	ART	Odds	Comment	Grade	Order of Finish
10-17^{11}	3-8	F	38.18	58½	3	8	7	5	4^{6}	38.62	2.90	*On outside*	(AA)	Copier, G.Frances. Zoom.Debbie
10-14^{12}	3-8	F	38.41	58	6	7	5	4	2^{1½}	38.52	2.50	*Crowded stretch*	(AA)	Copier, MelloMystic, L.G'sAres7
10-11^{8}	3-8	F	38.49	58½	7	6	5	1^{1}	1^{6}	38.49	3.40	*Drew out, wide*	(AA)	Bro.Adios, Fab.Whizzer, OBFan'e
10-7^{11}	3-8	F	38.57	58½	8	8	5	3	1^{1}	38.57	3.70	*Despite trouble*	AA	Bro.Gena, Me.Mystery, Ro.Regent
10-4^{12}	3-8	F	38.08	58½	8	8	8	6	4^{4}	38.34	12.30	*Wide front str*	AA	MelloMystic, Fariston, Zo.Debbie
10-2^{12}	3-8	F	38.22	58½	4	8	6	4	3^{7½}	38.74	4.20	*Wide thruout*	AA	T.Fakeroque, B.Adios, Mar.Lamb

2 (Blue) XANDRA

E. J. Alderson, owner
E. J. Alderson, trainer

Starts 3 · 1st 2 · 2nd 0 · 3rd 1
Tampa 4 · 1 · 1 · 1

64 Light Brin. B., Dec. 1964 Julius Caesar, Imp.—Je Nay's Empress

Date	Dist	Tk	Time	Wt	PP	Off	1/8	Str	Fin	ART	Odds	Comment	Grade	Order of Finish
10-17^{6}	3-8	F	38.13	63½	6	6	1½	1^{2}	1^{3}	38.13	.70	*Handily*	(AA)	BellCreek, IrishTray, GroveRock
10-14^{6}	3-8	F	38.19	63½	7	2	1^{3}	1^{5}	1^{3}	38.19	1.40	*Handily*	(AA)	Zo.Debbie, LGPhaet'n, W.Paisley
10-11^{11}	3-8	F	38.65	63	8	6	4	3	3^{2}	38.80	1.20	*Bumped curt tn*	(AA)	Mast.Mick, LB'sBil.Jeff, Gr.Rock
10-4^{4}s	5-16	F	30.82	63	4	2	2	1^{3}	1^{3}	30.82	.....	*Handily*		Fin.Effect, Wa.Paisley, CriReva6
Races Below Were Run at Tampa—Timed in 1/100ths of seconds														
9-20^{9}	5-16	F	31.32	63½	3	7	8	6	4^{8}	31.89	3.10	*Far back early*	A	Mr.Eli, TackSue, IrishMaiden

3 (White) POWDER ROCK

Deep Rock Kennel, owner
W. M. Glendenning, trainer

Starts 5 · 1st 2 · 2nd 1 · 3rd 0

73 Light Brindle D., July 1965 Jay Rock—Lou Rock

Date	Dist	Tk	Time	Wt	PP	Off	1/8	Str	Fin	ART	Odds	Comment	Grade	Order of Finish
10-17^{4}	3-8	F	38.57	73½	4	4	4	4	4^{3}	38.76	5.10	*Good effort*	(AA)	F.Whizzer, Ma.Mick, T.Faker'que
10-14^{4}	3-8	F	38.23	73	1	2	3	2	2^{1}	38.28	3.20	*Forward factor*	(AA)	Gr.Manor, G.Frances, M.Myst'y7
10-11^{10}	3-8	F	38.73	72	8	5	3	3	1^{hd}	38.73	14.40	*Up on inside*	(AA)	Broa.Gena, OldBalance, Pr.Molly
10-6^{11}	5-16	F	31.55	72	1	3	2	2	1^{1}	31.55	14.60	*Up on inside*	AA	Jus.Hint, TeenDog, IWsLumb'jk
10-2^{12}	3-8	F	38.22	72	1	3	5	6	5^{12}	39.05	15.90	*Dropped bk early*	AA	T.Fakeroque, Br.Adios, Clarless
9-28^{1}s	5-16	F	31.57	73	4	3	3	4	3^{4½}	31.89	.....	*On inside*		JollyJacoby, Shing, Mi.Fa.Storm

4 (Green) GRANNY'S PICK

D. Q. Williams, owner
D. Q. Williams, trainer

Starts 11 · 1st 7 · 2nd 2 · 3rd 1

52 Red Brindle B., June 1964 Coakfield Hero, Imp.—Betty Barr

Date	Dist	Tk	Time	Wt	PP	Off	1/8	Str	Fin	ART	Odds	Comment	Grade	Order of Finish
10-17^{12}	3-8	F	38.37	52	2	1	2	1^{1}	1^{3½}	38.37	.30	*Handily, wide*	(AA)	OldBalance, CoraCoker, Shing
10-14^{3}	3-8	F	37.95	52	2	1	2	1^{1½}	1^{4}	37.95	.30	*Drew out*	(AA)	BellCreek, Stel.Sango, Ho.Duke7
10-11^{12}	3-8	F	38.41	52	2	2	1^{3}	1^{4}	1^{6½}	38.41	.40	*Drew out*	(AA)	Roy.Regent, RubyRush, LG'sAres
10-7^{12}	3-8	F	38.37	52½	2	1	2	2	1^{2}	38.37	1.40	*Stretch drive*	AA	Mel.Mystic, IrishTray, Fin.Effect
9-30^{12}	3-8	F	38.37	52	4	7	8	5	3^{2½}	38.54	1.00	*Crowded, wide*	AA	Rib.Back, Zoo.Debbie, Coc.Susie
9-27^{12}	3-8	F	38.52	52	8	2	3	3	2^{hd}	38.54	1.30	*Bumped curt. tn.*	AA	Z. Debbie, F.Whizzer, CocosSusie

5 (Black) COPIER

Glen Garverick, owner
Ray Randle Kennel
Duane Randle, trainer

Starts 3 · 1st 3 · 2nd 0 · 3rd 0
FL 6 · 2 · 2 · 0

57 Red Brindle B., March 1965 Great Valor—Ed's Sizzle

Date	Dist	Tk	Time	Wt	PP	Off	1/8	Str	Fin	ART	Odds	Comment	Grade	Order of Finish
10-17^{11}	3-8	F	38.18	57½	6	6	2	1^{2}	1^{5}	38.18	1.50	*Drew out*	(AA)	G.Frances, Zoo.Debbie, Clarless
10-14^{12}	3-8	F	38.41	57	7	2	2	1^{2}	1^{1½}	38.41	1.90	*Handily*	(AA)	Clarless, MelloMystic, L.G'sAres7
10-11^{9}	3-8	F	38.48	57	2	2	1^{2}	1^{3}	1^{5½}	38.48	1.30	*Easily*	(AA)	Ho.Duke, LGPhaethon, Me.Myst'y
10-2^{1}s	5-16	F	31.30	58	5	3	2	3	4^{3}	31.50	.....	*Trouble thruout*		BellCreek, IrishTray, Fr.McCord
Races Below Were Run at Flagler—Timed in 1/100ths of seconds														
9-25^{12}	3-8	F	37.63	57½	6	2	1^{3½}	1^{3½}	1^{7}	37.63	2.20	*Drawing away*	A	Pranced, South.Flame, TwinSpin

6 (Yellow) MASTER MICK

Souza Bros. Kennel, owner
Robert O'Connell, trainer

Starts 14 · 1st 3 · 2nd 3 · 3rd 2

73 Red Brindle D., April 1965 Master Agent—Duck's Friend Dale

Date	Dist	Tk	Time	Wt	PP	Off	1/8	Str	Fin	ART	Odds	Comment	Grade	Order of Finish
10-17^{4}	3-8	F	38.57	73	2	3	2	2	2^{ns}	38.58	7.00	*Forward factor*	(AA)	F.Whizzer, T.Faker'que, Po.Rock
10-14^{11}	3-8	F	38.37	72½	6	2	1^{1½}	2	3^{8}	38.93	4.40	*Early speed*	(AA)	Fariston, Bratinella, JustaHint7
10-11^{11}	3-8	F	38.65	72	3	1	1^{2}	1^{2}	1^{1}	38.65	6.00	*Wire to wire*	(AA)	LB'sBil.Jeff, Xandra, GroveRock
10-7^{10}	5-16	F	31.48	72	2	3	5	5	3^{1}	31.56	7.90	*Blocked early*	AA	OldKim, Nei.McCoy, Zo.Debbie
10-4^{10}	5-16	F	31.14	72	3	4	6	6	5^{5½}	31.53	8.10	*Bumped early*	AA	M.Mystery, OldKim, JustaHabit
9-30^{11}	5-16	F	31.44	73	1	4	2	2	1^{1}	31.44	2.80	*Stretch drive*	(AA)	Or.McCoy, Broad.Go, Nei.McCoy

7 (Green & White) ZOOMING DEBBIE

Souza Bros. Kennel, owner
Robert O'Connell, trainer

Starts 15 · 1st 3 · 2nd 5 · 3rd 3

56 Red B., July 1965 Brook Charlie, Imp.—Zooming Rosey

Date	Dist	Tk	Time	Wt	PP	Off	1/8	Str	Fin	ART	Odds	Comment	Grade	Order of Finish
10-17^{11}	3-8	F	38.18	56½	1	2	3	3	3^{5½}	38.56	2.60	*Evenly*	(AA)	Copier, GallantFrances, Clarless
10-14^{6}	3-8	F	38.19	56	6	4	4	2	2^{3}	38.38	1.40	*Good effort, wide*	(AA)	Xandra, LGPhaethon, Wa.Paisley
10-11^{6}	3-8	F	38.36	55½	4	2	2	1^{1½}	1^{4}	38.36	.90	*Drew out*	(AA)	Gal.Frances, FInFront, Wa.Pais'y
10-7^{10}	5-16	F	31.48	55	8	1	6	6	4^{2}	31.61	5.70	*Bumped, wide*	AA	OldKim, Neim.McCoy, Mas.Mick
10-4^{12}	3-8	F	38.08	55	5	1	3	4	3^{3½}	38.32	4.30	*Wide thruout*	AA	MelloMystic, Fariston, Clarless
9-30^{12}	3-8	F	38.37	56	8	2	4	3	2^{1}	38.44	4.60	*Wide thruout*	AA	Ribb.Back, Gran.Pick, Coc.Susie

8 (Yellow & Black) FABULOUS WHIZZER

Charles Rink, owner
Charles Rink, trainer

Starts 13 · 1st 4 · 2nd 2 · 3rd 2

69 Black D., January 1966 Bustleton—Fabulous Spring

Date	Dist	Tk	Time	Wt	PP	Off	1/8	Str	Fin	ART	Odds	Comment	Grade	Order of Finish
10-17^{4}	3-8	F	38.57	69½	6	8	6	5	1^{ns}	38.57	2.00	*Str drive, wide*	(AA)	Mas.Mick, T.Faker'que, P.Rock
10-14^{10}	3-8	F	38.60	68½	6	8	5	3	1^{4½}	38.60	1.30	*Drew out*	(AA)	TYToDie, Hippodrome, OBTa.Kid
10-11^{8}	3-8	F	38.49	69½	6	8	8	6	3^{6½}	38.94	3.30	*Crowded, wide* .	(AA)	Clarless, Broad.Adios, OB'sFan'e
10-5^{10}	3-8	F	38.23	69	7	3	3	3	1^{1}	38.23	1.80	*Stretch drive*	A	CoraCoker, TeeJayF, How.Duke
9-30^{12}	3-8	F	38.37	69	2	8	6	4	5^{3}	38.59	14.90	*Crowded early*	AA	Rib.Back, Zo.Debbie, Grann.Pick
9-27^{12}	3-8	F	38.52	69	2	8	6	5	3^{2½}	38.70	25.00	*Steady gain wide*	AA	Z.Debbie, Gran.Pick, CocosSusie

WIN | PLACE | SHOW | PLACE | SHOW | SHOW

Handicapper's Selections—Granny's Pick, Xandra, Zooming Debbie

LG's Ada-1968

1968 DERBY PRESENTATION — WINNER: L.G.'S ADA

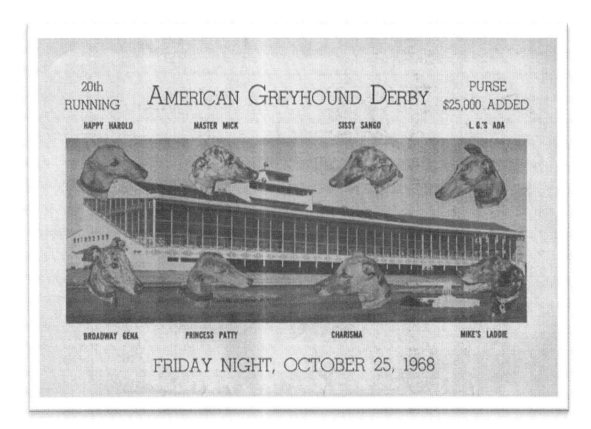

LG's Ada-1968

20th RUNNING AMERICAN GREYHOUND DERBY
Grade S

TWELFTH RACE

Please Call for Dog by Number

3/8 MILE
1980 FEET

TRACK RECORD
Donna Larsen 37.40

P. P.	Date	Dist	Tk	Time	Wt	PP	Off	1/8	Str	Fin	ART	Odds	Comment	Grade	Order of Finish

Red 1 — HAPPY HAROLD
73   Red Brindle D., June 1966   Rinaker—Lyrical
Francis Fulginiti, owner
Francis Fulginiti, trainer
Starts 14 1st 3 2nd 4 3rd 2

10-22¹¹	3-8	F	38.15	72½	8	6	3	3	2³½	38.40	2.50	Crowded crtn turn	S	Clarless, OldBalance, C.BillyBoy
10-19¹²	3-8	F	38.51	73	7	4	3	2	2ʰᵈ	38.53	2.50	Crowded crtn turn	S	PartIrish, Invaluable, Lottalike
10-16⁸	3-8	F	37.88	72½	2	1	1³	1⁸	1²	37.88	2.00	Handily	S	Princ.Patty, PartIrish, Mich.Ted
10-11¹²	3-8	F	38.0	73½		3	5	4	4³	38.30	5.90	Crowded crtn tn	AA	Broadf.Doll, Invaluable, L.G.Ada
10-7¹²	3-8	S	38.84	73½	8	6	3	3	3³	39.18	2.80	Crowded crtn tn	AA	M.Wewoka, Broa.Doll, Gal.Grant
10-3⁶	5-16	F	31.21	73	6	3	3	1³	15½	31.21	2.70	Easily	A	GoGlory, Granny.Pick, I.Hammer

Blue 2 — MASTER MICK
73   Red Brindle D., April 1965   Master Agent—Duck's Friend Dale
Souza Bros. Kennel, owner
Robert O'Connell, trainer
Starts 15 1st 4 2nd 5 3rd 3

10-22³	3-8	F	37.71	74½	6	1	1¹½	2	†2⁹	38.35	3.80	Dead heat place	S	L.G.Ada, C.B.Sm.Bite, C.M.Salty⁷
10-19⁹	3-8	F	38.42	72½	4	1	1³	1¹	1²	38.42	2.90	Wire to wire	S	Mich.Ted, M.W'woka, L.G.Ph'th'n
10-16⁹	3-8	F	38.51	73	4	1	1⁵	1⁵	1⁵	38.51	1.60	Easily	S	LightRay, H.Artistry, H.Flotation
10-12¹¹	5-16	F	30.83	73½	4	3	4	3	3⁸½	31.44	8.50	Blocked early	AA	T.Fakerogue, H.Switch, L.G.Chris
10-9¹¹	5-16	F	31.28	72½	6	3	5	4	3³½	31.52	8.70	Crd, steady gain	AA	Ev.Memory, D.Smiley, L.G.Chris
10-4¹¹	5-16	F	31.21	73	2	1	5	4	4²	31.35	7.70	Crowded 1st turn	AA	T.Fak'gue, E.Mem'y, S.P.I.W'kin

White 3 — SISSY SANGO
56   Brindle B., April 1965   Chief Pam—China Harjo
Lowland Kennel, owner
Harold Asman, trainer
Starts 12 1st 5 2nd 2 3rd 0

10-22⁵	3-8	F	37.95	56	1	1	1⁵	1⁵	1⁵	37.95	2.80	Wire to wire	S	M.Laddie, Stonebr'ker, Brocat'le⁷
10-19¹¹	3-8	F	38.44	56	6	6	6	5	5⁷½	38.96	4.40	Crowded early	S	Prin.Patty, T.Fakerogue, LastTim
10-16⁸	3-8	F	38.34	56	1	2	2	1ʰᵈ	1½	38.34	1.10	Up on outside	S	Ed.Nancy, GoGlory, Ceil.BillyBoy
10-12¹⁰	3-8	F	38.00	56	1	2	1¹	1³	1⁹	38.00	.90	Easily, wide	A	L.G.Phaethon, C.B.S.Bite, Explo
10-8¹²	3-8	F	37.96	56	4	6	5	4	2⁴½	38.27	1.70	Crowded turns	A	L.G.'sAda, NightRose, GoGlory
10-2¹²	3-8	F	38.90	56	7	7	4	2	2²	39.04	1.10	Blocked backstr.	A	Neptu.Pistol, Anisette, DerWolfe

Green 4 — L.G.'S ADA
56   Red Fawn B., May 1966   Westpark Hi Light, Imp.—Fluent Miss
Lloyd Clager, owner
Lloyd Clager, trainer
Starts 11 1st 5 2nd 2 3rd 1

10-22³	3-8	F	37.71	55½	5	6	2	1⁴	1⁹	37.71	1.80	Easily	S	Mas.Mick, C.B.S.Bite, C.M.Salty⁷
10-19⁶	3-8	F	38.09	55½	4	2	3	2	2½	38.12	2.70	Forward factor	S	E.LuckyPutty, Clarless, Charisma
10-16¹²	3-8	F	38.01	56	2	5	3	2	1¹½	38.01	2.70	Handily inside	S	Gall.Grant, Broadf.Doll, LastTim
10-11¹²	3-8	F	38.07	56	8	6	6	5	3²½	38.24	7.60	Good effort	AA	Broad.Doll, Invaluable, H.Harold
10-8¹²	3-8	F	37.96	56	5	8	3	1ʰᵈ	1⁴½	37.96	3.20	Drew out	A	SissySango, NightRose, GoGlory
10-3¹²	3-8	S	38.89	56	4	7	8	8	8¹⁴	39.86	12.30	Crowded early	AA	J.Bimbo, W.Melody, L.G.Ph'thon

Black 5 — BROADWAY GENA
55   Red Brindle B., July 1965   Rinaker—Broadway Donna
Michael R. Greco, owner
Michael R. Greco, trainer
Starts 7 1st 2 2nd 2 3rd 0

10-22¹²	3-8	F	38.30	55	8	2	2	2	2¹½	38.40	5.10	Chased winner	S	Broadf.Doll, Prin.Patty, La.Duke
10-19⁸	3-8	F	38.06	55½	7	4	3	3	2⁶	38.46	1.00	Best of rest	S	Vimco, C.M.Salty, DollOfB'dway
10-16⁵	3-8	F	38.14	55	8	2	2	2	1¹½	38.14	4.20	Handily, wide	S	Hon.Price, W.Melody, F.Whizzer
10-10¹¹	3-8	F	38.01	55½	1	1	1¹½	1²	1²	38.01	4.80	Wire to wire	A	D.Hammer, C.Coker, F.Whizzer⁷
10-7¹²	3-8	S	38.84	55	3	4	8	8	8¹⁴	39.85	11.00	Jammed early	AA	M.Wewoka, Broad.Doll, H.Harold
10-2¹¹	5-16	F	31.44	55½	8	3	8	7	7⁵	31.80	17.70	Carried wide	AA	LikeMagic, Nev.John, Broad.Doll

Yellow 6 — PRINCESS PATTY
58   Brindle B., January 1966   Hacker Hutch—Princess Idell
John Good, owner
David Smith, trainer
Starts 3 1st 1 2nd 1 3rd 1
Tampa 9 1st 2 2nd 3 3rd 2

10-22¹²	3-8	F	38.30	57	7	6	4	3	3²½	38.48	2.90	Good effort	S	Broadf.Doll, B'wayGena, La.Duke
10-19¹¹	3-8	F	38.44	57½	4	3	2	2	2¹½	38.44	1.90	Drew out	S	T.Fakerogue, LastTim, Obvi.Lass
10-16⁸	3-8	F	37.88	57½	1	2	3	2	2²	38.04	1.70	Good effort	S	Hap.Harold, PartIrish, Mich.Ted
10-11¹ˢ	5-16	F	30.67	58½	4	4	7	4	3¹¹	31.45	.....	Drpd back early		M.Mystery, Mich.Ted, Jol.Clown⁷
							Races Below Were Run at Tampa—Timed in 1/100ths of seconds							
10-9¹²	3-8	F	38.26	57	5	6	6	4	3¹	38.34	2.70	Closed fastest	A	Ribb.Back, Man.Jack, Nan.Vilas

Green & White 7 — CHARISMA
58   Dark Brindle B., March 1967   Cactus Noel—Lyrical
Francis Fulginiti, owner
Francis Fulginiti, trainer
Starts 15 1st 7 2nd 4 3rd 1

10-22⁴	3-8	F	37.81	58	5	5	2	1²½	1⁴	37.81	1.30	Drew out	S	Lottalike, W.Melody, Ed'sNancy⁷
10-19⁶	3-8	F	38.09	57½	3	6	5	6	4⁵	38.42	.90	Blocked backstr.	S	E.LuckyPutty, L.G.Ada, Clarless
10-16⁷	3-8	F	37.90	58½	5	3	2	2ⁿᵒ	37.91	1.80	Hard try	S	Stonebr'ker, Clarless, M.Wewoka
10-11¹¹	5-16	F	31.12	58	4	6	4	3	3¹	31.21	1.50	Close quarters	AA	Neva.John, J.R.Oleo, Gal.Susena
10-5¹²	3-8	F	38.04	58	3	6	5	6	5⁴½	38.36	1.20	Trouble thruout	AA	Nept.Pistol, Clarless, Abil.Annie
10-2⁶	5-16	F	31.62	58	5	8	7	7	5⁵½	32.00	.60	Bumped 1st turn	S	Duk.Smiley, Fr.Squire, N.Stinger

Yellow & Black 8 — MIKE'S LADDIE
70   Red Fawn D., August 1965   Solomon Sol—Peg The Damsel, Imp.
Souza Bros. Kennel, owner
Robert O'Connell, trainer
Starts 14 1st 4 2nd 1 3rd 1

10-22⁵	3-8	F	37.95	70	8	6	5	3	2⁵	38.31	6.40	Steady gain	S	S.Sango, Stonebreaker, Brocat'le⁷
10-19⁴	3-8	F	38.11	70½	2	5	3	2	1⁶	38.11	7.20	Drew out	S	O.Balance, N.Trader, Brocatelle⁷
10-16¹²	3-8	F	38.01	70½	1	7	8	8	6¹³	38.91	30.30	Never prominent	S	L.G.Ada, Gall.Grant, Broadf.Doll
10-12¹⁰	3-8	F	38.00	70½	4	8	8	8	8¹¹	38.78	8.50	Outrun	A	S.Sango, L.G.Ph'thon, C.B.S.Bite
10-8¹⁰	3-8	F	38.13	70½	5	8	6	2	1¹	38.13	7.00	Stretch drive	BB	BlueSmith, Ed'sNancy, Vimco
10-4¹⁰	3-8	F	38.11	71	5	7	7	7	7⁶½	38.57	5.70	Never prominent	A	M.Wewoka, Ni.Rose, H.Flotation

WIN   PLACE   SHOW   PLACE   SHOW   SHOW

Handicapper's Selections—Happy Harold, L.G.'s Ada, Charisma

Page TWENTY-ONE

Lucky Bannon-1969

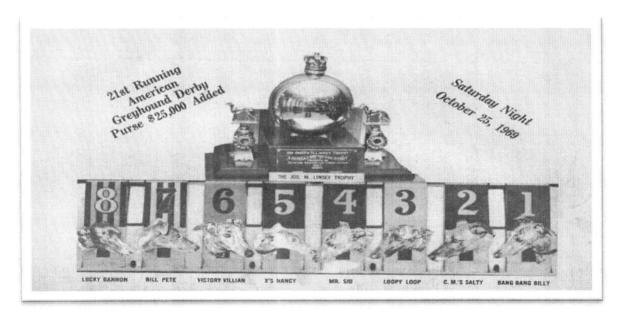

Lucky Bannon-1969

3/8 MILE

1980 FEET

21st RUNNING AMERICAN GREYHOUND DERBY

TWELFTH RACE

GRADE S

PLEASE CALL FOR DOG BY NUMBER

TRACK RECORD
Donna Larsen 37.40

Date · Dist · Tk · Time · Wt · PP · Off · 1/8 · Str · Fin · ART · Odds · Comment—Grade · *Schooled to Judges' Satisfaction · Order of finish

P. P. Red 1 — BANG BANG BILLY

Lowland Kennel, owner
Harold Asman, trainer

Starts 4 · 1st 4 · 2nd 0 · 3rd 0

69 Fawn Brindle D., May 1967 Sought After—L. L.'s Lizbet

Date	Dist	Tk	Time	Wt	PP	Off	1/8	Str	Fin	ART	Odds	Comment	Grade	Order of finish
10-22^{11}	3-8	F	37.80	67½	3	6	4	1^{2}	1^{9}	37.80	.60	*Breezing*	S	Mr.Sid, I.W'sQuartan, Fifi'sBones
10-18^{11}	3-8	F	37.98	68	8	4	5	2	1^{2}	37.98	.40	*Drew out*	S	BillPete, CrefogueDancer, Abil.Annie
10-15^{6}	3-8	F	37.74	68	8	4	3	2	$1^{\frac{1}{2}}$	37.74	1.10	*Stretch drive*	S	HitMe, Stonebreaker, SaintsRest
10-10^{11}	3-8	F	37.84	68	4	7	6	2	1^{6}	37.84	1.60	*Drew out rapidly*	AA	MerryWillow, PressOffer, L.A.Pix
10-6^{1}s	3-8	F	37.46	69	6	6	2	1^{2}	$1^{11\frac{1}{2}}$	37.46	.....	*Drawing away*		HerArtistry, HankBanner, BlueMaxine

Blue 2 — C. M'S SALTY

Don Chouinard, owner
Sam Benson, trainer

Starts 16 · 1st 4 · 2nd 5 · 3rd 4

63 Brindle B., April 1966 Toast The Prince, Imp.—Sun Kit

Date	Dist	Tk	Time	Wt	PP	Off	1/8	Str	Fin	ART	Odds	Comment	Grade	Order of finish
10-22^{5}	3-8	F	37.86	63	5	1	$1^{1\frac{1}{2}}$	2	2^{9}	38.51	12.00	*Set pace*	S	LuckyBannon, GeeYet, Bingham.Lassie
10-18^{9}	3-8	F	38.65	62½	6	3	3	3	1no	38.65	11.10	*Up at wire*	S	Explo, AgnesMcNutt, AlohaBlack
10-15^{8}	3-8	F	37.79	62½	2	2	2	3	4^{14}	38.77	21.10	*Early speed*	S	PrincessPalm, Explo, CrefogueDancer
10-9^{8}	3-8	F	38.48	63	5	4	2	2	$1^{1\frac{1}{2}}$	38.48	4.90	*Drew out*	BB	QueenDilly, Pra.Woman, Ne.Swamper
10-6^{12}	3-8	F	38.24	63	3	5	2	2	$2^{3\frac{1}{2}}$	38.49	5.00	*Crowded early*	BB	IrmaLou, WestyRebel, L.G'sJan
10-1^{12}	3-8	F	38.77	63½	1	3	3	2	$3^{1\frac{1}{2}}$	38.88	3.20	*Good effort*	BB	Winn.Count, Leis.Interlude, Carvalho

White 3 — LOOPY LOOP

Charles Rink, owner
Charles Rink, trainer

Starts 15 · 1st 5 · 2nd 3 · 3rd 1

58 White & Red B., December 1967 I.W's Owl—Quicken Quartet

Date	Dist	Tk	Time	Wt	PP	Off	1/8	Str	Fin	ART	Odds	Comment	Grade	Order of finish
10-22^{6}	3-8	F	38.02	58	4	2	1^{6}	1^{5}	1^{3}	38.02	2.40	*Handily*	S	BillPete, WhyBirch, HitMe
10-18^{5}	3-8	F	38.00	58	3	2	1^{2}	$1^{1\frac{1}{2}}$	$1^{1\frac{1}{2}}$	38.00	2.80	*Held safe lead*	S	SheikHarjo, Ardr.Echo, Nep.Swamper
10-15^{4}	3-8	F	37.99	58	4	3	2	1^{2}	1^{2}	37.99	5.30	*Handily*	S	BrightRuffle, Maddened, JerseyDonna
10-11^{11}	5-16	F	30.97	58	4	7	7	4	4^{7}	31.46	12.10	*Jammed early*	AA	Mr.Sid, SheikHarjo, He'sAPhantom
10-8^{11}	5-16	F	30.59	58	1	7	5	5	$5^{16\frac{1}{2}}$	31.77	6.60	*Bumped 1st turn*	AA	SheikHarjo, Mr.Sid, CaesarCommel
10-4^{11}	5-16	F	31.19	58	5	7	2	2	$1^{\frac{1}{2}}$	31.19	8.40	*Stretch drive*	S	T.Perfectionist, X'sKylaKay, Sh.Harjo

Green 4 — MR. SID

Mrs. Henrietta Furmanik, owner
Matthew Furmanik, trainer

Starts 15 · 1st 6 · 2nd 4 · 3rd 1

65 Brindle D., October 1967 Cactus Noel—Pallas Athena

Date	Dist	Tk	Time	Wt	PP	Off	1/8	Str	Fin	ART	Odds	Comment	Grade	Order of finish
10-22^{11}	3-8	F	37.80	65½	8	1	$1^{1\frac{1}{2}}$	2	2^{9}	38.42	3.30	*Set pace*	S	Ba.BangBilly, I.W.Quartan, Fifi.Bones
10-18^{12}	3-8	F	38.27	65	6	2	1^{4}	1^{4}	$1^{2\frac{1}{2}}$	38.27	4.20	*Handily*	S	BrightRuffle, IW.Quartan, Ben.Tench
10-15^{10}	3-8	F	38.24	64½	1	1	1^{hd}	1^{1}	1^{hd}	38.24	1.50	*Just lasted, wide*	S	BanditsCalla, Tr.Setter, D.B.Maverick
10-11^{11}	5-16	F	30.97	65	7	2	1^{2}	1^{4}	1^{2}	30.97	3.70	*Handily, wide*	AA	SheikHarjo, H.APhantom, LoopyLoop
10-8^{11}	5-16	F	30.59	65	4	4	4	3	2^{10}	31.30	11.10	*Wide thruout*	AA	SheikHarjo, CaesarCommel, BetterEnd
10-4^{11}	5-16	F	31.19	64½	2	3	5	6	$6^{1\frac{1}{2}}$	31.29	5.10	*Wide 1st turn*	S	LoopyLoop, T.Perfectionist, X.Ky.Kay

Black 5 — X'S NANCY

C. C. Wilson, owner
Kenneth Reid, trainer

Starts 14 · 1st 4 · 2nd 0 · 3rd 3

62 Brindle B., October 1966 Lupo Lad—Heidi Award

Date	Dist	Tk	Time	Wt	PP	Off	1/8	Str	Fin	ART	Odds	Comment	Grade	Order of finish
10-22^{12}	3-8	F	38.23	61	2	7	4	3	3^{6}	38.66	1.10	*Crowded early*	S	D.B'sMaverick, Explo, Stonebreaker
10-18^{6}	3-8	F	38.31	62	3	1	1^{3}	$1^{1\frac{1}{2}}$	1^{1}	38.31	9.40	*On inside*	S	Maddened, HitMe, RoyalPlus
10-15^{12}	3-8	F	38.39	60½	7	1	1^{2}	$1^{2\frac{1}{2}}$	$1^{2\frac{1}{2}}$	38.39	3.00	*Wire to wire*	S	HerArtistry, Fifi.Bones, AgnesMcNutt
10-9^{12}	3-8	F	38.39	61	3	5	4	4	$4^{3\frac{1}{2}}$	38.63	1.30	*Crowded, saved*	A	IrmaLou, Explo, WilliWeb
10-3^{10}	3-8	F	38.06	61½	8	2	2	2	$1^{1\frac{1}{2}}$	38.06	1.90	*Handily inside*	BB	MeanusMagic, MaBlakney, Danc.Dew
9-29^{11}	5-16	F	31.48	61	7	1	4	4	4^{4}	31.77	4.80	*Crowded early*	A	Neptu.Stinger, L.G.Chris, Cae.Commel

Yellow 6 — VICTORY VILLIAN

Lowland Kennel, owner
Harold Asman, trainer

Starts 7 · 1st 3 · 2nd 1 · 3rd 0

67 Black D., August 1966 Coffee Villian—Black Revo

Date	Dist	Tk	Time	Wt	PP	Off	1/8	Str	Fin	ART	Odds	Comment	Grade	Order of finish
10-22^{3}	3-8	F	38.05	66½	7	6	2	2	1^{2}	38.05	4.10	*Handily inside*	S	MelissaLynn, WilliWeb, SheikHarjo^{7}
10-18^{4}	3-8	F	38.15	67	7	5	$1^{2\frac{1}{2}}$	1^{5}	1^{5}	38.15	4.70	*Easily*	S	WhyBirch, MerryWillow, HankBanner
10-15^{3}	3-8	F	37.79	67½	3	5	6	6	6^{17}	38.97	3.80	*Never prominent*	S	PrincessPalm, Explo, CrefogueDancer
10-11^{6}	3-8	F	38.02	66½	7	3	2	2	1^{2}	38.02	5.60	*Drew out*	AA-A	Maddened, SanSavana, BroadfordDoll
10-7^{12}	3-8	F	38.10	67	4	6	3	3	2^{2}	38.26	17.50	*Blocked far turn*	AA	L.A.Pix, MelissaLynn, I.W'sQuartan
9-30^{11}	5-16	F	30.98	68	6	7	7	8	8^{15}	32.06	26.70	*Bumped 1st turn*	AA	DrishaneCastle, B.E'sSavage, JoePaul

Green & White 7 — BILL PETE

R. E. Thomas, owner
Frank Scott, trainer

Starts 3 · 1st 1 · 2nd 2 · 3rd 0
Tampa 8 · 2 · 1 · 1

70 Brindle D., February 1967 Tell You Why—Valoretta

Date	Dist	Tk	Time	Wt	PP	Off	1/8	Str	Fin	ART	Odds	Comment	Grade	Order of finish
10-22^{6}	3-8	F	38.02	70	8	6	2	2	2^{3}	38.21	3.80	*Chased winner*	S	LoopyLoop, WhyBirch, HitMe
10-18^{11}	3-8	F	37.98	69½	3	2	$1^{2\frac{1}{2}}$	1^{2}	2^{2}	38.12	3.30	*Outfinished*	S	BangBangBilly, Cre.Dancer, Ab.Annie
10-15^{9}	3-8	F	38.05	68½	5	4	4	2	1^{6}	38.05	.90	*Easily*	S	RoyalPlus, Nept.Swamper, L.G'sChris
10-10^{1}s	3-8	F	37.68	69	2	3	3	2	2^{3}	37.89	.....	*Blocked crtn turn*		BrightRuffle, AlohaBlack, ChipB.^{7}
Races Below Were Run at Tampa—Timed in 1/100ths of seconds														
10-7^{10}	3-8	F	38.36	70	8	3	2	2	1^{1}	38.36	12.20	*Caught leader*	A	L.B'sReply, MisterBerra, WillyNilly

Yellow & Black 8 — LUCKY BANNON

R. E. Thomas, owner
Frank Scott, trainer

Starts 3 · 1st 3 · 2nd 0 · 3rd 0
West Memphis 22 · 18 · 2 · 0

66 Red D., September 1967 Michigan Jack—Valoretta

Date	Dist	Tk	Time	Wt	PP	Off	1/8	Str	Fin	ART	Odds	Comment	Grade	Order of finish
10-22^{5}	3-8	F	37.86	66	2	6	3	1^{3}	1^{9}	37.86	.20	*Despite trouble*	S	C.M'sSalty, GeeYet, Bingham'sLassie
10-18^{3}	3-8	F	37.86	66	4	1	1^{5}	1^{10}	$1^{12\frac{1}{2}}$	37.86	.30	*All alone*	S	Bingha.Lassie, Anisette, D.B.Maverick
10-15^{11}	3-8	F	38.19	65	7	8	4	3	1^{hd}	38.19	.60	*Up at wire*	S	SheikHarjo, MelissaLynn, IrmaLou
10-10^{2}s	3-8	F	37.32	65	1	2	1^{2}	1^{3}	$1^{6\frac{1}{2}}$	37.32	.....	*Easily*		PrincessPalm, Tre.Setter, Cre.Dancer^{7}
Races Below Were Run at West Memphis —Timed in 1/100ths of seconds														
10-6^{2}s	AC	F	33.10	65½	1	1	1^{2}	1^{3}	1^{5}	33.10	.....	*Handily*		PrinceRocky^{2}

WIN · PLACE · SHOW · PLACE · SHOW · SHOW

Handicapper's Selections 1—8—3

Rising Queen-1970

1970 Winner—Rising Queen

THE RACING GREYHOUND

ON HIS OWN

There is one great distinction which separates greyhound racing from any other form of racing today.

In dog racing, there is no human element.

There are no jockeys, no drivers. Once a dog is in the starting box, he's on his own. And because the greyhounds do not pace themselves, from the moment the starting box opens each dog will run as fast as he can as long as he can.

Today's starting boxes are opened automatically by an electrical impulse when the lure reaches a specified point on the track. The lids of the boxes are molded into one solid piece, making it impossible for one box to remain closed while the others open.

No matter what happens during the course of a race, no matter how much a dog is bumped or interfered with, the finish will become official. For all practical purposes, only if a dog somehow catches the lure is a race ruled "no race" and all money wagered refunded to the public.

Since the lure is capable of speeds near 100 miles per hour, which is about 60 miles per hour faster than the fastest dog, the lure is rarely caught. When it is, it's usually due to a power failure.

The winner of a race is the dog whose NOSE reaches the finish line first. Often the leg of a greyhound will be in front of his nose at the finish line, but that does not enter into determining the order of finish.

SS Jeno-1971

SS Jeno-1971

⅜ MILE | **1980 FEET**

23rd RUNNING AMERICAN GREYHOUND DERBY

TWELFTH RACE
PLEASE CALL FOR DOG BY NUMBER

GRADE 5

TRACK RECORD Smokey Bar 37.27

P.P.	Date	Dist Tk Time Wt PP Off 1/8 Str Fin ART	Odds Comment—Grade *Schooled to Judges' Satisfaction	Order of finish

Red 1 — S. S. JENO
Edgar Trow, owner — Sam Benson, trainer — Starts 8, 1st 6, 2nd 1, 3rd 0
70 Brindle D., February 1970 Venerated—Kitty Hoss

11-16¹¹	3-8 F 37.50 70½ 2 2 1⁴ 1⁵ 1⁵ 37.50	1.00	*Easily*	*Cellanese, OddAir, EveningGlamour
11-13³	3-8 F 37.64 69½ 3 5 1⁵ 1⁸ 1¹³½37.64	.60	*All alone*	*NipaFly, GretaE.Eckert, GoWhiz
11-10¹¹	3-8 F 37.70 69½ 2 1 1⁵ 1³ 1⁴ 37.70	1.30	*Wire to wire*	*MonaleeMolly, Cara.Abbie, ShurLilly
11-4⁵	3-8 F 37.61 69½ 6 2 1² 1³ 1⁴ 37.61	1.10	*Easily*	AA CaravanAbbie, NipaFly, CountRebel
10-30¹¹	5-16 F 30.91 69 8 7 8 7 7⁸ 31.49	2.60	*Never prominent*	*Dot'sDoll, BlueDiamond, Carav.Abbie
10-27¹¹	5-16 F 31.04 70 5 4 3 2 2ⁿᵒ 31.05	3.20	*Crd., almost up*	*BlueDiamond, Dot'sDoll, Secr.Process

Blue 2 — C. C. TIM
Kenneth Reid, owner — Kenneth Reid, trainer — Starts 21, 1st 6, 2nd 4, 3rd 2
68 Fawn Brindle D., November 1969 Bulleree—Hi Troubles

11-16⁷	3-8 F 38.08 66 6 6 3 3 3²½ 38.25	4.10	*Boxed turn*	*S.S.Marg, SecretProcess, CountRebel
11-13⁴	3-8 F 38.19 67 2 3 2 1¹ 1¹ 38.19	1.20	*Lasted, wide*	*WestparkAnti, CountRebel, Mon.Bond
11-9¹¹	3-8 F 38.10 67 7 2 2 1½ 1¹½ 38.10	42.30	*Despite trouble*	*FriendWesty, Montag.Bond, Cellanese
11-5¹¹	5-16 F 31.11 67 8 6 6 4 4³ 31.33	8.20	*Gained backstr.*	AA Loud, MeanusMagic, Trousseau.Happy
11-2¹¹	5-16 F 30.88 66 7 6 8 7 7¹²31.70	15.20	*Much early trbl*	AA I.W.'sMardon, Loud, MeanusMagic
10-28⁵	3-8 F 38.25 67 5 1 1² 1²½1¹¹ 38.25	1.20	*Wire to wire*	A J.J.'sAllieDee, KaroKate, MaxieBaby

White 3 — NEPTUNE'S ECHO
Julliene Goble, owner — Amos Goble, trainer — Starts 21, 1st 4, 2nd 5, 3rd 4
67 Brindle D., September 1969 Bustleton—Neptune's Jewel

11-16¹²	3-8 F 37.97 67 1 1 1¹½2 2⁵ 38.32	2.20	*Set pace*	*MonaleeMolly, Car.Abbie, Whistl.Ray
11-13¹⁰	3-8 F 38.30 67 2 2 5 3 3³ 38.49	4.20	*Knocked back*	*SecretProcess, ShurLilly, BusyBee
11-10¹²	3-8 F 38.16 66½ 4 4 4 2 1³ 38.16	5.60	*Drew out inside*	*FaithfulMillie, Gr.E.Eckert, Gall.Fire
11-3¹¹	5-16 F 30.80 67 6 3 8 8 8¹² 31.62	40.10	*Blocked early*	AA BlueDiamond, Dot'sDoll, RuffUp
10-30¹¹	5-16 F 30.91 66½ 5 5 6 6 6⁶½ 31.36	13.60	*Crowded 1st turn*	*Dot'sDoll, BlueDiamond, Carav.Abbie
10-27⁵	5-16 F 31.12 67 7 1 1¾ 1² 1² 31.12	19.90	*Wire to wire*	*WestparkAnti, CaravanAbbie, RuffUp

Green 4 — DOT'S DOLL
Mrs. Harold Roderick, owner — Harold Roderick, trainer — Starts 23, 1st 3, 2nd 8, 3rd 8
56½ Dark Brindle B., September 1969 Westy Whizzer—Real Great

11-16³	3-8 F 37.82 55½ 6 3 1¹ 1½ 1¹ 37.82	3.10	*Withst'd challenge*	*S.S.Luki, FriendWesty, ShurLilly
11-13¹¹	3-8 F 37.95 55½ 4 2 1¹ 2 3³½ 38.19	2.20	*Early speed*	*Cellanese, MonaleeMolly, Mon.Duster
11-9⁵	3-8 F 37.57 55½ 3 1 1² 1² 1²½ 37.57	.70	*Wire to wire*	*ScobyKing, Bookie.Strike, Westp.Anti
11-6¹¹	5-16 F 30.79 55½ 5 6 4 4 3¹ 30.84	4.80	*Good effort*	AA I.W.'sMardon, Sunbury, BlueDiamond
11-3¹¹	5-16 F 30.80 56½ 1 1 2 2 2² 30.93	1.80	*Closed some*	AA BlueDiamond, RuffUp, Sockdolager
10-30¹¹	5-16 F 30.91 55½ 2 1 2 2 1½ 30.91	4.60	*Stretch drive*	*BlueDiamond, Car.Abbie, Sec.Process

Black 5 — SECRET PROCESS
Mrs. Harold Roderick, owner — Harold Roderick, trainer — Starts 23, 1st 4, 2nd 7, 3rd 7
54 Red Brindle B., September 1969 Westy Whizzer—Real Great

11-16⁷	3-8 F 38.08 54 2 1 1² 2 2½ 38.11	1.50	*Forward factor*	*S.S.Marg, C.C.Tim, CountRebel
11-13¹⁰	3-8 F 38.30 53½ 4 4 1⁴ 1³ 1¹ 38.30	1.60	*Lasted to win*	*ShurLilly, Neptune'sEcho, BusyBee
11-10⁵	3-8 F 38.03 54 2 4 2 3 2½ 38.07	1.20	*Hard try*	*NipaFly, S.S.Marg, OddAir
11-6⁵	3-8 F 37.51 54 3 5 3 3 3⁶ 37.92	1.50	*Evenly*	*FriendWesty, GreekPilot, Carav.Abbie
11-3⁵	5-16 F 31.02 54½ 2 1 1³ 1³ 1⁶ 31.02	1.50	*Easily*	AA Varied, Sunbury, JohnSample
10-30¹¹	5-16 F 30.91 53½ 7 4 4 5 4⁵½ 31.30	13.70	*No mishaps*	*Dot'sDoll, BlueDiamond, Carav.Abbie

Yellow 6 — CELLANESE
James E. O'Donnell, Jr., owner — M. Camelleri, trainer — Starts 4, 1st 2, 2nd 1, 3rd 0
55 Light Brindle B., July 1969 Rummystill—Aunt Mart

11-16¹¹	3-8 F 37.50 55½ 3 4 3 2 2⁵ 37.83	2.60	*Crowded crtn turn*	*S.S.Jeno, OddAir, EveningGlamour
11-13¹¹	3-8 F 37.95 55 1 3 2 1⁴ 1³ 37.95	2.30	*Drew out*	*MonaleeMolly, Dot'sDoll, Mont.Duster
11-9¹¹	3-8 F 38.10 54½ 4 6 5 5 4⁵ 38.43	1.60	*Much early trouble*	*C.C.Tim, FriendWesty, Montag.Bond
11-4¹¹	5-16 F 30.35 55 4 1 1ʰᵈ1² 1⁴½ 30.35	7.20	*Wire to wire*	AA Eve.Glamour, Mona.Molly, ScobyKing
11-1²ˢ	5-16 F 30.48 55 3 5 3 3 2² 30.63	.....	*Good effort*	MonaleeMolly, Book.Strike, GoWhiz⁷
10-29⁰ˢ	5-16 F 30.88 55 1 1 2 1 1⁴½ 30.88	.....	*Easily inside*	FaithfulMillie, Fahblee, CountRebel⁷

Green & White 7 — MONALEE MOLLY, Imp.
A. W. Kulchinsky, owner — George Sachar, trainer — Starts 4, 1st 1, 2nd 2, 3rd 1
58 Red B., June 1969 Monalee Champion—Mary's Chair

11-16¹²	3-8 F 37.97 58½ 8 5 2 1² 1⁵ 37.97	.90	*Easily*	*Neptun.Echo, Cara.Abbie, Whistl.Ray
11-13¹¹	3-8 F 37.95 58½ 7 4 3 2³ 38.16	2.60	*Off slowly*	*Cellanese, Dot'sDoll, MontagueDuster
11-10¹¹	3-8 F 37.70 58½ 6 6 3 2 2⁴ 37.99	2.60	*Good effort*	*S.S.Jeno, CaravanAbbie, ShurLilly
11-4¹¹	5-16 F 30.35 58 3 2 3 3 3⁶ 30.77	2.60	*Good effort*	AA Cellanese, Even'gGlamour, ScobyKing
11-1²ˢ	5-16 F 30.48 59½ 1 1 1³ 1⁴ 1² 30.48	.....	*Handily*	Cellanese, Bookie'sStrike, GoWhiz⁷

Yellow & Black 8 — CORK 'N CLEAVER
Henry Caswell, owner — Henry Caswell, trainer — Starts 18, 1st 6, 2nd 1, 3rd 4
70 Black D., November 1968 Spec Harmony—Wayside Cleo

11-16⁵	3-8 F 37.98 70 8 3 2 1⁴ 1⁵ 37.98	3.00	*Easily, wide*	*WestparkAnti, Velvadean, ScobyKing
11-13⁵	3-8 F 38.28 70 4 7 5 4 1ⁿᵒ 38.28	4.00	*Up on outside*	*Thunder.Moss, Eve.Glamour, Fr.Westy
11-9³	3-8 F 37.44 70 8 4 3 3³½ 37.69	4.20	*Good effort*	*Sockdolager, S.S.Luki, CountRebel
11-2⁵	3-8 F 37.74 70 6 3 5 4 3⁵ 38.08	3.10	*Steady gain, wide*	AAS&F'sTroy, S.S.Julie, Hushaway
10-29⁵ˢ	5-16 F 31.59 69½ 8 7 5 4 3⁴ 31.86	.....	*Wide late*	Mil.Garden, S.W.Buckat'r, L'ckluster⁷
10-25¹¹	5-16 F 31.19 69½ 6 8 7fl4 7³¹ 33.37	7.20	*Fell stretch*	AA JohnSample, S.S.Babs, S.S.Lad

WIN	PLACE	SHOW	PLACE	SHOW	SHOW

Handicapper's Selections 1 — 7 — 8

Twilight Belle-1972

Twilight Belle-1972

	American Greyhound Derby	GRADE S
3/8 MILE 1980 FEET	TWELFTH RACE	TRACK RECORD Smokey Bar 37.27

P.P.	Date	Dist	Tk	Time	Wt	PP	Off	1/8	Str	Fin	ART	Odds	Comment—Grade	*Schooled to Judges' Satisfaction	Order of finish

Red 1 — **NEPTUNE'S EL SIV**
Julliene J. Goble, owner — Amos Goble, trainer — Starts 20 1st 10 2nd 2 3rd 1
78 White & Red D., February 1970 I. W's Owl—Susan R. Imp.

11-15³	3-8	F	38.34	78	2	3stb	7	7	7¹¹½	39.14	.50	Stumbled early	s TwilightBelle, AlineGo, NumbahTen
11-11⁹	3-8	F	37.64	77½	2	1	1⁴	1⁵	1⁷	37.64	.80	Easily	s SurfireJohn, Repulsed, Elusive
11-7¹¹	3-8	F	37.91	78	1	1	1⁶	1⁵	1⁴	37.91	.80	Wire to wire	s Spe.Memory, CapPerfecta, Kes.Prince
11-4¹¹	5-16	F	30.93	77	4	1	4	5	6⁷	31.44	1.20	Collided 1st turn	s Mac.BlueBoy, Char.Char, Nep.ElTopo⁷
11-1¹¹	5-16	F	30.72	77½	5	5	4	3	2⁴	30.99	1.20	Blocked early	s S.S.Luki, Mac'sBlueBoy, CapPerfecta
10-27⁵	5-16	F	30.80	77½	2	1	1³	1⁸½	1⁶	30.80	.60	Drew out easily	s Mac'sBlueBoy, S.S.Groovy, NewLabel

Blue 2 — **CAP FULL**
Henry Caswell, owner — Henry Caswell, trainer — Starts 20 1st 3 2nd 3 3rd 3
60 Red Fawn B., April 1970 Caprioled—Super Fan

11-15¹¹	3-8	F	38.36	59½	7	4	1¹	1¹	1ⁿᵒ	38.36	17.70	Just lasted	s Elusive, Hubac, RabbitRun
11-11¹¹	3-8	F	37.74	60	2	1	1¹	3	5¹²	38.60	5.30	Crowded backstr.	s Invocation, CuttyCDay, Spec.Memory
11-7¹²	3-8	F	38.26	60	5	1	1⁵	1⁵	1²	38.26	10.20	Wire to wire	s S.S.Rob, Twili.Belle, O.K.MattWynn⁷
11-3⁷	3-8	F	37.96	60	8	4	3	3	3⁴½	38.27	3.20	Good effort	BB Shim.Miss, Mir.Image, Silhouet.Miss
10-31¹⁰	5-16	F	31.19	60	2	2	6	6	6⁹	31.82	13.10	Jammed early	A Ratjada, LiveEarth, S.S.Toga⁷
10-27²	5-16	F	31.25	60½	3	3	5	5	5¹⁰	31.95	8.10	Pinched back	A I.W.Maggie, Friend.Troubles, Ratjada

White 3 — **S. S. JENO**
Edgar Trow, owner — Marshall Rae, trainer — Starts 4 1st 2 2nd 1 3rd 1
70 Brindle D., February 1970 Venerated—Kitty Hoss

11-15¹²	3-8	F	38.31	71	1	3	1¹	1²	1¹	38.31	1.60	Lasted to win	s TampaMary, HandyCap, Mung.Queen
11-11¹²	3-8	F	37.93	69	6	1	1⁴	1¹½	3³	38.16	.60	Outfinished	s TampaMary, SecretProcess, HandyCap
11-8¹¹	3-8	M	38.28	70½	6	3	2	2	2⁶	38.68	1.40	Wide front stretch	s TalkOfTheTown, Exp.Choice, Hubac
11-2¹¹	5-16	M	31.28	70½	4	3	2	1⁴	1¹	31.28	1.30	Despite trouble	AA Seem.Certain, Josie.Daisy, NationalJet
10-25⁸s	5-16	F	31.31	71	3	3	1³	1⁴	1⁸½	31.31	.....	Easily	FieryCharger, Investor, Yamin
10-16⁸s	5-16	F	31.27	70½	7	6	2	2	2ⁿᵒ	31.28	.....	Cut in early	PowerPrinter, CorralBridge, Gr.Pilot⁷

Green 4 — **CAP PERFECTA**
Henry Caswell, owner — Henry Caswell, trainer — Starts 19 1st 3 2nd 4 3rd 6
68 Red Fawn D., April 1970 Caprioled—Super Fan

11-15⁷	3-8	F	38.44	68	8	5	2	1¹	1ⁿᵒ	38.44	3.10	Just lasted	s LittleCee, Repulsed, TobyFlint
11-11⁸	3-8	F	37.91	68½	1	5	4	2	2⁶	38.33	1.40	Crowded crtn turn	s S.S.Cher, SummerSparkle, Tiny.Sandy
11-7¹¹	3-8	F	37.91	68½	8	7	6	4	3⁷½	38.44	3.60	Steady gain	s Nept.ElSiv, Spe.Memory, Kesla.Prince
11-4¹¹	5-16	F	30.93	68	2	3	7	7	5⁷	31.42	16.10	Drpd back early	s Mac.BlueBoy, Char.Char, Nep.ElTopo⁷
11-1¹¹	5-16	F	30.72	68	7	7	6	5	4⁹½	31.39	21.60	Some gain	s S.S.Luki, Neptun.ElSiv, Mac.BlueBoy
10-27¹¹	5-16	F	31.10	69	3	7	5	4	3³	31.32	3.20	Steady gain	s JanetFirst, FairDollie, Tara'sHall

Black 5 — **NUMBAH TEN**
Richardson Kennel, owner — Bud Richardson, trainer — Starts 6 1st 1 2nd 1 3rd 1
54 Black Brindle B., June 1969 Westy Whizzer—Vistaril

11-15³	3-8	F	38.34	52	4	1	3	3	3³	38.54	15.20	Crowded crtn turn	s TwilightBelle, AlineGo, Spec.Memory
11-11¹⁰	3-8	F	38.15	52½	2	2	1¹⁴	1¹	1²	38.15	7.70	Handily	s SpecialNeed, JuneCap, MarquisGo
11-8¹²	3-8	M	38.67	53	2	2	2	2	2³	38.86	25.60	Chased winner	s KansasSneak, AlineGo, S.S.Cher
11-2⁹	3-8	M	38.33	54	6	3	5	4	5¹¹	39.08	18.20	Wide early	A S.S.Star, WinsomeLass, O.K.Ma.Wynn
10-27⁸s	3-8	B	38.26	54½	1	2	3	3⁶½	38.72	.....	Early speed	Invocation, Tiny'sSandy, Caroli.Rock⁵
10-23⁹	3-8	F	38.16	53	6	7	6	7	7¹²	38.98	6.10	No factor	A SpecialMemory, SurfireJohn, Han.Cap

Yellow 6 — **TWILIGHT BELLE, Imp.**
Teddy Meadows, owner — C. F. Williams, trainer — Starts 11 1st 6 2nd 0 3rd 1
60 Brindle B., May 1970 Money Grand—Pelican Queen

11-15³	3-8	F	38.34	59	8	7	1³	1²	1¹½	38.34	4.00	Handily	s AlineGo, NumbahTen, SpecialMemory
11-11⁷	3-8	F	37.80	58½	4	1	1³	1³	1²½	37.80	1.90	Wire to wire	s JuryLady, AlpineRock, MirrorImage
11-7¹²	3-8	F	38.26	59	4	3	3	3³½	38.51	1.50	Good effort	s CapFull, S.S.Rob, O.K.MattWynn⁷
11-4⁵	5-16	F	30.91	59½	1	2	6	6	7⁸	31.46	3.20	Much early trbl	AA BaseballCap, FairDollie, Neptune.Owl
10-31¹¹	5-16	F	30.96	60	1	5	6	6	6⁶½	31.42	1.20	Wide thruout	AA BaseballCap, Supre.Trac, Sec.Process
10-26⁵	3-8	F	38.07	59½	8	3	1⁴	1⁵	1⁷	38.07	3.70	Breezing	AA S.S.Cher, CuttyCDay, WinsomeLass

Green & White 7 — **S. S. CHER**
Edgar Trow, owner — Marshall Rae, trainer — Starts 16 1st 3 2nd 3 3rd 3
53 Brindle B., August 1970 L. L.'s Doug—S. W. Blondie Gal

11-15⁵	3-8	F	37.94	53½	3	2	1¹	1¹	1¹	37.94	2.20	Lasted to win	s TalkOfTheTown, Fearless, Spec.Need
11-11⁸	3-8	F	37.91	52½	2	2	1³	1⁵	1⁶	37.91	3.40	Easily	s CapPerfecta, Sum.Sparkle, Tiny.Sandy
11-8¹²	3-8	M	38.67	52	6	7	5	4	4⁶	39.10	5.10	Crowded turns	s KansasSneak, NumbahTen, AlineGo
11-3¹¹	3-8	F	37.86	52½	4	7	5	4	4⁵	38.19	3.60	Crowded early	s Desiring, TalkOfTheTown, Se.Process
10-30⁵	5-16	F	31.02	52	1	4	4	4	4¹	31.10	4.80	Wide 1st turn	AA S.S.Mike, I.W's Anlace, SurfireJohn
10-26⁵	3-8	F	38.07	52	2	4	4	4	2⁷	38.57	2.60	Trouble turns	AA TwilightBelle, CuttyCDay, Winso.Lass

Yellow & Black 8 — **INVOCATION**
Ryan Kennel, owner — John Ryan, trainer — Starts 3 1st 2 2nd 0 3rd 0
71 Red Brindle D., February 1970 Westy Whizzer—Wild Karen

11-15¹¹	3-8	F	38.36	71½	8	8	8	8	7⁹	38.99	.20	Trouble thruout	s CapFull, Elusive, Hubac
11-11¹¹	3-8	F	37.74	71½	8	8	4	1⁴	1¹¹	37.74	.90	All alone	s CuttyCDay, SpecialMemory, Rab.Run
11-8⁵	3-8	M	38.43	71	7	3	1³	1⁴	1³	38.43	2.00	Handily	s LittleCee, Elusive, TampaMary
11-3⁷s	3-8	B	38.14	71	3	1	2	2	1²½	38.14	.....	Drew out	LonesomeCougar²
10-27⁸s	3-8	B	38.26	71	5	3	1½	1³	1⁴	38.26	.....	Easily	Tiny'sSandy, NumbahTen, Caro.Rock⁵
10-23⁷s	3-8	F	37.91	71½	5	1	3	1¹	1²	37.91	.....	Handily	AlpineRock, Softer, DawstownHope⁵

WIN	PLACE	SHOW	PLACE	SHOW	SHOW

Handicapper's Selections   1 — 3 — 6

June's Tuffy-1973

1973 AMERICAN GREYHOUND DERBY — Winner: June's Tuffy

Resume' of 25th Annual Running of
THE AMERICAN GREYHOUND DERBY

TWELFTH RACE—3-8 Mile									Grade S
10-31³	June's Tuffy⁴	....72¼	3	1	1^½2	1½	37.71	6.80	*American Champion*
10-31⁹	Sky Tempo⁴²	....65¼	4	2	2	1¹ 2³	37.74	3.20	*Outfinished*
10-31⁵	Olympic Hero⁴³	...67	7	6	4	3⁴³	38.03	15.10	*Close qurtrs fr str.*
10-31⁷	Rapid Fire⁹	......71¼	6	3	6	5	4⁷	38.18	4.80	*Crowded front str.*
10-31⁹	Flirty Go¹⁵	.......60½	2	4	3	4	5⁷½	38.23	11.30	*Blocked far turn*
10-31⁹	Foil Valley⁴³	.....66¼	1	7	5	6	6⁸	38.28	9.40	*Early gain*
10-31¹¹	Berkley Kelou⁷	...59	8	8	8	7	7¹²	38.55	17.10	*No factor*
10-31¹¹	M.K.'s Ted Squirt²⁰	66¼	5	5	7	8	8¹⁸	38.81	1.50	*Crowded early*

Empire Kennel, Inc.'s, White & Brindle D., April '70. Ritemeir—Cool June

JUNE'S TUFFY	.... 15.60	7.40	4.20	Time 37.71—Fast
SKY TEMPO	....	5.80	4.00	3-4 Quiniela—42.20
OLYMPIC HERO	....		3.20	3-4-7 Trifecta—1,143.30

JUNE'S TUFFY broke on top—went some wide curtain turn and lost the lead but came on in a stretch drive to win on the rail. SKY TEMPO broke with winner and took the lead on the backstretch but was outfinished in the stretch. OLYMPIC HERO was in close quarters in the front stretch but made up ground to finish third. RAPID FIRE was near leader but was crowded back in the front stretch but came on to finish fourth. FLIRTY GO showed early speed, was blocked on far turn. FOIL VALLEY broke poorly and was never in contention. BERKLEY KELOU broke last and was never a threat. M. K.'S TED SQUIRT was knocked back early and could not recover.

American Greyhound Derby

June's Tuffy-1973

3/8 MILE
1980 FEET

TWELFTH RACE
TRACK RECORD—Smokey Bar 37.27

$29,000 American

1
White on Red

FOIL VALLEY, Imp.

James E. O'Donnell, Jr., owner
Edward Dolan, trainer

Starts	1st	2nd	3rd
6	2	1	0

67 White Fawn D., August 1970 Sally's Glory—Miss Angela

10-31^{9}	3-8	F	37.75	66	4	3	1^{1}	2	$2^{1/2}$	37.78	6.30	*Set pace wide*	S FlirtyGo, FaintHope, SkyTempo
10-28^{8}	3-8	F	37.93	66	1	1	2	2	1^{1}	37.93	4.30	*Drew clear*	S Hilda'sPride, Bullet, G.H'sMissPoco
10-25^{9}	3-8	F	38.26	66½	2	2	3	3	$1^{2 1/2}$	38.26	17.10	*Handily, wide*	S June'sTuffy, Suzette, TufMiler
10-20^{5}	3-8	F	38.04	67	5	2	4	5	6^{8}	38.59	12.30	*Steady fade*	AA June'sTuffy, GoldMoney, FlirtyGo
10-17^{9}	3-8	F	38.19	66½	7	7	6	6	7^{10}	38.90	12.00	*Wide front str.*	AA FancyMcWest, RapidFire, FlirtyGo
10-13^{7}	3-8	F	38.02	66	2	3	4	4	5^{11}	38.79	5.30	*No mishaps*	AA RapidFire, FancyMcWest, EveretBolt
10-10^{3}s	5-16	F	30.92	66	5	6	7	5	3^{14}	31.92	.....	*Crowded 1st turn*	WellTurned, I.W.'sMaggie, HansBolt

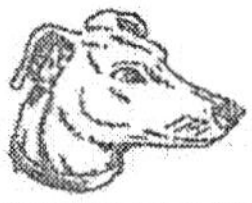

"Ed Dolan, my trainer, told me that never before in the history of this great Derby has a kennel finished with a first and a second place. I guess that between 'The Hero' and I we'll be able to set a new record for Mr. O. After all we do share the lead already."

2
White on Blue

FLIRTY GO

Rickbarb Kennel, owner
Arthur Alves, trainer

Starts	1st	2nd	3rd
15	4	2	3

60 Brindle B., October 1970 Ready Rob—Flirty J.

10-31^{9}	3-8	F	37.75	60	2	1	3	1^{hd}	$1^{1/2}$	37.75	6.20	*Up gamely*	S FoilValley, FaintHope, SkyTempo
10-28^{10}	3-8	F	37.94	60½	6	1	2	2	1^{1}	37.94	4.40	*Drew clear wide*	S OlympicHero, Suzette, S.S.Nico
10-24^{7}	3-8	F	37.93	61½	5	5	7	7	†4^{4}	38.22	3.20	*Crowded, DH*	S TampaMary, M.K.T.Squirt, FaintHope
10-20^{5}	3-8	F	38.04	61	6	3	2	2	$3^{2 1/2}$	38.22	6.30	*Good effort*	AA June'sTuffy, GoldMoney, Bitonto
10-17^{9}	3-8	F	38.19	61	4	3	2	2	$3^{2 1/2}$	38.36	8.20	*Good effort*	AA FancyMcWest, RapidFire, Bitonto
10-13^{11}	3-8	F	38.26	61½	5	2	3	4	$4^{2 1/2}$	38.43	9.30	*Bumped crtn turn*	S Suzette, JuryLady, M.K'sTedSquirt
10-10^{11}	3-8	F	38.34	60½	5	2	2	2	2^{3}	38.54	9.30	*Forward factor*	S Suzette, TampaMary, M.K'sTedSquirt

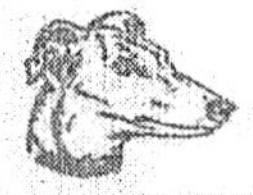

It sure is exciting—here I am in the best shape of my life, and I've won my last two qualifying races. Not only that but my trainer Arthur Alves told me that I'm the first in the history of the Rickbarb Kennel to make it to the finals.

3
Black on White

JUNE'S TUFFY

Empire Kennel, Inc., owner
Dan Ryan, trainer

Starts	1st	2nd	3rd
16	6	2	5

73 White & Brindle D., April 1970 Ritemeir—Cool June

10-31^{3}	3-8	F	37.58	73½	4	2	2	2	1^{1}	37.58	8.50	*Drew clear*	S S.S.Cyndi, WellTurned, Bullet
10-28^{11}	3-8	F	37.84	73½	3	2	4	4	3^{5}	38.18	5.20	*Crowded crtn turn*	S M.K.TedSquirt, SkyTempo, Lone.Billy
10-25^{9}	3-8	F	38.26	73	1	6	2	1^{hd}	$2^{2 1/2}$	38.44	1.80	*Crowded stretch*	S FoilValley, Suzette, TufMiler
10-20^{5}	3-8	F	38.04	73	3	1	$1^{1/2}$	1^{1}	1^{1}	38.04	2.70	*On inside*	AA GoldMoney, FlirtyGo, Bitonto
10-17^{11}	5-16	F	31.26	72½	6	4	3	3	3^{3}	31.49	8.20	*Bumped 1st turn*	AA JohnEgan, Bullet, ShellDaily
10-12^{11}	5-16	F	30.86	73	4	4	3	3	3^{3}	31.08	4.80	*Good effort*	AA JohnEgan, FlickerFlash, BonBonGo
10-6^{11}	5-16	F	31.24	73	1	4	2	1^{1}	1^{4}	31.24	2.10	*Easily, wide*	AA I.W.Islander, WarDemon, G.H.M.Poco

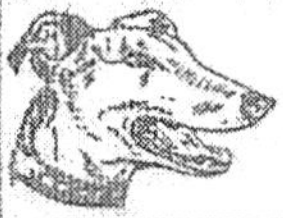

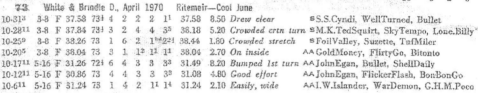

I know a lot of people have a great interest in this race but none will be more concerned than my boss John Malone, back in Denver. If you want to compare records—I guess I've had as successful a year as anyone. Since April I've had 38 starts and been in the money 32 times.

4
White on Green

SKY TEMPO

James C. Garber, owner
Don Garber, trainer

	Starts	1st	2nd	3rd
	4	2	1	0
Seabrook	*10*	*10*	*0*	*0*

66 Brindle B., May 1971 Michigan Jack—Sky Empress

10-31^{9}	3-8	F	37.75	65½	7	8	8	5	4^{3}	37.96	.20	*Crowded early*	S FlirtyGo, FoilValley, FaintHope
10-28^{11}	3-8	F	37.84	66½	5	4	3	2	2^{1}	37.92	.70	*Crowded, closing*	S M.K.TedSquirt, June.Tuffy, Lone.Billy
10-24^{11}	3-8	F	37.91	66½	8	3	4	3	$1^{1/2}$	37.91	.80	*Drew out*	S SpiritOfAmerica, GoldMoney, Bullet^{7}
10-20^{8}	3-8	F	38.00	67	5	4	3	2	$1^{1/2}$	38.00	1.50	*Stretch drive*	AA RapidFire, WellTurned, FancyMcWest
10-17^{1}s	3-8	F	37.85	66½	4	1	$1^{1 1/2}$	$1^{1 1/2}$	1^{5}	37.85	.....	*Drew out*	S.OfAmerica, C.F.Saluda, B.Quittacas^{7}
Races Below Were Run at Seabrook—Timed in 1/100ths of seconds													
10-12^{11}	YC	F	39.85	66	6	7	4	1^{1}	1^{3}	39.85	.80	*Was best*	A RedDeuce, Sec.H.Harry, EA.'sPickle

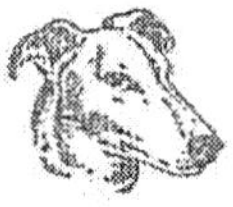

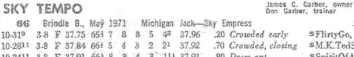

A lot of you fans will remember my Daddy, Michigan Jack—he ran in the '63 Derby. It's tough for a girl to live in foot steps but my records indicate that I can win this great race. At Seabrook I was undefeated in 10 starts and here at Taunton two wins, a second and a fourth.

Handicapper's Selections

35th GOLD COLLAR CHAMPIONSHIPS—NOV. 17

June's Tuffy-1973

Greyhound Derby

Grade S
Quiniela Betting This Race

$3. TRIFECTA
WAGERING IN THIS RACE

---

5 — Red on Black

M.K.'s TED SQUIRT

Souza Bros., owner
Peter Perrone, trainer

Starts	1st	2nd	3rd
14	5	1	3

65   Brindle D., April 1971   Westy Whizzer—Tim's Shamrock, Imp.

10-31¹¹	3-8	F	37.57	46	5	1	1⁸	1⁸	12½	37.57	2.20	*Wire to wire*	SSec.HandHarry, Lone.Billy, Ber.Kelou
10-28¹¹	3-8	F	37.84	65	2	1	1¹⁰	1⁴	1¹	37.84	2.50	*Long early lead*	SSkyTempo, June.Tuffy, LonesomeBilly
10-24⁷	3-8	F	37.93	65	7	1	1³	1³	2½	37.96	1.60	*Outfinished*	STam.Mary, F.Hope, O.A.Away, Fli.Go
10-20¹¹	5-16	F	30.76	65	4	1	1⁵	1⁶	1⁶	30.76	6.40	*Easily*	AAFairDollie, SuirLinda, CapFull
10-13¹¹	3-8	F	38.26	65	3	8	4	2	3²	38.41	3.20	*Good effort*	SSuzette, JuryLady, FlirtyGo
10-10¹¹	3-8	F	38.34	64½	7	4	4	3	4⁶	38.78	6.10	*Crowded turns*	SSuzette, FlirtyGo, TampaMary
10-6⁹	5-16	F	30.55	64	7	4	1³	1⁷	1¹¹	30.55	3.60	*Easily*	ASandyCash, BaseballCap, HeyGuy

"A lot of people thought that I was only a sprinter—but my boss Ed Souza knew better. Not only do I have the best sprint time of the season but also the best official 3-8th mile time as well. I'm lightning out of the box and they're going to have to catch me—not Rusty."

---

6 — Black on Yellow

RAPID FIRE

Lowland Kennel, owner
Dennis Andrews, trainer

Starts	1st	2nd	3rd
8	4	2	0

71   Brindle D., February 1971   L. L's Doug—Sara Bloom

10-31⁷	3-8	F	37.57	71½	1	1	2	2	1¼	37.57	.60	*Despite trouble*	SHilda.Pride, FarSuperior, TampaMary
10-28³	3-8	F	37.77	71	2	2	2	1²	1⁴	37.77	.50	*Easily*	SC.F.GoWell, Fan.McWest, Surfi.Kate⁷
10-25⁷	3-8	F	38.18	71½	4	8	7	6	5⁴	38.45	1.20	*Crowded early*	SGoSnipGo, Cam.O'Heather, S.S.Cyndi
10-20⁸	3-8	F	38.00	70½	3	6	5	3	2½	38.03	3.60	*Crowded early*	AASkyTempo, WellTurned, FancyMcWest
10-17⁹	3-8	F	38.19	70½	6	4	3	3	2¹¹	38.29	2.60	*Crowded, saved*	AAFancyMcWest, FlirtyGo, Bitonto
10-13⁷	3-8	F	38.02	71	4	1	3	1²	1⁸	38.02	3.30	*Despite trouble*	AAFancyMcWest, EveretBolt, GoldMoney
10-10¹¹	3-8	F	38.34	71	2	5	6	7	6⁸	38.90	2.20	*Crowded crtn turn*	SSuzette, FlirtyGo, TampaMary

It is really an honor being in the big race and in such great company. I have won my last two races and one was even despite trouble. My trainer Dennis Andrews says I've got the late speed to do it and I will.

---

7 — Black, Green, White

OLYMPIC HERO, Imp.

James E. O'Donnell, Jr., owner
Edward Dolan, trainer

Starts	1st	2nd	3rd
5	2	1	0

67   Red Fawn D., September 1971   Monalee Champion—Scoby

10-31⁵	3-8	F	37.65	67½	5	2	1²	1²	1¹	37.65	2.50	*Lasted to win*	SS.S.Cher, GoldMoney, FancyMcWest
10-28¹⁰	3-8	F	37.94	67	7	6	3	1ʰᵈ	2¹	38.03	1.60	*Forward factor*	SFlirtyGo, Suzette, S.S.Nico
10-24⁵	3-8	F	37.70	67	1	5	1ʰᵈ	12½	1⁵	37.70	1.60	*Easily*	STheSheikess, JuneCap, SandyCash
10-20⁵	3-8	F	38.04	67	8	4	3	3	5⁶	38.45	4.20	*Tired late*	AAJune'sTuffy, GoldMoney, FlirtyGo
10-16¹¹	3-8	F	38.20	68	8	5	7	8	8¹¹	38.98	2.30	*Outrun*	AATheSheikess, WarDemon, Berkl.Kelou
10-12¹s	3-8	F	37.41	67	3	3	2	1¹	2³	37.62	.....	*Good effort*	LuckyLee, ShanidPhil, FaintHope⁶
10-8²s	5-16	F	31.11	68	2	2	1³	1³	1³½	31.11	.....	*Handily*	HandyCap, GoldMoney, MiniDuke

"My room-mate Foil Valley tells it like it is—we've got the credentials and the experience. To toot my own horn a little, in my last twenty-seven races I have run first 8 times, second 7 times and about 7 other thirds & fourths. Besides, I have only started to run this track well."

---

8 — White, Black, Yellow

BERKLEY KELOU

Altino Gouveia, owner
Altino Gouveia, trainer

Starts	1st	2nd	3rd
16	3	3	2

59   Brindle B., July 1971   Sunnow, Imp.—Berkley June

10-31¹¹	3-8	F	37.57	59	8	8	6	5	4⁷½	38.09	2.30	*Steady gain*	SM.K.T.Squirt, Se.Ha.Harry, Lone.Billy
10-28⁴	3-8	F	37.86	59	4	4	3	2	1⁶	37.86	2.30	*Drew out easily*	SAhlo.Camelot, S.S.Cher, Tur.Trousers
10-24⁹	3-8	F	37.95	59½	2	4	3	3	1¹½	37.95	2.50	*Handily*	SWarDemon, Bitonto, Mac'sAngel
10-19⁸	3-8	F	38.36	59	5	3	4	2	2¹	38.41	4.20	*Crowded turns*	AAG.H.MissPoco, GoSnipGo, Tw.William
10-16¹¹	3-8	F	38.20	59	2	6	6	4	3⁵½	38.58	6.10	*Wide front str.*	AATheSheikess, WarDemon, Tw.William
10-11¹¹	5-16	F	31.21	59	8	8	6	7	7¹¹½	32.01	10.30	*No factor*	AASuirLinda, CapFull, TuffyStuff
10-6⁷	3-8	F	37.78	59½	8	7	4	3	2⁴½	38.09	11.20	*Steady gain*	AARapidFire, CamusO'Heather, FlirtyGo

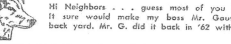

Hi Neighbors . . . guess most of you folks know me, as I live not too far from here. It sure would make my boss Mr. Gouveia happy to win another Derby right in our own back yard. Mr. G. did it back in '62 with the famed Cactus Noel.

---

5 — 4 — 3

Abella-1974

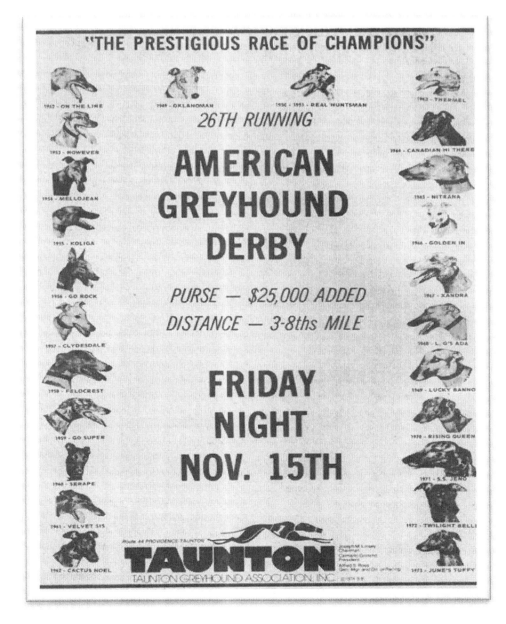

Abella-1974

3/8 MILE		
1980 FEET	TWELFTH RACE	$25,000 added American
	TRACK RECORD — Elite 37.02	

1 — RAZZ
White on Red

Bill Henthorn, owner
Bill Henthorn, trainer

Dist.	Starts	1st	2nd	3rd
3-8	4	1	1	0

70   Fawn D., July 1972   Valor—Dusty Shorty

11-12[11]	3-8	F	37.49	70	1	3	2	2	2²	37.65	4.80	*Chased winner*	(AA) Elite, LittleWishbone, BerkleySmiley
11-9[11]	3-8	F	37.52	69½	3	7	6	6	5¹²½	38.40	1.20	*Jammed early*	(AA) Clas.Whiz, MiniOfBr'way, Wyo.Dream
11-5[9]	3-8	M	37.56	69½	6	6	4	3	1²½	37.56	3.80	*Drew out*	(AA) M.K.TedSquirt, Clas.Fame, LadyStitch
11-2[5]	3-8	F	37.38	68½	8	7	7	7	7¹²	38.24	2.30	*No factor*	AA M.V.FromMars, Tsui, LittleWishbone
10-30¹s	3-8	F	37.33	69½	7	4	1ʰᵈ	1²	1³	37.33	....	*Handily*	S.S.Cyndi, ChampionMaeBee, Abella⁴

Races Below Were Run at Sodrac   Sodrac 20   6   4   2

| 9-15[6] | 3-8 | F | 39.14 | 70½ | 4 | 4 | 2 | 2 | 1⁶½ | 39.14 | 1.30 | *Going away* | A L.L'sInez, PedroPete, NoodlesMyPal |
| 9-11[11] | 3-8 | F | 39.24 | 70 | 1 | 1 | 1² | 1² | 1⁶ | 39.24 | 2.40 | *Going away* | A ZinZin, TKnee, ManteccaLinn |

2 — ABELLA
White on Blue

Keith Dillon, owner
Otto Mamino, trainer

Dist.	Starts	1st	2nd	3rd
3-8	3	2	0	0

60   Red Brindle B., December 1972   Lucky Bannon—Orange Ice

11-12[5]	3-8	F	37.83	60	8	4	4	4	1¹½	37.83	1.70	*Despite trouble*	(AA) M.V.FromMars, Teapot, LadyAnna
11-9[4]	3-8	F	37.47	59½	1	2	2	1²	1⁴½	37.47	6.50	*Drew out inside*	(A) Kans.Sensation, AnitaAnn, SlickJones
11-5[7]	3-8	M	37.92	60	1	3	6	6	5⁴½	38.23	2.60	*Crowded crtn tn*	(A) SueTerry, Gin.Mover, TimothyO'Toole
10-30¹s	3-8	F	37.33	60½	5	2	4	4	4⁶	37.74	....	*Drpd back early*	Razz, S.S.Cyndi, ChampionMaeBee⁴

Races Below Were Run at Southland   Southland 32   10   5   4

10-26[9]	SC	F	42.39	60	7	2	1¹	1¹½1ʰᵈ	42.39	7.20	*Derby Champ*	S Rocktown, IreneAnson, MC'sEmpress
10-22[8]	SC	F	42.31	60	3	1	1²	2	2¹	42.53	2.60	*Even effort*	S MCEmpress, WCDKid, H'son
10-18[7]	SC	F	41.98	60	8	3	3	3	3³½	42.24	2.60	*On outside*	S MCEmpress, TeAnson, TEvan

3 — TSUI
Black on White

J. C. Stanley, owner
Peter Perrone, trainer

Dist.	Starts	1st	2nd	3rd
5-16	3	0	0	1
3-8	12	5	1	3

71   Brindle D., June 1972   Blue Forge—Connie Admiral

11-12[3]	3-8	F	37.67	71½	5	1	3	3	3¹⁰	38.36	2.20	*Bumped 1st turn*	(AA) SlickJones, I.W.Reporter, K.Sensation
11-9[5]	3-8	F	37.61	71½	2	6	2	1²	1³	37.61	1.00	*Handily*	(AA) TimothyO'Toole, PaulaFlint, Suzette⁷
11-6[7]	3-8	F	37.27	71	1	1²	1²	1⁴	37.27	1.50	*Box to wire*	(AA) KansasSensation, Beulah, S.S.Cher
11-2[5]	3-8	F	37.38	71½	2	3	3	2	2²	37.52	3.60	*Blocked far turn*	AA M.V.F.Mars, L.Wishb'ne, MiniOfB'w'y
10-29[5]	3-8	F	37.69	71	6	1	5	4	3¹	37.75	4.20	*Steady gain*	AA M.V.FromMars, Cooley.Era, SmileJoey
10-26[9]	3-8	F	37.48	71	7	8	5	5	3⁴½	37.80	6.20	*Late gain*	AA M.V.FromMars, L.Wishbone, L.Scotch
10-23[11]	5-16	F	31.03	71	8	5	7	5	3²	31.15	13.10	*Blocked far turn*	AA DualUtah, S.S.Cher, AllStarBobby
10-17[7]	3-8	F	37.50	71	3	4	3	1¹	1²	37.50	4.80	*Despite trouble*	A ClassicWhiz, MiniOfBroadway, Suzette

4 — MINI OF BROADWAY
White on Green

Nova Kennel, owner
Hans Limmer trainer

Dist.	Starts	1st	2nd	3rd
3-8	18	3	5	2

59   Brindle B., March 1972   Bayside Noel—Broadway Cookie

11-12[11]	3-8	F	37.49	59	7	8	8	8	7¹¹	38.28	22.60	*No factor*	(AA) Elite, Razz, LittleWishbone
11-9[11]	3-8	F	37.52	58½	6	5	5	3-	2⁸	38.06	3.60	*Good effort*	(AA) ClassicWhiz, Wyo.Dream, Du.Discreet
11-5[5]	3-8	M	37.48	59	1	3	2	2	1¹	37.48	6.20	*Drew out*	(AA) OnieJones, SandCut, Swinger
11-2[5]	3-8	F	37.38	58½	5	1	2	4	4⁴	37.64	17.30	*No mishaps*	AA M.V.FromMars, Tsui, LittleWishbone
10-29[5]	3-8	F	37.69	59½	5	6	7	7	6⁷	38.19	9.40	*Bumped far turn*	AA M.V.FromMars, Cooleygorm.Era, Tsui
10-25[12]	3-8	F	37.46	59	2	1	1¹	1¹	1¹	37.46	4.40	*Box to wire*	A RoyalPrincess, ClassicWhiz, Beulah
10-20[12]	3-8	F	37.90	59	4	7	6	6	6¹¹½	38.71	2.60	*Never prominent*	A SurfireHerb, Class.Whiz, Roy.Princess
10-17[7]	3-8	F	37.50	59	7	6	8	5	3⁵	37.86	1.60	*Steady gain*	A Tsui, ClassicWhiz, Suzette

Handicapper's Selections

33rd BLUE RIBBON STAKES -- NOV. 30

Abella-1974

Greyhound Derby

Grade S
Quiniela Betting This Race

$3. TRIFECTA
WAGERING IN THIS RACE

5 Red on Black

SLICK JONES

R. L. Block, Inc., owner
R. L. Block, trainer

81 Brindle D., May 1972 Hoefer—Elsie Jones

Dist.	Starts	1st	2nd	3rd
3-8	3	2	0	0

11-12³	3-8	F	37.67	79½	4	8	1⁴	1⁷	1¹⁰	37.67	2.90	Benefited early	(AA) I.W.'sReporter, Tsui, KansasSensation
11-9⁴	3-8	F	37.47	80	6	8	4	4	4⁹½	38.14	1.50	Crowded early	(AA) Abella, KansasSensation, AnitaAnn
11-6⁵	3-8	F	37.35	80	4	4	3	1²½1⁴		37.35	2.50	On inside	(AA) AlDeLaney, I.W.Reporter, L.Wishbone
11-1¹s	3-8	F	36.95	80½	4	3	2	2	2⁶	37.36	.....	Rail thruout	Elite, OnieJones, AnitaAnn⁵

Races Below Were Run at Tampa   Tampa 4 2 0 0

10-25⁹	5-16	F	31.24	81	3	8	8	7	6⁹½	31.91	6.30	Off slow	ᴬ MontBaron, PsychicEnergy, Yuco
10-19⁶	5-16	F	31.01	80½	8	8	5	5	5⁹	31.64	6.70	Off slow	ᴬ Canyon, QueensMiss, SmmCumLaude
10-16⁹	5-16	F	31.47	81	5	6	4	2	1²	31.47	2.30	Bore in won	ᴬ GltrJerry, DrmltnMk, CincinnatiHry

6 Black on Yellow

ROYAL MARVEL

John Orkney, owner
Fred Soares, trainer

81 Light Fawn D., January 1973 Tim London—J.O.'s Cassy

Dist.	Starts	1st	2nd	3rd
5-16	5	1	0	1
3-8	15	3	5	2

11-12⁷	3-8	F	37.83	82	1	8	5	2	2¹	37.88	2.60	Inside far turn	(AA) SmileJoey, WegoSue, AnitaAnn
11-9⁷	3-8	F	37.80	82½	6	7	5	1¹	1¹½	37.80	2.50	Inside far turn	(A) IDid, AlDeLaney, KingRegal⁷
11-5³	3-8	M	37.79	82½	8	8	6	4	2½	37.83	3.20	Crd., came on	(A) LadyAnna, Suzette, BerkleySmiley
10-30¹¹	5-16	F	30.63	82½	6	8	8	6	6¹²	31.47	13.40	Never prominent	(AA) ClassicFame, FlickerFlash, AlpineStar
10-26⁷	5-16	F	30.68	82	8	8	8	5	4⁵	31.02	7.20	Rail thruout	(AA) JumpinRosie, Gold.Chance, DualUtah
10-23⁵	3-8	F	37.48	82½	2	8	8	6	6¹¹	38.24	3.60	Never prominent	AA Lit.Wishbone, M.V.F.Mars, Cin.Block
10-19¹¹	5-16	F	31.11	81½	5	8	6	4	1²½	31.11	16.10	Last to 1st	AA Class.Bound, Mant.Rose, I.W.Reporter
10-16⁷	3-8	M	37.57	81½	2	8	6	5	5⁶½	38.02	2.60	Close quarters	AA Tim.O'Toole, M.V.F.Mars, L.Wishbone

7 Black, Green, White

SAND CUT

George Thigpen, owner
Edna Dial, trainer

66 Red Brindle D., June 1972 Westy Whizzer—Edy Lou

Dist.	Starts	1st	2nd	3rd
3-8	3	1	0	2

11-12⁹	3-8	F	37.70	66	2	2	1⁵	1⁵	1¹½	37.70	5.10	Lasted to win	(AA) GoldMoney, AlDeLaney, IDid
11-9¹⁰	3-8	F	38.13	65	8	3	1¹	1¹	3²	38.25	.90	Speed to stretch	(AA) PeaceChance, WegoSue, LastScotch
11-5⁵	3-8	M	37.48	65	4	2	1⁴	1²	3⁴	37.78	.80	Speed to stretch	(AA) MiniOfBroadway, OnieJones, Swinger
11-1³s	5-16	F	30.34	66	2	1	1⁵	1⁵	1⁵	30.34	.....	Easily	GrannyCanuk, LovelyLegend, Huskee⁵

Races Below Were Run at Flagler   Flagler 8 3 1 2

10-26¹²	FC	F	37.77	65	8	5	1⁴	1²	1¹	37.77	3.90	Classic Champ	s AnitaAnn, Elite, PrettyPert
10-19¹¹	FC	F	37.56	65	6	5	6	4	3⁶½	38.01	5.90	Crowded break	SA AnitaAnn, Delos, WashingtonWalt
10-15¹¹	FC	F	37.79	65	7	8	6	4	4⁷½	38.31	2.10	Offstrided early	SA Elite, WashingtonWalt, Siege

8 White, Black, Yellow

ELITE

Merrimack Kennel, owner
John Owens, trainer

57 Black B., April 1971 Yellow Printer, Imp.—Aunt Mart

Dist.	Starts	1st	2nd	3rd
3-8	3	3	0	0

11-12¹¹	3-8	F	37.49	56½	8	4	1¹½1¹½	1²		37.49	.90	Handily	(AA) Razz, LittleWishbone, BerkleySmiley
11-9⁹	3-8	F	37.63	56	7	2	1²	1²	1²½	37.63	.90	Handily	(AA) Y.Clipper, M.K.T.Squirt, M.V.F.Mars⁷
11-6⁹	3-8	F	37.02	56½	5	1	1⁵	1⁴	1⁴	37.02	1.20	Track record	(A) L.A.Copper, PeaceChance, GoldMoney
11-1¹s	3-8	F	36.95	57	2	2	1⁴	1⁴	1⁶	36.95	.....	Easily	SlickJones, OnieJones, AnitaAnn⁵

Races Below Were Run at Flagler   Flagler 10 4 2 1

10-26¹²	FC	F	37.77	56	2	6	2	2	3³	37.96	4.60	Outfinished	s SandCut, AnitaAnn, PrettyPert
10-19¹¹	FC	F	37.56	57	5	3	5	6	8⁹½	38.21	1.40	Gradual fade	SA AnitaAnn, Delos, SandCut
10-15¹¹	FC	F	37.79	57	6	4	1³	1⁴	1⁶	37.79	1.40	Inside dricing	SA WashingtonWalt, Siege, SandCut

2 — 8 — 5

LADIES! SEE SUNDAY PROGRAM

1975

No Derby Run

P.L. Greer-1976

P.L. Greer-1976

AMERICAN GREYHOUND DERBY
TWELFTH RACE
Please Call for Dog by Number

GRADE S

⅛ MILE
1980 Ft. — 603.5 Meters

TRACK RECORD
Elite 37.02

P. P.	'76 Race Dis. Tk. Tm. Wt. PP Off 1-8 Str. Fin. RT Odds Grade	Sts. 1st 2d 3d 4th	Order of Finish with Comment

Red 1 — FLYING RIVER (55)
Red Brindle B., October 1974. Hoefer—Bea Barr
TAU 3 1 1 1 0 — Owner—R. J. Barber
PLN 22 7 6 3 2 — Trainer—John Woods
11-16⁵	3-8 F 38.63 54½ 8 4 3 3 3³½ 38.88 3.50 S	LivelyCount, Deb'sDustOff, ArcticFlower	[Inside bid⁷
11-13⁵	3-8 F 38.56 55 6 2 2 2 2¹ 38.63 8.00 S	RiverDee, LivelyCount, Arkle'sGift	[Winning effort⁷
11-10⁹	3-8 F 38.49 55 6 2 2 2 1¹ 38.49 58.40 S	ArcticFlower, P.L.Jackson, Leadership	[Up in stretch
11- 5⁶s	5-16 F 30.93 56 6 7 7 7 6¹⁴ 31.89	P.L.Greer, RiverChief, P.L.Jackson	[Never prominent
11- 2¹s	3-8 F 38.35 55 6 5 5 5 5²⁴ 40.04	RealDelight, StepProudly, TrialRun	[Out un rail⁵
(RACES BELOW WERE RUN AT PLAINFIELD)
| 10-20¹⁰ | 5-16 S 31.94 55 4 5 fell 7 7 OOP 25.30 SA | StoneyPrinter, GoldPiece, J.V.'sSpeedrock | [1st turn |

Blue 2 — REAL DELIGHT (71)
Red D., February 1974. Robichaux—Min White
TAU 3 1 1 0 0 — Owner—James Stanton
FLA 2 0 0 0 1 — Trainer—James Stanton
11-16³	3-8 F 38.34 71 4 4 4 5 6¹³ 39.27 1.60 S	RiverLass, DrainO, BlueDoll	[Saved
11-13¹¹	3-8 F 38.61 71 7 1 16 15 1ʰᵈ 38.61 3.60 S	Commentator, FreeMoments, Judianna	[Long early lead
11- 9⁹	3-8 F 37.94 70 7 2 2 2 2⁸ 38.50 7.10 S	P.L.Greer, Danbury, CountAxe	[Followed winner
11- 2¹s	3-8 F 38.35 71 4 2 1² 14 1³ 38.35	StepProudly, TrialRun, M.V.Scatty	[Easily⁵
(RACES BELOW WERE RUN AT FLAGLER)
| 10- 5⁷ | FC F 37.27 71 7 6 5 4 4¹¹ 38.02 13.20 SA | TeesTo, Ted'sBoomer, KC'sIlla | [No mishaps, outside |
| 10- 2⁵ | FC F 37.28 72 2 5 6 7 7¹² 38.14 24.30 SA | Ted'sBoomer, OddVenus, Mc'sCimmrn | [Wi early, no fat |

White 3 — RIVER DEE (60)
Fawn & White B., October 1974. Monalee Flybolt, Imp.—Irish Missy
TAU 3 2 1 0 0 — Owner—Frank Brothers
GM 10 2 5 1 0 — Trainer—Clarence Caswell
11-16¹¹	3-8 F 38.28 59 5 1 1² 13 1⁶ 38.28 6.50 S	Danbury, Commentator, T'sPrettyBoy	[Going away
11-13⁵	3-8 F 38.56 60 1 1 3 3 1¹ 38.56 2.70 S	FlyingRiver, LivelyCount, Arkle'sGift	[Up in stretch⁷
11-10¹¹	3-8 F 38.55 60 5 2 3 4 2ⁿᵈ 38.57 13.10 S	SuperLady, BlueDoll, SlippersBest	[Closed fast wide
11- 5⁶s	5-16 F 30.93 60½ 7 5 4 5 5⁹½ 31.61	P.L.Greer, RiverChief, P.L.Jackson	[Evenly
(RACES BELOW WERE RUN AT GREEN MOUNTAIN)
| 10-30¹⁰ | 3-8 F 38.78 61 5 2 2 2 2³ 39.00 4.30 A | RiverChief, ClintForrest, RuthNelson | [Chased winner |
| 10-24¹⁰ | x5-16 F 32.28 61 7 1 8 8 6⁵ 32.69 10.40 A | MidnightBdd., Clmb.Bill, PepperD. | [Shuffld, drpd back |

Green 4 — LIVELY COUNT (75)
Brindle D., February 1974. Count Rebel, Imp.—Lackluster
TAU 14 5 1 3 2 — Owner—Francis Fulginiti
BIS 7 3 2 1 0 — Trainer—Joseph Fulginiti
11-16⁵	3-8 F 38.63 75½ 5 2 1¹ 15 1³ 38.63 4.20 S	Deb'sDustOff, FlyingRiver, ArcticFlower	[Easily inside⁷
11-13⁵	3-8 F 38.56 75½ 5 5 5 4 3³ 38.78 1.40 S	RiverDee, FlyingRiver, Arkle'sGift	[Good effort⁷
11- 9⁷	3-8 F 38.12 74 6 7 6 3 2⁷ 38.62 1.80 S	T'sPrettyBoy, Deb'sDustOff, Judianna	[On inside
11- 5⁹	5-16 F 31.00 75 5 5 4 3 3³ 31.19 2.50 AA	FreeMoments, SuperLady, WhiteMajor	[Inside bid
10-30⁹	5-16 F 31.30 75 4 3 6 6 4¹ 31.34 3.50 S	SandHog, OldJessie, Timmie'sTip	[Despite trouble
10-27⁷	5-16 F 31.29 76 2 3 2 2 1¹ 31.29 1.80 S	Timmie'sTip, CountAxe, Chito	[Up rail
10-23⁹	5-16 F 30.85 74½ 6 8 2 1³ 1² 30.85 13.80 S	Fairness, OldJessie, Free Moments	[Handily rail

Black 5 — OFFICER SERMON (72)
Light Brindle D., July 1974. B. Whiz—Leah J.
TAU 3 1 1 0 1 — Owner—Paul Scheele
TAM 13 8 3 1 1 — Trainer—Paul Scheele
11-16⁷	3-8 F 38.78 71 5 2 4 5 .45 39.11 1.20 S	FashionSlipper, EasyPar, MermdPrinter	[Jammed far tn
11-13⁶	3-8 F 38.34 71½ 1 1 1² 16 1⁴ 38.34 1.60 S	ArcticFlower, EasyPar, SureGold	[Easily⁷
11-10⁷	3-8 F 38.17 72 7 6 2 3 2⁷ 38.64 5.40 S	HeatherScott, MelroseOlson, Bramble	[Good effort
11- 5³s	3-8 F 38.34 72 7 1 1½ 2 2²½ 38.52	GraceBrowning, Shella'sClock, Allou	[Collided crtn turn⁵
(RACES BELOW WERE RUN AT TAMPA)
| 10-30⁶ | 5-16 F 30.63 71 6 4 1¹ 1² 16 30.63 4.40 A | HaftaHurry, JamesTryon, Sheriff | [Drew away rail |
| 10-27⁶ | 5-16 F 30.96 71½ 7 4 2 2 2⁵ 31.32 4.40 A | Sheriff, HaftaHurry, LasansPronto | [Best of others |

Yellow 6 — P. L. GREER (64)
Red D., August 1973. S. S. Jeno—Colonel Vickey
TAU 3 3 0 0 0 — Owner—Richard Moran
CS 10 8 0 1 0 — Trainer—Mike Robinson
11-16⁹	3-8 F 38.21 64 7 2 15 16 1⁶½ 38.21 .50 S	RiverChief, StepProudly, Judianna	[Was best
11-13⁹	3-8 F 38.22 64 1 1 15 16 1⁶½ 38.22 .20 S	StepProudly, TerriJackie, Deb'sDustOff	[As he pleased
11- 9⁹	3-8 F 37.94 64 2 2 15 16 1⁸ 37.94 .50 S	RealDelight, Danbury, CountAxe	[Never challenged rail
11- 5⁶s	5-16 F 30.93 65 5 1 15 15 1³½ 30.93	RiverChief, P.L.Jackson, RiverLass	[All the way
(RACES BELOW WERE RUN AT COLORADO SPRINGS)
| 10-16⁸ | SC F 39.85 64 7 2 2 2 3²½ 40.27 .40 A | CindyGo, PurpleKat, XentureBabe | [Early speed |
| 10-13⁸ | SC F 39.62 64 7 4 2 14 15¹ 39.62 .40 A | SpryFinish, RomanHustler, OshkshCash | [Drew out |

Green & White 7 — T's PRETTY BOY (74)
Dark Brindle D., November, 1974. B Whiz—T's Perky.
TAU 26 9 2 2 4 — Owner—John Yamin
RAY 10 3 3 0 0 — Trainer—Gary Scott
11-16¹¹	3-8 F 38.28 73 1 6 5 5 4⁹½ 38.95 1.60 S	RiverDee, Danbury, Commentator	[Evenly
11-13⁴	3-8 F 38.55 73 1 2 2 2 1ⁿˢ 38.55 .60 S	RiverChief, TeesTo, DutchCertified	[Just up⁷
11- 9⁷	3-8 F 38.12 73 1 3 1² 14 1⁷ 38.12 1.70 S	LivelyCount, Deb'sDustOff, Judianna	[Drew out
11- 5¹⁵	5-16 F 31.52 73 6 2 3 1½ 2ⁿᵏ 31.55 4.50 AA	SurfireDolt, ArticKate, FazingRalph	[Caught stretch
11- 3⁹	3-8 F 31.32 73 6 5 4 3 2³ 31.52 2.50 AA	SurfireDolt, RSFriskie,, OldJessie	[Collided 1st turn
10-30⁷	3-8 F 38.11 73½ 7 4 3 3 4⁵ 38.44 2.20 AA	ChalkTalk, Arkle'sGift, ArcticFlower	[Forward factor
10-26⁷	3-8 F 38.34 72 1 2 1¹ 11 1⁴ 38.34 1.30 AA	FazingRalph, ChalkTalk, Commentator	[Drew clear

Yellow & Black 8 — RIVER LASS (60)
Brindle B., October 1974. Monalee Flybolt, Imp.—Irish Missy
TAU 3 1 1 0 1 — Owner—Frank Brothers
GM 10 6 2 1 0 — Trainer—Clarence Caswell
11-16³	3-8 F 38.34 60 3 1 2 14 1¹⁰ 38.34 4.40 S	DrainO, BlueDoll, StarPort	[Drew out
11-13⁶	3-8 F 38.53 60 1 1 1½ 13 2ⁿˢ 38.53 15.80 S	IvoryCoast, DebbieCap, Leadership	[Shuffled crtn turn
11- 3⁶	3-8 F 38.46 60 4 2 5 4 4⁵ 38.86 20.00 S	DebbieCap, FashnSlipper, SedroWooly	[Offstrided far tn
11- 5⁶s	5-16 F 31.54 60 1 4 5 4 4⁹ 31.54	P.L.Greer, RiverChief, P.L.Jackson	[Forward factor
(RACES BELOW WERE RUN AT GREEN MOUNTAIN)
| 10-27¹⁰ | 3-8 F 38.11 61 3 2 1 2 1¹½ 31.91 1.80 A | PattiShaw, Wood.Lady, Midnight Buddy | [Driving wide |
| 10-23¹⁰ | 3-8 F 38.11 61 1 2 1 1 1³ 38.86 .90 A | BrokeBell, Mr.Good, JohnnieMargo | [Box to wire |

*—Schooled to Judges' Satisfaction

WIN	PLACE	SHOW	PLACE	SHOW	SHOW

Handicapper's Selections
6 — 8 — 3 — 4

QUINIELA $3 SUPERFECTA

Downing-1977

FINAL CALLED "GREATEST"

"This is the greatest American Greyhound Derby in history."

That is the concensus of opinion of the banner crowds that watched the three qualifying rounds and were treated to a spectacular running performance by Downing, who more than upheld his reputation of being the greatest greyhound of the year.

True, the American Greyhound Derby has had some fine runnings since its inception in 1949. And there were many outstanding winners in the past as Oklahoman, Real Huntsman, On The Line, Feldcrest, Velvet Sis, Cactus Noel, S. S. Jeno and the Greyhound of 1976, P. L. Greer.

But never has the fancy of greyhound racing enthusiasts been as high as that shown for Downing, particularly in the final qualifying round when the grandson of the one-time Taunton favorite, Westy Whizzer, streaked around the 3-8ths mile course in the sensational new record time of 36.84, winning by 11 wide-open lengths.

Tomorrow night's Derby final is without doubt the greatest test Downing has been called upon to face. On his local performances the big red brindle will leave the starting box as the prohibitive favorite but as the field is arraged against him it may be a tougher task than it appears.

For instance, Malka has shown terrific come-from-behind speed as displayed in winning all three of her qualifying heats. Then there's Sultry Sister, winner of the Revere Derby; and Nadia, also outstanding in the pre-Derby trials; Taunton's White Desire; Colitta, River Chief and Keeter, all speedsters in their own rights.

The greatest American Greyhound Derby in history holds true and tomorrow night will prove it.

Downing-1977

3/8 MILE
1980 Ft. — 603.5 Meters

TRACK RECORD
Downing 36.84
11-10-77

$25,000 added American

P. P.	Date	Dis. Tk. Tm. Wt. PP Off 1-8 Str. Fin.	RT	Odds	Gr.	Comment	Sts. 1st 2d 3d 4th	Order of Finish

White on Red

1 MALKA (65) TAU 3 3 0 0 0 / WON 27 12 6 5 3   Owner—Mike Castellani, Inc. Trainer—Don Cuddy

Red B., January 1976. Yankee Clipper—Impeccable, Imp.

Date	Dis Tk Tm Wt	PP Off 1-8 Str Fin	RT	Odds	Gr	Comment	Order of Finish
11-10⁹	3-8 F 37.26 63	8 6 6	3 1² 37.26	.40	S	Driving wide	Colitta, IslaMae, DutchCappyAnn
11- 6⁹	3-8 F 37.97 64	3 6 6	2 1³ 37.97	.40	S	Big effort wide	MissAbigail, TK'sDelight, Mac'sGirl
11- 3¹²	3-8 F 37.60 64	8 6 2	14 15½ 37.60	1.40	S	Was best wide	ArticFlowr, DarkSpcial, ManchuPrnce
10-28¹s	3-8 F 37.75 64	8 6 7	6 44½ 38.07	....		Crowded early	RiverChief, SultrySister, RiverRose⁷
10-24¹s	5-16 F 30.85 65	6 5 5	1³ 19½ 30.85	....		Drew out wide	CrystalGypsy, WacoCrown, Mr. Tasmin

(RACES BELOW WERE RUN AT WONDERLAND)

9-26¹²	5-16 Sy 30.99 63	6 7 7	5 47½ 31.60	20.40	A	Late gain	Downing, RoosterCogburn, Nadia
9-22⁶	5-16 F 31.29 63½	5 1 8	5 2⁴ 31.59	1.60	A	Blocked break	DarkSpecial, Printer'sDolly, Durham
9-17¹¹	RC F 39.54 63½	2 3 4	2 1² 39.54	1.90	A	Long drive inside	SultrySister, IslaMae, Sheila'sClock
9-14¹¹	RC F 39.73 63	2 5 6	4 3³ 39.96	1.80	A	Blocked backstr	SultrySister, Adele, IslaMae

White on Blue

2 NADIA (61) TAU 3 2 1 0 0 / TAM 2 0 2 0 0   Owner—R.L. Block, Inc. Trainer—Alvin Rink

Red Brindle B., November 1975. Onie Jones—Play Dough

11-10⁷	3-8 F 37.39 61	2 7 4	2 2¹ 37.45	3.10	S	Closed rail	SultrySistr, BlazingRed, T.K.'sDelight
11- 6¹¹	3-8 F 37.99 61	1 6 1²	1³ 1² 37.99	2.60	S	Benefited break	SultrySister, G.R.Robin, ProprCascade
11- 3⁶	3-8 F 37.91 61	6 5 4	1¹ 15½ 37.91	1.10	S	Drew out rail	Colitta, DFAlethea, Leader'sMonalee
10-26¹s	3-8 F 38.02 61	7 8 2	2 1hd 38.02	....		Just up wide	Colitta, IsalMae, BlazingRed

(RACES BELOW WERE RUN AT TAMPA)

10-12⁷	5-16 F 31.02 60½	8 8 4	4 2¹³ 31.12	4.80	AT	Driving wide	MdwyCris, LnsmPrncess, WrghtAnchr
10- 7⁷	5-16 F 31.04 60½	7 5 5	4 2¹¹ 31.79	2.90	A	Driving wide	WrightAnchor, JetRun, MasterSctt
9-30¹s	5-16 F 31.51 61½	4 8 6	5 3¹ 31.57	....		Driving at end	GentleLady, Wagtail, CameronFlwr

(RACES BELOW WERE RUN AT WONDERLAND)

| 9-23¹² | 5-16 F 30.99 61 | 8 8 8 | 4 36½ 31.53 | 7.50 | A | Lacked early spd | Downing, RoosterCogburn, Malka |

Black on White

3 RIVER CHIEF (75) TAU 3 1 2 0 0 / GM 22 15 2 2 2   Owner—Frank Brothers Trainer—Jacqueline Alves

Red Fawn D., October 1974. Monalee Flybolt, Imp.—Irish Missy

11-10⁵	3-8 F 37.15 74½	5 2 2	15 15 37.15	1.00	S	Big effort inside	TopThat, SkimpySkamp, LdrsMnlee
11- 6³	3-8 F 37.73 75	4 2 2	2 2² 37.92	1.60	S	No room str turn	Colitta, DarkSpecial, Tovah
11- 3¹⁰	3-8 F 38.11 75	1 2 1¹	1¹ 2¹ 38.20	.80	S	Caught on rail	ProperCascade, Tovah, Chasing
10-28¹s	3-8 F 37.75 75	5 3 2	2 1² 37.75	....		Up on inside	SultrySister, RiverRose, Malka⁷

(RACES BELOW WERE RUN AT GREEN MOUNTAIN)

10-20⁷	3-8 F 38.26 75½	2 2 14	16 15 38.26	.50	A	Breezing along	M.KintoPat, TrudyGbsn., W.P.CherieK.
10-16¹²x3-8	F 38.76 75½	5 2 1²	15 12½ 38.76	.80	A	Set pace	Champ.Chet, W.W.Snpy.Lee, L.L.Pejr
10-10⁷x	3-8 F 37.91 75½	8 1 16	110 112 37.91	.40	B	New track recrd	CorkBoard, Nap'sOnrey, KennelDust
10- 6¹⁰	5-16 F 31.37 75½	7 8 6	5 4⁷ 31.89	1.60	A	Some gain	GHJanuary, PepperD., D.D.SnappyLee
10- 2¹⁰x	5-16 F 31.43 75	5 2 7	6 6⁹ 32.05	1.00	A	Crd ent backstr	Puzzle, Dixie'sRyan, PepperD.

White on Green

4 WHITE DESIRE (57) TAU 14 6 4 2 0   Owner—Charles Rink Trainer—Alan Rink

White & Red B., November, 1975. Hoefer's Boy—Cushie My, Imp.

11-10¹²	3-8 F 36.84 58	8 6 5	5 5¹⁵ 37.91	5.10	S	Collided str turn	Downing, SomethingVelvet, Keeter
11- 6⁶	3-8 F 37.77 57½	7 4 3	14 17 37.77	.70	S	Drew out wide	SkmpySkamp, IslaMae, DchCappyAnn⁷
11- 2⁸	3-8 F 37.80 57½	1 3 14	16 17½ 37.80	1.30	S	Was best wide	BlazingRed, SexySadie, IslaMae
10-28⁷	3-8 F 38.08 56	1 4 1¹	15 2hd 38.10	1.80	AA	Caught wide	ArticFlower, Chasing, ProudHiawatha
10-25⁷	3-8 F 37.74 57	5 4 2	2 2⁴ 38.03	3.50	AA	Outside bid	RiverLass, CashelBeauty, ArcticFlower
10-22⁸	3-8 F 37.22 57	3 5 2	2 3⁷ 37.72	3.10	S	Early factor wide	Chasing, ArcticFlower, SureGold
10-19⁷	3-8 F 37.90 57	2 5 4	2 3¹½ 38.01	.80	S	Around outside	SureGold, RSBlackhawk, SharonHobbs
10-15⁹	5-16 F 30.90 57	3 7 7	7 6⁵ 31.27	2.10	S	Wide	DarkSpecial, ProntoPoncho, TopThat
10-12⁷	5-16 F 30.75 57½	5 4 3	2 2² 30.89	.60	S	Worked thru	ProntoPoncho, Sgt.T.K., Contoe⁷
10- 8⁹	5-16 F 30.93 57½	8 7 2	14 17 30.93	.90	S	Breezing wide	Contoe, SgtT.K., BenAlly

Handicapper's Selections 5 — 1 — 6

36th BLUE RIBBON STAKE

QUINIELA **$2 TRIFECTA**

Downing-1977

Greyhound Derby

TWELFTH RACE (12)

GRADE S-AA

P.P	Date	Dis. Tk. Tm. Wt. PP Off 1-8 Str. Fin.	RT Odds Gr.	Comment	Sts. 1st 2d 3d 4th	Order of Finish

Red on Black 5

DOWNING (77) TAU 3 3 0 0 0 / WON 10 8 0 2 0 Owner—Pat Dalton Trainer—James Alves

Red Brindle D., March 1975. Big Whizzer—Hookers Flower

11-10[12] 3-8	F 36.84 77½ 7 1 1[6]	1[12] 1[11]	36.84	.10 S New track record	SomethingVelvet, Keeter, DmndsAstro
11- 6[12] 3-8	F 37.48 78 1 1 1[7]	1[10] 1[5]	37.46	.10 S As he pleased	BlazgRed, SmthgVelvet, R.S.Blkhawk
11- 2[12] 3-8	F 37.49 77½ 6 1 1[5]	1[6] 1[4½]	37.49	.10 S Total command rl	DiamondsAstro, Keeter, LisaLove
10-27[1s] 3-8	F 37.12 77½ 4 1 1[5]	1[9] 1[11]	37.12	Easily rail	Negligent[2]
10-21[3s] 5-16	F 30.22 78 1 4 1[7]	1[10] 1[20]	30.22	Much the best	HouseChamp, SayHelloMo, GoodbyeTu
(RACES BELOW WERE RUN AT WONDERLAND)					
9-26[12] 5-16	S 30.99 78 1 1 1[4]	1[3] 1[2½]	30.99	.20 A Box to wire	RoosterCogburn, Nadia, Malka
9- 5[12] 5-16	F 31.07 78½ 6 2 1[3]	1[4] 1[2]	31.07	.40 SA Denied rl cam on	Rstr.Cog., SF'sTain'tSo, WrightF.
9- 2[10] 5-16	F 30.55 77½ 3 1 1[3]	1[5] 1[10½]	30.55	.20 SA Breezing along	SilverCute, SullaneMiller, Stangl
8-30[11] 5-16	F 30.53 78 1 1 1[3]	1[4] 1[7]	30.53	.10 SA Much the best	Lacy'sJohnny, SilverCute, Malka[7]

Black on Yellow 6

SULTRY SISTER (62) TAU 3 2 1 0 0 / WON 30 21 6 2 1 Owner—Mike Castellani, Inc. Trainer—Don Cuddy

Red Fawn B., September 1975. B.B.'s Cracker—Odd Sister

11-10[7] 3-8	F 37.39 61 8 6 1[3]	1[5] 1[1]	37.39	.50 S Long early lead	Nadia, BlazingRed, T.K.'sDelight
11- 6[11] 3-8	F 37.99 62 2 2 7	3 2[2]	38.11	1.00 S Blocked break	Nadia, G.R.Robin, ProperCascade
11- 2[10] 3-8	F 38.03 61½ 6 4 1[3]	1[7] 1[4]	38.03	.60 S Easily mid-track	G.R.Robin, TopThat, SureGold
10-28[1s] 3-8	F 37.75 61½ 1 2 4	3 2[2]	37.89	Wide early	RiverChief, RiverRose, Malka[7]
10-21[1s] 3-8	F 37.90 62 8 4 1[4]	1[4] 1[3]	37.90	Easily inside	Negligent, PatCSilly, Becky'sImage
(RACES BELOW WERE RUN AT WONDERLAND)					
9-26[11] RC	Sy 39.99 61 5 7 4	1[1] 2[½]	40.04	.50 A Wide thruout	IslaM., NT'sMarshaA, Ldrs.Monalee
9-21[11] RC	F 39.66 59 2 2 1[3]	1[5] 1[5]	39.66	.40 A Was best	CarryAll, Adele, Sheila'sClock
9-17[11] RC	F 39.54 61 8 6 1[nk]	1[3] 2[2]	39.70	.70 A Long lead, caught	Malka, IslaMae, Sheila'sClock
9-14[11] RC	F 39.73 60 3 1 1[3]	1[3] 1[1]	39.73	.80 A Long early lead	Adele, Malka, IslaMae

Black, Green, White, 7

COLITTA (59) TAU 3 1 2 0 0 / TOP 3 3 0 0 0 Owner—North Shore Kennel Trainer—Mike Camilleri

Fawn B., November 1975. Frisco Bay—Ma Blakney, Imp.

11-10[9] 3-8	F 37.26 58½ 1 1 1[3]	1[2] 2[2]	37.41	2.10 S Outfin inside	Malka, IslaMae, DutchCappyAnn
11- 6[3] 3-8	F 37.79 59 6 1 1[2]	1[1] 1[2]	37.79	3.60 S Gamely inside	RiverChief, DarkSpecial, Tovah
11- 3[6] 3-8	F 37.91 59½ 2 1 2	2 2[5½]	38.30	1.60 S Pressing early rl	Nadia, DFAlethea, Leader'sMonalee
10-26[1s] 3-8	F 38.02 59½ 5 1 1[3]	1[2] 2nd	38.04	Outfinished insi	Nadia, IslaMae, BlazingRed
(RACES BELOW WERE RUN AT TOPSFIELD)					
10- 8[10] TC	F 39.60 59 4 2 1[1]	2 1[1½]	39.60	2.40 S Came again	LeadrMonalee, FlmishBronze, Cudgel
10- 5[10] TC	F 39.53 59 4 1 1[1]	1[1] 1[2]	39.53	3.60 A Never headed	FlemishBronuze, HouseChamp, Cudgel
10- 1[6] TC	M 41.01 59 4 2 1[1]	1[2] 1[3]	41.01	14.50 SB Rush to lead	Cudgel, CarryAll, Ragtone
(RACES BELOW WERE RUN AT WONDERLAND)					
9-26[9] RC	F 40.17 59 6 8 7	7 7[15½]	41.46	6.30 B Inside & outside	ArticFlwr, FlemishBrnz, FriendlyB.

White Black, Yellow 8

KEETER (56) TAU 3 1 0 2 0 / SEA 17 6 5 4 2 Owner—John Boyd Trainer—John Boyd

Red Fawn B., October 1975. Jake Predee—Stylish Checkers

11-10[12] 3-8	F 36.84 56 3 7 4	3 3[11]	37.62	21.00 S Evenly	Downing, SmethngVelvet, DmndsAstro
11- 6[5] 3-8	F 38.22 56 3 4 1[1]	1[5] 1[2]	38.22	1.20 S Handily inside	McSweeney, SheilaClock, Comntator[7]
11- 2[12] 3-8	F 37.49 56 5 5 4	3 3[14]	38.44	25.10 S On inside	Downing, Diamond'sAstro, LisaLove
10-26[2s] 3-8	F 38.49 56 3 7 4	3 3[5]	38.82	Good effort rail	TrimLass, Mr.McSweeney, Rustylbe[7]
(RACES BELOW WERE RUN AT SEABROOK)					
10-20[5x] 5-16	F 30.77 56 2 2 1[2]	1[5] 1[31]	30.77	.50 A Early command	Groaned, PepperPrinter, BrassyGold
10-15[10] 5-16	F 31.12 55 2 1 1[1]	1[4] 1[4]	31.12	.90 A Going away	L.A.Volare, DandyDart, JulyJan[7]
10-12[1s] 5-16	F 30.75 55½ 5 2 1[1]	1[1] 1[3]	30.75	Drawing away	Printer'sJud, DandyDart, FlashPrinter
10- 5[1s] 5-16	F 30.70 57 8 3 1[1½]	1[3] 1[5]	30.70	Brisk pace	SwedeRenick, T'sReddy, NiceGent
9- 3[10] YC	F 39.65 57 3 2 5	5 4[7½]	40.20	1.50 A Checked in lead	Lky.Twosp't, Picadil.Pete, Cor.Winnie

WIN	PLACE	SHOW		PLACE	SHOW		SHOW

QUINIELA

$2 TRIFECTA

Closing Night – November 30th

Blazing Red-1978

Blazing Red-1978

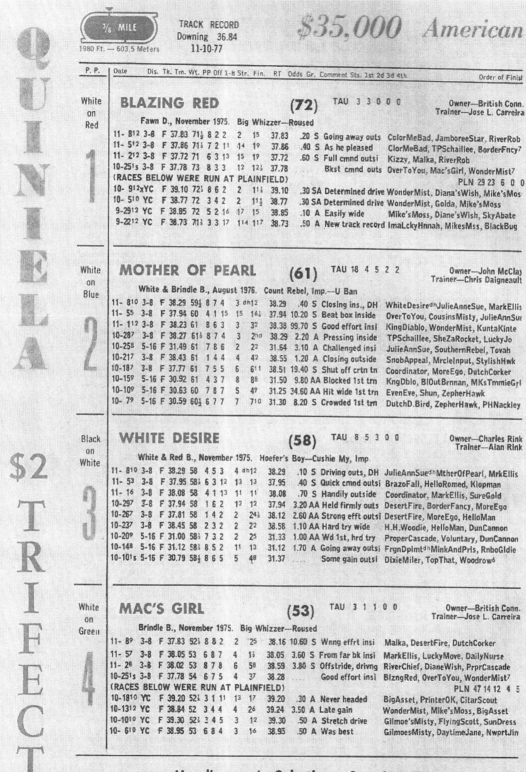

Blazing Red-1978

Greyhound Derby

TWELFTH RACE (12)

GRADE S-AA

P. P	Date	Dis. Tk. Tm. Wt. PP Off 1-8 Str. Fin.	RT Odds Gr. Comment Sts. 1st 2d 3d 4th	Order of Finish

Red on Black

5

COORDINATOR (72) TAU 19 4 3 3 5   Owner—Francis Fulginiti Trainer—Francis Fulginiti, Jr.

Brindle D., April 1976. Count Rebel, Imp.—Lackluster

11- 8¹¹	3-8 F 38.28 .72 5 4 3	3 1²	38.28 1.30 S	Lng drive outsi	SultrySister, TPSchaillee, HeloRomed
11- 5⁸	3-8 F 38.09 72½ 8 2 1²	1² 1³	38.09 1.70 S	Erly cntrl outsi	KuntaKinte, RNikie, JamboreeStar
11- 1⁶	3-8 F 38.08 72 3 2 3	4 2¹	38.16 4.30 S	Late rush outsi	WhiteDesire, MarkEllis, SureGold
10-28⁵	5-16 F 31.17 71½ 5 5 8	7 5⁸	31.72 6.20 AA	Jammed 1st turn	HonorCode, SteelBridge, CheerflLady
10-21¹²	3-8 F 37.48 71 4 2 6	7 4¹⁵	38.55 7.30 S	Late dri outsi	DesertFire, KingDiablo, MoreEgo
10-18⁷	3-8 F 37.77 71 3 1 1³	1² 15¹	37.77 12.70 S	Nvr headed outs	MoreEgo, DutchCorker, DesertFire
10-15⁵	3-8 F 38.29 70½ 4 4 6	5 2ⁿˢ	38.30 2.20 A	Strng rush outsi	Ard, Tovah, SheZaRocket
10-12¹²	3-8 F 37.54 70 8 7 7	6 3⁹	38.16 3.90 A	Late rush wide	DesertFire, ClrgnsOwen, SheZaRocket
10- 7⁷	3-8 F 37.89 70 4 3 6	5 3²	38.03 2.20 A	Closing fast outsi	MantecaCinder, LuckyFind, Ard
10- 4¹⁰	5-16 F 30.98 70½ 3 7 7	7 5¹¹	31.72 16.50 AA	Forced out bkstr	Ashmont, RealLikeable, NumbersUp

Black on Yellow

6

MALKA (66) TAU 3 2 0 1 0   Owner—Mike Castellani, Inc. Trainer—Stanley Morrill

Red B., January 1976. Yankee Clipper—Impeccable, Imp.

11- 8⁹	3-8 F 37.83 66 1 7 4	3 1⁵	37.83 .90 S	Pulling away ots	Mac'sGirl, DesertFire, DutchCorker
11- 5⁶	3-8 F 37.95 66 4 6 7	4 1⁵	37.95 .80 S	Pwrful dry outs	ThndrStrk, RiverChief, SSSlinkySlew
11- 2¹²	3-8 F 37.72 65½ 4 7 7	6 3¹¹	38.50 1.80 S	Forced out early	BlazingRed, Kizzy, RiverRob
10-27¹s	3-8 F 37.85 66 7 4 4	2 14½	37.85	Pulling awy outsi	ColorMeBad, JmbreeStar, SltrySistr⁴

(RACES BELOW WERE RUN AT WONDERLAND) WON 8 4 3 0 0

10-21¹¹	RC F 39.97 64½ 8 8 8	6 2ⁿˢ	39.98 1.00 A	Blocked, cmng on	SultrySister, SilentSea, RumorFlash
10-16²s	5-16 F 30.81 66 2 3 4	3 2²	30.97	Closed gap wide	Nrly.Nrml., Strvn.Artist, Cmron.Daisy⁵
10- 6¹s	5-16 F 31.08 66½ 7 5 3	3 3³	31.34	Even effort	GB'sMatthew, DromlaraHino, RedRita⁷
6- 3¹²	WC F 44.76 65 2 8 6	4 2³½	45.02 .30 SA	Lacked early spd	HiddenPower, Ardent, BeautySpec
5-30¹¹	WC F 44.94 64 8 2 4	2 1¹½	44.94 .30 SA	Up on inside	Tatania, Erratic, LarkSong

Black, Green, White,

7

KING DIABLO (72) TAU 22 13 5 2 1   Owner—Charles Rink Trainer—Alan Rink

Red D., August 1976. Stretch—Laura Leads

11- 8¹²	3-8 F 37.83 72 7 7 4	5 7⁹½	38.50 5.60 S	Tiring outside	BlazingRed, ClorMeBad, JambreeStar
11- 5¹⁰	3-8 F 38.11 72 1 3 3	1⁴ 1³	38.11 .90 S	Bkstr cmnd outsi	Diane'sWish, SultrySister, RiverRob
11- 1¹²	3-8 F 38.23 72 4 2 2	2 1½	38.23 3.00 S	Strong drive outs	WndrMist, MothrOfPearl, KuntaKinte
10-29⁵	5-16 F 31.17 72 6 6 5	3 1²	31.17 .70 AA	Plling away outs	P.D.Q.Jupiter, LeadOn, Contoe
10-26⁹	5-16 F 30.85 71½ 8 8 4	3 3⁴	31.12 .60 AA	Stdy gain outsi	PrprCscde, FrgnDiplomat, LilRedLnzy
10-21¹²	3-8 F 37.48 71½ 1 3 2	2 2⁶	37.90 1.30 S	Strng efft outsi	DesertFire, MoreEgo, Coordinator
10-18¹²	3-8 F 37.86 72 1 5 4	4 2⁵	38.21 1.00 S	Steady gain outs	BorderFancy, JulieAnnSue, SpecBond
10-15⁹	5-16 F 30.92 71½ 2 4 4	4 1²	30.92 1.40 AA	Strong rush wi	BailOutBrennan, MKsTmmieGrl, Prfme
10-12⁷	3-8 F 37.55 71½ 1 5 6	5 4⁸	38.10 .40 AA	Even effort outsi	BorderFancy, MoreEgo, DutchCorker
10- 9⁷	3-8 F 37.92 71½ 5 6 1¹	1² 1⁴	37.92 1.20 AA	Going away outsi	CosAmu, S&SSlinkySlew, DesertFire

White Black, Yellow

8

COLOR ME BAD (68) TAU 3 1 2 0 0   Owner—Christine Daigneault Trainer—Don Daigneault

Brindle D., April 1976. S.S. Jeno—Little One

11- 8¹²	3-8 F 37.83 68 1 1 1¹	1ⁿs 2⁵	38.17 6.30 S	Outfinished insi	BlazingRed, JamboreeStar, RiverRob
11- 5¹²	3-8 F 37.86 66½ 2 5 3	3 2⁹	38.47 2.00 S	Driving inside	BlazingRed, TPSchaillee, BorderFncy⁷
11- 1¹⁰	3-8 F 37.71 67 4 1 1⁴	1⁷ 1¹¹	37.71 2.90 S	Box to wire ins	CosAmu, RomanBest, SSSlinkySlew
10-27¹s	3-8 F 37.85 68 5 3 2	1² 2⅘	38.16	Outfinished insi	Malka, JamboreeStar, SltrySister⁴
10-23¹s	3-8 F 38.29 68½ 5 7 2	2 3¹	38.34	Forced pace insi	BeeQuick, JamboreeStar, MsSwftSailr

(RACES BELOW WERE RUN AT WONDERLAND) WON 19 6 5 2 0

10-19¹¹	RC F 39.71 67 8 5 3	3 3⁵	40.12 3.10 A	Raced inside	SuisseCredit, WiseSlew, FirstDebnture
10-13¹⁰	TC F 39.87 67 7 7 7	8 8¹³	40.85 .60	No factor	JerseyJane, MajorMoon, Willowette

(RACES BELOW WERE RUN AT TOPSFIELD) TOP 1 0 0 0 0

10- 3¹¹	RC F 39.58 67 5 7 8	8 8⁹½	40.37 2.10 A	Collided turn	SultrySister, Prance, WaxDoll

WIN	PLACE	SHOW		PLACE	SHOW	SHOW

Closing Night – November 30th

QUINIELA

$2

TRIFECTA

Texas Brass-1979

**JOSEPH M. LINSEY
...and the Trophy**

THE MAN WHO
STARTED IT ALL

Super purses for Greyhound races in the United States were unheard of until Joe Linsey came up with his idea of having a race for the very best in the World, his race of races, the American Greyhound Derby. It has become the true showcase for the best of the best, as you can see for yourself tonight. It is proper that the Joseph M. Linsey trophy be given to the Champ.

Texas Brass-1979

¼ MILE
1980 Ft. — 603.5 Meters

TRACK RECORD
Downing 36.84
11-10-77

$35,000 America...

P. P.	Date	Dis. Tk. Tm. Wt. PP Off 1-8 Str. Fin.	RT Odds Gr. Comment Sts. 1st 2d 3d 4th	Order of F...

White on Red

1

TEXAS BRASS (73) TAU 22 9 9 2 0
Owner—Otto Ma...
Trainer—Paul Be...

Red D., August 1976. Ebony Wall, Imp.—Gertie Nebo

11- 7¹⁰ 3-8 F 38.19 71 4 7 6 3 3²½ 38.37 .90 S Blkd erly, drvng	WinWthWndy, OkldArst, Ldr...
11- 4¹⁰ 3-8 F 37.83 71½ 8 7 3 13 15½ 37.83 2.40 S Bkstr cmnd mdtr	NightBloom, KingAlfrd, ND...
11- 1¹² 3-8 F 38.23 71½ 1 3 2 12 15 38.23 2.60 S Late cmnd insi	DeviousLdy, PierRovr, Cptn...
10-27¹⁰ 5-16 F 31.49 72 8 5 6 6 2⁵½ 31.87 1.20 AA Dspt tble 1st tn	MsStrdeOnBy, BrzoPrya, Pl...
10-23⁹ 5-16 F 31.22 72 4 4 4 4 3⁴ 31.49 1.10 AA Blkd wd, drvng	MsStrdOnBy, SrfrSpcl, Plcnt...
10-19⁷ₓ 3-8 F 38.01 71½ 1 4 2 12 2³ 38.20 1.30 AA Outfinishd mdtk	OkldArrst, SfreSpcl, J.A.M.P...
10-13⁹ 5-16 F 30.81 72 7 6 8 8 5⁸ 31.36 1.30 AA Shut off 1sb tn	EarlyFctr, FatDmnck, PlcnK...
10-10⁹ₓ 5-16 F 31.55 71½ 7 4 2 2 2² 31.70 1.40 AA Good effort mdtk	EarlyFactr, GdTmKlly, CnT...
10- 6⁹ 5-16 F 30.99 72 2 5 3 2 2¹ 31.06 .EC AA Closing fast insi	EarlyFactr, PelicnKing, NeroHero...
10- 3¹⁰ₓ5-16 F 31.05 72 5 2 1ʰᵈ 12 14 31.05 1.60 AA Pulling awy mdtk 9.52 RmbInGuy, ShortBolt, LttieL...

White on Blue

2

COLOR ME BAD (68) TAU 19 6 2 0 2
Owner—Christine Daign...
Trainer—Donald Daign...

Brindle D., April 1976. S.S. Jeno—Little One

11- 7⁶ 3-8 F 38.24 67 3 2 1² 12 1ʰᵈ 38.24 2.00 S Just lasted insi	MoreEgo, CsnsTrbl, SndyH...
11- 4⁵ 3-8 F 38.05 67 8 2 1³ 15 14½ 38.05 4.09 S Early cntrl insi	MteeSndhr, LdgfldSny, LteL...
10-31¹² 3-8 F 38.47 68 5 2 8 8 8¹⁵ 39.51 2.10 S Frcd wd fr str	WinWithWill, Zig, NeroHere...
10-27⁷ 3-8 F 38.66 67½ 6 2 13 14 2ⁿᵏ 38.69 3.10 AA Long lead inside	Blessed, OklndArrest, PierR...
10-23⁷ 3-8 F 38.15 67 6 7 6 7 8¹⁵ 39.19 2.80 AA Crd crtn trn	OklndArrst, DtchCrkr, JAMP...
10-16⁷ 3-8 F 38.14 67 3 3 5 6 7¹⁵ 39.22 1.50 AA Weakened insi	GnaGe, LdgfldSny, S&SSIk...
10-13⁷ 3-8 F 37.83 67 5 1 1³ 12 1½ 37.83 2.50 AA Held gamly insi	S&SSInkySlw, ElsvHze, BnB...
10- 8¹² 3-8 F 38.61 67 5 2 2 5 8⁹ 39.22 3.80 S Weakened inside	JackRosch, DtchCorker, Mo...
10- 5⁷ₓ 3-8 F 37.75 67½ 2 1 14 13 1¹ 31.75 5.00 AA Nver headed insl	MoreEgo, J.A.M.Poppy, Cla...
9-30⁷ₓ 3-8 F 37.96 68 3 1 16 16 1⁹ 37.96 2.30 A Box to wire insi	DtchBrbB, JckRsch, MteeS...

Black on White

3

STEAM TRAIN (71) TAU 7 3 0 2 1
Owner—Stephen V...
Trainer—John S...

Light Brindle D., March 1977. B. Whiz—Leah J.

11- 7⁴ 3-8 F 37.99 70 5 1 1² 15 16¹ 37.99 5.10 S Box to wre outsi	S&SSInkySlw, CptnPte, Nr...
11- 4⁶ 3-8 F 37.71 70½ 6 2 4 5 4¹¹ 38.46 7.30 S Drftd wd frt str	LegActn, NghtenGale, Elsv...
11- 1⁶ 3-8 F 38.33 70 5 1 5 3 1¹½ 38.33 11.80 S Strng dri outsi	WinWithWndy, Zaggy, Rc...
10-26²ˢ 5-16 F 31.88 72½ 5 2 8 8 5¹⁶ 32.99 .... Never prom mdtk	ECsSlvr, ClssicJ, SprrwFl...
10- 19ₓ 5-16 F 31.15 69½ 4 7 8 8 8¹² 32.00 5.20 AA No factor outsi	MyTracy, DixieMan, SueS...
9-25⁵ₓ 5-16 F 30.95 70 4 2 6 6 3⁶ 31.37 6.80 AA Late surge mdtr	DoFreDke, FatDmnck, Str...
9-22⁶ₓ 5-16 S 32.06 71½ 4 2 4 4 3⁵½ 32.45 5.20 AA Closing wide	Condoned, QuckBrny, Ldgf...
9-18¹ₓ 5-16 F 31.58 71 5 7 3 4 1¹ 31.58 6.80 A Out 1st, driving	KittnHawk, DoltBandit, Ho...
9-14²ˢ 5-16 F 31.67 71 7 6 5 3 1² 31.67 .... Str drive mdtrk	Bird'sEye, Silt, PeachyGla...

White on Green

4

WIN WITH WILL (61) TAU 3 1 2 0 0
Owner—Brad Coc...
Trainer—Brad Coc...

Brindle D., May 1977. Friend Westy—Mary E.

11- 7⁸ 3-8 F 38.18 60½ 5 1 14 14 2² 38.31 1.30 S Caught late insi	LsleRedToy, Zaggy, Rocky...
11- 4⁹ 3-8 F 37.63 60 8 1 2 2 2¹¹ 38.39 1.20 S Good effort insi	MFAngel, RockyKnox, Sndy...
10-31¹² 3-8 F 38.47 60½ 7 1 1³ 16 1ʰᵈ 38.47 1.30 S Lastd gamly insi	Zig, NeroHero, LadyFlyer
10-28¹ˢ 3-8 F 38.53 61 5 1 1⁷ 16 16½ 38.53 .... Box to wire insi	LsliesRdTy, LndGddss, Leg...

(RACES BELOW WERE RUN AT BISCAYNE)   BIS 13 4 3...

10-20⁹ BC F 33.55 60 7 8 6 7 6⁸½ 34.14 10.50 A No mishaps	Millie'sSpecial, HyLorded, Count...
10-17¹⁰ BC F 33.40 60 5 3 3 3 3¹½ 33.48 6.50 A Bumped slt turn	DocMnshadow, MddsBddy, Millie...
10-13⁶ BC F 33.69 61 1 2 2 2 2² 33.84 2.30 A Fllwed pace insi	DocMnshdow, SteveWhz, Wstwrd...
10-10⁶ BC F 33.69 61 6 1 14 14 14 33.30 .90 A All the way insi	WstwrdWind, KCBernese, MarK...
10- 5¹² BC F 33.19 61 7 2 7 7 6¹⁰ 33.87 14.50 SA Close qtrs early	SteveWhiz, BlackBnnie, DocsMn...

Handicapper's Selections 5 — 1 — 3

38th BLUE RIBBON STAK...

Texas Brass-1979

reyhound Derby   **TWELFTH RACE (12)**

GRADE S-AA

	Dis. Tk. Tm. Wt. PP Off 1-8 Str. Fin.	RT	Odds Gr. Comment Sts. 1st 2d 3d 4th	Order of Finish

NIGHT BLOOM   **(57)**   TAU 3 2 1 0 0   Owner—H. R. Castellani / Trainer—Norman Penny

Brindle B., April 1977. Carry On—Cooladine Shara, Imp.

	Dis	Tk	Tm	Wt	PP	Off 1-8	Str	Fin	RT	Odds	Gr	Comment	1st 2d 3d 4th
11-712	3-8	F	38.16	56½	6	4 2	2	1nk	38.16	2.10	S	Just up mdtrk	Zig, DeviousLady, MiteeSandbar
11-410	3-8	F	37.83	57	7	8 7	4	25½	38.22	1.40	S	Stdy gn mdtrk	TexasBrss, KingAlfrd, NDBannon
11-110	3-8	F	38.35	58	2	5 4	3	12½	38.35	.90	S	Drwng away insi	Devoneyeda, JllyJmbo, NghtnGle
11-253s	3-8	F	38.48	57	3	1 14	15	17½	38.48	....		Box to wire insi	SndwnRhndo, Zaggy, CFsNlsn5

(RACES BELOW WERE RUN AT WONDERLAND)   WON 51 14 9 10 7

11-2512	RC	F	39.31	57½	8	5 2	3	25½	39.69	3.00	A	Early factor	GoldieGiver, SelfService, CousnsTrbl
11-137	RC	F	39.32	57	6	5 5	4	34½	39.65	3.30	A	Some wide	PrntrPddy, CsnsTrouble, DeviousLady
11-1011	RC	F	39.31	57	2	1 13	11	12	39.31	1.30	A	Beat the box	Kochia, PrntrPddy, RssprPass
11-812	RC	F	39.45	56½	7	8 6	6	56	38.89	1.50	A	Pinched bk brk	GB'sTwoBoy, RossportPass, PrntrPddy
8-2512	RC	F	39.12	56½	1	6 2	2	27	39.62	.80	A	Followed pace	DeviousLady, IRsJoshua, TooMuch

GUNNERY BUCK   **(72)**   TAU 3 1 1 0 0   Owner—R.J. Barber / Trainer—Bob Gluck

White & Brindle D., January 1977. President Day—Rocking Ronda

11-74	3-8	F	37.99	72	8	8 8	7	816	39.10	1.10	S	No factor insi	StmTrn, S&SSInkySlw, CptnPte
11-412	3-8	F	38.40	72½	2	1 5		38.40	2.30	S	Drwng away insi	SueShe, ElusiveHaze, ShortyT
11-3110	3-8	F	38.49	70	11	2 3	2	21	38.57	2.10	S	Pressing inside	SndyHope, MoreEgo, SomeMona
11-222s	3-8	F	38.52	71½	1	2 0	1hd	13½	38.52	....		Plling away insi	TM'sQuickStep, CashWay3

(RACES BELOW WERE RUN AT PENSACOLA)   PEN 1 1 0 0

9-2310xNC	F	30.98	71	5	3 2	11	12	30.98	1.00		Driving, wide	DiggedyDag, Welty, DutyBound
9-172s	NC	F	30.93	71	2	2 4	2	22½	31.11	....		Despite trbl brk	EastrnLeadr, RstlsMike, KpOnSmiln

LESLIE'S RED TOY   **(62)**   TAU 3 2 0 0 0   Owner—Frederick Tatro / Trainer—Kenneth Tatro

Red B., July 1977. Big Whizzer—Kitty's Kandi

11-74	3-8	F	38.18	61	3	2 2	2	12	38.18	4.40	S	Up near wr insf	WinWithWill, Zaggy, RckyKnox
11-43	3-8	F	38.18	61½	2	1 3	6	64½	39.50	3.20	S	Bmpd crin turn	BnBnDart, SSZee, WinWithWndy
11-313	3-8	F	38.29	62	3	2 13	11½	1ns	38.29	13.50	S	Just lstd mdtrk	OklndArrst, LndGdss, BnBnBnDt
11-254s	3-8	F	38.53	62	7	3 2	2	26½	38.98	....		Good effort insf	WnWthWll, LndGddss, LegActn4

(RACES BELOW WERE RUN AT SOUTHLAND)   SOU 11 2 3 0

11-2010	AC	F	32.56	61	2	6 6	6	44½	32.89	32.20	A	Slight gain	PollyFancy, WilcffAlma, McMoonmist
11-512	AC	F	32.67	60	3	7 7	7	77	33.19	12.80	A	Wide coil 1st trn	GHTfany, MCSpmaster, Fadra
9-15	AC	F	32.86	60	3	5 7	7	75½	33.24	5.20	A	No mishaps	Bravery, MCSpmaster, KAAngD
11-6x	AC	F	32.78	60	3	3 2	2	11	32.78	2.00	B	Driving outside	BubJones, PiHawk, GoldDelta
1-234	AC	F	32.68	60	2	2 2	2	2hd	32.70	8.00	B	Pressing winner	MrPcJerry, Rebellion, CarMiss

WIN WITH WENDY   **(61)**   TAU 3 1 1 1 0   Owner—Brad Cochrane / Trainer—Brad Cochrane

Red Fawn B., May 1977. Friend Westy—Mary E.

11-710	3-8	F	38.19	61	1	1 13	15	11	38.19	7.90	S	Lsted gamly insi	OklndArrst, TexsBrss, LadyFlyer
11-41	3-8	F	38.18	61½	5	2 1hd	13	31½	38.28	3.60	S	Overtaken insi	BonBonDart, SSZee, LoneClone
11-14	3-8	F	38.33	61½	1	4 13	13	21½	38.44	2.10	S	Caught late insi	StmTrn, Zaggy, RckyKnox
11-254s	3-8	F	38.74	61	5	1 2	12	23	38.96	....		Outfinished insi	MFAngel, BlueMane, ShortyT5

(RACES BELOW WERE RUN AT BISCAYNE)   BIS 11 3 1 2

10-134	BC	F	33.78	61½	3	5 3	2	31½	33.86	2.20	A	Outfinished insi	Locomotor, MC'sGypsyJinx, JesikaS.
10-910	BC	F	33.74	61½	8	2 11	12	1ns	33.74	12.30	TA	Held gamely, insi	Doc'sMellowOne, SandyTNT, DETerrie
10-12	BC	F	33.79	62	5	7 2	13	12½	33.79	4.60	B	Easy win, inside	DesertFire, LuckyBones, Perfumed
10-29	BC	F	33.41	61½	3	5 7	6	611	34.15	23.80	A	Bumped 1st trn	DocMoonshadow, SLTanya, MddsBddy
10-51	BC	F	33.53	61	1	5 3	5	54½	33.82	12.60	SA	No mishaps	WiseSasha, LuckyBones, DesertFire

PLACE	· SHOW	PLACE	SHOW	SHOW

Sunday Matinee — December 16

QUINIELA   **$2**   **TRIFECTA**

Position-1980

American Greyhound Derby Tradition

The American Greyhound Derby is one of the most traditional stake races in the country. Over the year the greyhounds that have graced the winner's circle of this prestigious event, let alone the also rans and non-derby finalists, are among the sports all time greats.

Just how great were those that triumphed? Let's take a look. At present, 5 winners have been installed into the Greyhound Hall of Fame, one earned the Rural Rube Award winner (nation's best sprinter), three were given the Flashy Sir Award (nation's best distance runner), 13 winners were selected to the All-American Team of which 3 captained, and last year's winner was selected as the World's top middle distance runner. Here they are:

ALL AMERICAN		HALL OF FAME	
Year won	Greyhound	Year won	Greyhound
1986	Prince Proper**	1977	Downing
1985	Dutch Bahama	1958	Feldcrest
1984	Dutch Bahama *	1952	On The Line
1982	Mr. Wizard	1950-51	Real Huntsman
1980	Position	1949	Oklahoman
1978	Blazing Red		
1977	Downing *		Flashy Sir
1976	P.L. Greer *	1984	Dutch Bahama
1974	Abella	1978	Blazing Red
1969	Lucky Bannon	1976	P.L. Greer
Greer 1967	Xandra		
1966	Golden In		Rural Rube
1963 (first year)	Thermal	1977	Downing

'All American Captain
**All World Mid Distance Greyhound.

Devon Unocopy-1981

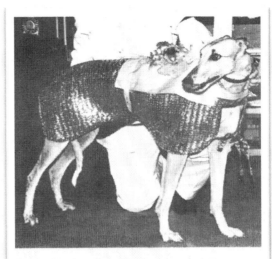

to the winner: a Sequin
topcoat--and Orchids!

Every Derby winner gets a blanket of Sequins and
Orchids--plus $20,000, of course. Devon Unocopy, last
year's winner, loved the loot, especially because so
few gave him a shot at winning. The Payoff: $81.60.

The year of the LONGSHOT

Very few people gave Devon Unocopy much of a
chance to win the Derby in 1981, but the Tony
Salpietro trained runner finished on top to pay
$81.60. That's Tony standing behind the trophy with
Derby founder Joe Linsey. The gold sequin blanket
and orchids on Devon Unocopy is standard fare for
the Derby.

Devon Unocopy-1981

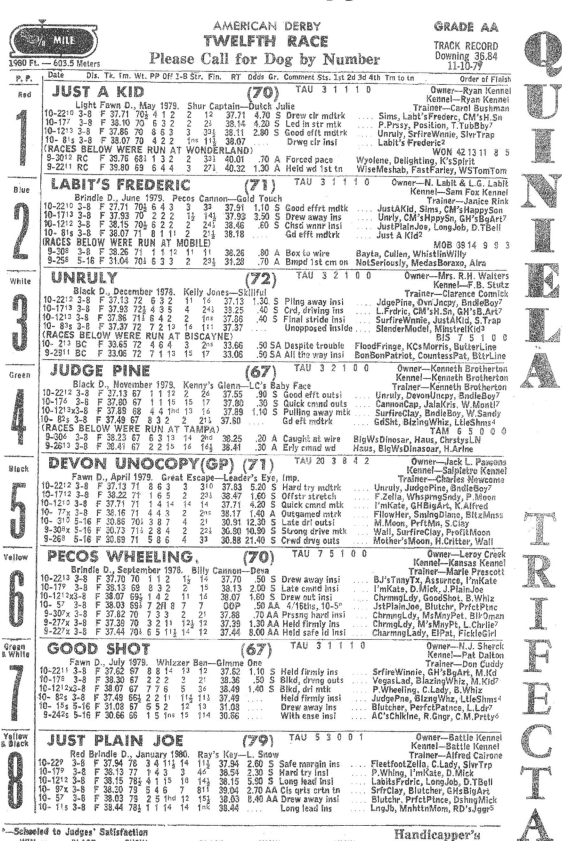

The Derby moves to its new home at Raynham Park located in Raynham, Ma.

The Raynham Years
(1982-1985)

Mr Wizard-1982

and NOW...

**Taunton Greyhound
proudly presents**
America's most prestigious
Greyhound race

Tonight we come to the Grand Finale of the $350,000 Northeast Triple Crown, a series of Super Purse Stakes races that started at Lincoln, R. I., moved down to Wheeling, W. Virginia, and, fittingly, winds up at the Taunton meet where big Greyhound purses got their start.

This final leg, The American Greyhound Derby, is the Granddaddy of all Stakes races. It carries a purse of $35,000, and provides a $1,000 payoff to even the last place finisher, a reward for surviving the gruelling Qualifying rounds to make the Championship Final.

Classic Kennel's Stormy Encounter won the first race at Lincoln, and John Seastrom's Mr Wizard prevailed at Wheeling, breaking the track record while winning. Obviously, there's no way of one Greyhound winning all three Finals. But if one Greyhound had won all three Legs of the series, that Greyhound would have received a bonus of $200,000, the biggest bonus offering in Greyhound racing.

This Northeast Triple Crown is a tough assignment for even the best of Greyhounds. Many a favored Greyhound has been defeated in the rough competition over the demanding 3/8th mile distance. Many kennels have tried to bring along outstanding Sprinters to the point where they could race the extra distance of the 3/8th, and many have been unable to handle the added yardage. There also have been a number of 7/16th Marathon standouts who have tried to win over the Northeast distance. Few have been successful. The 7/16th distance may require more endurance, but the 3/8th requires a combination of speed and endurance. Greyhound trainers will tell you it's the toughest distance in Greyhound racing because it's too long for the majority of Greyhounds, who are 5/16th Sprinters, and not long enough for the precious few Greyhounds who seem to be able to run forever, but hardly at the lightning-like speeds of the Sprinters.

So tonight you are witnessing perhaps the truest test of the modern Greyhound. Speed and stamina are both necessary to win. And with such a select field, racing luck is a major factor. Greyhounds of this calibre can shake off a slight bump over the distance, but if they are to put their speed and stamina to the best use, they cannot get tangled up for very long.

The three tracks that sponsor this series, Lincoln, Wheeling and Taunton, are delighted to have been able to bring you so many outstanding Greyhounds.

May you be successful in selecting the best of all of them this evening.

Happy Superfecta!

Mr Wizard-1982

RACE 12 HOW THEY HAVE BEEN RACING OF LATE

1 RED

Stingy Star 37.96 [A B] (58)

TAU 20 10 1 5 1 Owner:Marguerite Reist
RAY 10 1 3 1 0 Ken'l:Otto Mamino
Train:Jim Prescott

White Brindle B., March 1980. Whizzer Ben--Telethon

Race	Dis	TC	Time	Wt	B	O	1/8	St	Fin	RunTm	Odds	Gd	How Performed	Opponents' Finish Order 10/23^{12}
10/20^{5}	3/8	F	38.48	58	2	7	6	5	3^{4}	38.74	0.70	SA	Off Slow	BblngButy MsHarttrb SeaKsdGrl^{7}
10/16^{3}	3/8	F	38.56	58	8	1	1^{2}	1^{4}	1^{3}	38.56	0.60	SA	All The Way Ins	JockosJsn JamsHugh MercQueen^{7}
10/12^{5}	3/8	F	38.37	59	2	1	3	2	1^{3}	38.37	10.60	SA	Strch Drive Ins	Nana Gert MothsMoon TorchSong
10/ 3^{11}x	3/8	F	37.96	57	5	1	1^{7}	1^{8}	1^{5}	37.96	7.50	A	All The Way Ins	MsHarttrb GrgsProft PacePrncr
9/27^{11}	3/8	F	38.30	58	8	1	2	1^{2}	1$^{3\frac{1}{2}}$	38.30	2.30	A	Late Comm Ins	BlueRaven PipsAmbDk TenderTot
9/21^{12}	3/8	F	38.48	57	2	4	6	5	3^{2}	38.60	1.70	A	No Room Crt Trn	LteLteMry SunPartnr BlueRaven
9/17^{11}	3/8	F	38.93	57½	8	4	7	7	6^{6}	39.36	0.90	A	Dropped Bk Erly	TsIdluvta PipsAmbDk PssnPansy

2 BLUE

Mr Wizard 38.12 [A A] (73)

TAU 3 2 1 0 0 Owner:John Seastrom
Ken'l:John Seastrom
Train:James Bagley

Brindle D., December 1979. Tuf Miler--JM's Mod C

10/20^{10}	3/8	F	38.60	72¼	4	1	3	2	1^{6}	38.60	0.40	SA	Going Away Mdtk	TorchSong Firing RGsMahogy
10/16^{11}	3/8	F	38.71	72¼	4	3	3	3	2^{2}	38.85	0.50	SA	No Room Turns	SunPartnr MothsMoon NancyLttl
10/13^{11}	3/8	F	38.12	72	5	1	1^{3}	1^{3}	1^{3}	38.12	3.80	SA	Never Headed Md	NsIrshStu Vidalia AlpneRngr
10/ 9^{6}s	3/8	M	38.92	73	1	1	1^{7}	1^{6}	1$^{4\frac{1}{2}}$	38.92	. . .		All The Way Ins	KipKsJese NsIrshStu SwetAsHny^{5}
[Races Below were run at Wheeling Downs]														WD 12 6 3 0 0
10/ 1^{11}	K	F	37.98	73½	1	1	1^{3}	1^{3}	1^{3}	37.98	0.90	A	New Track Recrd	SaucyTbsc MercryQue MyProblem
9/28^{11}	K	F	38.67	74	8	6	5	4	4^{5}	39.04	0.80	A	Bumped Up Some	SwetAsHny KsMoon LadyLloyd

3 WHITE

Torch Song 38.93 [A A] (55)

TAU 3 1 1 0 1 Owner:Franklin M. Pike
Ken'l:Frank Pike
Train:CarleenBoutsianis

Red Brindle B., December 1979. Electric Torch--Hi Bail

10/20^{10}	3/8	F	38.60	53	3	6	4	4	2^{6}	39.01	16.10	SA	Bpd Crt Tn,Drvn	Mr Wizard Firing RGsMahogy
10/16^{8}	3/8	F	38.93	54	3	7	2	2	1ns	38.93	3.20	SA	Final Strde Out	RorngRook HubrtDecn SndyKlutz^{7}
10/12^{5}	3/8	F	38.37	53	6	3	4	3	4$^{4\frac{1}{2}}$	38.68	9.20	SA	Good Efft Outs	StingyStr Nana Gert MothsMoon
10/ 9^{5}s	3/8	M	39.19	55	8	4	4	4	4^{11}	39.98	. . .		Coll Str Turn	MercQueen RorngRook AlpneRngr^{5}
[Races Below were run at Wonderland]														WON 45 6 8 6 4
10/ 1^{12}	R	F	40.35	53	8	4	3	3	2$^{8\frac{1}{2}}$	40.94	15.40	A	Some Wide	GlmngJula EnglsLdy FoxyRed
9/22^{10}	R	F	39.16	53	7	7	5	3	2^{8}	39.74	22.60	A	Some Wide	IjspInwnr Firing EnglshLdy

4 GREEN

Bubbling Beauty 38.48 [A A] (59)

TAU 3 1 1 1 0 Owner:E & R Beckner
Ken'l:North Shore
Train:Stan Morrill

Brindle B., April 1980. K's Flak--Jolly Reid

10/20^{5}	3/8	F	38.48	58½	7	4	3	2	1^{2}	38.48	2.40	SA	Drew Away Mdtrk	MsHarttrb StingyStr SeaKsdGrl^{7}
10/16^{4}	3/8	F	38.25	58	6	1	1^{4}	1hd	3^{7}	38.73	3.40	SA	Tired Strtch In	DerlrDee CsnsStaci Erma Lee
10/12^{9}	3/8	F	38.30	58	8	4	3	3	2^{4}	38.57	6.30	SA	Blkd,Drvng Ins	MsHarttrb SuperBeam P's Legal
10/ 9^{7}s	3/8	M	38.70	59½	7	3	3	2	2^{5}	39.07	. . .		Blocked Early	PecosCrsn HubrtDecn MyCrtLady^{4}
[Races Below were run at Wheeling Downs]														WD 4 0 0 1 0
9/24^{8}	K	F	38.22	58	5	2	8	8	7$^{12\frac{1}{2}}$	39.09	10.60	A	Bump Escape Trn	SaucyTbsc WyldeJone LadyLloyd
9/21^{10}	K	S	38.75	58	5	8	3	4	3$^{4\frac{1}{2}}$	39.07	13.00	A	Game Efft Insde	PecosCrsn MakeMeWnr CbsFPards

5 BLACK

M's Heartthrob 38.30 [A M] (60)

TAU 21 9 3 2 3 Owner:Frank Hanifl
RAY 7 0 3 1 2 Ken'l:Marion Currier
Train:Grace Schaefer

Dark Brindle B., December 1980. Big Ziggy--Holly Jones

10/20^{5}	3/8	F	38.48	59	5	3	1^{5}	1^{4}	2^{2}	38.62	7.10	SA	Outfinished Ins	BblngButy StingyStr SeaKsdGrl^{7}
10/16^{5}	3/8	F	38.51	60	3	2	1^{6}	1^{1}	5^{7}	39.01	1.90	SA	Set Pace Insde	DtchCrolS GrgsProft Vidalia^{6}
10/12^{9}	3/8	F	38.30	59	3	7	2	1^{2}	1^{4}	38.30	7.80	SA	Late Control In	BblngButy SuperBeam P's Legal
10/ 8^{11}	3/8	M	39.67	59	7	8	4	4	5^{11}	40.42	5.80	A	Even Effort	BlueRaven Skiddy SuperBeam
10/ 3^{11}x	3/8	F	37.96	60	3	8	2	2	2^{5}	38.33	3.60	A	Chased Winner	StingyStr GrgsProft PacePrncr
9/27^{7}	5/16	F	31.04	59½	1	1	2	1½	1^{5}	31.04	1.30	A	Going Away Ins	Chekit Frizado MshnsRvng
9/21^{11}x	5/16	F	31.30	59	2	3	6	5	4^{4}	31.55	1.40	A	Blocked 1st Trn	MadsMitns HondoJade Make Good

6 YELLOW

Dutch Carol S 38.51 [A A] (61)

TAU 3 1 1 0 0 Owner:Herb Koerner
Ken'l:Herb Koerner
Train:Richard Calabro

Red Brindle B., February 1981. Sod Buster--Dutch Cappy Ann

10/20^{4}	3/8	F	38.58	60	3	7	5	4	2^{2}	38.72	1.70	SA	Blk, Clsng Ins	MercQueen GrgsProft Denbow
10/16^{5}	3/8	F	38.51	61	5	4	4	3	1$^{1\frac{1}{2}}$	38.51	3.80	SA	Up Between Ldrs	GrgsProft Vidalia TmeStitch^{6}
10/13^{9}	3/8	F	38.24	60½	8	6	8	7	5^{8}	38.80	1.90	SA	Wide Crtn Turn	DerlrDee RGsMahogy Mintage
10/ 9^{4}s	3/8	M	39.12	61	5	5	5	3	2^{2}	39.29	. . .		Off Slow,Closng	TmeStitch LilMsMrkr JamsHugh^{5}
[Races Below were run at Lincoln]														LGP 27 9 7 6 2
10/ 5^{10}	5/16	F	31.48	61	5	6	8	7	3$^{4\frac{1}{2}}$	31.80	1.90	A	Pinchd Back Brk	BeePrdPpr GoldenGns ShandnIke
10/ 1^{10}	5/16	F	31.40	61½	6	7	8	4	1^{2}	31.40	4.80	A	Outran Field	SrfreMona QuenOfWnt BettyBck

7 GREEN & WHITE

Derailer Dee 38.24 [A A] (71)

TAU 3 3 0 0 0 Owner:Karelitz Corp
Ken'l:Karelitz Kennel
Train:Sandra Keevin

White Ticked Brindle D., March 1980. Geronimo Go--Cindy Go

10/20^{8}	3/8	F	38.77	71	2	4	5	3	1^{1}	38.77	0.50	SA	Up On Inside	PecosCrsn NsIrshStu JamsHugh
10/16^{4}	3/8	F	38.25	71	7	3	2	2	1^{5}	38.25	2.00	SA	Drawing Away In	CsnsStaci BblngButy Erma Lee
10/13^{9}	3/8	F	38.24	71	7	4	3	1^{1}	1^{3}	38.24	7.60	SA	Dspt Erly Trbl	RGsMahogy Mintage Firing
10/ 9^{8}s	3/8	M	39.09	71	3	1	1^{2}	1^{4}	1$^{6\frac{1}{2}}$	39.09	. . .		Box To Wire Ins	PenrseSkl BonitaJne JimmyCoin^{5}
[Races Below were run at Wonderland]														WON 44 14 6 5 6
10/ 1^{11}	5/16	F	31.68	71	8	7	6	5	5^{9}	32.33	16.20	A	No Threat	OKTroy RAFleur RghnckGrl
9/28^{12}	5/16	F	32.23	71	2	1	5	3	1^{2}	32.23	1.40	B	Thru On Rail	WllKtchm WallyBll HubrtDecs

8 YELLOW & BLACK

Pecos Cruisin 38.56 [A A] (75)

TAU 3 1 1 0 0 Owner:Kansas Kennel
Ken'l:Kansas
Train:Robin Nash

Red Brindle D., June 1979. Pecos Cannon--Zig Zag, Imp.

10/20^{8}	3/8	F	38.77	74	6	3	2	2	2^{1}	38.84	9.10	SA	Hard Try Outs	DerlrDee NsIrshStu JamsHugh
10/16^{6}	3/8	F	38.56	73½	5	3	1^{2}	1^{3}	1^{1}	38.56	6.90	SA	Hld Sfe Mrgn Md	S R O ScndOpin WillieTln^{7}
10/13^{9}	3/8	F	38.24	73	6	3	6	6	7$^{9\frac{1}{2}}$	38.89	3.60	SA	Crowded Early	DerlrDee RGsMahogy Mintage
10/ 9^{7}s	3/8	M	38.70	58	3	1	1^{8}	1^{10}	1^{5}	38.70	. . .		All The Way	BblngButy HubrtDecn MyCrtLady^{4}
[Races Below were run at Wheeling Downs]														WD 5 1 1 0 0
9/28^{11}	K	F	38.67	74½	7	5	6	7	8$^{13\frac{1}{2}}$	39.62	8.60	A	Bumped 1st Turn	SwetAsHny KsMoon LadyLloyd
9/24^{8}	K	F	38.22	74	7	7	7	6	8^{13}	39.14	4.50	A	Faded Midtrack	SaucyTbsc WyldeJans LadyLloyd

SELECTIONS
7
1
2
3

Anxious Wait-1983

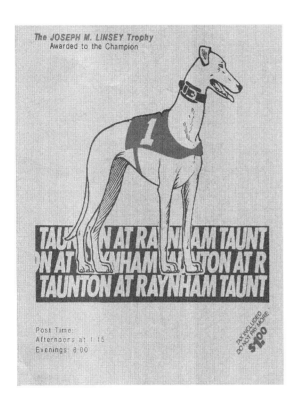

This is the combination that took away last year's Derby loot: Trainer Norman Penny and Derby Champ Anxious Wait.

Anxious Wait-1983

RACE 12	AMERICAN GREYHOUND DERBY SUPERFECTA!! QUINIELA	3/8 Mile Grade S

	Race	Dis	TC Time	Wt	B.O 1/8 St Fin	RunTm	Odds Gd	How Performed	Opponents' Finish Order

Anxious Wait 38.00 [A A] (61) TAU 3 1 0 1 0
OWNER: Mike Castellani KEN'L: Mike Castellani TRAIN: Norm Penny

Blue Brindle B., February 1981. K's Flak—Malka

10/19¹² 3/8	F 38.00	60	5 5 4	1·⁵ 1³	38.00	14.10 SA	Drawing Away Ot	StokerAce JamsHugh FlaksT
10/15⁵ 3/8	F 38.42	61	1 5 5	5 3ᴴᴰ	38.44	4.00 SA	Late Rush Outs	KipKsMnny MstrBckwt Son
10/12¹¹ 3/8	M 39.26	60	4 4 8	7 5⁹	39.87	11.60 SA	Flew 1st Turn	StokerAce BJGntleJm AutmnF
10/ 7⁴ₛ 3/8	F 38.07	61	6 5 5	5 5⁷·⁵	38.59	. . .	Even Efft Outs	JamsHugh PrttyHny Astound

Races below were run at WONDERLAND WON 29⁹ 8 3 5 7

| 10/ 1⁷ | R | F 39.90 | 61 | 5 8 4 | 2 2ᴺˢ | 39.91 | 3.10 A | Winng Efft Outs | SmeoneNew TinyPiece MCEₛ |
| 9/28⁹ W | F 45.14 | 61 | 7 4 4 | 3 4⁷ | 45.64 | 1.80 TA | No Mshps Sm Wd | SmeoneNew MDGayle Che |

RED

Three Steps 38.04 [A A] (59) TAU 3 1 0 1 0
OWNER: Oxley Langford KEN'L: Oxley Langford TRAIN: Harold Roderick

Brindle B., February 1981. Empire—Peaceful Lady

10/19¹² 3/8	F 38.00	60	3 3 7	6 5⁸	38.58	8.40 SA	Even Effort Ins	AnxiousWt StokerAce Jams
10/15¹ 3/8	F 38.04	60	3 4 1³	1⁴ 1⁴·⁵	38.04	8.60 SA	Erly Cmmd Mdtrk	DevotdPrs JockosJsn Extro
10/12¹ 3/8	M 39.20	60	6 4 2	2 3²	39.35	9.40 SA	Good Effort Ins	ExtraHrnt PlsntView Jams
10/ 7⁷ₛ 3/8	F 38.36	60	1 2 2	2 5⁷·⁵	38.89	. . .	Crowded Str Trn	AutumnFns Karlis FlaksTig

Races below were run at BISCAYNE BIS 5 0 1 1 0

| 9/21¹¹ B | F 33.59 | 60 | 4 4 8 | 7 8⁷·⁵ | 34.10 | 9.10 SA | Bumped Early | JagurRckt SouthrDrf RsRong |
| 9/17¹¹ B | F 33.64 | 58⅟ | 1 3 6 | 6 6⁶·⁵ | 34.08 | 9.80 SA | Tired Early | SouthrDrf BLsJacb Spider |

BLUE

LS Black Mike 37.64 [A B] (71) TAU 5 3 0 2 0
OWNER: W Or D Schmitt KEN'L: Herb Koerner TRAIN: Bill Nihan

Black D., August 1980. Jennie's Rouge—LS's Misty Morn

10/19¹¹ 3/8	F 37.83	69	3 4 1⁴	1⁶ 1³	37.83	0.50 SA	Easily Inside	AnnsPrsnt HubrtsDec Reasne
10/15⁷ 3/8	F 37.64	70	2 4 2	1⁴ 1⁶	37.64	1.30 SA	Late Cmmd Ins	BJGntleJm Hicksvill Reasne
10/12⁷ 3/8	M 38.49	70	3 7 3	1² 1⁷	38.49	2.40 SA	Going Away Ins	PrttyHny P's Legal Hubrts
10/ 3¹¹ 3/8	F 38.33	70	5 7 7	4 3⁶·⁵	38.78	1.30 A	Dropped Bk Erly	JockosJsn TakeAShot Sonys
9/28¹¹ 3/8	F 38.75	71	6 8 6	5 3⁴·⁵	39.06	0.70 A	Good Effort Ins	TakeAShot JockosJsn AbvRe
9/23¹ₛ 5/16	F 30.99	72	5 6 3	2 1ᴴᴰ	30.99	. . .	Up At Wire Ins	CrrncyGme DocsZebra Krml

WHITE

Mr Flint 37.88 [A A] (64) TAU 3 1 1 0 0
OWNER: Jimmy G. Brown KEN'L: Triangle Kennel TRAIN: Ted Chotain

Dark Brindle D., November 1981. Mike Whiz—Jerena

10/19⁶ 3/8	F 37.88	63	5 1 1⁴	1⁵ 1¹	37.88	28.60 SA	Box To Wire	StingyStr GigiTrail SeaKsdGrl
10/15¹² 3/8	F 38.24	64	2 1 1²	2 2⁴	38.53	33.20 SA	Set Pace Outs	FoxieMppt Tkyrbstst AntioRos
10/12³ 3/8	M 38.56	63	7 4 4	4 6²²	40.12	16.90 SA	Never Prominent	BblngButy StingyStr FoxieMp
10/ 7⁷ₛ 3/8	F 38.29	64	1 1 1¹	3 3⁸	38.86	. . .	Tiring, Wide	P's Legal GigiTrail SLissaDll

Races below were run at LINCOLN LGP 37 12 7 2 1

| 10/ 4¹⁸ 5/16 | F 31.39 | 64 | 6 4 7 | 7 8⁷·⁵ | 31.92 | 3.30 A | Bmpd Wd 1st TrnSuprmespd | PenrseSkl D |
| 9/30¹⁸ 5/16 | F 31.18 | 64 | 8 3 1² | 1¹ 1·⁵ | 31.18 | 4.20 A | Handily Mdtrk | ShesAHrt KipKsMnny PenrseS |

GREEN

Karlis 37.75 [A A] (64) TAU 3 2 0 1 0
OWNER: Dixieland Kennel KEN'L: Randle Kennel TRAIN: Robert Ackles

Brindle B., October 1981. Firelite—Lace

10/19³ 3/8	F 37.75	63⅟	7 6 3	3 1¹	37.75	0.90 SA	Strch Drv Outs	PrttyHny MellwMusc LasVegsJ
10/15³ 3/8	F 37.78	64	6 2 1⁷	1⁷ 1⁸	37.78	1.20 SA	Erly Cmmd Outs	Tangina PlsntView BySurprse
10/12⁵ 3/8	M 38.84	64	4 7 5	3 3¹·⁵	38.95	2.10 SA	Steady Drv Outs	LasVegsJm Sandak Freedm
10/ 7⁷ₛ 3/8	F 38.36	63⅟	7 5 4	4 2⁸·⁵	38.60	. . .	Late Drive Ins	AutumnFns FlaksTigr BySrprise

Races below were run at WONDERLAND WON 13 6 1 2 1

| 10/ 3⁹ | R | F 39.08 | 63 | 2 6 2 | 1¹ 1² | 39.08 | 2.70 A | Ld On Outside | BySurprse TracysJet GHsAllst |
| 9/27⁶ 5/16 | F 31.22 | 63⅟ | 1 6 5 | 5 4⁸·⁵ | 31.84 | 1.80 A | Carr In Early | GinFah MagnumFrk Big |

BLACK

Flak's Tiger 39.10 [A A] (75) TAU 3 1 0 1 1
OWNER: NCole&RynldsGryhn KEN'L: Fredericks Kennel TRAIN: Richard Childs

Brindle D., May 1981. K's Flak—Cushie Muppet, Imp.

10/19¹² 3/8	F 38.00	75	7 7 3	3 4⁷	38.50	7.70 SA	Blocked For Trn	AnxiousWt StokerAce JamsH
10/15⁴ 3/8	F 37.93	75⅟	7 8 6	5 3⁸	38.51	1.10 SA	Good Effort,Wde	MellwMusc RGsMahgny DocsZe
10/12¹² 3/8	M 39.10	74⅟	8 5 1⁴	1⁵ 1⁶	39.10	4.30 SA	Easily Outside	AntioRosi Milliscnd Reasnett
10/ 7⁷ₛ 3/8	F 38.36	75	8 4 5	5 3⁶	38.76	. . .	Wide Thruout	AutmnFnst Karlis BySurprse

Races below were run at LINCOLN LGP 21 6 8 2 1

| 10/ 1¹² O | F 38.82 | 75 | 4 8 5 | 3 2³ | 39.01 | 2.00 A | Clsd Well Outs | GigTrailr BeePetrPn JJsJocka |
| 9/28¹² O | F 38.95 | 75⅟ | 4 4 4 | 2 1·⁵ | 38.95 | 1.80 A | Drvng To Win | GigTrailr MrrstwnCl RckySlly |

YELLOW

Stingy Star 37.96 [A B] (58) TAU 15 8 2 0 2
OWNER: Marguerite Reist KEN'L: Otto Mamino TRAIN: Jim Smires

White Brindle B., March 1980. Whizzer Ben—Telethon

10/19⁶ 3/8	F 37.88	58⅟	2 2 3	3 2¹	37.94	0.50 SA	Crwd 1st Tn Cls	Mr Flint GigiTrail SeaKsdGrl
10/15⁹ 3/8	F 37.96	58	3 1 1⁴	1⁷ 1⁸·⁵	37.96	0.70 SA	All The Way Ins	Red Rang GigiTrail Milliscnd
10/12³ 3/8	M 38.56	58	4 1 2	2 2²	38.69	1.30 SA	Chased Winner	BblngButy FoxieMppt AnnsPrs
10/ 8¹¹ 3/8	F 38.56	57	4 2 5	2 1⁵	38.56	0.90 A	Going Away Insd	WndrngJny D'Accord Reasnet
10/ 1² 3/8	F 38.15	58	1 2 2	1² 1⁴·⁵	38.15	1.60 A	Late Commnd InsExtraHrnt GrandFind OKActvA
9/24¹¹ₓ 3/8	F 38.03	57⅟	6 8 2	2 1⁵	38.03	2.60 A	Going Away Ins	LeadmnTed LeisreTlk OKActvA
9/17¹¹ 3/8	M 38.49	58	6 6 7	6 6¹¹	39.27	4.10 A	Blkd Crt Turn	BrzoBluCh LeadmnTed Mors

GREEN WHITE

Stoker Ace 37.83 [A A] (72) TAU 3 2 1 0 0
OWNER: Franklin M. Pike KEN'L: Frank Pike TRAIN: CarleenBoutsianis

Black D., November 1981. Dillard—Jamie Lee

10/19¹² 3/8	F 38.00	71	6 8 6	5 2³	38.19	0.90 SA	Off Slowly	AnxiousWt JamsHugh FlaksTig
10/15¹¹ 3/8	F 37.83	72	2 5 3	1² 1⁵	37.83	0.30 SA	Late Cmmn Outs	P's Legal FreedmFor Mintage
10/12¹¹ 3/8	M 39.26	71	5 6 5	5 1²·⁵	39.26	1.10 SA	Str Drvie Out	BJGntleJm AutmnFnst JamsH
10/ 7⁷ₛ 3/8	F 37.94	73	5 4 3	2 1¹¹	37.94	. . .	Going Away Ins	ReblsRtrn ToulnOzzy MstrBck

WON 18 6 7 5 0

| 9/27¹¹ | R | F 39.64 | 73⅟ | 3 8 4 | 3 2²·⁵ | 39.81 | 0.90 A | Slow Start | TnyPcs YkmoGrl ChrlC |
| 9/20⁹ | R | F 39.68 | 73 | 4 8 6 | 5 2³ | 39.87 | 1.70 A | Late Gain | StlnEmbrc BigJC GHslnkS |

YELLOW BLACK

SELECTIONS: 3 8 7 5

Dutch Bahama-1984

TAUNTON GREYHOUND
ASSOCIATION

Proudly
Presents

THE AMERICAN GREYHOUND DERBY
35th running for a purse of $50,000 added
and the Joseph M. Linsey trophy to the winner

raced over 3/8th of a mile
RAYNHAM/TAUNTON
greyhound park
SATURDAY EVENING OCT. 20, 1984

Master of Ceremonies

Derby Founder Linsey handles the chores of a championship presentation while Mrs. Linsey assists Irving Epstein in providing the winner with well-deserved orchids.

Dutch Bahama-1984

35th RUNNING
THE AMERICAN GREYHOUND DERBY

HOMSPUN ROWDY

	37.69 [A A]	(71)	TAU 3 2 0 0 0	OWNER:	JBugnerCPevehouse	
				KEN'L:	John Bugner	
				TRAIN:	John Bugner	

1 RED

White Tckd Red Brndle D., August 1982. Oshkosh Champ--Homspun Anne

10/17⁵	3/8	F 37.69	70½	4 11² 1² 1³	37.69	1.30 SA	Box To Wire	StokerAce Fast Toby APrfctTen
10/13¹³	3/8	F 37.94	70	5 18ᶠ⁻⁸ 8	OOP	1.50 SA	JudgeOK 10/15s	DtchBahma StokerAce Interface
10/10⁹	3/8	F 38.31	70½	5 3 4 2 1³·⁵	38.31	0.60 SA	Drew Away Insde	Greenie Unruled KayasLnce
10/ 5²s	3/8	F 38.39	71½	3 13 3 2⁵	38.43	. . .	Beat Box	AnxusWait SilverStn FireFirst⁴

Races below were run at LINCOLN   LGP 35 20 5 3 2

10/ 2¹²	O	F 38.13	71	2 21³ 1⁴ 1⁶	38.13	0.30 SA	Never In Doubt	TipToeLee Drucker SmmrFntsy
9/26¹²	O	F 38.36	70	5 11³ 1³ 1⁶	38.36	0.70 AA	Easy Win Inside	BrwnDrbGo TipToeLee MistyStrd

Homspun Rowdy figured high after winning the Rhode Island Derby, but he fell in the second round, facing a must-win situation in the third round to make the finals.

EILAND

	38.14 [A A]	(68)	TAU 3 2 0 0 0	OWNER:	Dixieland Kennel	
				KEN'L:	Ray&Chris Randle	
				TRAIN:	Bob Ackles	

2 BLUE

Red Brindle D., October 1981. Firelite--Lace

10/17⁹	3/8	F 38.12	67	5 4 3 5 5⁹·⁵	38.78	0.50 SA	No Mishaps	PatrotDle Drucker Interface
10/13¹¹	3/8	F 38.22	67	6 11⁶ 1⁸ 1⁵·⁵	38.22	1.10 SA	All The Way Ins	AnxusWait DtchNncyB FoxieMppt
10/10⁴	3/8	F 38.14	67	1 11⁵ 1⁴ 1¹	38.14	0.20 SA	Lasted On Insde	FoxieMppt Nabel LasVegsJm
10/ 6⁶s	3/8	F 38.59	68	8 31⁸ 1⁶ 1²	38.59	. . .	Erly Commnd Ins	FoxieMppt Greenie SmmrFntsy⁴

Races below were run at WONDERLAND   WON 34 20 4 2 3

9/27¹⁰	R	F 39.49	67½	4 11⁵ 1⁸ 1⁸	39.49	0.70 AA	Breezing Inside	Sofarsogd StokerAce OpusNmbrO
9/21¹⁰	R	F 39.93	67	5 8 6 5 4⁶	40.36	0.80 AA	Off Bad	StokerAce OpusNmbrO AnxiouWat

Eiland won the first New England Futurity last year and has been a big factor in Greyhound racing ever since. He's a littermate of Karlis, another Derby finalist.

A PERFECT TEN

	38.41 [A A]	(64)	TAU 3 1 1 0 1	OWNER:	James Powers	
				KEN'L:	Paul Scheele	
				TRAIN:	Karen Knapp	

3 WHITE

Brindle B., December 1981. Factual--Trouble Maker Imp

10/17⁵	3/8	F 37.69	63	7 7 6 6 4⁹·⁵	38.35	5.80 SA	Steady Gain Ins	HmspnRwdy StokerAce Fast Toby
10/13³	3/8	F 38.56	63½	3 3 3 3 2⁵	38.60	0.50 SA	Crwd, Closng In	GabeRobrt Boa Canei Nabel
10/10¹¹	3/8	F 38.41	64	8 6 3 2 1¹	38.41	1.70 SA	Drew Clear Ins	JWsBettyP MsEyelght MissSophi
10/ 4¹s	5/16	F 30.74	64	1 21¹ 1⁵ 1¹²	30.74	. . .	All Alone Insde	HondoMrdr CrusnHack ShesATrct⁴

Races below were run at TAMPA   TAM 1 0 1 0 0

9/29⁴	5/16	F 31.14	64	5 7 5 4 2ᴺˢ	31.15	1.70 A	Just Missd Rail	TyrasBest LBsDooley MdIndFncy
9/25¹s	5/16	F 31.26	64½	7 1 2 1·⁵ 1³	31.26	. . .	Came Again	Yodel Ganton PeantsEck⁷

Although her last race before the American was at Tampa, Fla., A Perfect Ten attracted real attention at Daytona Beach where she finished first in 19 of 36 races.

DRUCKER

	37.57 [A A]	(65)	TAU 3 1 1 0 0	OWNER:	Leslie Bolling	
				KEN'L:	Rickbarb Kennel	
				TRAIN:	John August	

4 GREEN

Brindle D., October 1982. Strata Rocket--Bernita Rose

10/17⁹	3/8	F 38.12	64½	1 1 4 3 2¹	38.18	3.40 SA	Hard Try Inside	PatrotDle Interface AnxusWait
10/13¹¹	3/8	F 38.22	64	1 3 8 8 6¹³	39.12	1.00 SA	Shutoff Early	Eiland AnxusWait DtchNncyB
10/10¹	3/8	F 37.57	65	8 4 1⁶ 1⁷ 1⁶	37.57	2.10 SA	All Alone Insde	MsCrlyMar HastyLght DtchDWest
10/ 5⁵s	5/16	F 30.94	65	7 31·⁵ 1⁶ 1¹⁴	30.94	. . .	Going Away Insd	OrntlButy MissMinet SurfrDela³

Races below were run at LINCOLN   LGP 30 8 2 5 4

10/ 2¹²	O	F 38.13	64	6 8 7 5 3⁶·⁵	38.59	9.90 SA	Gradual Gain Md	HmspnRwdy TipToeLee SmmrFntsy
9/28⁷	O	F 38.42	64½	8 31ᴺᴷ1⁶ 1⁸·⁵	38.42	4.60 A	Going Away Ins	KayasRacr SrfreMona LavacaJoy

Drucker's Lincoln record was not overly impressive but he obviously took to the Raynham/Taunton track from his first schooling effort.

SELECTIONS: 2 1 3 7

Dutch Bahama-1984

Distance: 3/8th Mile
Grade: SA

SUPERFECTA
Quiniela Wagering

BROWN DERBY GOGO

5 BLACK

			38.20 (58)	TAU	3	2	1	0	0	OWNER:	Jimmy G. Brown
			[A A]							KEN'L:	Triangle Kennel
										TRAIN:	Leo Desmairais

Brindle B., July 1982. Bill Whiz––Bellisle Spec Imp

10/17¹¹ 3/8	F 38.32	57	362	1·⁵	1⁴	38.32	7.10	SA	Drawg Away Ins	Karlis	KayasLnce	DtchBahma⁷
10/13⁵ 3/8	F 38.27	57	366	4	2²	38.42	3.60	SA	Stretch Drv Ins	KayasLnce Fast Toby	TipToeLee
10/10⁵ 3/8	F 38.20	56½	162	2	1⁴	38.20	5.50	SA	Drawg Away Mdtk	StingyStr GabeRobrt BlueLegnd
10/ 6⁴s 3/8	F 38.16	57	334	3	3³	38.35	. . .		Good Effort Ins	Karlis Fast Toby MsCrlyMar⁴

Races below were run at LINCOLN   *LGP* 39 10 10 2 7

9/29¹²	O	F 38.75	55½	277	6	4⁴	39.04	2.70	AA	No Room Turns	TipToeLee FlakTiger MstyStard⁷
9/26¹²	O	F 38.36	57	233	3	2⁶	38.78	7.10	AA	Up For Place Md	HmspnRwdy TipToeLee MistyStrd

Brown Derby Gogo really got surprisingly hot here at Raynham/Taunton and came out of the qualifying races tied with Karlis for the best record.

GABE ROBERTS

6 YELLOW

			38.34 (66)	TAU	17	7	4	3	1	OWNER:	B. H. Cole
			[A A]							KEN'L:	B. H. Cole
										TRAIN:	Wally Souza

Red Brindle D., May 1982. Pecos Greyeagle––Classic Gift

10/17² 3/8	F 37.98	65½	411¹	1·⁵	2⁴	38.26	3.80	SA	Led To Stretch	FreedmFor Proud Sis BlueLegnd
10/13³ 3/8	F 38.56	66	111⁸	1⁸	1·⁵	38.56	4.60	SA	Lasted On Insde	APrfctTen Boa Canei Nabel
10/10⁵ 3/8	F 38.20	66	831¹	1	3⁶	38.61	4.20	SA	Set Pace Inside	BrwnDrbGo StingyStr BlueLegnd
10/ 6¹¹x 3/8	F 38.34	66	321²	1³	1²·⁵	38.34	2.20	A	Handily Inside	StingyStr JiveyMiss Food Mart
9/29¹¹x 3/8	F 38.43	67	164	3	4⁸	38.97	4.30	A	Crowded For Trn	StingyStr Food Mart MssWndrld
9/22¹¹ 3/8	F 38.75	67	721⁶	1⁵	1¹	38.75	1.30	A	Lasted On Ins	DavesElli LdyWthAPs MsHllyHtc
9/16⁴x 5/16	F 31.13	67	247	6	6¹⁴	32.13	1.50	A	Coll Ent Bkstr	Be Daring Pepsi Red SpceltTwc

Gabe Roberts raced in many stakes, most of them at 5/16ths of a mile. Few Greyhounds have established themselves as the fast breaker as Gabe has at this track.

DUTCH BAHAMA

7 GREEN WHITE

			37.94 (76)	TAU	3	2	0	0	1	OWNER:	Herb Koerner
			[A A]							KEN'L:	Herb Koerner
										TRAIN:	Bill Nihan

White Fawn D., January 1982. Hairless Joe––Dutch Debit

10/17¹¹ 3/8	F 38.32	76	121³	2	4⁵·⁵	38.70	0.50	SA	Set Pace Inside	BrwnDrbGo Karlis KayasLnce⁷
10/13¹³ 3/8	F 37.94	76	621⁷	1⁶	1⁴	37.94	4.20	SA	Easily Inside	StokerAce Interface Millescnd
10/10¹² 3/8	F 38.23	76	862	1³	1ᴴᴰ	38.23	0.60	SA	Just Lasted Ins	JuneSales Proud Sis OrntlButy
10/ 6¹s 5/16	F 30.54	76	811⁵	1⁸	1¹²	30.54	. . .		Breezing Inside	LasVegsJm BsPapSki DtchDlusn⁴
10/ 3¹s 5/16	F 30.53	76	131¹	1⁴	1³·⁵	30.53	. . .		Easily Inside	MsHllyLas TopProfit MsCrlyMar⁴

Races below were run at BISCAYNE   *BIS* 11 5 2 0 1

8/18⁶	B	F 33.39	75	123	4	4⁴	33.64	1.90	A	Early Factr Ins	MyUnicorn Magnify StrobFnz

Dutch Bahama won the Irish–American at Biscayne, Fla., by seven lengths on August 3. He broke in here at Raynham/Taunton and is trained by Brockton native Bill Nihan.

KARLIS

8 YELLOW BLACK

			37.88 (65)	TAU	3	2	1	0	0	OWNER:	Dixieland Kennel
			[A A]							KEN'L:	Ray&Chris Randle
										TRAIN:	Bob Ackles

Brindle B., October 1981. Firelite––Lace

10/17¹¹ 3/8	F 38.32	64	654	4	2⁴	38.59	2.10	SA	Steady Drive Mt	BrwnDrbGo KayasLnce DtchBahma⁷
10/13¹ 3/8	F 38.19	65	144	2	1¹·⁵	38.19	0.50	SA	Stretch Drv Out	StingyStr FreedmFor JiveyMiss
10/10³ 3/8	F 37.88	65	112	1	1⁴	37.88	0.30	SA	Drawg Away Outs	Millescnd Boa Canei Food Mart⁷
10/ 6⁴s 3/8	F 38.16	65	842	1ᴴᴰ	1²·⁵	38.16	. . .		Handily Inside	Fast Toby BrwnDrbGo MsCrlyMar⁴

Races below were run at WONDERLAND   *WON* 29 12 5 4 1

10/ 1¹¹	R	M 40.78	65	688	4	4¹¹	41.55	1.80	AA	Shutoff Esc Trn	OrintlBty Shydr PennyCndl
9/24¹²	R	F 39.89	65	355	4	2³·⁵	40.15	0.80	AA	Drv Place Mdtrk	OrintlBty StolnEmbr GHsPl

Karlis is a kennelmate of another American finalist, Eiland. She tied with Brown Derby Gogo with the best record in the three qualifying rounds for the Derby.

Dutch Bahama-1985

TWICE AS NICE

Back Row (R-L): Thomas Whalen, Robert Kelly, Kelley Carney, George Carney and Mrs. Carney. *Front Row (L-R):* Mrs. Thelma Linsey, Mrs. Joanne Koerner, Mr. Joe Linsey, Herb Koerner, Rich Calabro and Kathy C.

TWICE AS NICE

Last year's winner, Dutch Bahama pictured above with his official entourage accomplished a feat that only the great Real Huntsman had before him and that was to win the American Greyhound Derby twice. Real Huntsman did it in 1950 and '51. Dutch Bahama repeated it in 1984 and '85.

Dutch Bahama-1985

RACE 12 — 36th RUNNING
THE AMERICAN GREYHOUND DERBY

DUTCH BAHAMA

1 RED

38.17
[A A]　(76)　TAU　3　2　1　0　0

Owner: Herb Koerner
Kennel: Herb Koerner
Trainer: Richard Calabro

White & Fawn M., January 1982. Hairless Joe--Dutch Debit

10/16⁹	3/8	F 38.35	77	8 6 2	1⁴	1⁶	38.35	0.50 SA	Going Away Mdtk	Kiowa Tip Proud Sis DancinDoe⁷
10/12¹¹	3/8	F 38.54	77	1 5 2	1²	2ᴺᴷ	38.57	0.20 SA	Caught Late Ins	RwdyRuffn WhlsInMtn LadyDelit⁷
10/ 9¹²	3/8	F 38.17	77	6 3 1²	1⁴	1²	38.17	1.00 SA	Handily Inside	Proud Sis SilverStn TargtZack
10/ 4⁶s	5/16	F 31.39	76	1 2 1²	1³	1⁴	31.39	. . .	All The Way Ins	OSSFIshbk PaidToWin BNBsZanPr⁴
9/30¹s	5/16	F 30.58	76	4 3 2	1³	1⁶	30.58	. . .	Late Contrl Mdk	MteeWldfr Chcno Wst Elliceman⁶

Races below were run at WONDERLAND

WON 5 3 1 0 1

8/31¹²	R	F 39.68	75	6 4 4	3	2¹	39.75	3.50 SA	Drive To Plc In	SprtnSun Rustica RBsBounty

Dutch Bahama's accomplishments won her the captaincy of the All America greyhound team. Derby champ in '84, she seeks to be the 2nd dog in history to win it twice.

KIOWA TIP

2 BLUE

38.64
[A A]　(62)　TAU　3　1　2　0　0

Owner: Kay E Smith
Kennel: Lingle Kennel
Trainer: Ray Brownlee

Brindle M., January 1984. Streak--AK's Be Even

10/16⁹	3/8	F 38.35	61¾	3 4 1.5 2	2⁶	38.78	3.00 SA	Next Best Mdtrk	DtchBahma Proud Sis DancinDoe⁷
10/12⁴	3/8	F 38.64	62	3 1 1²	1³	1¹	38.64	1.40 SA	Never Headed In	LillieBlk DGsDriftr DancinDoe⁷
10/ 9⁷	3/8	F 38.29	62	8 1 1²	1²	2¹	38.35	6.40 SA	Caught Late Mdt	MsExcalbr Della EDJStetsn
10/ 3²s	3/8	F 38.99	62	7 4 4	4	3¹⁰	39.67	. . .	Steady Efft Out	Timesfour BostnTrad DGsDriftr⁴

Races below were run at LINCOLN

LGP 15 6 1 1 1

9/25¹²	O	F 38.24	61	4 1 1⁴	1²	1.5	38.24	7.20 SA	Drew Out Early	MagicGift KiowaJoe MstyStrd
9/20⁶	5/16	F 31.47	62	6 3 5	5	5⁶.5	31.93	1.70 AA	Crrd Wd 1st Trn	MnhttnDd BrwnDrbyG ChargLrm

Kiowa Tip has a reputation as a tough-to-catch fast breaker who showed Lincoln fans that foes who made mistakes would find him too far in front to catch.

DOLEFUL DOE

3 WHITE

38.05
[A A]　(58)　TAU　14　6　2　1　2

Owner: Alvin Rink
Kennel: Alvin Rink
Trainer: Jim DiRocco

Brindle B., March 1983. More Ego--White Desire

10/16⁷	3/8	F 38.48	57	8 2 1.5 3	4⁴	38.77	3.80 SA	Offstrd Crtn Tn	PlacdStyl DGsDriftr Please Do
10/12⁷	3/8	F 38.62	57¾	1 1 1⁶	1⁴	1¹	38.62	1.60 SA	Long Early Lead	Elliceman PrssyPldg BoaChlant⁷
10/ 9⁹	3/8	F 38.49	57	2 1 1⁵	1³	1¹	38.49	3.70 SA	Under Prssre In	BostnTrad DancinDoe PrncsChce
10/ 4¹s	3/8	F 38.83	58	5 2 2	2	2².5	39.00	. . .	Always Close In	WhlsInMtn Please Do TargtZack⁵
9/13¹¹	3/8	F 38.50	57	4 2 5	8	8¹³	39.40	7.00 A	Muzzle Hanging	ManorEarl CheerJull JiveyMiss
9/ 7¹¹	3/8	F 38.22	57	2 2 8	8	8¹⁰	38.94	0.60 A	Crowded 1st Trn	CrmnsPrty Road West BrssyTrg
9/ 2¹²x	3/8	F 37.77	58	2 1 1⁴ 2	2¹⁰.5	38.51	1.40 A	Set Pace Inside	Proud Sis FanComndr SwansDown

Doleful Doe is Rowdy Ruffian's sister. Her father is More Ego, winner of the New Hampshire Great Greyhound Race, and her mother is White Desire, 1978 Derby finalist.

PRINCESS CHOICE

4 GREEN

38.04
[A A]　(57)　TAU　3　2　0　0　1

Owner: Wade Mayfield
Kennel: Henry Caswell
Trainer: Angelo Marchione

Fawn F., February 1983. Desert Fire--So Smart

10/16⁵	3/8	F 38.04	56¾	6 4 3	1⁴	1⁷	38.04	0.70 SA	All Alone Outs	Elliceman Road West PrssyPldg
10/12¹²	3/8	F 38.15	56	1 2 2	1⁵	1⁶	38.15	7.00 SA	Easily Outside	Please Do HmspnRwdy SpartanSn
10/ 9⁹	3/8	F 38.49	57	1 7 8	6	4³.5	38.73	2.70 SA	Steady Gain Out	DoleflDoe BostnTrad DancinDoe
10/ 4⁷s	5/16	F 31.68	57	1 3 3	2	1³.5	31.68	. . .	Strtch Drv Outs	ShrHppyHr EDJStetsn BNBsGgmGl⁴

Races below were run at LINCOLN

LGP 52 16 7 13

9/25¹⁰	5/16	F 30.91	56	3 7 4	4	2¹	30.97	3.50 AA	Drove To Place	PaidToWin KiowaBmby TaIntLnsy
9/21¹⁰	5/16	F 30.97	56¾	4 6 8	6	4²	31.10	9.10 AA	From Last Outs	HondoBarb BoaChiant ValleyPro

Princess Choice became an especially popular Lincoln greyhound because she created many exciting finishes by usually taking the long way around on the outside.

Dutch Bahama-1985

Distance: 3/8th Mile
Grade: SA

SUPERFECTA
Quiniela Wagering

▪5 WHEELS IN MOTION

BLACK

		38.36 [A A]		(71)		TAU	3 2 0 1 0		Owner: Augstein&Perrault

Black M., April 1983. Straight Three---Late Breeze
Kennel: Jandean Kennel
Trainer: Bob Antunes

Date		Dist								Time	Odds	Gr	Comment	1st/2nd/3rd
10/16[11]	3/8	F	38.54	70	7	2	2	2	1[NS]	38.54	5.50	SA	Just Lasted Ins	RBsBounty LiteSensr LadyDelit
10/12[11]	3/8	F	38.54	71	2	3	6	4	3[9.5]	39.21	8.80	SA	Crowd Erly,Drvg	RwdyRuffn DtchBahma LadyDelit[7]
10/ 9[5]	3/8	F	38.36	71	5	1	1[3]	16	14.5	38.36	5.70	SA	All The Way Ins	EJ Dowd Timesfour Elilceman
10/ 4[1]s	3/8	F	38.83	71	3	1	1[1]	1[2]	12.5	38.83	. . .		Held Safe Lead	DoleflDoe Please Do TargtZack[5]

Races below were run at LINCOLN

												LGP	41 9 6 12 1	
9/30[7]	O	F	38.41	70	2	2	1[2.5]	12	1[3]	38.41	1.70	A	Easily Mdtrk	Colibri KiowaEnrg HondoTrbl
9/25[2]	5/16	F	31.01	71	1	7	7	5	3[1]	31.10	2.00	A	Steady Gain Mdt	Folkfest JessleMnt BoldVicki

Wheels In Motion always rated high at Lincoln, but when he defeated RB's Bounty, Rhode Island Derby champ, in the 3rd Derby round here his stock soared.

▪6 RB'S BOUNTY

YELLOW

		37.82 [A A]		(66)		TAU	3 2 1 0 0		Owner: Rose A Bernard

Fawn M., January 1983. Drif's Fast---Carolina Rose
Kennel: Sunshine Kenl Inc
Trainer: Robert Towk

Date		Dist								Time	Odds	Gr	Comment	1st/2nd/3rd
10/16[11]	3/8	F	38.54	65½	2	5	6	3	2[NS]	38.55	0.40	SA	Long Gain Mdtrk	WhlsInMtn LiteSensr LadyDelit
10/12[9]	3/8	F	37.82	65½	6	4	3	14	1[8]	37.82	0.60	SA	Late Command In	SilverStn Road West LiteSensr[7]
10/ 9[4]	3/8	F	38.26	66	6	7	6	3	11.5	38.26	0.90	SA	From Far Back	FrmdblDvn Road West EvanSlctr
10/ 4[4]s	3/8	F	38.52	66	3	2	2	15	1[13]	38.52	. . .		Going Away Insd	PlacdStyl ValleyPro Astatsman[3]

Races below were run at DAYTONA

												DB	9 6 3 0 0	
9/27[13]	3/8	F	38.03	67	5	3	2	2	2.5	38.07	0.80	A	Forced Pace	CEsEasyWy APrfctTen DancrPlyg
9/20[13]	3/8	F	37.45	67	8	2	1[1]	13	1[1]	37.45	1.90	A	New Trck Record	PoloGenie CEsEasyWy CollenTru

RB's Bounty won the Rhode Island and Daytona Beach derbies, and raced sensationally in the first Derby rounds. Despite trouble in the 3rd round he almost got up to win.

▪7 ROWDY RUFFIAN

GREEN WHITE

		37.93 [A B]		(72)		TAU	9 4 1 1 0		Owner: Alvin Rink
						RAY	29 7 4 7 4		Kennel: Alvin Rink

Red D., March 1983. More Ego---White Desire
Trainer: Jim DiRocco

Date		Dist								Time	Odds	Gr	Comment	1st/2nd/3rd
10/16[3]	3/8	F	38.18	71½	2	1	2	2	1[2]	38.18	2.60	SA	Strch Drive Md	BostnTrad LillieBlk SilverStn[7]
10/12[11]	3/8	F	38.54	71	4	7	3	2	1[NK]	38.54	10.80	SA	Up Gamely Mdtrk	DtchBahma WhlsInMtn LadyDelit[7]
10/ 9[3]	3/8	F	37.93	71½	3	3	3	1[2]	17	37.93	10.80	SB	Going Away Mdtk	PlacdStyl PrssyPldg Rustica
10/ 5[11]	3/8	M	38.61	71	5	8	8	7	6[7]	39.10	8.90	A	No Mishaps	LiteSensr Road West PrssyPldg
9/29[11]x	3/8	F	38.18	71	1	4	5	4	3[3]	38.40	6.60	A	Steady Drv Mdtk	Proud Sis FrmdblDvn PrssyPldg
9/23[2]s	5/16	F	31.78	72	8	4	7	6	4[1]	31.84	. . .		Clsng Fast Mdtk	Gil Stone MteeWldfr Osterman
9/20[3]s	5/16	F	31.26	72	4	3	6	3	3[6]	31.66	. . .		Evenly Midtrack	ComeOnMgl SunryScrp Rose'sBid[6]

Rowdy Ruffian is the brother half of the first brother-sister act in Derby championship history. He and Doleful Doe are from a More Ego-White Desire litter.

▪8 BOSTON TRADER

YELLOW BLACK

		38.69 [A A]		(72)		TAU	3 1 2 0 0		Owner: R H Walters Jr

Black M., May 1983. Unruly---Crackle
Kennel: R H Walters Jr
Trainer: Carl Petricone

Date		Dist								Time	Odds	Gr	Comment	1st/2nd/3rd
10/16[3]	3/8	F	38.18	72	5	2	1[4]	1.5	2[2]	38.33	2.50	SA	Caught Late Out	RwdyRuffn LillieBlk SilverStn[7]
10/12[1]	3/8	F	38.69	72	2	2	3	11.5	14	38.69	0.90	SA	Drawing Away In	CrmnsPrty SrgtSpark FrmdblDvn
10/ 9[9]	3/8	F	38.49	71½	4	2	3	2	2[1]	38.54	3.00	SA	Dspte Wide Trns	DoleflDoe DancinDoe PrncsChce
10/ 3[2]s	3/8	F	38.99	72	1	1	1[2]	11	2[2]	39.13	. . .		Wde Trns Costly	Timesfour Kiowa DGsDriftr[4]

Races below were run at WONDERLAND

												WON	19 7 2 4 2	
9/30[10]	R	F	39.74	71	4	4	2	3	3[3]	39.97	3.10	AA	Frcd Early Pace	PleaseDo Rustica MarineTrd
9/24[8]	R	F	39.47	71	2	1	1[NK]	11	11.5	39.47	39.47	AA	Came Again Outs	PleaseDo SpartanSn Rustica

Boston Trader is the outstanding son of one of the outstanding greyhounds of all time, Unruly. At Wonderland he was known as a real speedster who often raced outside.

The Derby is moved to Lincoln Greyhound Park located in Lincoln, RI.

The Lincoln Years
(1986-2008)

Prince Proper-1986

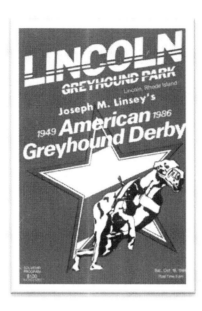

Prince Proper-1986

$50,000 AMERICAN

TWELFTH RACE

2010 Feet  OCEAN COURSE

Grade S

SUPERFECTA & QUINIELA WAGERING ON THIS RACE

PostPos.	Race	Dis.	Tk	Tm.	Wt.	PP	Off 1-8	Str	Fin	RT	Odds	Gr	FTT	Sts	1	2	3	4		Order of Finish

1 — RED — VIEW FINDER (74)
LGP 3 2 1 0 0 / RAY 5 0 1 1 0
White & Red M., April, 1983. La Tortuga—Tropicana.
Owner—Peter Eremich / Kennel—B. H. Cole[72] / Trainer—Tom Floody

Race	Dis.	Tk	Tm.	Wt.	PP	Off 1-8	Str	Fin	RT	Odds	Gr		Order of Finish
10-14[3]	O.C.	F	38.43	74	3	8 3	2	1½	38.43	3.90	S	---- Won drvng ins	IndioAmber,Trapman,JOsMoe
10-10[2]	O.C.	F	38.43	74	3	1 11½	11	11	38.43	1.30	S	---- Held firm inside	EachAMystry,ECGrg,AnitaSelectr
10- 7[2]	O.C.	F	38.28	74	2	2 2	2	27	38.79	4.30	S	---- Prssd erly ins	RBsBounty,HeartsCode,Ambria
10- 2[1s]	O.C.	F	38.42	74½	5	2 2	2	12½	38.42	...		---- Came on str ins	Thundrr,BedfrdsBst,CeboCalcult[4]

(BELOW AT RAYNHAM-TAUNTON, MA, 1986)

9-28[11]	3-8	F	38.85	73	4	4 4	4	2[nk]	38.88	2.90	A	---- Despite trouble	BrassyTargt,ECLII,KiowaBeautifl
9-24[11]	3-8	F	37.61	73	7	6 7	8	8[14]	38.55	19.50	SA	---- Cls qrtrs early	MajorMoves,HomspunRowdy,Ambrai
9-20[7]	3-8	F	38.72	73	4	6 2	6	67½	39.25	13.40	SA	---- Bumped crtn trn	Moonhaze,PrinceProper,KiowaCindy
9-17[2]	3-8	F	37.77	74	2	7 4	3	34½	38.08	6.10	SA	---- Crowded 1st drv	WheelsInMotin,Moonhaz,TalentMc
9-12[4x]	3-8	F	38.50	74	5	3 3	3	58½	38.95	9.60	A	---- Factor to str	KiowaTip,EliIceman,RBsJustice

2 — BLUE — RB'S BOUNTY (68)
LGP 3 1 1 0 1 / RAY 4 1 1 1 0
Fawn M., January 27, 1983. Drif's Fast—Carolina Rose.
Owner—Rose A. Bernard / Kennel—Rose A. Berard[63] / Trainer—Roberta Nurse

10-14[1]	O.C.	F	38.54	68	6	3 4	4	46½	38.99	.80	S	---- Trbl twice mtk	CheDavid,Thunderer,MistyStardust
10-10[3]	O.C.	F	38.26	67	4	7 4	3	27	38.76	1.50	S	---- Svd trns wd str	Trapman,Exception,RestlessRocket
10- 7[2]	O.C.	F	38.28	68	1	1 12	12½	17	38.28	.80	S	---- Str command ins	ViewFinder,HeartsCode,Ambria
10- 2[6s]	O.C.	F	38.39	68½	8	1 2	2	1[hd]	38.39	...		---- Up at wire mtk	TipToeBuster,PrinceProper[3]

(BELOW AT RAYNHAM-TAUNTON, MA, 1986)

9-24[4]	3-8	F	37.73	68	6	6 5	3	3[2]	37.85	1.90	SA	---- Steady drive ins	FlordJck,WheelsInMtn,StrobsErln
9-20[9]	3-8	F	38.20	67½	2	4 2	2	21	38.26	1.70	SA	---- Chased winner	MdkMajorMovs,WheelsInMotin,RckQn
9-17[11]	3-8	F	38.03	67	7	7 7	6	68	38.57	.90	SA	---- Driving hrd blkd	MajorMoves,DegrateOne,HeartsCd
9- 7[4]	3-8	F	38.52	66½	6	5 4	2	11	38.52	.70	A	---- Long drive mtk	KiowaTip,DegrateOne,CookiScltr

3 — WHITE — THUNDERER (74)
LGP 3 1 2 0 0 / WON 28 7 8 0 3
Red Brindle M., July, 1984. Jimmy's Smile—Tanda.
Owner—Mike Castellani, Inc / Kennel—Mike Castellani, Inc.[71] / Trainer—Steve Zack

10-14[1]	O.C.	F	38.54	74	8	4 13	12½	23	38.76	10.00	S	---- Wide str ovrtkn	CheDavid,MistyStardust,RBsBounty
10-10[10]	O.C.	F	39.35	74	8	4 4	4	1[hd]	39.35	.90	S	---- Up in str mtk	FleetfootFrnk,MaudeDalli,JellyTt
10- 6[2]	O.C.	F	38.21	74½	6	1 3	11½	21	38.27	5.20	S	---- Otfnshd sm wd	JellyTt,TipToeBustr,TammiesFncy
10- 2[1s]	O.C.	F	38.42	74	1	1 13	11½	22½	38.60	...		---- Wide stretches	ViewFndr,BedfrdsBst,CeboCalcult[4]

(BELOW AT WONDERLAND, MA, 1986)

9-25[4]	5-16	F	30.90	73	4	4 4	2	22½	31.08	18.80	AA	---- Wntd rl early	PresntHrmny,HondoBarbrn,PlntBy
9-19[11]	5-16	F	31.09	72	3	2 2	12	12½	31.09	2.30	A	---- Up on outs	VideSgnl,GiveMewnnr,JackisMyLv
9-14[4]	5-16	F	31.44	73	5	4 3	2	2[hd]	31.46	3.20	A	---- Late bid inside	PatricRshn,VideSgnl,TennesseCrmn
9- 9[9]	5-16	F	30.91	73	5	8 8	8	8[12]	31.77	11.60	AA	---- Shtf 1st turn	KachinEgl,MidnitGrc,PraislyPrnc
9- 5[9]	5-16	F	30.95	73	3	1 6	7	69	31.57	12.10	AA	---- Ofstrd 1st turn	MidnitGrc,KachinEgl,PraislyPrnc

4 — GREEN — SARA SARA (63)
LGP 43 22 5 8 2 / PLN 2 0 0 0 0
Brindle F., September 14, 1984. World Wide—Minaret.
Owner—Ray & Chris Randle / Kennel—Ray & Chris Randle[7] / Trainer—Anthony Pella

10-14[12]	O.C.	F	38.23	63	2	2 12	13	11	38.23	3.80	S	---- Handily mtk	HomspunRowdy,PleaseDo,BlowSmoke
10-10[4]	O.C.	F	38.67	63	2	4 4	4	510	39.37	1.80	S	---- Never varied mtk	MsExcalibre,BlowSmoke,PleaseDo
10- 6[4]	O.C.	F	38.66	63	3	1 15	17	13	38.66	1.60	S	---- Wire to wire	BrimSton,StrobesErlen,DGsDriftr
10- 2[5s]	O.C.	F	38.37	63½	3	1 12½	11½	22	38.53	...		---- Outfinished mtk	RBsJustice,JDsTrisha[3]
9-24[4]	5-16	F	30.98	63	6	8 8	6	37½	31.51	.20	AA	---- Gained show outs	TXsWinchstr,FantasiaD,EPsMtthw
9-20[12]	5-16	F	30.98	62½	1	4 4	2	16½	30.98	.50	AA	---- Going away mtk	FantasiD,TXsWnchster,PTsTomflry[7]
9-16[10]	5-16	F	31.10	62½	5	3 3	11½	14	31.10	.40	AA	---- Svd bks drew out	MaryvilleDrm,VallyPr,MorningStrk
9-10[3]	5-16	F	30.90	63	6	2 3	11½	16½	30.90	.40	AA	---- Easily best mdtk	MorningsBy,TXsWinchest,EPsJhn
9- 1[10]	5-16	F	31.00	63	6	2 12	15	16	31.00	.90	AA	9.09 Command in bkstr	MagicGift,PaidToWin,DGsDrifter
8-28[10]	5-16	F	30.92	63	3	2 2	12	15	30.92	1.90	AA	---- Str contrl mtk	KiowaTp,CountryGatr,CharStarlt

SELECTIONS: 5—7—2—4

Prince Proper-1986

GREYHOUND DERBY

TWELFTH RACE

SUPERFECTA & QUINIELA WAGERING ON THIS RACE

 OCEAN COURSE 2010 Feet

Grade S

PostPos.	Race	Dis.	Tk	Tm.	Wt.	PP	Off 1-8	Str	Fin	RT	Odds	Gr	FTT	Sts	1	2	3	4		Order of Finish
5 BLACK	**TRAPMAN** (73)												LGP RAY	3 4	2 1	0 2	1 1	0 0		Owner—Roland F. McLeroy Kennel—Ray & Chris Randle7 Trainer—Anthony Pella
	Brindle M., April, 1984. K's Clown—Goodnight Irene.																			
	10-14³	O.C.	F	38.43	73	5	3	5	4	3¹½	38.55	.50	S	----	Blkd closed outs				ViewFinder,IndioAmber,JOsMoe
	10-10³	O.C.	F	38.26	72	2	4	1²	1³	1⁷	38.26	1.50	S	----	Str command mtk				RBsBonty,Exceptin,RestlessRockt
	10-6³	O.C.	F	38.49	73	6	3	3	2	1¹½	38.49	.80	S	----	Won drvg mtk				JazzBand,BlowSmoke,TejasAbe
	10-2³s	O.C.	F	37.84	73	3	1	1⁶	1⁷	1¹⁰	37.84	...		----	Quick cmmnd mtk				MaudeDallia,ClareAnn³
	(BELOW AT RAYNHAM-TAUNTON, MA, 1986)																			
	9-24⁶	3-8	F	37.96	72	3	4	2	2	2⁵	38.00	8.70	SA	----	Almost up mdtrk				KiowaTp,PrincePropr,EachAMystry
	9-20¹¹	3-8	F	38.35	73	7	6	5	4	3⁵	38.72	2.10	SA	----	Despite trouble				HomspnRowdy,RandomChoice,KWTp
	9-17⁷	3-8	F	37.65	72½	8	5	3	2	2⁵	38.02	1.10	SA	----	Stdy drive mdtk				ProudSis,ECGreg,ProudFuture
	9-13¹¹x	3-8	F	38.34	72	7	7	4	3	1ⁿˢ	38.34	1.90	A	----	Final stride mdt				CheerJulie,Fireworks,FncyNncyR⁷
6 YELLOW	**M'S EXCALIBRE** (69)												LGP RAY	3 24	2 15	0 1	0 2	0 2		Owner—Marion Currier Kennel—Marion Currier69 Trainer—David Currier
	Brindle M., December, 1983. Steve Whiz—M's Miss Ethel.																			
	10-14²	O.C.	F	38.62	70½	2	5	5	5	5³	38.85	.50	S	----	Crwd brk bpd tn				MajorMovs,MaudeDalli,NavyRespons
	10-10⁴	O.C.	F	38.67	69½	4	2	1¹½	1³½	1⁴½	38.67	2.10	S	----	Easy win outside				BlowSmok,PleaseD,WheelsInMotin
	10-6¹²	O.C.	F	38.58	69	6	3	1²	1⁴	1⁷½	38.58	5.20	S	----	Beneftd drew out				FiestGrl,Seeinandbeinsn,Exceptn
	10-2²s	O.C.	F	38.58	70	2	2	2	3	3²½	38.76	...		----	Led frnt str mtk				PleaseDo,BrimStone,RandomChoice⁴
	(BELOW AT RAYNHAM-TAUNTON, MA, 1986)																			
	9-27¹²	3-8	F	38.46	68	7	7	4	4	4⁴	38.72	1.80	SA	----	Blocked far turn				Moonhz,WheelsInMotn,HomspnRwdy
	9-24⁹	3-8	F	37.51	68	2	2	1³	1⁸	1¹¹	37.51	.60	SA	----	Breezing mtk				HeartsCod,Moonhaz,FrequentFlyr
	9-20¹	3-8	F	38.03	70	4	1	3	1⁵	1⁵½	38.03	.30	SA	----	Drew away outs				PTsHushPuppy,HeartsCode,ECGreg
	9-17⁶	3-8	F	38.04	68½	8	3	2	4	4⁴	38.33	.60	SA	----	Bumped curtn trn				HiddenFire,Ambria,PrinceProper
7 GREEN-WHITE	**PRINCE PROPER** (75)												LGP RAY	3 3	2 0	0 1	1 2	0 0		Owner—Francis Fulginiti Kennel—Fulginiti Kennels,Inc.65 Trainer—Mike Camilleri
	Red Brindle M., August, 1984. Placid Ace—Maid's Day Off.																			
	10-14⁴	O.C.	F	38.37	75	1	5	6	5	3⁶½	38.84	.60	S	----	Blkd erly wd trn				HeartsCod,PTsHushPppy,CapoDiCap
	10-10¹²	O.C.	F	38.73	74	7	5	2	1³½	1⁶	38.73	1.80	S	----	Going away mtk				HmspnRwdy,CapoDCp,Seeinandbensn
	10-7¹²	O.C.	F	38.19	74	5	1	1³	1⁴	1⁶	38.19	1.70	S	----	Easily best outs				PleaseDo,AnitaSelector,Moonhaze
	10-2⁶s	O.C.	F	38.39	74½	6	3	3	3	3²	38.52	...		----	Sm late gain mtk				RBsBounty,TipToeBuster³
	(BELOW AT RAYNHAM-TAUNTON, MA, 1986)																			
	9-24⁷	3-8	F	37.96	75½	1	2	4	3	3³½	38.20	.50	SA	----	Despte erly trbl				KiowaTip,Trapman,PrinceProper
	9-20⁷	3-8	F	38.72	75	2	2	3	3	2²	38.88	.80	SA	----	Crowd erly drvng				Moonhaze,KiowaCindy,OrntlExpress
	9-17⁵	3-8	F	38.04	75	4	6	3	3	3¹½	38.15	1.30	SA	----	Despite trouble				HiddenFire,Ambria,MsExcalibre
	9-12²s	3-8	F	38.54	75	5	4	4	3	2³	38.77	...		----	Steady drive mtk				PleaseDo,Macho,DotsDash⁴
8 YELLOW-BLACK	**RB'S JUSTICE** (72)												LGP RAY	3 5	2 2	0 0	0 1	0 1		Owner—Rose A. Bernard Kennel—Rose A. Bernard63 Trainer—Roberta Nurse
	Black M., May, 1984. Mr. Please—Carolina Rose.																			
	10-14¹²	O.C.	F	38.23	71	6	8	6	5	5⁵	38.59	1.70	S	----	Wide frnt str				SaraSara,HomspnRowdy,PleaseDo
	10-10⁸	O.C.	F	38.75	72½	8	8	3	1¹½	1³½	38.75	1.00	S	----	Drew out mtk				Diamondizr,NavyRespons,TalentMc
	10-7⁴	O.C.	F	38.61	72	2	5	3	3	1²	38.61	4.30	S	----	Driving str mdtk				MajorMoves,TalentMac,KwikKayo
	10-2⁵s	O.C.	F	38.37	72	1	2	2	2	1²	38.37	...		----	Str drive mtk				SaraSara,JDsTrisha³
	(BELOW AT RAYNHAM-TAUNTON, MA, 1986)																			
	9-24⁷	3-8	F	37.90	71	6	8	7	7	7⁷	38.39	7.10	SA	----	Trouble turn				Fireworks,PleaseDo,ECGreg
	9-20³	3-8	F	38.32	71½	7	6	4	2	1ⁿᵏ	38.32	.70	SA	----	Despite trouble				JosMoe,Exception,StrobesErlene⁷
	9-17⁹	3-8	F	37.79	71	5	4	7	5	4⁵	38.16	6.90	SA	----	Blkd 1st driving				KiowaTip,RandomChoice,GBsGeeGee
	9-12⁴x	3-8	F	38.50	72	3	7	5	6	3⁴½	38.80	2.80	A	----	Despite trouble				KiowaTip,Eliiceman,HiddenFire
	9-7²	7-16	F	44.26	71	2	1	1²	1²	1⁴	44.26	.80	A	----	Box to wire				Deniset,ShrEstrlily,OrntlCyndy

SELECTIONS: 5—7—2—4

Fuel's Stargazer-1987

A Star Is Born

In 1987 Josef & Sherck's Fuel's Stargazer qualified second yet left the startin at nearly 10 to 1. With plenty of FUEL to spare she left the re   the field STARGAZING all the way to the winner's circle. Pictured here with last year's champ are the Lincoln Leadouts (back row), and (l to r) Al Ross, Richard Josef, Mr. & Mrs. Ben Silberman, Joseph and Thelma Linsey and Mrs. Karen Ross. Holding a tight lead on Fuel's Stargazer is Assistant Racing Secretary Gary Liberatore.

JOSEPH M. LINSEY TROPHY
"The Most Prestigious Award in Greyhound Racing"

American Greyhound Derby Tradition

The American Greyhound Derby is one of the most traditional stake races in the country. Over the year the greyhounds that have graced the winner's circle of this prestigious event, let alone the also rans and non-derby finalists, are among the sports all time greats.

Just how great were those that triumphed? Let's take a look. At present, 5 winners have been installed into the Greyhound Hall of Fame, one earned the Rural Rube Award winner (nation's best sprinter), three were given the Flashy Sir Award (nation's best distance runner), 13 winners were selected to the All-American Team of which 3 captained, and last year's winner was selected as the World's top middle distance runner. Here they are:

ALL AMERICAN		HALL OF FAME	
Year won	Greyhound	Year won	Greyhound
1986	Prince Proper''	1977	Downing
1985	Dutch Bahama	1958	Feldcrest
1984	Dutch Bahama '	1952	On The Line
1982	Mr. Wizard	1950-51	Real Huntsman
1980	Position	1949	Oklahoman
1978	Blazing Red		
1977	Downing '	Flashy Sir	
1976	P L. Greer '	1984	Dutch Bahama
1974	Abella	1978	Blazing Red
1969	Lucky Bannon	1976	P.L. Greer
Greer 1967	Xandra		
1966	Golden In	Rural Rube	
1963 (first year)	Thermal	1977	Downing

'All American Captain
''All World Mid Distance Greyhound

Ico Evan-1988

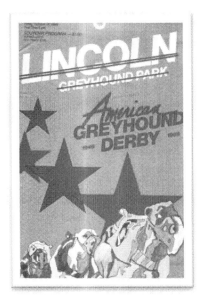

Ico Evan-1988

$50,000 AMERICAN

TWELFTH RACE

2010 Feet OCEAN COURSE

Grade S

SUPERFECTA & QUINIELA WAGERING ON THIS RACE

PostPos.	Race	Dis.	Tk	Tm.	Wt.	PP	Off 1-8	Str	Fin	RT	Odds	Gr	FTT	Sts	1	2	3	4	Order of Finish

1 RED — ICO EVAN (79)
LGP 3 2 0 0 0 — WON 40 10 9 7 0
Owner—A. E. or Ann T. Nienow
Kennel—Harlan Kennel
Trainer—Elizabeth Keevin
Brindle M., March 8, 1986. PV's Fred—Keyme Cathy

Race	Dis.	Tk	Tm.	Wt.	PP	Off 1-8	Str	Fin	RT	Odds	Gr	FTT	comment	Order of Finish
10-10¹²	O.C.	F	38.10	78	2	1	1³	1³	1²½	38.10	1.30	S	----	Wire to wire mtk	ScenicBty,ChicgJll,PraislyPrnc
10- 7³	O.C.	F	39.04	79½	3	2	4	5	54½	39.36	1.90	S	----	Trouble thruout	PerfectJob,Mazak,FranksAward⁷
10- 3¹²	O.C.	F	38.37	78	5	1	1¹½	12½	12	38.37	4.40	S	----	Handily inside	GiggiDear,KacyEasy,BahamaTip
9-29²s	5-16	F	31.29	79½	7	3	3	3	2³½	31.54	. . .		----	Coll closed ins	LateApprasl,KcyEsy,ColorMeMrcll⁵

(BELOW AT WONDERLAND, MA, 1988)

Race	Dis.	Tk	Tm.	Wt.	PP	Off 1-8	Str	Fin	RT	Odds	Gr	FTT	comment	Order of Finish
9-20⁴	RC	F	39.66	79	6	1	1³½	1½	2¹	39.73	2.60	AA	----	Cght lt str mdtk	TorreyPns,SportingTms,Implictd
9-14¹¹	RC	F	39.66	77½	6	1.	1²	1²	1²½	39.66	3.20	AA	----	Box to wr sm wd	SprtngTms,TMsTcktHm,JATlknTlnt
9-10⁹	RC	F	39.78	78½	3	5	6	5	5⁹	40.41	1.00	AA	----	Wide 1st turn	RacingRae,TMsTicketHome,BokToy
9- 6⁴	RC	F	39.45	78	2	1	1¹	3	2²½	39.62	2.40	AA	----	Fctr thrut sm wd	TMsTicketHm,TorreyPns,Millimcrn
9- 1⁴	RC	F	38.85	79½	1	4	2	2	2¹²	39.68	2.50	AA	----	Held place ins	TorreyPins,Millimicrn,PerfectJb

2 BLUE — LATE APPRAISAL (62)
LGP 3 1 1 0 0 — RAY 15 3 2 2 1
Owner—Texesbee Greyhounds & L. Perry
Kennel—B. H. Cole
Trainer—Wally Souza, Jr.
Brindle F., November 1, 1985. Bon Bon Patriot—Party Lace.

Race	Dis.	Tk	Tm.	Wt.	PP	Off 1-8	Str	Fin	RT	Odds	Gr	FTT	comment	Order of Finish
10-10⁶	O.C.	F	37.95	62	2	1	1¹½	2	25	38.28	1.20	S	----	Pacesetter ins	CutsGambler,MookieFinn,GiggiDear
10- 7³	O.C.	F	39.04	62½	4	4	6	6	78	39.62	3.30	S	----	No room at break	PerfectJob,Mazak,FranksAward⁷
10- 3²	O.C.	F	38.41	61	5	4	1¹½	12	14	38.41	4.10	S	----	Extended lead	GdPlly,JATalknTlnt,PhlpsExcllr⁷
9-29²s	5-16	F	31.29	61½	2	4	14	14	1³½	31.29	. . .		----	Easily inside	IcoEvan,KacyEasy,ColorMeMarcell⁵

(BELOW AT RAYNHAM-TAUNTON, MA, 1988)

Race	Dis.	Tk	Tm.	Wt.	PP	Off 1-8	Str	Fin	RT	Odds	Gr	FTT	comment	Order of Finish
9-23¹¹x	5-16	F	31.20	62	6	4	8	8	8²³½	32.83	5.00	A	----	Hit 1st turn	PatCHeMan,StarcrossedGal,Kook
9-17¹¹x	5-16	F	31.18	61½	7	1	2	5	4³½	31.41	4.40	A	----	Forced erly pace	DarkSunshine,ECSam,PatCHeMan
9-11¹¹x	5-16	F	31.26	61½	8	1	4	4	3³	31.47	6.20	A	----	Blocked 1st turn	PatCHeMn,DarkSunshin,KBsMyMnply
9- 5⁹x	5-16	F	30.55	61½	6	3	1ns	3	2³½	30.78	3.40	A	----	Set pace inside	Chicopee,JustCrockett,KiowaDime
8-31⁷	5-16	F	31.06	61½	8	2	4	4	5⁸½	31.65	9.30	SA	----	Bumped 1st turn	DublinShadow,MCGraw,Sunburn

3 WHITE — VODAR (69)
LGP 54 15 7 11 10 — LGP 40 10 5 5 7
Owner—Roland F. Mc Leroy
Kennel—Chris Randle
Trainer—Richard Marchione, Jr.
Brindle M., December 3, 1985. C.'s Mickey—Goodnite Irene.

Race	Dis.	Tk	Tm.	Wt.	PP	Off 1-8	Str	Fin	RT	Odds	Gr	FTT	comment	Order of Finish
10-10⁴	O.C.	F	37.77	68½	5	1	1¹½	14	14½	37.77	2.50	2A	----	Control in bkstr	FamousWn,Leftfild,JATalkinTalnt
10- 7¹⁰	O.C.	F	38.97	67½	6	1	3	3	2ns	38.98	3.60	2A	----	Closing fast wd	FlashToWin,MarionsLuck,DJsSheba⁷
10- 3¹¹	O.C.	F	38.33	68	1	4	3	4	3⁴	38.63	3.60	2A	----	Evenly outside	MountnBlsh,TdCpwll,BarryProftbl
9-29⁴	O.C.	F	38.55	68½	6	1	1³	13	14	38.55	3.90	SA	----	All the way outs	KiowaBbs,ChicagoJll,BlackieBck
9-24²	O.C.	F	38.75	68	5	8	6	5	3¹	38.83	2.50	A	----	Steady gain wd	GiggiDear,LadyRust,Sasuma
9-21¹²x	O.C.	F	38.96	67½	8	4	4	4	3⁴	39.23	1.80	A	----	Good effort outs	Leftfield,LadyRust,FuelAGoGo
9-15¹²	O.C.	F	38.74	67	4	4	6	5	3⁵	39.07	1.50	A	----	Erly trbl wd	RoadTrip,TallyHee,MissHandy
9-12¹²	O.C.	F	38.67	68	4	3	7	7	4¹²½	39.55	2.60	AA	----	No gain wide	ReoBossMn,ChicagoJll,MaxistarDo⁷
9- 2¹²	O.C.	F	38.84	68	6	7	6	5	4⁷	39.32	6.40	AA	----	Some gain wide	CutsGamblr,ReoBossMn,MaxistarDo
8-26¹²	O.C.	F	38.84	67	8	1	8	8	8	OOP	4.80	AA	----	Judged OK 8-30	Itchabon,CutsGambler,FancyNikki

4 GREEN — TED CAPWELL (78)
LGP 38 18 5 5 3 — RAY 3 0 2 0 0
Owner—Richard B. Flanagan
Kennel—Leo Desmarais
Trainer—Danny Therrien
Brindle M., August 26, 1986. K's Flak—Seana's Sunshine.

Race	Dis.	Tk	Tm.	Wt.	PP	Off 1-8	Str	Fin	RT	Odds	Gr	FTT	comment	Order of Finish
10-10¹⁰	O.C.	F	37.59	78	7	1	16	18	19	37.59	.80	2A	----	New track record	DixieRose,MarionsLuck,ReoBossMan⁷
10- 7¹²	O.C.	F	38.35	77½	8	4	12½	15	15	38.35	2.50	2A	----	Easy win outside	TorreyPines,Leftfield,IonPayDirt
10- 3¹¹	O.C.	F	38.33	78½	3	5	2	2	2½	38.37	3.70	2A	----	Late threat outs	MountainBlsh,Vodr,BarryProfitabl
9-27¹⁰	5-16	F	31.12	78	8	4	6	3	12	31.12	1.40	AA	----	Driving winner	LungMoon,NicksEcho,RemsNoble
9-23¹²	O.C.	F	38.32	77	6	6	4	3	3⁶½	38.77	4.40	2A	----	Evenly outside	BahamaTip,TallyHee,ScenicBeauty
9-17¹²	O.C.	F	38.48	78	8	6	3	3	37	38.99	2.40	AA	----	Good effort outs	BahamaTp,EdgetownHrry,CutsGamblr
9-14¹⁰	5-16	F	31.06	78	4	6	8	7	4⁶	31.47	3.20	AA	----	Bumped 1st turn	BahamaTip,CharCruiser,WCPearl
9- 3¹⁰	5-16	F	31.18	79	2	3	7	6	2³	31.37	.60	AA	----	Erly trbl drvng	LungMn,FabledPenelp,MarcusCttn
8-31¹⁰	5-16	F	30.86	77½	2	3	3	2	16	30.86	2.40	AA	----	Going away ins	LadyBss,MarcusCottn,BlancasWsh
8-27¹⁰	5-16	F	30.64	77	6	8	3	2	2⁴	30.91	1.50	AA	----	Outside route	DexDextr,FabledGazzell,CrossCt

Ico Evan-1988

GREYHOUND DERBY

TWELFTH RACE

TRACK RECORD - 37.59
Ted Capwell — October 10, 1988

SUPERFECTA & QUINIELA WAGERING ON THIS RACE

Grade S

PostPos.	Race	Dis.	Tk	Tm.	Wt.	PP	Off 1-8	Str	Fin	RT	Odds	Gr	FTT	Sts	1	2	3	4	Order of Finish
5 BLACK																			

5 BLACK — DIXIE ROSE (62)
LGP 3 1 1 0 0 — WON 44 10 9 4 9
Owner—C. C. Lightfoot · Kennel—Slatex · Trainer—Kevin Dalton
Red Fawn F., April, 1986. Barry Lyndon—Weezie The Clown.

Race	Dis.	Tk	Tm.	Wt.	PP	Off 1-8	Str	Fin	RT	Odds	Gr	FTT	Order of Finish
10-10	10	O.C.	F	37.59	62	6	3	2	2	2^9	38.20	7.10	S	Best of others	TedCapwll,MarionsLck,ReoBossMn7
10- 7	10	O.C.	F	38.97	61	8	6	6	5	5^6	39.39	3.90	S	No real threat	FlashToWin,Vodar,MarionsLuck7
10- 3	3	O.C.	F	38.36	62	2	3	4	3	1^{ns}	38.36	6.50	S	Came on str rail	ScenicBeaty,Itchabn,SkimarGayl
9-29	1s	5-16	F	31.16	62	7	4	1^1	4	4^4	31.44	...		Set pace mdtrk	PraisleyPrnc,MarinsLck,FlyingQul5
(BELOW AT WONDERLAND, MA, 1988)
9-26	9	5-16	F	31.40	$61\frac{1}{2}$	8	5	2	2	1^1	31.40	7.80	AA	With rush outs	RomanArena,MCGraw,BahamaLine
9-22	9	5-16	F	31.45	61	2	1	4	4	$5^{1\frac{1}{2}}$	31.56	9.80	AA	Fctr thru ins	HondoAudacios,PyrmidEliRly,MCGrw
9-16	2s	5-16	F	31.22	62	4	5	5	3	$4^{7\frac{1}{2}}$	31.76	...		Late factor	GHsSnappr,DinnerDrss,LocalPioner
8-27	13	RC	F	39.69	$61\frac{1}{2}$	7	6	5	2	$2\frac{1}{2}$	39.73	13.60	S	Coming fast	IcoEvn,ColorMeMarcll,TorreyPins
8-23	9	RC	F	39.66	61	8	3	3	4	$4^{7\frac{1}{2}}$	40.19	4.50	AA	Even effrt mdtk	PerfctJb,WestprkRnOn,WestPontr

6 YELLOW — SCENIC BEAUTY* (58)
LGP 45 11 8 3 8 — PLN 3 0 0 0 1
Owner—Pat Dalton · Kennel—Pat Dalton · Trainer—David O'Keeffe
Black F., May 19, 1985. Security Alert—Miss Peel.

Race	Dis.	Tk	Tm.	Wt.	PP	Off 1-8	Str	Fin	RT	Odds	Gr	FTT	Order of Finish
10-10	12	O.C.	F	38.10	58	8	2	2	2	$2^{2\frac{1}{2}}$	38.27	3.70	2A	Next best inside	IcoEvn,ChicagoJll,PraisleyPrinc
10- 7	4	O.C.	F	38.68	$58\frac{1}{2}$	4	1	1^2	12	$12\frac{1}{2}$	38.68	1.40	2A	Never headed ins	FamosWn,OrientlPtP,JATalkinTlnt
10- 3	3	O.C.	F	38.36	58	5	2	$11\frac{1}{2}$	11	2^{ns}	38.37	2.60	2A	Winning effort	DixieRose,Itchabon,SkimarGayla
9-28	12	O.C.	F	38.59	58	4	2	2	12	1^4	38.59	3.90	AA	Drew away inside	FancyNikki,GiggiDear,ReoBossMan
9-23	12	O.C.	F	38.32	$57\frac{1}{2}$	4	3	5	4	4^7	38.81	5.00	2A	Stayed even ins	BahamaTip,TallyHee,TedCapwell
9-17	12	O.C.	F	38.48	58	7	7	7	8	7^{13}	39.40	3.50	AA	Offstrd early	BahamaTp,EdgetownHrry,TedCapwll
9-14	12	O.C.	F	38.64	58	3	2	3	$12\frac{1}{2}$	$17\frac{1}{2}$	38.64	2.90	AA	Thru in bks ins	Wobble,FranksAward,YawlEnjoyMe
9- 3	12	O.C.	F	38.74	58	3	2	1^2	12	1^1	38.74	3.70	2A	Held firm ins	KiowaBbs,SuperEclips,RumPontlnn
8-31	12	O.C.	F	38.81	57	6	3	2	2	1^{hd}	38.81	2.50	A	Up near wire ins	FranksAward,RoadTrip,JosTippy
8-27	12	O.C.	F	38.80	58	5	3	3	2	2^1	38.86	4.40	A	Gaining in str	TallyHee,RoadTrip,SpeakOut

7 GREEN-WHITE — BARRY PROFITABLE (66)
LGP 3 1 1 0 1 — WON 46 6 6 8 11
Owner—S. Benners & R. Trochman · Kennel—Agganis and Stanton · Trainer—Thomas Guerra
Brindle F., Fenruary, 1986. Barry Lyndon—Belinda Sue.

Race	Dis.	Tk	Tm.	Wt.	PP	Off 1-8	Str	Fin	RT	Odds	Gr	FTT	Order of Finish
10-10	3	O.C.	F	37.82	$66\frac{1}{2}$	2	1	15	13	$2^{1\frac{1}{2}}$	37.93	5.30	S	Long lead ovrtkn	IonPayDirt,Winterfest,FancyNikki7
10- 7	8	O.C.	F	39.01	67	3	1	14	12	1^{ns}	39.01	7.80	S	Just lasted mtk	ChicagoJill,MookieFinn,GiggiDear
10- 3	11	O.C.	F	38.33	66	5	2	4	3	4^5	38.68	7.90	S	Wd early ins bks	MountainBlush,TedCapwell,Vodar
9-29	7s	O.C.	F	38.90	$66\frac{1}{2}$	3	1	2	2	$2\frac{1}{2}$	38.94	...		Late bid inside	GoodPlly,OrientalPtP,ProsStormr5
(BELOW AT WONDERLAND, MA, 1988)
9-16	2s	5-16	F	31.22	67	6	6	8	7	$6^{10\frac{1}{2}}$	31.96	...		Lckd erly spd	GHsSnappr,DinnerDrss,LocalPioner
9- 1	4	RC	F	38.85	65	7	3	6	6	5^{16}	39.97	9.00	AA	Evenly ins	TorreyPines,IcoEvan,Millimicron
8-28	4	RC	F	39.13	$64\frac{1}{2}$	1	1	2	2	$2^{1\frac{1}{2}}$	39.23	1.60	AA	Prssd winner ins	HomeRunHank,Katja,ValiantSon
8-23	4	RC	F	39.73	65	5	3	2	2	$3\frac{1}{2}$	39.77	12.20	AA	Fctr thruout	ColorMMrcll,PrsStrmr,EstCstAndy
8-19	11	RC	F	39.71	65	5	2	4	4	5^9	40.34	4.60	S	Wanted ins erly	TMsTicktHm,HomRnHnk,OrientlRmb

8 YELLOW-BLACK — ION PAY DIRT (69)
LGP 3 2 0 0 1 — RAY 12 6 3 1 1
Owner—James P. Miller · Kennel—John Lingle · Trainer—Mark Dunnuck
Red Fawn M., August 1, 1986. BJ's Justin—Cashmaker.

Race	Dis.	Tk	Tm.	Wt.	PP	Off 1-8	Str	Fin	RT	Odds	Gr	FTT	Order of Finish
10-10	3	O.C.	F	37.82	$68\frac{1}{2}$	7	5	2	2	$1^{1\frac{1}{2}}$	37.82	1.00	S	Driving wnnr ins	BarryProfitbl,Wintrfst,FancyNkk7
10- 7	12	O.C.	F	38.35	$67\frac{1}{2}$	4	6	5	4	$4^{13\frac{1}{2}}$	39.29	2.10	S	Offstrd far trn	TedCapwell,TorreyPines,Leftfield
10- 3	8	O.C.	F	38.43	$68\frac{1}{2}$	8	4	2	2	$1^{4\frac{1}{2}}$	38.43	2.50	S	Drew clear str	HomeRunHank,LeesDash,BikiniBabe
9-29	3s	O.C.	F	39.10	$68\frac{1}{2}$	2	4	4	4	4^5	39.47	...		Crd bumped erly	PhelpsExcellor,Mazak,TorreyPines5
(BELOW AT RAYNHAM-TAUNTON, MA, 1988)
9-22	4x	3-8	F	38.36	68	8	3	2	2	1^2	38.36	.60	A	Str drive ins	EtchAFuture,StrobesCopy,BrnyAnn
9-17	7x	3-8	F	38.25	69	8	4	2	12	$1^{5\frac{1}{2}}$	38.25	1.20	A	Extending ins	KacyBodck,IwinkatthstRs,Wntrfst
9-10	7x	3-8	F	37.67	$68\frac{1}{2}$	1	2	2	13	$1^{6\frac{1}{2}}$	37.67	.80	A	Going away ins	IndioSmallTalk,KacyBodock,KWCcsh
9- 4	11	3-8	M	39.40	68	5	5	5	3	3^1	39.47	1.90	A	Blocked far turn	StrobesCopy,PattiGleason,TmBifrn
8-31	12	3-8	F	38.59	67	3	5	3	2	$1^{1\frac{1}{3}}$	38.59	.90	A	Stretch drve ins	PattiGleason,TeamoBifrn,StrbsCpy7

SELECTIONS 1-2-4-8

Winterfest-1989

Winterfest-1989

$50,000 AMERICAN

THIRTEENTH RACE

2010 Feet  OCEAN COURSE

SUPERFECTA & QUINIELA WAGERING ON THIS RACE

Grade S

PostPos.		Race	Dis.	Tk.	Tm.	Wt.	PP	Off	1-8	Str	Fin	RT	Odds	Gr	FTT	Sts	1	2	3	4		Order of Finish	LGP 10/14/89/E/13

1 RED — ALLEGIS (78)

LGP 3 3 0 0 0 — WON 11 8 2 0 1

Owner—R. H. Walters, Jr.
Kennel—Mike Castellani
Trainer—Steve Zack

Brindle M., August, 1986. Dutch Bahama—Satisfied.

Race	Dis.	Tk.	Tm.	Wt.	PP	Off	1-8	Str	Fin	RT	Odds	Gr	FTT	Comment	Order of Finish
10-10^{12}	O.C.	F	38.93	76½	6	3	2	2	1^5	38.93	.40	S	----	Won impressively	SportsCannon,AJ'sTropicstorm,MuggsyBogues^7
10- 6^{13}	O.C.	F	38.73	77	3	4	3	3	1^3	38.73	.80	S	----	Driving winner	KacyBodock,FrontCover,BabyDoll
10- 2^{12}	O.C.	F	38.01	77	7	5	3	1^2	1^7	38.01	.80	S	----	Was best rail	MyOlivia,AJ'sTropicstorm,SillyBilly
9-28^{10}s	O.C.	F	38.54	78½	6	2	11½	1^3	1^6	38.54	...		----	Going away rail	AJ'sTropicstorm,SportsMission,FrontCover^4
(BELOW AT WONDERLAND, MA, 1989)															
9-23^{11}	RC	F	38.37	77½	4	1	11½	1^6	1^{11}	38.37	.40	AA	----	Drew out ins	ProfitsGold,DixieRose,SuperGirl^7
9-19^6	RC	F	38.37	78	1	1	1^3	1^7	1^{12}½	38.37	.40	AA	----	New track record	DAndM'sXpress,ProfitsGold,Magee
9-14^4	RC	F	39.59	77	7	1	2	1^{nk}	1^{hd}	39.59	.90	AA	----	Won late duel rl	RapidoGal,HondoTracer,HomeRunHank
9- 8^4	RC	F	39.30	78	6	1	3	2	2^{4}½	39.61	.80	AA	----	Chasd wnnr ins	RapidoGal,Cowpoodle,SlicksLifeste
9- 1^4	RC	F	39.53	78½	6	1	1^2	1^5	1^{6}½	39.53	.50	AA	----	All the way ins	Cowpoodle,Linville'sLad,OrientalSilver

2 BLUE — MAGEE (69)

LGP 3 1 1 0 0 — WON 22 6 7 3 2

Owner—Mike Castellani
Kennel—Mike Castellani
Trainer—Steve Zack

Light Brindle M., October, 1987. Ramblewood—Assertive.

Race	Dis.	Tk.	Tm.	Wt.	PP	Off	1-8	Str	Fin	RT	Odds	Gr	FTT	Comment	Order of Finish
10-10^4	O.C.	F	39.20	67½	7	8	8	8	8	OOP	4.40	S	----	Judged OK	SillyBilly,JustCan'tLose,Winterfest
10- 6^4	O.C.	F	38.82	67½	8	8	5	5	1^1	38.82	5.40	S	----	Rail trns cme on	MyOlivia,BoligeeCapone,FabledCharlie
10- 2^8	O.C.	F	38.98	68	1	8	5	5	2^1	39.07	6.60	S	----	Closing late ins	KiowaMatilda,Kelso'sAce,SassyWinner
9-28^{9}s	O.C.	F	38.47	69½	7	4	4	4	3^9	39.09	...		----	Raced inside	QuickSack,JustCan'tLose,KiowaMatilda^4
(BELOW AT WONDERLAND, MA, 1989)															
9-19^6	RC	F	38.37	68½	3	7	6	4	4^{13}½	39.32	6.10	AA	----	Late gain inside	Allegis,DAndM'sXpress,ProfitsGold
9-12^4	RC	F	40.06	68	8	7	6	3	2^1	40.15	.60	AA	----	Late bid outs	SlicksInk,PrettySmart,ZavtikZephyr
9- 6^4	RC	F	40.20	68	3	7	3	2	2^{4}½	40.53	1.40	AA	----	Saved turns	SuperGirl,Tuckaprofit,GreetMe^7
8-30^4	RC	F	39.59	67	6	8	3	2	2^{hd}	39.61	3.10	AA	----	Benf 1st cmg rl	BarryProfitable,LuckyLadyLisa,QuickSack
8-26^{13}	RC	F	39.58	66	4	5	6	5	5^5	39.95	20.50	S	----	Evenly inside	RapidoGal,Bartie,FrontCover

3 WHITE — MIST BEHAVIN (62)

LGP 23 8 5 4 3 — RAY 1 0 0 0 1

Owner—Roland F. Mc Leroy
Kennel—Chris Randle
Trainer—Maurice Henvey

Dark Brindle F., December, 1987. HD's Eli—Goodnite Irene.

Race	Dis.	Tk.	Tm.	Wt.	PP	Off	1-8	Str	Fin	RT	Odds	Gr	FTT	Comment	Order of Finish
10-10^{10}	O.C.	F	39.57	61	7	8	6	5	1^{hd}	39.57	4.40	SAA	----	Fast finish wide	ZavtikZephyr,HomeRunHank,DoctorRandy
10- 6^{13}	O.C.	F	38.73	61½	7	7	8	8	8^9	39.36	4.30	SAA	----	Never prominent	Allegis,KacyBodock,FrontCover
10- 2^4	O.C.	F	39.43	62	1	3	8	6	1^{ns}	39.43	2.60	SAA	----	From last outs	JessieFlanagan,KacyBodock,SR'sSwinger
9-29^{1}s	5-16	F	31.17	62	2	8	7	6	4^6	31.58	...		----	Lacked erly spd	KingBell,SassyWinner,FabledGazzelle
9-26^{12}	O.C.	F	38.14	61½	5	5	4	2	1^4	38.14	5.10	AA	----	Mzzl off driving	Cut'sGambler,CashForChris,SillyBilly
9-22^2	O.C.	F	38.41	62	8	2	2	1^2	1^{6}½	38.41	4.20	A	----	Mzzl off drw out	FabledCharisma,CatesUpFront,ChasquinLatrela
9-15^2	O.C.	F	39.09	62	2	2	11½	1^2	1^8	39.09	1.70	BB	----	Str command wide	DreamAlibi,Blackeyes,Didazz
8-31^{12}	O.C.	F	38.79	62	8	7	5	4	2^1	38.85	2.50	BB	----	Steady gain	ECCyclone,DollarBill,Labit'sShelby
8-26^2	O.C.	F	38.79	61½	7	8	4	4	2^1	38.84	2.50	BB	----	Gained plce drvn	ToteTheLoad,WatchNLearn,ECCyclone
8-22^9	O.C.	F	38.96	62	2	1	7	4	3^6	39.39	1.80	BB	----	Closed for show	SportsDate,JO'sAnne,AtwoodNike

4 GREEN — CASH FOR CHRIS (71)

LGP 44 12 5 5 7 — PLN 3 0 0 1 1

Owner—W. O'Connell & M. Barber
Kennel—Anthony Tutalo
Trainer—Ken Richard

Brindle M., September, 1986. Sports Special—Strange Asset.

Race	Dis.	Tk.	Tm.	Wt.	PP	Off	1-8	Str	Fin	RT	Odds	Gr	FTT	Comment	Order of Finish
10-10^{10}	O.C.	F	39.57	69	2	3	4	4	5^{4}½	39.89	2.00	SAA	----	Shutoff early	MistBehavin,ZavtikZephyr,HomeRunHank
10- 6^{12}	O.C.	F	38.97	69½	4	2	1^3	1^4	1^{2}½	38.97	3.70	SAA	----	Quick commnd mtk	MuggsyBogues,BarryProfitable,HN'sHampshire^7
10- 2^6	O.C.	F	39.02	70	3	4	2	2	1^1	39.02	5.90	SAA	----	Came on stretch	LaserLightning,Winterfest,PrettyMaggie
9-26^{12}	O.C.	F	38.14	69½	8	3	1^2	1^2	3^5	38.47	5.80	AA	----	Overtkn in str	MistBehavin,Cut'sGambler,SillyBilly
9-22^{13}	O.C.	F	39.23	70	3	2	5	5	4^2	39.37	3.30	AA	----	Shuffled back	SillyBilly,SportsDate,TBElvira
9-18^{12}	O.C.	F	38.75	70	1	5	1^1	1^4	1^{4}½	38.75	4.10	AA	----	Drew clear bkstr	Robin'sEdge,SportsDate,TBElvira
9- 4^{13}	O.C.	F	38.80	70	3	7	7	7	7^{11}	39.57	5.40	AA	----	Blkd crtn turn	RoadTrip,TBElvira,SpeedoMr.Earl
8-30^{12}	O.C.	F	38.55	70	3	3	4	4	3^6	38.55	3.50	AA	----	Gained for show	RoadTrip,SillyBilly,TBElvira
8-26^{13}	O.C.	F	38.95	70	8	8	3	1^2	2^1	39.00	2.50	AA	----	Forced late pace	RoadTrip,OrientalViolet,SpeedoMr.Earl
8-23^{12}	O.C.	F	38.62	69½	8	5	4	5	7^9	39.23	4.60	AA	----	Trbl aftr break	SpeedoMr.Earl,RoadTrip,CatesUpFront

Winterfest-1989

GREYHOUND DERBY

THIRTEENTH RACE

SUPERFECTA & QUINIELA WAGERING ON THIS RACE

TRACK RECORD—37.59
Ted Capwell—October 10, 1988

Grade S

PostPos.	Race	Dis.	Tk.	Tm.	Wt.	PP	Off	1/8	Str	Fin	RT	Odds	Gr	FTT	Sts	1	2	3	4	Order of Finish	LGP 10/14/89/E/13

5 WHITE-BLACK — WINTERFEST (74)

														LGP	3	1	0	2	0	Owner—Chris Randle

RAY 43 5 5 8 6 — Kennel—Chris Randle (Raynham) — Trainer—Timothy Andrews

Brindle M., September, 1986, Placid Ace—Domilee.

10-10⁴	O.C.	F	39.20	72½	2	4	3	2	3½	39.23	1.20	S	----	Never far back	SillyBilly,JustCan'tLose,CatnsUpFront
10- 6¹⁰	O.C.	F	38.56	73	5	1	1³	1³	1³	38.56	7.50	S	----	Wire to wire mtk	AJ'sTropicstorm,LaserLightning,SurfireGail
10- 2⁶	O.C.	F	39.02	74	8	7	4	3	3¹½	39.13	6.10	S	----	Closed gap ins	CashForChris,LaserLightning,PrettyMaggie
9-26⅝	O.C.	F	38.57	73	7	2	1¹½	1¹½	1³	38.57	...		----	Held safe margin	HomeRunHank,FabledCharlie,IfYouSayGo⁴

(BELOW AT RAYNHAM-TAUNTON, MA, 1989)

9-21³	5-16	F	30.43	73	2	7	1⁴	1⁷	1¹⁰	30.43	1.90	°C	----	Much the best	Fandango,PanamaSpot,RanchoSuzyQ
9-18²ₓ	3-8	F	38.01	74	3	2	4	4	3⁶	38.44	3.10	C	----	Stdy effort insd	Bab'sDallas,Mena,Memories
9-10¹²ₓ	3-8	F	38.66	72	6	1	2	1¹	2¹½	38.75	3.50	C	----	Outfnshed insd	Ric'sRiddle,LisaBonet,Mena
9- 6²ₓ	5-16	F	31.71	73	4	2	4	2	1¹½	31.71	...		----	Stretch drv insd	WinsomeWench,SecondShrm,MsHiFlvn

6 YELLOW — BOLIGEE CAPONE (69)

LGP 3 2 0 1 0 — Owner—Doris G. Greene

PLN 31 13 8 5 0 — Kennel—Bay Point — Trainer—Graydon Robtoy

Dark Brindle M., March, 1987, Rooster's Sput—Credit Good.

10-10³	O.C.	F	38.79	68½	4	2	1⁶	1⁶	1⁵	38.79	4.80	S	----	Far the best mtk	KacyBodock,Robin'sEdge,PrettyMaggie
10- 6⁴	O.C.	F	38.82	68	2	6	4	4	3⁴	39.08	2.10	S	----	Closing blocked	Magee,MyOlivia,FabledCharlie
10- 2³	O.C.	F	39.32	68	5	3	5	3	1¹	39.32	1.30	S	----	Trbl kpt driving	GiggiDear,RoyalGolinda,SpeedoRalph
9-26⅝	O.C.	F	38.54	69	6	2	3	3	3¹	38.63	...		----	Despite trouble	KacyBodock,YKnotGayle,SirDonaldTrump⁴

(BELOW AT PLAINFIELD, CT, 1989)

9-23¹⁰	YC	F	39.00	67½	1	4	2	2	1²½	39.00	.90	°A	----	Driving finish	TM'sDetermined,TuffTiffy,BckikTshb
9-19¹⁰ₓ	YC	M	38.75	68	8	1	1	1⁴	1⁴½	38.75	1.00	°A	----	Won going away	TM'sDetermined,TuffTiffy,AlyeStp
9-13¹⁰	YC	F	39.11	67½	8	6	2	1²	1⁷	39.11	1.00	°A	----	Strong finish	SuzieRules,DJ'sCherry,TM'sFlgRar
9- 7⁶	YC	F	39.52	68	2	1	1⁴	1⁴	1⁴	39.52	1.00	°A	----	Alwys on top ins	DJ'sCherry,SuzieRules,ChmpgMldy

7 GREEN-WHITE — SPORTS CANNON (72)

LGP 3 1 1 0 0 — Owner—B.H. Cole

RAY 37 13 8 7 3 — Kennel—B.H. Cole (Raynham) — Trainer—Wally Souza, Jr.

Red Brindle M., March, 1987, Ben Green—DJ Hutan.

10-10¹²	O.C.	F	38.93	73	8	7	4	3	2⁵	39.26	7.20	S	----	Gradual gain wd	Allegis,AJ'sTropicstorm,MuggsyBogues⁷
10- 6⁸	O.C.	F	38.89	72	5	2	2	2	1¹	38.89	8.20	S	----	Late drive mdtk	Robin'sEdge,IntenseTime,DoctorRandy
10- 2¹²	O.C.	F	38.01	71½	3	8	7	7	7¹⁹	39.33	6.30	S	----	Never prominent	Allegis,MyOlivia,AJ'sTropicstorm
9-28⅝	O.C.	F	38.55	71½	8	3	2	2	1½	38.55	...		----	Came on str mdtk	KiowaHumphry,HN'sHampshire³

(BELOW AT RAYNHAM-TAUNTON, MA, 1989)

9-22²	7-16	F	43.70	71	5	1	1³	1⁴	1⁵½	43.70	1.80	TA	----	Box to wire	MistyRed,Kelodius,WhatAboutWin
9-17¹¹½	3-8	F	37.73	71	8	7	8	8	5⁹	38.09	2.20	A	----	Trouble thruout	BabyDoll,HWatt,EtchAFuture
9-13⁷	5-16	F	31.30	71	1	5	5	4	3²½	31.46	1.10	A	----	Steady drive mtk	OT'sBananaRoll,CourtSd,BtchRdrck
9- 6¹¹	5-16	F	31.11	71	6	6	7	3	3⁶	31.54	4.40	A	----	Crowded brk drvg	DarkSunshine,ToTheTip,PatCEsyLss
9- 3¹²	7-16	F	44.11	70½	5	1	1²	1²	1²	44.11	6.00	SA	----	Gold Collar Chmp	AJ'sTropicstorm,FlehyAc,WhtAbtWn

8 YELLOW-BLACK — ROYAL GOLINDA (58)

LGP 3 1 0 2 0 — Owner—Johnny Biehle

RAY 31 6 7 3 3 — Kennel—Steve Merlock — Trainer—Steve Merlock

White & Black F., November, 1987, Barry Lyndon—Ken's Lady.

10-10⁷	O.C.	F	39.33	57	8	5	2	2	3ʰᵈ	39.35	14.90	S	----	Almost up rail	SportsMission,BabyDoll,MooMoo
10- 6²	O.C.	F	38.96	57	4	2	1½	1¹½	1½	38.96	9.70	S	----	Gamely inside	MajorDemon,QuickSack,JessieFlanagan⁷
10- 2³	O.C.	F	39.32	58	2	1	1²	1¹½	3¹	39.40	12.90	S	----	Overtkn late str	BoligeeCapone,GiggiDear,SpeedoRalph
9-28⅝	O.C.	F	38.57	58	2	3	4	4	4⁹	39.22	...		----	No trouble ins	SR'sSwinger,WaveSounds,IntenseTime⁴

(BELOW AT RAYNHAM-TAUNTON, MA, 1989)

9-24⁹	3-8	F	38.45	57	4	2	3	2	2⁴	38.75	2.50	°B	----	Forward fctr ins	LashingSleet,FnshngSprt,RnchRsty
9-21¹¹ₓ	3-8	F	37.56	57½	7	2	6	7	7¹³½	38.50	36.80	A	----	Hit 1st turn	FabledCharlie,MadRoman,GullsCndy
9-15¹¹ₓ	3-8	F	37.55	57½	4	3	7	6	6⁸½	38.16	27.80	A	----	Early trouble	AlyceR'sLoulu,Sadiesindn,KcyBdck
9- 9²ₓ	3-8	F	37.57	58	2	3	6	6	6¹⁷	38.76	5.10	A	----	Close qtrs early	KacyBodock,Gull'sCindy,SunnysMjr

SELECTIONS: 1—2—6—4

Swedish Episode-1990

AMERICAN DERBY AT A GLANCE

DISTANCE	3-8ths of a mile, 2010-ft Ocean Course. by **Ted Capwell**, 37.59 on October 10, 1988.
QUALIFIERS & AVERAGE RACE TIMES	(1) Swedish Episode, , 38.99; (2) **Advice**, 38.85; (3) **Legs Maverick**, 39.24; (4) **Chet**, 38.55; (5), I's On Top, 38.86; (6) **EZ Quest**, 39.09; (7) **Pretty Maggie**, 38.83; (8) **Flying Vince**, 38.53.
ENTRIES BY POST POSITION	(1) **Swedish Episode** represents the Marion Currier Kennel and Raynham/Taunton Park, (2) **Advice** is from the Chris Randle Kennel and Raynham/Taunton Park, (3) **Legs Maverick** represents the Steve Merlock Kennel and Raynham/Taunton Park, (4) **Chet** represents the Cuddy-Randle Kennel of Raynham/Taunton Park, (5) **I's on Top** is from the Paul Paulk Kennel and Lincoln Greyhound Park, (6) **EZ Quest** represents the Nanci Caswell Kennel and Lincoln Greyhound Park, (7) **Pretty Maggie** is from the Mike Castellani Kennel and Wonderland Park, (8) **Flying Vince** is from the Fortune Kennel and Wonderland Park.
PURSE DISTRIBUTION	**Winner**, $30,000; **second**, $10,000; **third**, $5,000; **fourth**, $3,000; **fifth** through **eighth**, $1,500. Total added: $54,000.
COMPETITION BREAKDOWN	Swedish Episode did not defeat a Derby finalist, **Advice** did not defeat a derby finalist, **Legs Maverick** defeated **Swedish Episode**, **Chet** defeated **Flying Vince**, **I's On Top** defeated **EZ Quest**, EZ Quest did not defeat a Derby finalist, **Pretty Maggie** defeated I's On Top and EZ Quest, Flying Vince defeated **Chet**.
AVERAGE BETTING ODDS THROUGH THREE ROUNDS	Swedish Episode, .30, **Advice**, 5.20, **Legs Maverick**, 11.10, **Chet**, 2.80, I's On Top, 1.90; EZ Quest, 2.30; **Pretty Maggie**, 4.60; **Flying Vince**, 1.80.
PREVIOUS DERBY CHAMPIONS AT LINCOLN	1989 – Chris Randle's Winterfest by 1 length in 38.27 1988 – Harlan Kennel's Ico Evan, by five lenghts in 38.45 1987 – Josef & Sherck Kennel's Fuel's Stargazer, by 3 1/2 lengths in 38.36. 1986 – Fulginiti Kennel's Prince Proper, by one length in 38.52.
FASTEST DERBY QUALIFYING TIME	38.20 by Rosebud Christie.
LARGEST DERBY WIN PAYOFF	Devon Uncopy paid $81.60 in 1981.
VICTORY MARGIN Longest Shortest	Feldcrest, by eight lengths, 1958. Twilight Bell in 1972, and Devon Uncopy in 1981, both by a nose.

Swedish Episode-1990

THIRTEENTH RACE

 OCEAN COURSE 2010 Feet

$50,000 AMERICAN

Grade S

TRACK RECORD—37.59
Ted Capwell—October 10, 1988

SUPERFECTA & QUINIELA WAGERING ON THIS RACE

PostPos.	Race	Dis.	Tk.	Tm.	Wt.	PP	Off	1-8	Str	Fin	RT	Odds	Gr	FTT	Sts	1	2	3	4	Order of Finish	LGP 10/05/90/E/13

1 RED — SWEDISH EPISODE (68)
LGP 3 2 1 0 0 — Owner—Marion W. Currier
RAY 25 19 1 2 1 — Kennel—Marion Currier — Trainer—Grace Schaffer
White Red F., November, 1987. Dutch Bahama—Meter Maid.

10- 2[12]	O.C.	F	39.51	66½	7	6	4	4	2ns	39.52	.40	S	---- Trbl closing lte	LegsMaverick,Tracy'sBest,OtherMethod[7]
9-28[13]	O.C.	F	39.08	67	2	5	1¹	1²	15½	39.08	.30	S	---- Late command mtk	LaserLightning,Kakadu,JK'sDapperDan
9-24[12]	O.C.	F	38.37	66½	2	3	1⁶	1⁷	19½	38.37	.20	S	---- Unchallenged mtk	TBElvira,Winterfest,CommonDestiny
9-20½	5-16	F	30.55	68½	5	2	1³	1⁴	15½	30.55	...		---- Easily inside	SportsCannon,TM'sCameo³

(BELOW AT RAYNHAM-TAUNTON, MA, 1990)

9- 8⁷½	3-8	F	38.31	66½	2	4	1ns	13½	11½	38.31	.60	A	---- Saved 1st wd str	PrettyEllie,PanamaRich,SprtsMssn
9- 4¹¹½	3-8	F	38.17	66½	5	4	8	7	4⁷	38.65	.40	A	---- Frcd wd thruout	RearStep,SportsMission,PrettyEll

(BELOW AT WONDERLAND, MA, 1990)

8-25[12]	RC	F	38.04	66½	4	4	5	4	6⁸	38.60	1.60	S	---- Hit hard 1st tm	Bartie,RosebudChristie,TomQuick
8-21[11]	RC	F	38.97	67	3	5	6	3	37½	39.50	.20	S	---- Shtf ofstrd erly	KidOctane,TM'sCameo,TeamoChamp

2 BLUE — ADVICE (65)
LGP 3 1 1 0 0 — Owner—Chris Randle
RAY 21 5 2 6 2 — Kennel—Chris Randle (Raynham) — Trainer—Tim Andrews
Red M., December, 1988. Home Computer*—Summin Up.

10- 2³	O.C.	F	38.53	65	4	4	6	6	58½	39.12	2.20	S	---- Crd erly wd aftr	SportsCannon,Angwish,JK'sDapperDan
9-28³	O.C.	F	38.67	65½	6	2	2	1¹½	1³	38.67	3.60	S	---- Led outs drw clr	BoligeeCapone,Bob'sBolster,Cut'sGambler⁷
9-24⁹	O.C.	F	38.75	65	1	2	1¹½	1¹½	2ns	38.76	9.90	S	---- Almost held on	TomQuick,Tracy'sBest,Angwish
9-20½	O.C.	F	38.18	65	4	1	4	4	3¹⁰	38.90	...		---- Drppd back early	FlyingVince,Bob'sNiel,JK'sDapperDan⁴

(BELOW AT RAYNHAM-TAUNTON, MA, 1990)

9-16⁷	3-8	F	38.03	65	2	2	4	5	45½	38.43	4.70	A	---- Cls qtrs early	Angwish,AnniePace,KountryPlayer
9-12⁷	3-8	F	38.36	63½	4	3	6	3	11½	38.36	2.60	A	---- Late control mtk	AnniePace,Pa'sDreaming,BadgerGam
9- 7⁷½	3-8	S	38.46	65½	7	6	6	6	64½	38.79	2.50	A	---- Cls qtrs early	MountainRumor,AnniePace,PasDrmng
9- 1⁴	3-8	F	38.38	65	4	5	7	4	3⁴	38.67	3.00	A	---- Dsp crwd bkstr	BadgerGame,Pa'sDreaming,LngTllPt
8-27⁴	3-8	F	38.20	65	8	5	3	2	2ns	38.21	5.50	A	---- Hard try inside	PanamaRich,Pa'sDreaming,ChinaTwn

3 WHITE — LEGS MAVERICK (64)
LGP 6 2 1 1 0 — Owner—Patsy Green
RAY 47 8 6 11 8 — Kennel—Steve Merlock — Trainer—Steve Merlock
White & Black M., July, 1988. Jock's Warrior—Desto Diane.

10- 2[12]	O.C.	F	39.51	62	8	5	2	1nk	1ns	39.51	13.90	S	---- Gamely some wd	SwedishEpisode,Tracy'sBest,OtherMethod⁷
9-28⁹	O.C.	F	38.99	63	7	4	2	2	1½	38.99	8.20	S	---- Frcd pace cm on	SirDonaldTrump,Intergrate,SassyWinner⁷
9-24⁷	O.C.	F	38.76	63½	3	3	4	5	5⁷	39.23	11.10	S	---- Close qtrs early	I'sOnTop,BoligeeCapone,TBMariah
9-20½	O.C.	F	38.60	64	5	3	2	3	3⁴	38.86	...		---- Erly bid some wd	PrettyMaggie,Intergrate³

(BELOW AT RAYNHAM-TAUNTON, MA, 1990)

9-14[12]	7-16	F	43.89	64	1	4	1¹	2	39½	44.54	6.80	TA	---- Erly leader outs	Warhol,Aprisa,PanamaRico⁷
9- 9²	7-16	F	44.44	64½	8	1	2	1³	11½	44.44	1.30	TB	---- Lastd gamely mtk	MDSportsMan,SweetyBird,DenisetDb
9- 2²	7-16	F	44.04	64	1	7	3	2	3¹	44.12	10.40	TB	---- Led in bkstr mtk	PanamaRico,DenisetaDeb,AnniePace
8-29⁷	7-16	F	43.51	62	2	6	5	6	7¹²½	44.39	11.70	SB	---- Crowded crl trn	CommonDestiny,Aprisa,GullsBrgndy⁷
8-25²	7-16	F	43.01	63½	2	6	4	2	3¹¹	43.79	8.60	SB	---- Lost place duel	SportsCannon,NightHaven,PatCEstl⁷

4 GREEN — CHET (79)
LGP 3 1 2 0 0 — Owner—W.L. Lowrence
RAY 21 13 6 1 0 — Kennel—Cuddy - Randle — Trainer—Don Cuddy
Red Brindle M., August, 1988. Understood—Sterrett.

10- 2⁷	O.C.	F	38.73	79½	1	3	2	3	2³	38.95	1.10	S	---- Good eff some wd	FlyingVince,KB'sFlora,CS'sCashaticket
9-28²	O.C.	F	38.27	79½	5	2	1¹½	1¹½	12½	38.27	1.90	S	---- Late control mtk	FlyingVince,Regatta'sPride,Bob'sNiel
9-24⁵	O.C.	F	38.20	80	6	1	2	2	23½	38.44	5.30	S	---- Pressing early	RosebudChrisie,CuddlesColleen,IAmGoinPlaces
9-20½	O.C.	F	38.71	79½	6	3	2	1¹½	2¹	38.80	...		---- Ofstrd cght ins	KidOctane,SirDonaldTrump,HeyAustin⁴
9-10½	5-16	F	30.79	80	2	6	4	3	36½	31.25	...		---- Saved stretches	PlayfulMood,VelvetDutchman,IAmGoinPlaces

(BELOW AT RAYNHAM-TAUNTON, MA, 1990)

7-19⁴	3-8	F	38.19	79	3	5	3	1¹½	12½	38.19	.30	A	---- Split ldrs bkstr	KountryPlayer,RoyalJBsTry,BoyDll
7-12[11]	5-16	M	31.74	78	2	2	4	2	2½	31.84	1.00	A	---- Closed gap late	GraceQuigley,MatchTheCat,MllrWhz
7- 4⁴	3-8	F	37.68	79	5	2	2	1¹½	12½	37.68	.80	A	---- Drew clear mdtk	Bab'sDallas,KountryPlayr,MllrWhz⁷
7- 1½	3-8	F	38.45	79½	6	1	1⁸	1⁵	15½	38.45	.90		---- Mch the best mtk	RoyalJB'sTroy,MoellrWhz,GllsHrvy

Swedish Episode-1990

Grade S

SUPERFECTA & QUINIELA WAGERING ON THIS RACE

TRACK RECORD—37.59
Ted Capwell—October 10, 1988

PostPos. | Race | Dis. | Tk. | Tm. | Wt. | PP | Off | 1-8 | Str | Fin | RT | Odds | Gr | FTT | Sts | 1 | 2 | 3 | 4 | Order of Finish | LGP 10/05/90/E/13

5 — WHITE-BLACK

I'S ON TOP (72) — LGP 26 9 6 4 3 — SEA 3 0 0 1 1

Owner—Paul Paulk
Kennel—Paul Paulk
Trainer—Brian Sanchez

Light Blue Brindle M., December, 1987. Seeinandbeinseen—Ski Squaw.

Race	Dis.	Tk.	Tm.	Wt.	PP	Off	1-8	Str	Fin	RT	Odds	Gr	FTT	Comment	Order of Finish
10- 2^{9}	O.C.	F	38.75	72	1	5	2	2	3^{2}	38.88	2.50	SAA	----	Chased winner	Intergrate,PrettyMaggie,TomQuick
9-28^{4}	O.C.	F	38.93	72½	2	2	1^{5}	1^{4}½	2^{hd}	38.95	1.50	SAA	----	Big lead overtkn	OtherMethod,TomQuick,TBElvira
9-24^{7}	O.C.	F	38.76	71	4	6	5	3	1^{1}	38.76	1.60	SAA	----	Long drive rail	BoligeeCapone,TBMariah,Intergrate
9-18^{12}	O.C.	F	39.26	71½	8	6	2	3	5^{6}	39.70	2.50	AA	----	Thrt to str bmpd	EZQuest,SpeedoSweetpea,ScotchLad
9-14^{13}	O.C.	F	39.29	71	5	8	4	2	1^{2}	39.29	3.00	AA	----	Saved drove thru	SpeedoSweetpea,TBMariah,*IAmGoinPlaces
9-10^{2}	O.C.	F	38.47	72	5	4	1^{8}	1^{9}	1^{8}	38.47	.70	A	----	Impressively ins	RioDarlaE,RB'sStarBuck,Regatta'sPride
9- 5^{7}	5-16	F	31.25	72½	1	3	4	4	3^{7}	31.73	1.20	A	----	Blocked twice	GetDownMama,BoldExpress,OftenFey
(BELOW AT SEABROOK, NH, 1990)															
8-28^{10}	5-16	F	30.23	72	7	7	7	6	4^{4}½	30.55	21.20	S	----	Late dash mid	CCBigOne,MaxLance,DJ'sMr.CoCo^{7}
8-24^{12}	5-16	F	30.71	72	4	8	8	5	3^{9}½	31.36	6.30	S	----	Desp blkd far tn	Bob'sRadar,PleasantGrove,OneSitn

6 — YELLOW

EZ QUEST (70) — LGP 26 9 4 4 3 — PLN 6 2 2 0 0

Owner—Nanci Lee Caswell
Kennel—Nanci Caswell
Trainer—Jimmy Rae

Brindle M., May, 1987. Quotation—Closing Night*.

Race	Dis.	Tk.	Tm.	Wt.	PP	Off	1-8	Str	Fin	RT	Odds	Gr	FTT	Comment	Order of Finish
10- 2^{9}	O.C.	F	38.75	69½	4	4	5	5	5^{3}	38.97	3.60	SAA	----	Ran evenly mdtrk	Intergrate,PrettyMaggie,I'sOnTop
9-28^{12}	O.C.	F	38.73	69½	7	5	4	2	2^{11}	39.48	1.20	SAA	----	Saved ground bks	IAmGoinPlaces,ScotchLad,Robin'sGlory^{7}
9-24^{11}	O.C.	F	38.82	69	1	3	2	2	1^{1}	38.82	2.00	SAA	----	Won driving mdtk	CS'sCashaticket,Cut'sGambler,PrettyEllie
9-18^{12}	O.C.	F	39.26	69½	2	4	3	1^{1}	1^{3}½	39.26	1.70	AA	----	Svd bks drew out	SpeedoSweetpea,ScotchLad,SassyWinner
9-14^{9}	5-16	F	31.58	70	6	8	6	6	3^{1}	31.64	2.50	AA	----	Late rush mdtrk	JD'sTraxx,JR'sCassiusRe,BlueGrassBank
9-10^{4}	5-16	F	31.01	70	3	8	5	4	2^{1}	31.09	3.10	AA	----	Saved 1st drvng	CuddlesColleen,OrientalGreen,JR'sCassiusRe
9- 5^{4}	5-16	F	30.82	70	5	6	5	4	2^{3}	31.03	2.10	AA	----	Steady drive	CuddlesColleen,JR'sCassiusRe,AMatterOfTime^{7}
9- 1^{9}	5-16	F	31.34	69½	7	8	8	7	7^{2}	31.50	1.60	AA	----	Off slow wd trn	CuddlesColleen,JR'sCassiusRe,OrientalGreen
8-28^{9}	5-16	F	31.44	70½	2	2	6	5	3^{2}	31.58	1.80	AA	----	Gained steadily	CuddlesColleen,RidgeRule,RDTexasToot
8-22^{9}	5-16	F	31.09	70	2	2	3	2	1^{3}	31.09	4.40	AA	----	Coll kpt driving	RidgeRule,MakeMineWine,Encourage

7 — GREEN-WHITE

PRETTY MAGGIE (63) — LGP 3 1 1 0 0 — WON 25 4 6 6 4

Owner—Mike Castellani
Kennel—Mike Castellani
Trainer—Steve Zack

Red F., October, 1987. Keefer—Sea Sprite.

Race	Dis.	Tk.	Tm.	Wt.	PP	Off	1-8	Str	Fin	RT	Odds	Gr	FTT	Comment	Order of Finish
10- 2^{9}	O.C.	F	38.75	62	3	3	3	3	2^{1}½	38.85	10.00	S	----	Gained grnd ins	Intergrate,I'sOnTop,TomQuick
9-28^{9}	O.C.	F	38.99	62	2	6	6	5	5^{6}	39.43	2.20	S	----	Even effort ins	LegsMaverick,SirDonaldTrump,Intergrate^{7}
9-24^{2}	O.C.	F	38.23	62½	1	1	2	2	1½	38.23	1.40	S	----	Came on stretch	ScotchLad,MistBehavin,Bob'sNiel
9-20^{4s}	O.C.	F	38.60	63	2	1	1^{2}½	1^{2}	1^{2}	38.60	...		----	Safe margin ins	Intergrate,LegsMaverick^{3}
(BELOW AT WONDERLAND, MA, 1990)															
9-15^{4}	RC	F	39.34	63	3	1	1^{3}	2	2^{3}½	39.60	6.40	AA	----	Erly ldr sm wd	TomQuick,Bob'sBolster,Sirenian
9- 8^{4}	RC	F	39.13	63	5	5	6	4	3^{11}	39.89	11.70	AA	----	Up for show	RosebudChristie,TomQuick,Minisin
9- 2^{4}	RC	F	39.20	63	3	7	7	7	6^{7}½	39.72	4.80	AA	----	No threat	Tracy'sBest,KidOctane,DJLightning
8-29^{9}	RC	F	38.99	63	8	3	1^{nk}	1^{5}	1^{6}	38.99	5.70	AA	----	Pulled away ins	KidOctane,Tracy'sBest,DJLightning
8-25^{9}	RC	F	38.61	63	5	3	4	3	2½	38.66	10.20	AA	----	Late bid ins	Bob'sBolster,DJLightning,TeamoChamp

8 — YELLOW-BLACK

FLYING VINCE (73) — LGP 3 2 1 0 0 — WON 35 11 7 7 3

Owner—John Alves
Kennel—Fortune (Wonderland)
Trainer—Jimmy Fortunato

White Brindle M., November, 1987. Dutch Bahama—China Gal.

Race	Dis.	Tk.	Tm.	Wt.	PP	Off	1-8	Str	Fin	RT	Odds	Gr	FTT	Comment	Order of Finish
10- 2^{7}	O.C.	F	38.73	73	3	6	4	2	1^{3}	38.73	2.20	S	----	Drove thru ins	Chet,KB'sFlora,CS'sCashaticket
9-28^{2}	O.C.	F	38.27	73½	4	8	4	3	2^{2}½	38.45	1.40	S	----	Gradual gain ins	Chet,Regatta'sPride,Bob'sNiel
9-24^{4}	O.C.	F	38.41	73	5	4	3	2	1^{2}	38.41	1.70	S	----	Up in str outs	JessieFlanagan,JK'sDapperDan,FanDan
9-20^{4s}	O.C.	F	38.18	73	8	3	2	1^{2}	1^{7}	38.18	...		----	Str command ins	Bob'sNiel,Advice,JK'sDapperDan^{4}
(BELOW AT WONDERLAND, MA, 1990)															
9-13^{4}	RC	F	39.91	72	8	8	4	1^{nk}	1^{3}	39.91	.40	A	----	Determined ins	MadisonBlue,SCChargInAce,GH'sPortland
9- 6^{9}	5-16	F	31.20	72½	3	8	7	6	5^{4}	31.50	6.00	AA	----	Slow start	Omigosh,SirFredTavano,PassingTrax
8-30^{9}	5-16	F	30.91	72	5	8	5	4	4^{7}	31.39	6.90	AA	----	Railrunner	DiviMagicRuler,MainLimit,TeamoChamp
8-25^{12}	RC	F	38.04	72	6	5	8	7	7^{11}	38.81	17.00	S	----	Trbl 1st turn	Barrie,RosebudChristie,TomQuick
8-21^{4}	RC	F	39.09	72½	8	4	3	1½	1^{1}	39.09	2.60	S	----	Led on inside	Bob'sNeptune,Salinas,SmileySchool

SELECTIONS: 1–4–8–6

Pro's Hi Gear-1991

Pro's Hi Gear-1991

JOSEPH M. LINSEY'S
1991 AMERICAN GREYHOUND DERBY

Ocean Course

SUPERFECTA WAGERING
THIRTEENTH RACE
QUINIELA Wagering on This Race

Grade S
Track Record 37.59
Ted Capwell
10/10/88

Post & Dist Recd	Date	Race	Dist	Tk	WinTm	Wt	PP	Off	1-8	Str	Finish	ActualTm	Odds	Grade	TnTm		Sts	1st	2nd	3rd	4th	Finish Order	Kennel #

RED — 1 — AA 3 2 0 1

TOM QUICK (82)
Black Male, January 4, 1988, Prince Proper-Tingler
$0 LGP 3 2 0 1 0 WON 35 6 9 11 3
Owner-Donald R. Ryan
Kennel-Ryan Kennel (WON)
Trainer-Henry Chin #76

Date	Dist	Tk	WinTm	Wt	PP	Off	1-8	Str	Finish	ActualTm	Odds	Grade		Comment	Finish Order
10-01 5	O.C.F	38.45	81½	2 8 6	4		1½	38.45	2.90	SAA	.....	Strong finish	AirMajor,DakotaSummer,Sabana
9-27 9	O.C.F	38.26	81	4 8 7	6		34½	38.57	3.90	SAA	.....	Closed well mtk	GreysLadybullet,WhiteLadyBJ,NFrits
9-23 5	O.C.F	37.76	82	5 8 3	1²		16½	37.76	1.20	SAA	.....	Pulling away ins	SPPsExplorer,DNsVodka,EganNite
9-19 7 s	O.C.F	38.11	82	7 4 3	2		1¹	38.11	....		.....	Svd erly came on	Turnagain,TracysFantasy,SweetLaura 4

1991 Races Below at Wonderland

9-12 9	RC F	39.32	81	6 8 7	4		4¹⁰	40.01	8.50	AA	.....	Lacked early spd	PrettyMaggie,ArizonaSun,HarpoonLoe
9-08 11	RC F	38.57	81	5 7 6	4		3⁹	39.19	4.70	AA	.....	Up for show	ArizonaSun,PrettyMaggie,HarpoonLoe
9-02 5	RC F	39.30	81½	5 7 6	3		2³	39.49	1.90	AA	.....	Late gain inside	WhiteLadyBJ,ProsYoungMC,GrysBlntne
8-28 4	RC F	38.88	81	3 8 5	3		3hd	38.90	5.40	AA	.....	Late bid inside	TracysFantasy,WhiteLadyBJ,Amarit

BLUE — 2 — AA 3 2 1 0

ADVICE (66)
Red Male, December 16, 1988, Home Computer*-Summin Up
$0 LGP 3 2 1 0 0 RAY 34 10 8 1 5
Owner-Chris Randle
Kennel-Chris Randle (RAY)
Trainer-Tim Andrews #53

Date	Dist	Tk	WinTm	Wt	PP	Off	1-8	Str	Finish	ActualTm	Odds	Grade		Comment	Finish Order
10-01 7	O.C.F	38.48	65	2 1 2	2		1²	38.48	1.20	SAA	.....	Driving winner	KlssSidkick,SprtsCdillc,JATgAWrrir
9-27 3	O.C.F	37.82	66½	3 1	1¼ 1¼	1⁴¼	37.82	1.00	SAA	.....	Wire to wire mtk	BobsTorch,SPPsExplorer,AirMajor
9-23 3	O.C.F	37.72	66	1 1 2	2		2³	37.91	1.20	SAA	.....	Next best mdtrk	PrettyMaggie,BobsTorch,QuinelaJrry
9-19 9 s	O.C.F	38.23	66	5 1 3	3		2½	38.27	....		.....	Gaining in str	ProsHiGear,BobsTorch,Elias 4

1991 Races Below at Raynham-Taunton

9-13 12	3/8 F	38.63	64½	2 2 6	3		2²½	38.81	3.60	A	.....	Crwd early drvng	MasterGame,PasPerfect,KBsFlora
9-08 12	3/8 F	38.01	65½	6 4 3	3		2²½	38.18	1.40	A	.....	Hard try mdtrk	StayBackJack,WCsPerfectTn,SnpptsSs
9-01 12	3/8 F	38.38	66	2 8 7	6		6⁸	38.95	2.60	SA	.....	No threat to ldr	Turnagain,BabsDallas,MasterGame
8-28 2	3/8 F	38.18	65	3 1	1hd 2	1ns	38.18	.40	SA	.....	Erly ld cm again	RearStep,RoyalJBsLujk,LsssEZGng

WHITE — 3 — AA 3 1 2 0

GREYS LADYBULLET (59)
Fawn & Brindle Female, August 25, 1989, Dutch Bahama-Rifle Lady
$0 LGP 3 1 2 0 0 WON 31 12 6 2 2
Owner-Ernest J. Butler
Kennel-Greymeadow Kennel (WON)
Trainer-Steve Perkins #73

Date	Dist	Tk	WinTm	Wt	PP	Off	1-8	Str	Finish	ActualTm	Odds	Grade		Comment	Finish Order
10-01 12	O.C.F	38.09	59	1 2 2	2		2³	38.30	2.20	SAA	.....	Second best rail	ArizonaSun,IAmGoinPlaces,WildPrfit
9-27 9	O.C.F	38.26	59½	1 5 3	3		1²	38.26	1.30	SAA	.....	Driving on rail	WhiteLadyBJ,TomQuick,NoFruits
9-23 9	O.C.F	38.41	59	3 4 3	3		2⁵	38.77	3.10	SAA	.....	Rail stretches	KaraYoung,PatCHometown,DJsPete
9-19 6 s	O.C.F	38.05	59½	4 1 1³	11½ 11		38.05	....		.....	Held firm rail	Matchable,DJsPete,MDLaken

1991 Races Below at Wonderland

9-12 4	5/16F	31.00	58½	4 1 1³	12½ 12½	31.00	2.40	AA	.....	Box to wire ins	ModernWorld,StormyHary,FabensVictr
9-08 4	5/16F	30.73	58½	3 5 6	6		59½	31.39	.80	AA	.....	No mishaps ins	HotShotCasey,HzerSlider,ModernWrld
9-02 2	5/16F	30.61	58½	8 2 1⁵	15	1⁷	30.61	.50	AA	.....	Quick commnd ins	SeaTrader,BobsSprad,Celebrity
8-24 9	5/16F	30.42	59½	8 6 1⁴	14	15½	30.42	1.30	AA	.....	Like a shot ins	MerryBand,JALylFlyer,FaysLark

GREEN — 4 — AA 3 2 0 1

ARIZONA SUN (77)
Fawn Male, September 18, 1989, Dutch Bahama-Dreamers Island
$0 LGP 3 2 0 1 0 WON 28 10 8 2 1
Owner-R. Belcastro Or A. Conger
Kennel-J.A. Fortune
Trainer-John Alves #24

Date	Dist	Tk	WinTm	Wt	PP	Off	1-8	Str	Finish	ActualTm	Odds	Grade		Comment	Finish Order
10-01 12	O.C.F	38.09	77½	2 1 1³	15	1³	38.09	1.50	SAA	.....	Wire to wire ins	GreysLadybllt,IAmGinPlcs,WildPrfit
9-27 5	O.C.F	37.99	78½	2 3 2	12½ 1³	37.99	.90	SAA	.....	Took control bks	WildProfit,WitNGrit,Newcomb
9-23 7	O.C.F	37.69	77½	6 5 4	3		3⁸½	38.28	2.20	SAA	.....	Good effort ins	ProsHiGear,Lavish,Turnagain
9-19 3 s	O.C.F	38.31	78	1 2 2	1nk 1½	38.31	....		.....	Won lng duel mtk	PrettyMaggie,PatCHometown

1991 Races Below at Wonderland

9-12 9	RC F	39.32	76½	4 1 1⁴	1²	2hd	39.34	1.40	AA	.....	Long ld cght ins	PrettyMaggie,HarpoonLoe,TomQuick
9-08 11	RC F	38.57	76	3 1 1³	15	1⁶	38.57	2.70	AA	.....	Impressively ins	PrettyMaggie,TomQuick,HarpoonLoe
9-04 11	RC F	39.21	77	1 6 5	2		1nk	39.21	1.10	AA	.....	Shffld 1st cm on	CTHorton,HarpoonLoe,PrettyMaggie

Pro's Hi Gear-1991

JOSEPH M. LINSEY'S 1991 AMERICAN GREYHOUND DERBY

Post & Dist Recd | Date Race Dist Tk WinTm Wt PP Off 1-8 Str Finish ActualTm Odds Grade TnTm | Sts 1st 2nd 3rd 4th | Finish Order | Kennel #

BLACK **5** — **WHITE LADY BJ** (59) $0
White,Fwn & Brdl Female,September 14,1988,BJ Gentleman Jim -Eppie
LGP 3 1 1 0 0 / WON 45 10 7 7 3
Owner-Philip J. Recker, Kennel-Nova Kennel (WON), Trainer-Richard Arno — #62

Post & Dist Recd	Date Race	Dist	Tk	WinTm	Wt	PP	Off	1-8	Str	Finish	ActualTm	Odds	Grade	TnTm		Finish Order	
	10-01^{5}	O.C.	F	38.45	58½	6	1	4	6	$6^{6½}$	38.91	3.10	SAA	.....	Erly spd drpd bk	TomQuick,AirMajor,DakotaSummer	
AA 3 1 1 0	9-27^{9}	O.C.	F	38.26	59	3	1	2	2	2^{2}	38.40	6.50	SAA	.....	Erly leader mtk	GreysLadybullet,TomQuick,NoFruits	
	9-23^{11}	O.C.	F	38.22	58	6	1	$1^{1½}$	$1^{1½}$	1^{2}	38.22	6.00	SAA	.....	Wire to wire	Sabana,FrankJG,KelsosSidekick	
	9-19^{4} s	O.C.	F	38.23	58	8	2	2	2	1^{1}	38.23	....		.....	Came on str mdtk	DNsVodka,RunningChamp	3
	1991 Races Below at Wonderland																
	9-15^{1} s	RC	F	39.70	58	8	1	1^{4}	1^{2}	1^{nk}	39.70	....		.....	Long ld held ins	SalsawSwfty,HisArrival,KelssSprkle	
	9-06^{11}	RC	F	38.35	57½	7	6	8	7	7^{18}	39.64	3.00	AA	.....	No threat inside	ProsHiGear,Amarit,TMsRnAWay	
	9-02^{5}	RC	F	39.30	57	2	1	1^{2}	1^{2}	$1^{2½}$	39.30	2.50	AA	.....	All the way ins	TomQuick,ProsYoungMC,GrysBlntne	
	8-28^{4}	RC	F	38.88	58	5	1	1^{1}	1^{1}	2^{ns}	38.89	12.50	AA	.....	Game try some wd	TracysFantasy,TomQuick,Amarit	

YELLOW **6** — **KLONDY** (58) $11,867
Dark Brindle Female,March 31,1989,P's EZ Strider-Knitz
LGP 45 11 10 9 2 / RAY 6 0 2 0 1
Owner-Chris Randle, Kennel-Chris Randle, Trainer-Mike Tremblay — #7

Post & Dist Recd	Date Race	Dist	Tk	WinTm	Wt	PP	Off	1-8	Str	Finish	ActualTm	Odds	Grade	TnTm		Finish Order	
	10-01^{9}	O.C.	F	38.53	57	1	1	$1^{4½}$	$1^{1½}$	$1^{½}$	38.53	13.80	SAA	.....	Box to wire mdtk	Matchable,ProsHiGear,TracysFantasy	
AA39 9 10 8	9-27^{7}	O.C.	F	38.17	57	5	2	$1^{3½}$	$1^{½}$	2^{3}	38.37	4.50	SAA	.....	Set pace ovrtkn	KaraYoung,JohnnyBadboy,Turnagain	7
A 3 1 0 0	9-23^{5}	O.C.	F	37.76	57	3	4	7	7	7^{11}	38.57	13.90	SAA	.....	Blkd aftr break	TomQuick,SPPsExplorer,DNsVodka	
BB 1 1 0 0	9-16^{12}	O.C.	F	38.46	57½	1	2	2	2	3^{3}	38.69	2.00	TAA	.....	Good efft mtk	JATugAWarrior,DakotSmmr,OwincFirst	
	9-12^{12}	O.C.	F	39.13	57	2	2	2	6	6^{6}	39.56	4.30	TAA	.....	Erly speed mtk	JATugAWarrior,WildProfit,DakotSmmr	
	9-07^{13}	O.C.	F	38.17	57	6	4	2	2	3^{4}	38.44	3.70	AA	.....	Threat to str	AeroWarrior,WildProfit,NoFruits	
	9-03^{12}	O.C.	F	38.59	57	3	6	8	8	6^{13}	39.49	2.50	AA	.....	No room aftr brk	WildProfit,IAmGoinPlaces,UnclVinny	
	8-30^{13}	O.C.	F	38.58	57	5	1	$1^{2½}$	$1^{1½}$	1^{1}	38.58	3.60	AA	.....	Was best mdtrk	WildProfit,IAmGoinPlacs,JATgAWrrir	
	8-24^{13}	O.C.	F	38.51	57	1	1	1^{2}	1^{1}	2^{1}	38.58	1.90	TAA	.....	Overtaken mdtrk	QuinelaJerry,WildProfit,GunnerNGo	

GREEN & WHITE **7** — **PRO'S HI GEAR** (68) $0
Brindle Male,September 22,1989,My Unicorn-Labits Della
LGP 3 2 0 1 0 / WON 29 9 7 2 0
Owner-Propst & Wheeler Cuzziere, Kennel-C & W Kennel, Inc. (WON), Trainer-John Liberatore — #68

Post & Dist Recd	Date Race	Dist	Tk	WinTm	Wt	PP	Off	1-8	Str	Finish	ActualTm	Odds	Grade	TnTm		Finish Order	
	10-01^{9}	O.C.	F	38.53	67½	4	2	3	3	3^{3}	38.74	.80	SAA	.....	Crd bmpd crt trn	Klondy,Matchable,TracysFantasy	
AA 3 2 0 1	9-27^{12}	O.C.	F	37.95	67	3	1	1^{3}	1^{7}	1^{5}	37.95	1.20	SAA	.....	With ease mdtrk	Matchable,Sabana,QuinelaJerry	
	9-23^{7}	O.C.	F	37.69	67	2	1	1^{4}	$1^{2½}$	$1^{2½}$	37.69	4.60	SAA	.....	Led box to wire	Lavish,ArizonaSun,Turnagain	
	9-19^{9} s	O.C.	F	38.23	67½	3	2	$1^{2½}$	$1^{2½}$	$1^{½}$	38.23	....		.....	Safe margin mtk	Advice,BobsTorch,Elias	4
	1991 Races Below at Wonderland																
	9-14^{4}	RC	F	39.00	67	2	2	1^{3}	1^{4}	$1^{1½}$	39.00	2.90	AA	.....	Long lead lasted	Amarit,JillyMac,GreysSmpsn	
	9-10^{9}	RC	F	38.59	67	3	4	7	8	8^{14}	39.59	1.00	AA	.....	Outrushed sm wd	Amarit,JillyMac,MntnBuster	
	9-06^{11}	RC	F	38.35	67	5	1	1^{5}	1^{7}	$1^{6½}$	38.35	1.60	AA	.....	Quick trip sm wd	Amarit,TMsRnAWay,JillyMac	
	8-30^{11}	RC	F	38.78	67½	5	2	1^{3}	1^{6}	1^{10}	38.78	4.30	A	.....	Overdrive sm wd	KystnBgler,MerryMonth,GRsMstrmr	

YELLOW & BLACK **8** — **KARA YOUNG** (66) $7,611
Black Female,February 19,1989,Kansas Drifter-Dottie Line
LGP 45 9 8 10 5 / LGP 2 0 0 1 0
Owner-Richard Alves, Kennel-Rickbarb, Trainer-Arthur M. Alves — #20

Post & Dist Recd	Date Race	Dist	Tk	WinTm	Wt	PP	Off	1-8	Str	Finish	ActualTm	Odds	Grade	TnTm		Finish Order	
	10-01^{7}	O.C.	F	38.48	66	8	5	7	6	5^{10}	39.22	4.50	SAA	.....	Bumped frcd wd	Advice,KelsosSidekick,SportsCdillc	
AA12 3 1 3	9-27^{7}	O.C.	F	38.17	65	2	3	2	2	1^{3}	38.17	10.10	SAA	.....	Drove thru mdtk	Klondy,JohnnyBadboy,Turnagain	7
A 13 2 3 3	9-23^{9}	O.C.	F	38.41	64½	7	8	2	2	1^{5}	38.41	63.80	SAA	.....	Driving drw away	GreysLadybullet,PatCHometwn,DJsPte	
BB 4 1 1 1	9-18^{9}	5/16	F	31.17	64½	1	7	8	8	6^{5}	31.50	15.90	AA	.....	Lacked erly spd	Itsallgreektm,GPlyEckrt,SpcilVisin	
B 2 1 1 0	9-14^{13}	O.C.	F	38.29	64½	5	3	4	4	3^{5}	38.65	17.60	TAA	.....	Closed outside	AeroWarrior,JAHighFlight,FrankJG	
	9-11^{12}	O.C.	F	38.95	65	7	7	7	7	6^{5}	39.29	11.90	AA	.....	Wide aftr break	SPPsExplorer,RegalRanee,AeroWarrir	
	9-06^{13}	O.C.	F	38.44	65½	8	3	2	$1^{1½}$	1^{2}	38.44	2.70	A	.....	Drove thru fr tn	WilbeDun,ChalasEasyGor,NikiMyFrind	
	9-03^{2}	O.C.	F	38.05	65½	7	4	3	2	2^{3}	38.28	6.00	A	.....	Saved ground bks	NoFruits,SportsCorvett,NikiMyFrind	
	8-28^{12}	O.C.	F	38.37	66	7	7	6	6	6^{11}	39.13	1.50	A	.....	No room aftr brk	CatesUpFrnt,GrndKidsPick,ChlsEsyGr	

Selections 2 1 7 4

Boligee Champ-1992

Joseph M. Linsey's
AMERICAN GREYHOUND DERBY

1949
Saturday,
November 14, 1992
Post Time 8 p.m.

1992
Souvenir Program
$1.25
Tax Included
Off-Track $1.50

LINCOLN
GREYHOUND PARK
LINCOLN, RHODE ISLAND

"Joseph M. Linsey's

American

Greyhound Derby"

The American Derby is the nation's first "big stakes" greyhound race. The race originated at the Taunton Greyhound Track and was the brainstorm of Taunton's President, Joseph M. Linsey.

The first American Greyhound Derby was run on May 14, 1949, and attracted the finest greyhounds from two continents as champions from both Ireland and America gathered for the event.

The American Greyhound Derby is the predecessor of all modern stakes challenges and can be said to be greyhound racing's "Grandaddy of them all". The prestige of this event has grown throughout the four decades of it's existence, and the coveted Joseph M. Linsey Trophy remains the one owners and trainers most want to win.

The Derby and it's great tradition moved to Rhode Island and the Lincoln Greyhound Park oval in October of 1986. We at Lincoln strive to carry on the great tradition of this fall classic. And in keeping with that tradition, Lincoln Greyhound Park has dedicated the running of the American Greyhound Derby to it's founder --

Joseph M. Linsey

Boligee Champ-1992

JOSEPH M. LINSEY'S $60,000
1992 AMERICAN GREYHOUND DERBY

Ocean Course

SUPERFECTA WAGERING
THIRTEENTH RACE

QUINIELA Wagering on This Race

Grade S
Track Record 37.59
Ted Capwell
10/10/88

Post & Dist Recd	Date Race Dist Tk WinTm Wt	PP Off 1-8 Str Finish ActualTm Odds Grade	TnTm	Sts 1st 2nd 3rd 4th	Finish Order	Kennel #

RED 1 — 3 2 1 0

BOLIGEE CHAMP (68) $920
Brindle Male, August 18, 1990, Rooster's Spur-Boligee Darcy
Owner-T.A. Greene
Kennel-Bay Point Kennel
Trainer-Graydon Robtoy
LGP 3 2 1 0 0 / PLN 37 22 4 7 3 — #44

Date	Dist	WinTm	Wt	PP Off 1-8	Str	Finish	ActualTm	Odds	Grade	Comment	Finish Order
11-09 9	O.C.F	38.79	67½	4 2 3	3	1 2	38.79	5.80	SAA	Came on str mdtk	BXsClaudette,PatCJonesy,OkieGwen
11-06 3	O.C.F	38.39	68	1 6 4	3	2 2	38.55	.50	SAA	Gd effort mdtrk	MysticHero,CrystinFran,CCBlueBaby
11-02 5	O.C.F	39.04	67½	6 5 4	2	1 2	39.04	3.00	SAA	Up in str mdtrk	OkieGwen,BroomsPookie,PleasantKtie
10-29 6 s	O.C.F	38.70	68	2 3 1³	12½	2³	38.89	....		Outfinished ins	Sabana,PleasantKatie,CrystinFran
				1992 Races Below at Plainfield							
10-24 10 x	YC F	38.47	68	3 1 1⁵	1⁸	1¹⁵	38.47	.80	A	Six in a row rl	AGsAimHigh,MiniDon,DonnaKelly
10-21 6 x	YC F	38.75	68	3 3 2	1⁵	1 4½	38.75	.90	A	Extended the ld	BeAAngel,MinnieMaker,DonnaKelly
10-16 12	YC F	39.06	68	3 2 2	2	1 1½	39.06	.70	A	Stretch victory	GullsUptown,JKTrtnJhnny,DnnKlly
10-10 10 x	YC F	39.33	68	3 2 2	1⁴	1¹	39.33	1.20	A	Shrinking lead	JoesBet,DonnaKelly,MinnieMaker

BLUE 2 — 3 2 0 0

PHANTOM LASS (61) $1,226
Brindle Female, July 1, 1990, Torrey Pines-Semi Pro
Owner-Ryan Farms Kennel
Kennel-Ryan Kennel
Trainer-Henry Chin
LGP 3 2 0 0 0 / WON 49 15 7 7 7 — #52

Date	Dist	WinTm	Wt	PP Off 1-8	Str	Finish	ActualTm	Odds	Grade	Comment	Finish Order
11-09 9	O.C.F	38.79	60	3 1 2	2	5³	38.98	.50	SAA	Evenly late mtk	BoligeeChamp,BXsClaudette,PatCJnsy
11-06 5	O.C.F	38.40	61½	4 2 12½	1²	1²	38.40	1.60	SAA15.49	Held safe margin	RockysLady,BXsClaudett,HrdlyPffing
11-02 7	O.C.F	39.06	60½	1 2 1²	1³	1³	39.06	.80	SAA	Handily mdtrk	TracysFantasy,Klondy,SixteenDelits
10-29 3 s	O.C.F	38.66	60	1 1 2	1²	1⁷	38.66	....		Drawing away mtk	SweepingChange,TracysFantasy
				1992 Races Below at Wonderland							
10-24 12	RC F	39.04	60½	2 4 4	3	4 3½	39.29	3.90	S	Followd pace ins	JSIronLeige,GreysStatesman,ProsGor
10-20 4	RC F	35.92	60½	1 2 1⁴	1³	1²	38.92	1.70	S	Long erly ld ins	BabyEmileeAnn,Susanetta,Banbridge
10-16 7	RC F	38.92	61	2 2 2	2	2ns	38.93	1.50	S	Just missed ins	MeadowsBullet,KiowaAnico,BobsSprd
10-12 4	RC F	38.85	61	8 4 1nk	1²	1⁴	38.85	2.90	S	Rushed to ld ins	ECAimHigh,ComancheToni,ProsYoungMC

WHITE 3 — 3 2 0 1

BOLIGEE NICKY (75) $1,226
Black Male, July 3, 1990, Nicky Finn-Cheryl's Ditto
Owner-Doris G. Greene
Kennel-Bay Point Kennel
Trainer-Graydon Robtoy
LGP 3 2 0 1 0 / PLN 33 22 3 4 1 — #44

Date	Dist	WinTm	Wt	PP Off 1-8	Str	Finish	ActualTm	Odds	Grade	Comment	Finish Order
11-09 11	O.C.F	38.96	75	7 8 6	4	3³	39.15	1.10	SAA	Off slow gained	BobsSprad,TracysFantasy,Bellereve
11-06 16	O.C.F	38.80	75	4 7 4	3	1ns	38.80	.80	SAA	Blkd long drive	TracysFantasy,OkieGwen,LimitedAmnt
11-02 12	O.C.F	38.93	74½	8 6 2	1 1½	1⁶	38.93	1.20	SAA	Pulling away ins	MysticHero,AeroWarrior,Sabana
10-29 2 s	O.C.F	38.44	76	4 2 1³	1⁵	1⁷	38.44	....		Easily on rail	MysticHero,BXsClaudette,PrechrRllo
				1992 Races Below at Plainfield							
10-23 12	YC F	38.63	74½	2 2 2	1⁴	1 8½	38.63	.10	A	As expected ins	HawthornHwk,HtshtXprss,ChynnLsbr
10-17 6 x	YC F	38.68	74½	7 7 2	1³	1⁶	38.68	.40	A	Drv to lead bkst	MiniDon,Devilishandmdn,HtshtXprss
10-11 12 x	YC F	38.66	74	5 5 2	1²	1⁵	38.66	.10	A	Six times on top	ProsRoylJwl,Dvlshndmdn,AGsAimHigh
10-06 12 x	YC F	38.48	73½	6 7 3	1²	1³	38.48	.10	A	Quick trip	AGsAimHigh,WhipItUp,KilmarneyWh

GREEN 4 — A 3 2 1 0

MYSTIC HERO (74) $13,719
White & Black Male, June 5, 1990, Dutch Bahama-Gortnaminch Wish*
Owner-Francis Flavin
Kennel-Pat Dalton
Trainer-David O'Keeffe
LGP 45 13 10 5 12 / WON 4 0 0 1 2 — #5

Date	Dist	WinTm	Wt	PP Off 1-8	Str	Finish	ActualTm	Odds	Grade	Comment	Finish Order
11-09 7	O.C.F	38.81	73	5 6 4	1¹	1 ½	38.81	1.90	SAA	Held gamely outs	Sabana,BluegrassBrandy,BroomsPookie
11-06 3	O.C.F	38.39	72½	2 3 2	1 1½	1²	38.39	2.70	SAA	Led in bks outs	BoligeeChamp,CrystinFran,CCBlueBby
11-02 12	O.C.F	38.93	72½	5 4 1 1½	2	2⁶	39.33	12.40	SAA	Set pace outside	BoligeeNicky,AeroWarrior,Sabana
10-29 2 s	O.C.F	38.44	73½	8 3 2	2	2⁷	38.93	....		Chased winner	BoligeeNicky,BXsClaudett,PrchrRllo
10-23 13	5/16	30.70	73	4 8 7	3	3¹¹	31.48	20.00	AA	Some bkstr gain	RockysLady,DakotaSummer,Peleke
10-19 11	5/16	31.11	73	7 6 3	2	2¹	31.20	10.70	AA	Never far back	PlayTheWind,TipisMagic,DakotaSummr
10-16 13	5/16	30.99	73	1 5 8	8	4¹⁰	31.72	18.90	AA	Wide thruout	PyrmidHardboby,NastyAlli,PlyThWind
10-12 13 x	5/16	30.56	73	5 5 6	4	4⁸	31.10	7.10	SAA	Wide stretches	PyrmidHardboby,DakotSmmr,PlyThWind
10-09 10	5/16	31.41	73	3 6 2	2	1 2½	31.41	1.90	SAA	Wide came on str	PyrmidLearJet,LamarsFred,SamLogan

Boligee Champ-1992

JOSEPH M. LINSEY'S $60,000 1992 AMERICAN GREYHOUND DERBY

Post & Dist Recd	Date	Race Dist Tk	WinTm	Wt	PP Off 1-8 Str	Finish	ActualTm	Odds	Grade	TnTm		Sts 1st 2nd 3rd 4th	Finish Order	Kennel #

BLACK

5 — ROCKY'S LADY (60) $12,656

Red Fawn Female, April 22,1990, Do Rocky Do-Divot Stomper

Owner-C. Murphy Or Hart Kennel
Kennel-Mel Langford Ent,Inc.
Trainer-Michael Roderick   #12

LGP 70 21 7 3 4
LGP 11 4 0 2 1

AA	6	3	1	1	11-09 4	O.C.F 38.50	60	6 3 1⁴	1⁵	1³	38.50 2.60 SAA ..... In command early	StarLightSis,LimitedAmount,NstyLiz
BB	2	0	0	0	11-06 5	O.C.F 38.40	59½	5 1 2	2	2²	38.55 4.50 SAA ..... Main threat mtk	PhantomLass,BXsClaudtt,HrdlyPffing 7
B	1	0	0	0	11-02¹¹	O.C.F 39.15	61	1 3 2	3	34½	39.46 1.80 SAA ..... Followed pace	PayLuckyLucy,PatCJonesy,NastyLiz 7
					10-30¹³	5/16F 31.21	60	3 1 5	4	2²	31.34 5.40 AA ..... Closed gap mdtk	PlayTheWind,TupeloGenie,AirMajor
					10-26¹¹	5/16F 31.16	60½	7 5 5	4	2½	31.20 4.20 AA ..... Crwd stdy drive	LamarsFred,PlayTheWind,FrankJG
					10-23¹³	5/16F 30.70	60½	6 2 2	1¹	17½	30.70 11.40 AA ..... Strong finish wd	DakotaSummer,MysticHero,Peleke
					10-19¹¹	5/16F 31.11	60	3 1 7	7	8⁷	31.61 6.30 AA ..... Outrshd crowded	PlayTheWind,MysticHero,TipisMagic
					10-14 7 x 5/16F 30.93		61	7 3 1ⁿᵏ	1⁵	1⁶	30.93 1.10 AA 9.04 Easily best outs	FrontMarker,FrankJG,PayBraveDave
					10-09¹⁴	5/16F 31.27	60	2 6 6	5	3²	31.42 5.40 SAA ..... Coll driving wd	PlayTheWind,PyrmidHardboby,IbxBABe

YELLOW

6 — BLUEGRASS BRANDY* (68) $6,442

Brindle Male, August 13,1990, Mr John Dee-Lovely Wish

Owner-Kerry Hills Kennels
Kennel-Kerry Hills
Trainer-Gerard Ryan   #11

LGP 41 12 4 4 5
WON 5 1 0 2 0

AA	4	1	1	1	11-09 7	O.C.F 38.81	67½	2 7 5	4	3⁴	39.07 2.60 SAA ..... Gradual gain mtk	MysticHero,Sabana,BroomsPookie
A	1	1	0	0	11-06¹¹	O.C.F 38.71	68	6 5 4	3	2¹	38.77 .60 SAA ..... Saved coming on	CultHero,SalvoNite,BabyEmileeAnn
					11-02 3	O.C.F 38.83	68	1 2 1⁴	1⁶	1⁶	38.83 1.90 SAA 15.43 Easy winner ins	DLBsInaLee,JABabyMagic,WiseMemory

1992 Races Below at Wonderland

10-24¹¹	RC F 38.86	67	7 6 6	6	6¹¹	39.65 4.00 S ..... No change ins	BobsTray,MeadowsBullet,NiceDelivry
10-20 9	RC F 39.17	67½	1 4 4	5	54½	39.48 2.90 S ..... Shutof far trn	ProsYoungMC,BobsTray,WiseMemory
10-16 5	RC F 38.68	67½	7 1 1⁴	14	18½	38.68 6.00 S ..... All the way out	DJsSalem,Bambridge,MyBlackMirah 7
10-12 7	RC F 38.64	66½	1 3 4	4	3¹⁰	39.38 10.50 S ..... Up for show ins	WickedSpeed,JSIronLeige,SportsIsse
10-06 4	RC F 40.36	68	7 4 4	4	3²	40.48 24.30 S ..... Closing outs	Celebrity,SpeedSampler,MPsRuth

GREEN & WHITE

7 — BX'S CLAUDETTE (58) $797

White & Red Female, October 7,1989, Dutch Bahama-GH's Eleanor

Owner-Bobby W. Brand
Kennel-Slatex Kennel
Trainer-Richard Arno   #42

LGP 3 1 1 1 0
WON 46 6 12 4 4

3	1	1	1	11-09 9	O.C.F 38.79	57½	7 3 1²	11½	2²	38.91 7.10 SAA ..... In & out overtkn	BoligeeChamp,PatCJonesy,OkieGwen
				11-06 5	O.C.F 38.40	58	3 3 3	3	3⁴	38.69 18.30 SAA ..... Close erly ins	PhantomLass,RockysLady,HrdlyPffing 7
				11-02 2	O.C.F 39.36	58	7 4 1⁷	1⁶	1²	39.36 11.10 SAA 15.82 Easily trbl bhnd	HrdlyPffing,OwincFirst,KlssSidkick
				10-29 2 s O.C.F 38.44		58	2 1 3	3	37½	38.97 .... Ran evenly ins	BoligeeNicky,MysticHero,PrechrRllo 4

1992 Races Below at Wonderland

10-22¹¹	RC F 39.35	58	5 4 3	3	2³	39.57 2.20 AA ..... Fctr thruout ins	RadarLock,Kavort,GreysDonovan
10-15 4	RC F 39.15	58	5 1 1⁴	1⁵	1⁵	39.15 6.10 TA ..... Spd to spare ins	GreysBallentine,Scrutinear,RadrLck
10-10 9 x 5/16F 30.86		58½	4 7 6	5	5⁹	31.47 6.70 A ..... Wide 1st turn	Recollection,GrysHndsDwn,FbnsFlint
10-05 4	RC F 39.83	56	7 3 4	5	45½	40.22 1.90 AA ..... Clsg blkd str tn	RoseLodge,GreysBallentine,BbsBlstr

YELLOW & BLACK

8 — SABANA (61) $736

Light Brindle Female, June 2,1989, Dutch Bahama-Someone New

Owner-Mrs. R.H. Walters
Kennel-Mike Castellani, Inc.
Trainer-Steve Zack   #49

LGP 3 1 1 0 1
WON 50 11 12 8 5

3	1	1	0	11-09 7	O.C.F 38.81	60½	1 5 3	2	2½	38.84 2.20 SAA ..... Pressing lte mtk	MysticHero,BluegrassBrndy,BrmsPkie
				11-06¹³	O.C.F 38.72	60	1 4 4	2	1²	38.72 1.60 SAA ..... In & out driving	OwincoFirst,HornetHope,PatCJonesy 6
				11-02¹²	O.C.F 38.93	60½	2 3 6	5	4¹⁰	39.64 4.90 SAA ..... No real threat	BoligeeNicky,MysticHero,AeroWarrir
				10-29 6 s O.C.F 38.70		61	4 1 2	2	1³	38.70 .... Came on str mdtk	BoligeeChamp,PleasntKti,CrystinFrn 4

1992 Races Below at Wonderland

10-24¹²	RC F 39.04	60	5 2 7	5	5⁷	39.52 10.30 S ..... Outrshd to trn	JSIronLeige,GreysStatesman,PrsHiGr
10-20¹¹	RC F 38.77	60½	3 1 1½	1⁵	1⁹	36.77 4.60 S ..... Xtnding mrgin in	LJsLawanna,TwoJakes,JaneAnacin
10-16 5	RC F 38.66	60½	4 4 6	5	5¹⁴	39.66 2.20 S ..... No mshps sm wd	BluegrassBrandy,DJsSlm,DistntDrmmr
10-12 9	RC F 38.87	60½	5 2 2	1⁵	1⁹	38.87 3.90 S ..... Led rl esc drwt	GreysGayle,DjsSalem,DistantDrummer

Selections 3 1 2 6

Wiki Wiki Peka -1993

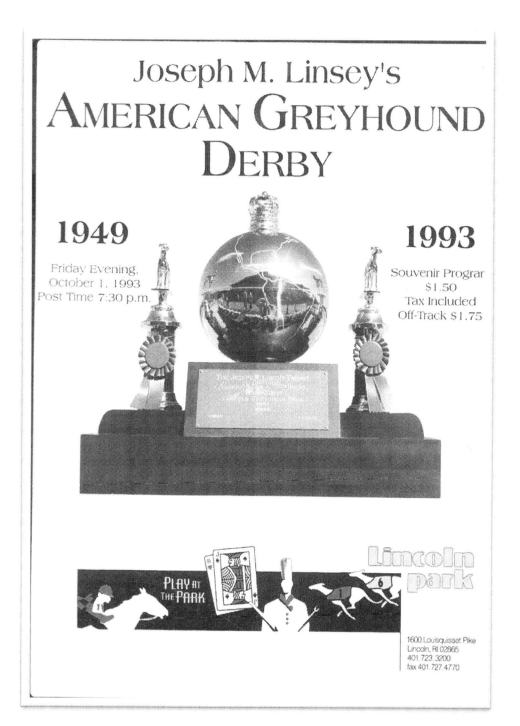

Wiki Wiki Peka -1993

JOSEPH M. LINSEY'S $60,000 1993 AMERICAN GREYHOUND DERBY

2010 FEET — **TWELFTH RACE** — **GRADE S**

OCEAN COURSE

2ND HALF LATE DOUBLE & SUPERFECTA WAGERING

Trifecta & Quiniela Wagering

TRACK RECORD
Vision King
37.44 (09/20/93)

PP · Event · Trk · Dst · TC · Time · Wt · PP · Off · 1/8 · Str · Fin · ART · Odds · Grade · Comment · Opponents Finish Order · LI10/01E12

1 — 20-1 Jet Jaynes (AA) — 72

LI 43 12 6 9 5

Kennel: Nanci Caswell Kennel [3]
Owner: David J. Jeswald
Trainer: Angelo Marchione

White & Red M, May 1, 1991. Bahama Tip-What About Win — $7706

	Event	Trk	Dst	TC	Time	Wt	PP	Off	1/8	Str	Fin	ART	Odds	Grade		Comment	Opponents Finish Order
	09/27 E7	LI	2010 F		37.94	72	7	6	3	3	2 2½	38.10	4.10	SAA		Gradual Gain Mtk	WikiWikiPk, WyOfthDrgn, BlgChmp
	09/24 E10	LI	2010 F		38.39	72	7	4	1 2	1 6	1 4	38.39	5.10	SAA	15.49	Command In Bkstr	ProperLeader, BolgNcky, AJsBlGm
	09/20 E7	LI	2010 F		38.64	73	3	2	6	5	5 6	39.05	4.30	SAA		Blckd Crtn Turn	FabledShockNXS, Tingaling, EJsKr
	09/17 A4	LI	2010 F		39.45	72½	4	8	8	4	3 1	39.52	3.10	TAA		Gained Grnd Mdtk	OhpasBdbybl, NncCnOnc, DwyStlln
	09/11 E12	LI	2010 F		38.32	72	3	3	2	1 2	1 6½	38.32	3.70	TA		Going Away Mdtrk	FbldShckNXS, XqzmSwty, ShbrnNcl
	09/03 E7	LI	2010 F		38.99	72	7	7	6	5	6 7½	39.51	4.70	AA		Ran Evenly Mdtrk	AJ'sShelby, QualityZip, BWHghTm
	08/28 E7	LI	2010 F		38.07	72	3	5	4	4	4 11½	38.88	5.10	AA		Bmpd Erly Ofstrd	AJ'sShelby, TasseDee*, CharlieD
	08/25 E7	LI	2010 F		38.61	72½	8	3	8	8	8 13	39.52	5.10	AA		Bumped Frnt Str	ValsPorsche, HollyBaham, BWHghTm
	08/20 E13	LI	2010 F		38.38	72	8	5	1 1	1 2½	1 4	38.38	2.10*	TA		Drawing Away Str	FabledShockNXS, DrB'sCmm, OnBhm
	08/14 E13	LI	2010 F		37.95	72	3	8	4	4	5 13	38.86	6.70	TAA		Crwd Aftr Break	BWHighTime, BrotherSabu, HllyBhm
	08/11 E12	LI	2010 F		38.60	71½	7	6	6	5	4 12	39.45	1.60*	TAA		Frcd Wd Frnt Str	CCKwikKim, Bellereve, DrB'sCamm
Red	08/06 E7	LI	2010 F		38.21	71½	3	8	7	6	5 14	39.18	4.20	AA		Off Slow Wd Erly	QualityZip, HollyBahama, CharlD

2 — 9-2 Vision King (AA) — 70

LI 3 2 0 0 0
WO 19 3 3 5 2

Kennel: Fulginiti Kennel, Inc. [56]
Owner: John Melillo or Francis Fulginiti
Trainer: Bill Nihan

Black M, Sep 1, 1991. Chevy Montecarlo-Dashing Baby — $1231

	Event	Trk	Dst	TC	Time	Wt	PP	Off	1/8	Str	Fin	ART	Odds	Grade		Comment	Opponents Finish Order
	09/27 E3	LI	2010 F		38.21	70	6	7	5	6	7 10½	39.37	2.50	SAA		Crwd Bmpd Early	TollFree, CharlieD, ShibrenNicol
	09/24 E11	LI	2010 F		38.59	70	3	3	2	1 3	1 8	38.59	7.10	SAA		Best Again Inside	WyOfthDrgn, BBsDtchBy, InPckgDl7
	09/20 E1	LI	2010 F		37.44	70	8	5	2	1 1	1 nk	37.44	14.90	SAA		New Track Record	TollFree, QualityZip, AJ'sBluGm
	09/16 S8	LI	2010 F		39.01	69½	8	1	1 1½	1 ½	4 6	39.43	·		15.51	Overtkn Ent Str	WayOftheDragn, KdCrl, DMsLckyStr4
											Races below at Wonderland						
	09/09 E11	WO	1650 F		30.73	69½	6	4	5	4	3 3	30.96	3.10	AA		Hld Wd 1st Clsd	SR'sBucuti, MohicanSpcl, CMRckvw
	09/05 E11	WO	1650 F		30.62	69	7	5	4	4	4 9½	31.28	5.60	AA		Evenly Inside	KidCreole, Katalist, Alfredson7
	09/01 E1	WO	1650 F		31.08	70	7	1	1 2	1 2	1 3	31.08	1.50	A		Box To Wire Ins	Whozini, JimPallis, Kelso'sCnsrt
	08/28 A11	WO	1650 F		30.84	70	8	6	5	6	6 8	31.47	3.90	A		Hld Wd 1st Trn	Bill'sBomber, OnEydDndy, DvdFrncs
	08/24 E7	WO	2045 F		38.82	70	3	1	2	2	2 8	39.39	20.70	SA		Best Of Rest Mtk	BoligeeChamp, RngOfTrth, DJsBss
	08/20 E2	WO	2045 F		39.32	70	7	3	2	7	7 16½	40.63	17.80	SA		Held Wd 1st Trn	Wisememory, Boasted, Headinghome
Blue	08/16 E9	WO	2045 F		39.64	70	1	1	1 4	1 nk	3 1	39.71	2.90	SA		Pcstr Cgt Str Lt	Kelso'sLolita, BmsWrnng, JchJns7

3 — 3-1 Kid Creole (AA) — 72

LI 3 2 0 0 1
WO 20 8 5 1 0

Kennel: Keota Kennel [47]
Owner: Carl A. Petricone
Trainer: Kevin Walker

Black M, Dec 11, 1991. Kail-Shiny Stockings — $1231

	Event	Trk	Dst	TC	Time	Wt	PP	Off	1/8	Str	Fin	ART	Odds	Grade		Comment	Opponents Finish Order
	09/27 E3	LI	2010 F		38.21	72	5	8	7	6	4 13	39.12	2.10*	SAA		Shutoff Erly Rail	TollFree, CharlieD, ShibrenNcl
	09/24 E1	LI	2010 F		38.17	71	2	3	2	1 1½	1 hd	38.17	1.00*	SAA		Led Rail Held On	Boasted, BetterButch, GlassDrm*7
	09/20 E10	LI	2010 F		38.18	70½	1	2	1 3	1 3	1 4	38.18	1.50	SAA	15.58	Easy Win Inside	WikiWikiPeka, BoligNcky, MssClly
	09/16 S8	LI	2010 F		39.01	72	2	3	3	3	2 3	39.22	·			Closing Ins Blkd	WayOfthDrgn, DMsLckyStr, VsnKng4
											Races below at Wonderland						
	09/11 E11	WO	1650 F		31.10	71½	6	8	8	6	6 3½	31.36	1.80	AA		Slw Strt Blkd 1st	Bill'sBomber, Yuspp, JpySlmDnk
	09/05 E11	WO	1650 F		30.62	70½	1	3	3	1 2½	1 3	30.62	0.50	AA		Driving On Ins	Katalist, Alfreson, Visionking7
	08/31 E11	WO	1650 F		30.99	70	1	1	1 1	1 2	1 4	30.99	1.00	AA		Drew Clear Ins	Reinsplash, Jetsetty, PebblePup
	08/26 E11	WO	1650 F		30.69	70	6	2	4	4	3 1½	30.81	3.60	AA		Wntd Rl Erl Clsg	BeNice, FieldersChoice, Strathm
	08/22 E11	WO	1650 F		31.23	70½	2	4	5	3	1 1	31.23	2.90	AA		Up On Inside	PawsativelyBeth, FieldersChoic, BNc
	08/18 E11	WO	1650 F		30.99	70½	1	2	8	6	5 6	31.57	1.30	AA		Shtf Stmbld 1st	BeNice, JSNeonRider, StrngSttmnt
White	08/13 E2	WO	1650 F		30.43	70	8	8	6	3	2 4	30.71	2.50	AA		Drv To Plc Rl	Smashing, DarkDanger, JSNeonRider

4 — 6-1 Wiki Wiki Peka (AA) — 62

LI 47 10 10 7 7
WO 4 0 0 1 1

Kennel: Frederick's Kennel [13]
Owner: Fredericks & P. Miller
Trainer: George Nurse

Brindle F, Apr 6, 1991. Jeremys Jaguar-Kwik Kyleen — $7709

	Event	Trk	Dst	TC	Time	Wt	PP	Off	1/8	Str	Fin	ART	Odds	Grade		Comment	Opponents Finish Order
	09/27 E7	LI	2010 F		37.94	63½	8	1	2	2	1 2½	37.94	3.30	SAA		Won Driving Mdtk	JetJaynes, WayOfthDrgn, BlgChmp
	09/24 E3	LI	2010 F		38.27	63	2	1	1 3½	1 3	1 2	38.27	5.80	SAA	15.48	Took Control Erly	ValsPorsch, HDsCglty, DwnngSpr
	09/20 E10	LI	2010 F		38.18	62	4	7	4	3	2 4	38.46	7.30	SAA		Gradual Gain Mtk	KidCreole, BoligeeNcky, MssClly
	09/15 E7	LI	2010 F		38.40	62	3	6	4	4	3 4½	38.73	3.60	TAA		Gained Show Ins	DowningSpur, HummnHrmn, DghtnJnS
	09/10 E7	LI	2010 F		37.98	63	2	1	1 6	1 6	1 4½	37.98	4.60	TA	15.45	Never In Doubt	DowningSpur, OwincoFirst, CharliD
	09/04 A13	LI	2010 F		38.71	63½	6	5	2	1 3	1 6½	38.71	4.40	BB		Bks Drv Drew Off	NipperRover, JABabyMagic, NFrts
	08/30 A12	LI	2010 F		38.73	63½	1	3	5	2	1 3	38.73	3.80	B		Won Driving Mdtk	Smoothrnnndv, MybltWsM, GrtWrks
											Races below at Wonderland						
	08/20 E1	WO	2045 F		38.72	62	5	8	8	7	8 13	40.33	13.20	SB		No Factor	RongJones, DJ'sTony, IndianWarrior
	08/16 E11	WO	2045 F		39.55	62	3	8	8	5	4 3½	39.80	13.90	SB		No Rm Erl Clsng	RongJones, Boasted, Rovinhunter
	08/11 E4	WO	2045 F		39.48	62	1	6	4	5	5 4	39.74	13.60	SB		Raced Inside	RingOfTruth, Sr'sRollsRoyce, TollFr
Green	08/05 E9	WO	2045 F		38.89	62	4	7	6	5	3 6½	39.48	20.50	A		Closing Outs	StephanieN, FeistyFlossie, BolgChmp

CONTINUED ON NEXT PAGE

Wiki Wiki Peka -1993

JOSEPH M. LINSEY'S $60,000 1993 AMERICAN GREYHOUND DERBY

CONTINUED FROM PREVIOUS PAGE

PP	Event	Trk	Dst	TC	Time	Wt	PP	Off	1/8	Str	Fin	ART	Odds	Grade	Comment	Opponents Finish Order	LI10/01E12

2-1 — 5 — Rastro Ricky (AA) — 76

LI 30 15 5 2 3 · WO 4 0 0 1 1

Kennel: Nanci Caswell Kennel [3] · Owner: David J. Jeswald · Trainer: Angelo Marchione

White & Brindle M, May 1, 1991. Bahama Tip-What About Win · $8866

Event	Trk	Dst TC	Time	Wt	PP	Off	1/8	Str	Fin	ART	Odds	Grade	Comment	Opponents Finish Order
09/27 E11	LI	2010 F	37.93	76	4	5	4	3	1 5	37.93	0.80*	SAA	Coll Long Drive	ProperLeader, BB'sAce, OwincFrst
09/24 E12	LI	2010 F	38.07	75½	7	6	4	1 1½	1 10	38.07	0.80*	SAA	Far The Best Mdtk	BlazngBrndy, AnthrCk, HDsAglty7
09/20 E12	LI	2010 F	38.56	75½	1	8	7	6	2 ½	38.61	1.60*	SAA	Strong Finish Mtk	CharroSwifty, BB'sAce, PlsBddy
09/17 A7	LI	2010 F	37.98	75½	2	6	3	1 2	1 8½	37.98	0.90*	AA	Best Again Outs	ShesaPib, HollyBahama, ShibrnNcl
09/11 E7	LI	2010 F	38.25	76	6	5	5	3	1 4	38.25	1.60*	AA	Driving Drew Off	HollyBahama, DLB'sEudor, QltyZp
09/03 E13	LI	2010 F	38.73	75	3	7	3	1 1½	1 10½	38.73	2.10*	TAA	Strong Finish Mtk	OwncFrst, DktRdBrn, FbldShckNXS
08/28 E13	LI	2010 F	37.84	75½	5	4	4	2	1 1½	37.84	3.80	TA	Driving On Outs	FabledShockNXS, Bellrv, JABbyMgc
													Races below at Wonderland	
08/20 E6	WO	2045 F	39.23	75½	2	6	7	6	3 8	39.79	9.60	SA	Shftf 1st Up Show	MystclMmry, ApchDsrtdg, ChldPrdgy
08/15 E9	WO	2045 F	39.31	75	8	7	4	4	4 4½	39.63	13.00	SA	Blkd In Bks Clsng	StephenisN, WsMmry, TmmyThtndr
08/11 E4	WO	2045 F	39.48	76	8	7	7	7	7 8	39.89	16.40	SAA	No Threat Sm Wd	RingOrTruth, SR'sRollsRyc, TllFr
Black 08/07 E4	WO	2045 F	39.44	75	8	7	8	6	5 9½	40.10	11.00	AA	Blkd Rl Fr Tn	TollFree, Sketched, BeamsWarning

8-1 — 6 — Already Gone (AA) — 61

LI 3 2 0 0 0 · SL 46 7 11 6 2

Kennel: Elite Kennel [57] · Owner: Busemann Kennels or Tim A. Balakas · Trainer: David Tatro

White & Fawn F, Jul 17, 1990. Land-Dateland · $616

Event	Trk	Dst TC	Time	Wt	PP	Off	1/8	Str	Fin	ART	Odds	Grade	Comment	Opponents Finish Order
09/27 E1	LI	2010 F	38.74	61½	5	5	1 4	1 6	1 5	38.74	4.10	SAA15.70	With Ease Rail	RanchoJolly, StarLghtSs, DwnngSpr
09/24 E13	LI	2010 F	38.62	61	3	6	1 3	1 8	1 2½	38.62	12.50	SAA15.50	Full Command Ins	BeAlive, HollyBahama, BWHighTim
09/20 E4	LI	2010 F	38.71	61	6	8	5	3	6 7	39.21	7.00	SAA	Closing Ins Blckd	Boasted, DowningSpur, ProprLdr
09/16 S6	LI	2010 F	38.57	60½	6	4	3	2	2 7½	39.09	-		Good Effort Ins	PaulsBddy, ChrrSwfty, ItsThWldmn4
													Races below at Plainfield	
09/11 S1	PL	2040 F	39.39	60	8	3	1 2	1 8	1 16	39.39	-		In A Romp	DLB'sRojo, GNCBabyFace, CheyenneSz
													Races below at Seabrook	
09/04 E12	SE	1650 F	30.04	60	1	5	7	6	6 10	30.74	7.10	SA	Jammed Early Rl	SportsShwcs, Sntsgft, WyOfthDrgn
09/01 E12	SE	1650 F	30.61	60	8	4	4	2	1 1	30.61	6.70	SA	Determined Mid	RealEconomy, JLGatrAd, SprtsShwcs
08/28 E6	SE	1650 F	30.60	60½	2	4	3	1 1½	1 3	30.60	9.80	SA	Drove Thru On Rl	AceChaser, MrChappie, JLGaterAd7
08/25 E6	SE	1650 F	30.28	59	7	8	5	4	3 4½	30.61	22.00	SA	Clsd For Shw Ins	SportsShwcs, WyOfthDrgn, Frtrss
Yellow 08/21 E6	SE	1650 F	30.49	59½	7	6	6	4	2 6½	30.87	15.00	A	Drove To Place	DutchAlfie, BlinkisPrncr, Sthrnlc

5-1 — 7 — Toll Free (AA) — 76

LI 3 2 1 0 0 · WO 47 9 3 9 7

Kennel: Aline Kennel [41] · Owner: Sydney A. Gasche · Trainer: Richard Arno

Red M, Feb 1, 1991. Bj's Justin-Katsu Top Seed · $924

Event	Trk	Dst TC	Time	Wt	PP	Off	1/8	Str	Fin	ART	Odds	Grade	Comment	Opponents Finish Order
09/27 E3	LI	2010 F	38.21	75½	4	1	1 2	1 4½	1 7	38.21	3.40	SAA15.63	Extending Margin	CharlieD, ShibrenNicole, KidCrl
09/24 E8	LI	2010 F	38.41	75	2	1	2	2	1 1	38.41	1.00*	SA	Came On Str Mdtrk	CreamSalute, CharlieD, LehsJgr
09/20 E1	LI	2010 F	37.44	76	4	2	1½	2	2 nk	37.47	4.10	SA 14.67	Game Try Mdtrk	VisionKing, QualityZip, AJ'sBluGm
09/16 S7	LI	2010 F	38.84	76½	7	3	2	1 1	1 1	38.84	-		Thru Far Trn Ins	BoligeeChamp, RadrLck, BllsBmbr4
													Races below at Wonderland	
09/10 E2	WO	1650 F	30.99	75½	6	2	8	7	7 10½	31.72	5.90	SA	Ofstr 1st Trn	StrongStatement, FarwyFx, Phppsbrg
09/06 E11	WO	1650 F	30.79	75	4	2	3	3	3 3	31.01	7.00	SA	Fllwd Pc Sm Wd	Stratham, MeadowsBullet, Camway
08/29 E4	WO	1650 F	31.22	74½	5	2	5	6	5 3	31.44	2.80	A	Some Wd Trns	StrongStatement, PhnxPrk, FrytlTwst
08/25 E4	WO	2045 F	39.23	75	8	3	4	4	4 8	39.66	4.40	AA	Rshd Up Ofst 1st	HeadingHome, J'sDimndDst, Ssntt
08/20 E1	WO	2045 F	38.72	75	3	4	4	4	4 14	39.70	5.10	SAA	Wide 1st Trn	RongJones, DJ'sTony, IndianWarrior
Green 08/15 E11	WO	2045 F	38.94	76	8	4	7	6	6 10	39.64	2.80	SAA	Outrushed Erly	ScalperPie, Cass, SR'sRollsRoyce
White 08/11 E4	WO	2045 F	39.48	75	7	4	5	4	3 3	39.69	1.30	SAA	Late Gain Outs	RngOftrth, SRsRllsRyc, WyOfThDrgn

15-1 — 8 — Boligee Baby (AA) — 70

LI 3 2 0 0 0 · PL 44 11 10 5 4

Kennel: Bay Point Kennel [43] · Owner: T. A. Greene · Trainer: Graydon Robtoy

Brindle M, Jul 2, 1991. Boligee Flak-Big Aida · $616

Event	Trk	Dst TC	Time	Wt	PP	Off	1/8	Str	Fin	ART	Odds	Grade	Comment	Opponents Finish Order
09/27 E9	LI	2010 F	37.90	70	1	1	1 6	1 3	1 1½	37.90	3.60	SAA15.40	Drew Out Erly Ins	HDsCglty, BttrBtch, FbldShckNXS7
09/24 E1	LI	2010 F	38.17	70	5	5	6	6	6 14½	39.17	3.60	SAA	Trbl Twice Erly	KidCreole, Boasted, BetterButch7
09/20 E11	LI	2010 F	38.18	69	1	2	1 2½	1 3	1 4	38.18	6.70	SAA15.65	Was Best Inside	BeAlive, CharlieD, RadarLock
09/16 S3	LI	2010 F	38.83	69½	7	3	2	2	2 3	39.05	-		Closest Threat	PhaserLaser, EJ'sKari, StephanieN4
													Races below at Plainfield	
09/12 A1	PL	2040 F	39.50	69	8	3	2	2	1 ns	39.50	0.70	TA	Up By A Nose	Starlightwally, Minniemkr, DktSprn
09/06 A1	PL	2040 F	38.75	69	1	3	2	2	2 1½	38.86	0.60	A	Chased Winner Rl	BoligeStrm, ChlsPrM, StrlghtOlg
08/29 A5	PL	2040 F	38.60	68	2	4	2	2	2 1	38.66	4.00	A	Good Pursuit Ins	AJ'sBlueGem, BoligStrm, DktSprn
													Races below at Wonderland	
08/24 E9	WO	2045 F	38.83	69	6	8	7	6	6 17	40.02	11.90	SA	Trouble Turns	RongJones, BeAlive, Wisememory
Yellow 08/20 E4	WO	2045 F	39.35	69	4	1	1 2½	1 2	1 2½	39.35	10.70	SA	Held Firmly	AggressiveNeal, Dalanda, KelsosCtn
Black 08/15 E9	WO	2045 F	39.31	68	6	5	6	5	5 7½	39.85	15.90	SAA	Evenly Inside	Stephanien, Wisememory, TmmythTndr

Computer: 5-6-4-3

Tm's Rescue Me-1994

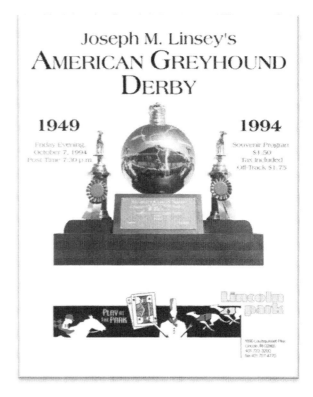

The Inside Track . . .

A THANK YOU TO THE FANS

All the preparations are complete for our premiere event of the season.

Tonight we hope you will enjoy the 45th running of Joseph M. Linsey's American Greyhound Derby. The management of Lincoln Park would like to thank all those who made this event possible. A special thank you to Mr. Joseph M. Linsey for all he has meant to this sport. A thank you to our Derby entrants who have provided such an outstanding field of competition.

But most of all we would like to thank you, the fans, for your support throughout the years. Your interest and enthusiasm have made this much more than just a great race.

Enjoy this night, as our talented field competes in this year's fall classic - The 45th Running of Joseph M. Linsey's American Greyhound Derby.

A very special welcome to all of our fans and honored guests.

Tm's Rescue Me-1994

JOSEPH M. LINSEY'S $60,000
1994 AMERICAN GREYHOUND DERBY

2010 FEET — OCEAN COURSE

FOURTEENTH RACE

SUPERFECTA WAGERING!

Trifecta & Quiniela Wagering

GRADE S

TRACK RECORD
Vision King
37.44 (09/20/93)

LI10/07E14

1 (Red) — 10-1 — TM's Rescue Me (AA) — 75

LI 3 2 0 0 0 / WO 46 7 12 12 8

Kennel: Teddy Meadows Kennel [50]
Owner: Teddy Meadows
Trainer: Richard Carbone

Red M, Feb 29, 1992. Perceive-Freada Salfity — $964

Event	Trk	Dst	TC	Time	Wt	PP	Off	1/8	Str	Fin	ART	Odds	Grade	Comment	Opponents Finish Order
10/03 A2	LI	2010	F	38.18	75	5	3	3	3	1 ½	38.18	5.20	SAA	With Rush Sm Wide	JamaicnBlck, BigNcky, MrtyPwrs
09/30 E5	LI	2010	F	38.30	76	4	3	7	7	5 4½	38.63	2.70	SAA	Knckd Back Early	BWHighTime, DD'sMax, AgentGeno
09/26 E1	LI	2010	F	38.34	75	8	7	3	2	1 3½	38.34	8.60	SAA	Str Drive Mdtrk	HilaryMiss, MyRooster, DogtwnHzl
09/22 S2	LI	1650	F	31.01	75½	8	3	3	3	1 1½	31.01	-		Drove Btwn Leadrs	MohicanKurt, FastEddieD, Negrl 4
Races below at Wonderland															
09/16 E11	WO	1650	F	30.99	75	4	4	4	4	3 2½	31.16	7.10	AA	Some Wd 1st Clsd	Phippsburg, FredBasset, MrqMths
09/11 E1	WO	1650	F	31.17	74	6	8	6	6	3 4	31.47	3.50	AA	Drv To Shw Outs	PenninePass, GreysBlueFox, Sysst
09/06 E11	WO	1650	F	30.94	74	5	8	5	6	3 ½	30.99	10.40	AA	Closing Outs	Roseanetta, Negril, DreamStrollin
Races below at Mile High															
08/30 E12	MH	2050	F	39.14	74½	5	4	4	2	2 3	39.35	6.20	TA	Gallant Pursuit	PtCCldbrst, AgentGeno, Oshkshldz 7
08/26 E7	MH	2050	F	39.19	73½	4	7	8	6	5 7½	39.72	9.10	TA	Crowded Early	PtCMntcrlo, OshkshAfar, OshkshFrny
08/23 E3	MH	2050	F	39.31	75	5	2	5	4	3 8½	39.75	7.10	TA	Solid Gain Mtk	Oshkshldz, PalBrseino, BmrBrmda

2 (Blue) — 20-1 — Shyland Tramp (AA) — 77

LI 3 1 1 0 0 / MH 7 0 1 1 2

Kennel: Three B Ent. Kennel [52]
Owner: Bussman Kennels or T. Balakas
Trainer: David Tatro

Brindle M, Mar 17, 1992. Thomas Michael-Quote Chick — $1446

Event	Trk	Dst	TC	Time	Wt	PP	Off	1/8	Str	Fin	ART	Odds	Grade	Comment	Opponents Finish Order
10/03 A2	LI	2010	F	38.18	77½	4	6	8	7	6 13	39.10	3.30	SAA	No Contender	TM'sRescueMe, JamaicanBlck, BigNcky
09/30 E3	LI	2010	F	38.17	77	1	3	2	2	1 2½	38.17	2.80	SA	Fcd Pce Up In Str	JamacnBlck, MyRstr, ChlssBbybp 6
09/26 E3	LI	2010	F	38.52	77½	2	3	3	3	2 ns	38.53	9.10	SA	Closing Jst Missd	DD'sMax, Ang'sMomSandy, MssBsc
09/22 S13	LI	2010	F	38.39	77	4	1	1 3	1 3	1 2	38.39	-		Erly Control Ins	MissBasic, BoligeeDixie, 3
Races below at Mile High															
09/03 E9	MH	2050	F	39.20	78	7	5	6	7	6 6½	39.66	9.20	A	Never Close Ins	OgalalaLnd, WhskrFsh, OshkshFrny
08/26 E8	MH	2050	F	39.19	78	6	8	7	8	8 12	40.02	25.30	TA	Off Slow Ran Ins	PtCMntcrl, OshkshAfr, OshkshFrny
08/23 E13	MH	2050	F	38.77	78	7	7	5	4	3 12	39.60	60.10	TA	Some Late Gain Md	PtCClodbrst, AgntGn, ECLghtnng 7
08/19 E9	MH	2050	M	39.68	77½	2	5	8	8	7 8	40.24	10.20	TA	Shuffled Bck Erly	SanTnRsty, OshkshKpr, BrmrBrmd
08/16 E9	MH	2050	F	39.25	77	1	4	5	3	2 1	39.32	18.20	A	Catching Up Insde	PtCCldbrst, OgalalDc, BrmrBrmd
08/09 E7	MH	2050	F	39.52	77½	7	8	7	6	4 17	40.70	4.50	A	Too Far Back Erly	OshkshFny, BrmrBrmuda, HeartFr

3 (White) — 7-2 — Pat C Montecarlo (AA) — 72

LI 3 2 1 0 0 / MH 14 9 2 1 1

Kennel: Pat Collins Kennel [47]
Owner: Patrick Collins
Trainer: Rebecca Chamberlain

Black M, Apr 21, 1992. Chevy Montecarlo-Pat C Adora — $1446

Event	Trk	Dst	TC	Time	Wt	PP	Off	1/8	Str	Fin	ART	Odds	Grade	Comment	Opponents Finish Order
10/03 A7	LI	2010	F	38.42	71	7	4	5	3	1 hd	38.42	5.90	SAA	Came On Late Rail	DD'sMax, WikiWikiPeka, Syrah
09/30 E13	LI	2010	F	38.29	71½	6	2	4	1 1	1 2½	38.29	0.90*	SAA	Rail Bks Drew Clr	DakotaCommander, MdStt, SRsJmc
09/26 E11	LI	2010	F	38.27	72	4	3	2	2	2 3½	38.52	1.60	SAA	Second Best Ins	ScenicStar*, Mello, Nita'sSusie
09/22 S11	LI	2010	F	38.63	72	1	2	1 2½	1 2½	1 1	38.63	-		Handily On Inside	Nita'sSusi, JsTppr, ExprssChrs 4
Races below at Mile High															
09/03 E12	MH	2050	F	39.29	70	8	2	1 2	1 1	1 ½	39.29	3.40	AT	Columbine Champ	AgentGeno, OshkoshKper, PtCRvltn
08/30 E9	MH	2050	F	39.23	70	3	1	1 4	1 4	1 6½	39.23	0.40*	TA	Easy Prelim Win	OshkshKper, OgalalaDoc, SnTnRsty
08/26 E7	MH	2050	F	39.19	70½	8	4	2	1 2	1 1	39.19	1.30*	TA	Worked Up Ins	OshkoshAfar, OshkshFrny, BeebobJan
08/23 E9	MH	2050	F	38.74	70½	2	1	1 3½	1 1½	2 3	38.96	0.50*	TA	Speedy Pace Cght	OshkshAfar, OshkshTry, JkrtEpsd 7
08/19 E3	MH	2050	M	39.95	72	1	1	1 4	1 3	1 3½	39.95	0.60*	TA	Shot To Ld Coastd	OgalalaDoc, MegaMorris, KCDoc
08/12 E9	MH	2050	F	39.88	72	2	3	4	3	4 9	40.52	0.20*	A	Shuffled Came On	BrmrBrmuda, Oshkshldlz, HeartFr

4 (Green) — 6-1 — DD's Max (AA) — 70

LI 8 3 4 1 0 / BI 9 3 1 1 0

Kennel: DQ Williams Kennel [18]
Owner: D. Davidson or D.Q. Williams
Trainer: Richard Calabro

Brindle M, Sep 7, 1991. Harry's Ace-EC Lill — $4422

Event	Trk	Dst	TC	Time	Wt	PP	Off	1/8	Str	Fin	ART	Odds	Grade	Comment	Opponents Finish Order
10/03 A7	LI	2010	F	38.42	70½	2	1	1 3½	1 2	2 hd	38.44	4.20	SAA	Cght Final Stride	PatCMontecarlo, WikiWkPk, Syrh
09/30 E5	LI	2010	F	38.30	70	3	1	1 3½	1 4	2 1	38.36	1.60*	SAA	Outfinished Ins	BWHighTime, AgentGeno, Wtsndlmgn
09/26 E3	LI	2010	F	38.52	70	7	2	2	2	1 ns	38.52	2.60	SAA	Frcd Pace Just Up	ShylndTrmp, AngsMmSndy, MssBsc
09/21 A12	LI	2010	F	38.01	70½	6	1	1 3	1 2	2 1	38.07	3.70	AA	Overtkn On Ins	ChelseasBbybp, ARsLrtt, TdsAbbyGl
09/16 E12	LI	2010	F	37.76	70	1	1	1 8	1 6	1 1	37.76	2.60	AA	Drew Off Erly Ins	BWHighTime, DDsJll, ChlssBbybp
09/10 E7	LI	2010	F	38.39	70	3	1	1 1	1 1½	2 nk	38.42	4.90	AA	Winning Effort	ChelseasBabybop, LuLost, MyRoostr
09/02 E12	LI	2010	F	38.49	70	7	2	3	3	3 3½	38.75	6.30	AA	Closing Ins Blckd	ChelseasBabybp, ARsLrtt, BigDk
08/29 E7	LI	1650	F	30.57	69	6	3	1 1	1 2½	1 4	30.57	3.00	AA	Handily Inside	CharLKingcobra, PrssvPggy, DrBsBn
08/25 S1	LI	1650	F	30.30	70	8	1	1 1	3	3 4	30.58	-		Set Pace Some Wd	JakesLite, CollierBay, Ric'sCpr
Races below at Biscayne															
08/06 A11	BI	1815	F	33.68	70	4	1	1 5	1 6	1 7	33.68	0.90*	B	Box To Wire Mdtrk	OleJim, RndrWhtcld, RilDon
08/02 E1	BI	1815	F	33.67	70	8	1	2	2	2 4½	33.97	1.90*	B	Followed Pace Ins	PrmBhamaEv, GreysCesna, ShgnRs

CONTINUED ON NEXT PAGE

Tm's Rescue Me-1994

JOSEPH M. LINSEY'S $60,000
1994 AMERICAN GREYHOUND DERBY

CONTINUED FROM PREVIOUS PAGE

LI10/07E14

5 — 8-5 — Black

Johnny Canoe (AA) 74

LI 3 3 0 0 0
RT 27 14 5 5 2
$1928

Kennel: Fortunato & Sarney Kennel [54]
Owner: Arthur J. Fortunato
Trainer: Jimmy Fortunato

Fawn M, Nov 18, 1991. Arizona Sun-Carol Dobson

Event	Trk	Dst	TC	Time	Wt	PP	Off	1/8	Str	Fin	ART	Odds	Grade	Comment	Opponents Finish Order
10/03 A9	LI	2010	F	37.81	74	3	3	2	1 1½	1 5½	37.81	0.50*	SAA	Pulling Away Mdtk	HollyBhm, RtPckAnthny, BWHghTm
09/30 E7	LI	2010	F	37.87	74	3	2	1 6	1 8	1 7	37.87	0.80*	SAA	Never In Doubt	RatPackAnthony, JamsCIV, MrtyPwrs 7
09/26 E9	LI	2010	F	38.61	74	5	1	3	1 2	1 4	38.61	2.20	SAA	Bks Drv Drew Out	JamaicnBlck, HzFlmt, HbsBckdrft 7
09/22 S7	LI	2010	F	38.21	74	5	2	1 7	1 10	1 7½	38.21	-		Easily Best Mdtk	MartyPwrs, SwbckSln, SnpsStrBrd 4
											Races below at Raynham-Taunton				
09/18 S1	RT	1650	F	31.40	74	7	2	2	2	1 1	31.40	-		Stretch Drive Ins	Junkanoo, CMBluGlry, PtCClssfd
09/15 S1	RT	1650	F	31.22	73½	5	8	5	4	2 8	31.78	-		Driving Hard Mdtk	FancyIowa, SolomonSonic, SkmrM
08/03 A2	RT	1980	F	38.66	74	8	8	3	2	3 4	38.94	0.80*	A	Prssd Nipped Plc	StarlightGold, JsscPrtr, LndsWy
07/29 A12	RT	1980	F	38.83	73	8	5	4	3	2 2	38.98	0.60*	A	Factr Thruout Mtk	AirsMeAgain, HezWhspr, BllsChc
07/24 A12	RT	1980	F	38.36	72½	3	5	3	1 3	1 4½	38.36	1.00*	A	Late Command Mtk	BellsChoice, HeezaWhisper, RdCr
07/20 E11	RT	1980	F	38.52	72	5	5	4	3	3 6	38.95	1.00*	A	Crwd 1st Gaining	Linda'sWay, BllsChc, StrlghtJln

6 — 12-1 — Yellow

Jamaican Black (AA) 58

LI 3 0 3 0 0
WO 33 11 7 3 5
$964

Kennel: Anawan Kennel, Inc. [51]
Owner: Carl A. Petricone
Trainer: Kevin Walker

Black F, Dec 11, 1991. Kail-Shiny Stockings

Event	Trk	Dst	TC	Time	Wt	PP	Off	1/8	Str	Fin	ART	Odds	Grade	Comment	Opponents Finish Order
10/03 A2	LI	2010	F	38.18	57	3	2	1 6	1 3	2 ½	38.23	2.50*	SAA	Long Lead Caught	TM'sRescueMe, BlgNcky, MrtyPwrs
09/30 E3	LI	2010	F	38.17	57½	2	1	1 1½	1 1	2 2½	38.35	3.70	SAA	Overtkn Ent Str	ShylandTramp, MyRstr, ChlssBbybp 6
09/26 E9	LI	2010	F	38.61	58	8	6	2	2	2 4	38.90	7.30	SAA	Frcd Pace In Bks	JohnnyCanoe, HzFlmt, HbsBckdrft 7
09/22 S1	LI	1650	F	31.12	58	4	3	3	2	3 2	31.27	-		Saved Stretches	MyBoyMitch, Mello, 3
											Races below at Wonderland				
09/19 S3	WO	1650	F	31.33	58	8	5	5	5	6 8½	31.92	-		Raced Inside	Polaroid, AlreadyALegend, PavTcktHm 7
08/09 E11	WO	2045	F	38.82	57	3	3	2	2	3 6½	39.29	7.80	SAA	Follwd Pce Ins	Drycide, GreysSpincity, BeAlive
08/05 E2	WO	2045	F	38.88	57	7	4	4	5	5 17	40.08	7.90	SAA	Wanted Ins 1st Tn	BeAlive, Ypsilanti, Reminisce
08/01 E7	WO	2045	F	39.06	58	5	2	1 4	1 4	1 2½	39.06	9.10	SAA	Held Safe Ld Ins	Raspber, Reminisce, MHDeannti
07/25 E4	WO	2045	F	39.02	56	7	4	3	3	4 3	39.24	5.40	AA	Bmpd 1st Rushed	MHDeannti, Reminisce, Rasper
07/20 E7	WO	1650	F	31.12	58	2	5	3	4	4 7	31.62	1.70	AA	Frwd Fctr Ins	GreysBlueFox, Phippsbrg, DrmStrlln

7 — 9-2 — Green White

Scenic Star* (AA) 62

LI 25 14 1 3 3
WO 3 0 0 0 2
$11989

Kennel: Pat Dalton Kennel [5]
Owner: Edward W. Barlow
Trainer: David O'Keeffe

Black F, Jan 19, 1992. Dereen Star-Scenic Beauty

Event	Trk	Dst	TC	Time	Wt	PP	Off	1/8	Str	Fin	ART	Odds	Grade	Comment	Opponents Finish Order
10/03 A11	LI	2010	F	38.35	61½	4	8	6	5	4 4½	38.68	1.60*	SAA	Slow Start Shtoff	DktCmmndr, PtCCldbrst, StrlghtRp
09/30 E9	LI	2010	F	38.31	62	1	5	4	2	1 3½	38.31	0.40*	SAA	Driving Drew Off	StarlightRip, BoligeDx, BlgChmp
09/26 E11	LI	2010	F	38.27	62	3	1	1 3	1 3	1 3½	38.27	1.50*	SAA	Wire To Wire Ins	PatCMontecarlo, Mello, Nita'sSs
09/21 A2	LI	2010	F	38.34	62	2	5	3	2	1 2½	38.34	1.00*	A	Led Str Drw Clear	Pa'sPhntm, RnchlcLdy, BlckBndt
09/16 E12	LI	2010	F	37.76	61	4	5	6	5	5 6	38.19	3.30	AA	Shutoff Frnt Str	DD'sMax, BWHighTime, DD'sJill
09/07 A12	LI	2010	F	38.46	61½	3	5	4	4	4 2½	38.62	1.40*	AA	Followed Pace	WikiWikiPeka, AR'sLrtt, ChlssBbybp
09/02 E12	LI	2010	F	38.49	61½	4	8	7	7	7 8	39.04	1.20*	AA	Much Erly Trble	ChelseasBabybop, AR'sLrtt, DDsMx
08/27 A12	LI	2010	F	38.41	61½	5	8	1 3½	1 6	1 7	38.41	1.40*	AA	Rushed Won Easy	CharlieD, ChelsesBbybp, XqzmSwty
08/22 E2	LI	1650	F	31.31	61½	6	3	7	3	1 1½	31.31	0.90*	A	Stretch Drive Mdk	PasAnnBrzn, DktTppy, SprtsTrbt
08/17 A1	LI	1650	F	31.17	62½	5	3	6	5	3 2½	31.35	1.10*	A	Steady Gain Mdtrk	MinuteInAHuff, TipiDee, JJSarh
											Races below at Wonderland				
08/05 E2	WO	2045	F	38.88	63	2	5	3	3	4 14	39.87	7.40	SA	Frwd Fctr Sm Wd	BeAlive, Ypsilanti, Reminisce

8 — 8-1 — Yellow Black

Mello (AA) 58

LI 3 2 0 1 0
WO 35 7 2 8 2
$1253

Kennel: Teddy Meadows Kennel [50]
Owner: C. Meadows & R. Carbone
Trainer: Richard Carbone

Black F, Jun 9, 1991. TM's Ticket Home-Cam's Lady Isis

Event	Trk	Dst	TC	Time	Wt	PP	Off	1/8	Str	Fin	ART	Odds	Grade	Comment	Opponents Finish Order
10/03 A4	LI	2010	F	37.90	58	6	2	2	2	1 1½	37.90	5.80	SAA	Stretch Drive Mtk	ChelsesBbybp, Ngrl, AngsMmSndy
09/30 E1	LI	2010	F	38.08	58½	1	1	1 1½	1 2	1 1½	38.08	3.60	SAA	Never Headed Mdtk	Negril, ArdentSon, BoligeeNcky
09/26 E11	LI	2010	F	38.27	59	6	4	6	4	3 12	39.10	8.30	SAA	Dspt Erly Trble	ScenicStar*, PatCMontecrl, NtsSs
09/22 S1	LI	1650	F	31.12	59½	1	2	2	3	2 1½	31.24	-		Closed Late Mdtk	MyBoyMitch, JamaicanBlack, 3
											Races below at Wonderland				
09/13 E4	WO	2045	F	39.17	58½	5	1	1 4	2	2 2½	39.36	2.90	AA	Set Erly Pace	HeadingHome, RJsMaiTai, PJ'sKelly
09/04 E12	WO	2310	F	44.02	58	4	1	1 2½	4	4 7½	44.55	2.90	SAA	Pacesetter Sm Wd	MyVwrsGd, GrysSprngcty, AcrssThBy
08/31 E4	WO	2045	F	39.08	59	5	2	4	5	5 6½	39.67	4.80	AA	Evenly Sm Wd	Syrah, MidState, RjsMaiTai
08/23 E4	WO	2045	F	39.35	58	3	7	2	1 ½	1 ½	39.35	1.40*	AA	Ld Str Sm Wd	MohicanFreedom, Evzen, Cloudygem
08/17 E4	WO	2045	F	39.93	59	4	6	4	2	1 1	39.93	1.00*	AA	Up On Outside	MHQuicklyNcky, AcrssThBy, ElCbrDst 7
08/13 E12	WO	2045	F	38.58	57½	3	3	7	6	6 12	39.44	12.30	SAA	Outrushed Erly	Drycide, Evzen, MyRooster

Computer: 3-7-4-1

Pat C Anguish-1995

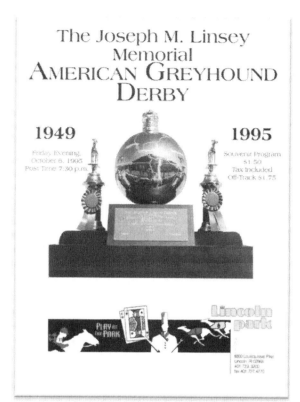

The Joseph M. Linsey Memorial AMERICAN GREYHOUND DERBY

1949   **1995**

Friday Evening,
October 6, 1995
Post Time 7:30 p.m.

Souvenir Program
$1.50
Tax Included
Off-Track $1.75

PLAY at the PARK   Lincoln park

5800 Louisquisset Pike
Lincoln, RI 02865
401-723-3200
Fax 401-727-4770

Joseph M. Linsey
1899 - 1994

FRIDAY EVENING OCTOBER 6 1995 • POST TIME 7:30 PM

*This event has been renamed
'The Joseph M. Linsey Memorial American Greyhound Derby'
in honor of its' founder who passed away on November 29, 1994 at the age of 95. Mr. Linsey
certainly lived a full life and his philanthropic deeds remain well known and highly regarded.*

*Mr. Linsey donated millions of dollars to Brandeis University where the sports center is
named in his honor. He established the Joseph M. Linsey Foundation and gave generously to the
Massachusetts Eye and Ear Infirmary, Beth Israel Hospital and numerous other Boston area
institutions.*

*He was the owner of the former Taunton Dog Track - the birthplace of the American
Greyhound Derby in 1949. That first "big stakes" greyhound race on May 14 in '49 attracted the
finest greyhounds from two continents as champions from both Ireland and America gathered for
the event.*

*The American Greyhound Derby is the predecessor of all modern stakes challenges and can
be said to be greyhound racing's "Granddaddy of them all". The prestige of this event has grown
throughout the decades of its' existence, and the coveted Joseph M. Linsey Trophy remains the one
owners and trainers most want to win.*

*The Derby and its' great tradition moved to Rhode Island and the Lincoln Park oval in
October of 1986. We will do our best to carry on the great tradition of this fall classic - especially
this year, our first without Mr. Linsey.*

*Our special thanks to Joseph M. Linsey for his years of
generosity & countless contributions to the sport of greyhound
racing. Tonight's special event has evolved from his brainstorm 46
years ago. We are proud to present The Joseph M. Linsey
Memorial American Greyhound Derby.*

Pat C Anguish-1995

"THE 1995 $60,000 JOSEPH M. LINSEY MEMORIAL AMERICAN GREYHOUND DERBY"

2010 FEET — OCEAN COURSE

FOURTEENTH RACE

3RD RACE OF THE $1.00 PICK 3

SUPERFECTA, Trifecta, Quiniela, Win, Place, & Show Wagering

GRADE S
TRACK RECORD
Vision King
37.44 (09/20/93)

LI10/06E14

1 — 10-1 — Red

Pat C Cloudburst (AA)

38.29 AA AA 69 — LI 3 1 1 1 0 — MH 21 9 8 0 0 — $1013

Brindle M, Jun 29, 1992. Pat C Rambuntous-AJ's Tropicstorm

Kennel: Pat Collins Kennel [59]
Owner: Patrick Collins
Trainer: Rebecca Chamberlain

Event	Trk	Dst	TC	Time	Wt	PP	Off	1/8	Str	Fin	ART	Odds	Grade	Comment	Opponents Finish Order
10/02A4	LI	2010	F	37.85	69	8	3	4	3	3 6½	38.25	3.30	SAA	Evenly For Show	Dominatin, EltsDnnl, StrlghtTwty
09/27A2	LI	2010	F	37.56	69½	8	5	6	6	2 6½	38.01	1.10*	SAA	Belated Gain Mtk	DLB'sWam, TwilitSldr, BrthlssBb
09/23E9	LI	2010	F	38.29	69½	7	4	2	2	1 1	38.29	2.10	SAA	Driving Wnnr Mdtk	DarlnDlt, DrwnsMyth, ABPwrRngr
09/20S11	LI	2010	F	38.05	69	7	3	3	3	2 9	38.69	-		Even Pace Mdtrk	PatCAnguish, PatCMontecarlo, 3
Races below at Mile High															
09/15E12	MH	2050	F	39.02	68	4	2	2	2	2 4½	39.32	4.50	A	Game Effort Md Wd	PtCAnglsh, KwJcktnns, PtCMntcrl
09/11A8	MH	2050	F	39.64	68	4	4	8	8	8 14	40.63	0.20*	TA	Obstructed Esc Tn	KwJckharts, OshkoshKper, KCFrs
09/07A12	MH	2050	F	39.68	68	3	1	2	2	2 1½	39.78	0.79*	TA	In Hot Pursuit	ArjPenn, EnzoBio, OshkoshCpon
09/04A8	MH	2050	F	39.66	68	4	1	1 4	1 5	1 6	39.58	0.70*	TA	Pullng Away Md Wd	SkdyKnight, Prncassly, ArjPnch
08/31E10	MH	2050	F	39.27	69	6	1	1 2½	1 5	1 7½	39.27	0.80*	TA	Breezing Wd	PO'sOpenRd, TwltSldict, OshkoshCpon
08/19E12	MH	2050	F	39.36	69½	6	2	3	2	2 1	39.40	2.60	A	In Hot Pursuit Md	ArjoPenn, KCFries, KwCelebrate
08/15E8	MH	2050	F	39.67	69	4	2	2	1 1	2 hd	39.69	0.20*	TA	Caught Late Md Wd	BetsyVnG, AgstThWnd, OshkshCpn

2 — 12-1 — Blue

Elite's Donnalee (AA)

37.94 AA A 62 — LI 6 1 3 0 2 — PL 56 18 14 10 6 — $1580

Red Brindle F, Mar 11, 1993. Braddy-Gloria Haley

Kennel: Regall Sports [10]
Owner: Dynamic Racers
Trainer: Carlos Barbosa

Event	Trk	Dst	TC	Time	Wt	PP	Off	1/8	Str	Fin	ART	Odds	Grade	Comment	Opponents Finish Order
10/02A4	LI	2010	F	37.85	61½	4	1	1 3½	1 2½	2 ½	37.90	11.10	SAA	Caught Late Mdtk	Domntn, PtCCldbrst, StrlghtTwty
09/27A3	LI	2010	F	37.94	61½	6	2	3	3	1 hd	37.94	12.80	SA	Up Near Wire Mtk	PineDrive, SR'sSeville, Allegt*
09/23E7	LI	2010	F	38.14	61	7	3	5	5	4 7	38.62	4.90	SA	No Mishaps Mdtk	JakesLite, PatCMontecarl, IndnRn
09/19A12	LI	2010	F	38.08	62	1	1	1 4	1 3	2 1½	38.17	3.10*	A	Set Pace Overtkn	StmrllrS, NdkLdybrd, PlntyOfStyl*
09/15E12	LI	2010	F	38.56	61	4	1	1 5	1 6	2 1	38.64	2.50*	TA	Long Lead Caught	SteamrllrS, DtchJcb, RnchWhstht
09/12A12	LI	2010	F	38.09	62	5	8	6	5	4 9½	38.74	2.80	A	Slight Gain Mtk	ABPowerRangr, RdHllBggls, SfrDwn
09/06S10	LI	2010	F	38.72	61½	6	2	2	1 3	1 6	38.72	-		Pulling Away Mdtk	NodakPat, ABMavrck, SplnddThng7
09/02S1	LI	1650	F	30.96	62	5	3	6	7	7 11½	31.75	-		Crwd Aftr Break	CheckitSally, OkieNadi, UltrRdnt
Races below at Plainfield															
08/25E12	PL	2040	F	39.09	61	3	7	5	3	1 ½	39.09	1.60*	A	With A Rush Rail	CheyneSusanna, Ol'sMane, SCsFm
08/19A10	PL	2040	F	38.90	62	2	2	1 2	1 1	1 2	38.90	2.40	A	Held Advantage	BellaCarissima, GoToltGlnd, Dtntn
08/15A8	PL	2040	F	38.82	62½	2	8	6	4	3 7	39.31	2.50	A	Lacked Early Sped	Ric'sAndrea, WondrWhls, ChrVnc

3 — 7-2 — White

Syrah (AA)

37.67 AA AA 62 — LI 3 2 0 0 0 — WO 19 13 1 1 1 — $1360

Dark Blue Brindle F, Dec 10, 1991. Video Signal-Kim's Nifty*

Kennel: North Shore Kennel [54]
Owner: W.H. O'Donnell
Trainer: James M. O'Donnell

Event	Trk	Dst	TC	Time	Wt	PP	Off	1/8	Str	Fin	ART	Odds	Grade	Comment	Opponents Finish Order
10/02A4	LI	2010	F	37.85	62	3	4	8	7	7 10½	38.59	0.60*	SAA	Crd Erly Frcd Out	Dominatn, EltsDnnl, PtCCldbrst
09/27A15	LI	2010	F	37.67	62	1	6	3	1 3	1 1½	37.67	0.70*	SAA	Arnd Leaders Bks	SeeyaByeSolng, PsPhntm, MdwsDlt
09/23E11	LI	2010	F	37.73	62½	8	4	1 4	1 7	1 5	37.73	1.00*	SAA	Much The Best Mtk	TM'sTooTrue, Domintn, RynsFlyn
09/19S10	LI	2010	F	38.54	62	1	3	2	1 2	1 2½	38.54	-		Saved Trns Ld Ins	StrlghtTwty, CrwnsTrvlr, JhnMClssAct4
Races below at Wonderland															
09/10E4	WO	2045	F	38.54	62½	2	1	1 6	1 10	1 15½	38.54	1.40*	AA	In A Romp Ins	MarqueSinatra, PJsKelly, MissBasc
09/04E9	WO	2045	F	39.09	62½	7	6	2	1 2½	1 6½	39.09	0.80*	TAA	Led Far Tn Drwout	MyViewersGuid, MssBsc, MrqSntr7
08/27E7	WO	2045	F	39.50	62	3	8	5	2	2 3	39.70	1.30*	AA	Slow Start	MissBasic, Homeroom, Easy'sPearlMn
08/23E4	WO	2045	F	38.59	62	4	5	1 nk	1 4	1 3½	38.59	1.50	AA	Rshd To Lead Outs	Ryan'sFlyin, Homeroom, MrqSntr
08/15E11	WO	2045	F	38.55	61½	7	8	6	8	7 11	39.33	1.50*	SAA	Shutoff Early	PineDrive, Ceeya, Forteza
08/11E7	WO	2045	F	38.57	62½	6	4	2	3	3 3½	38.82	1.40*	SAA	Follwed Pc Sm Wd	Morella, Dick'sHeadach, SprkMrk7
08/07E6	WO	2045	F	38.85	62½	1	4	2	1 4	1 4½	38.85	0.40*	SA	Led Rl Ent Bkstr	LALacey, RovnStrwbrry, SRsAllnt

4 — 6-1 — Green

Morella (AA)

37.63 AA AA 62 — LI 3 2 0 1 0 — WO 48 22 7 5 0 — $893

White & Red F, Jan 11, 1993. Mac Leroy-Salem Pride

Kennel: Mike Castellani Kennel [47]
Owner: Mike Castellani Kennel
Trainer: Steve Zack

Event	Trk	Dst	TC	Time	Wt	PP	Off	1/8	Str	Fin	ART	Odds	Grade	Comment	Opponents Finish Order
10/02A13	LI	2010	F	37.88	61½	3	4	2	2	1 5	37.88	2.70	SAA	Going Away Inside	OurPepperHot, RynsFlyn, IndnRn
09/27A5	LI	2010	F	37.63	62½	3	1	1 4	1 5	1 8½	37.63	1.10*	SAA	Much The Best Ins	DarlinDelta, TMsEsyNw, NtsFrnd
09/23E3	LI	2010	F	37.68	62	4	2	2	2	3 6½	38.13	0.80*	SAA	Close Erly Evenly	Pa'sPhantom, DLB'sWam, MdwsDlt
09/19S9	LI	2010	F	38.32	62	8	1	1 6	1 6	1 6	38.32	-		Wire To Wire Ins	TM'sEasyNw, BlgAlbm, StrlghtHnk4
Races below at Wonderland															
09/14E4	WO	2045	F	38.44	62	7	1	1 4	1 5	1 7	38.44	1.90*	AA	All The Way Ins	MarqueSinatra, PavSassy, Minicnt
09/06E13	WO	2045	F	38.66	62	2	2	2	2	2 ½	38.71	1.10*	AA	Closing On Ins	Rassluss, Forteza, SayNow7
09/02E4	WO	2045	F	39.12	63	7	1	1 6	1 5	1 4½	39.12	1.80	AA	Handily Inside	Forteza, Rassluss, PJsKelly
08/29E4	WO	2045	F	38.68	63	4	1	1 5	1 5	1 3	38.68	2.80	AA	Full Command Ins	SRsSeville, MarqSntr, SnnsFntsy
08/25E4	WO	2045	F	39.07	62	3	1	2	2	1 nk	39.07	2.60	TAA	Up On Rail	Rassluss, Yearbook, RJsMalTaj
08/19L1	WO	2045	F	38.42	62	3	2	6	6	6 19	40.55	4.00	SAA	Ofstrd Stmbld 1st	PineDrive, KidCadillac, Rsslss
08/15E13	WO	2045	F	38.42	62	5	2	2	2	2 2½	38.60	3.80	SAA	Chased Wnner Ins	Rassluss, RovinCalico, Hyarj

CONTINUED ON NEXT PAGE

Pat C Anguish-1995

"THE 1995 $60,000 JOSEPH M. LINSEY MEMORIAL AMERICAN GREYHOUND DERBY"

CONTINUED FROM PREVIOUS PAGE

PP	Event	Trk	Dst	TC	Time	Wt	PP	Off	1/8	Str	Fin	ART	Odds	Grade	Comment	Opponents Finish Order	LI10/D6E14

2-1 John M Class Act (AA) — 37.55 / 69 — LI 3 3 0 0 0 — AA AA — RT 36 10 8 4 5 — $1360
Kennel: Salpietro Kennel [55] — Owner: John M. McCarthy — Trainer: Anthony Salpietro

Black F, Apr 1, 1993. Chevy Montecarlo-Pay Penny

5

Date	Trk	Dst TC	Time	Wt	PP	Off	1/8	Str	Fin	ART	Odds	Grade	Comment	Opponents Finish Order
10/02 A7	LI	2010 F	37.74	69	4	1	1⁶	1⁵	1nk	37.74	1.80*SAA		Drew Out Erly Mtk	SeeyaByeSolong, MidStat, JksLt
09/27 A13	LI	2010 F	37.55	67½	1	1	1⁵	1⁵	1⁵¾	37.55	1.60*SAA		Wire To Wire Mdtk	TorridZone, PopsEiln, RynsFlyn7
09/23 E13	LI	2010 F	37.81	68	6	2	1³½	1⁶	1³½	37.81	16.50 SAA		Easy Win Mzzl Off	PtCAngsh, StrightTwty, BbySndy
09/19 S10	LI	2010 F	38.54	68½	3	1	1½	3	4⁸½	39.13	-		Cght Far Trn Mdtk	Syrah, StrightTwty, CrwnsTrvlr4

Races below at Raynham-Taunton

09/14 A11	RT	1650 F	31.06	67½	3	2	2	1⁶	1⁷	31.06	1.40*A		Extending Lead	JCsCountyLine, Montnlrn, EbnyTrnd
09/08 A4	RT	1650 F	31.29	69½	7	4	3	1¹	1⁶¾	31.29	0.90*A		Late Control Mdtk	VegasRoller, NatalieBlak, Tdlm
09/02 E12	RT	1650 F	31.60	67	2	4	6	8	8⁶¾	32.04	9.00*A		Jammed 1st Turn	Montanalron, ArjoCinch, Donna'sB
08/27 S1	RT	1650 F	30.98	69	3	1	1⁴	1¹⁰	1¹⁴½	30.98	-		Outclassed Field	HayeFaye, PatCRaceCr, JAMmryBnk6
08/23 S1	RT	1650 F	31.04	69	3	2	1²	1⁴	1⁶½	31.04	-		With Ease Midtrk	JohnnyCanoe, NitasFrnd, PtCRcCr
07/20 A11	RT	1650 F	30.97	68	8	3	4	2	2ns	30.98	1.60 A		A Nose Shy Mdtrk	MrPractitionr, LtnNrmn, JhnnyCn
07/14 E4	RT	1650 F	30.75	66	3	5	2	1⁵	1⁸½	30.75	1.00*A		Full Of Run Insde	Wahuggana, PatCWhtsOn, RbsSylr6

Black

4-1 Okie Nadia (AA) — 37.50 / 57 — LI 36 20 0 5 2 — AA M — LI 5 2 1 1 0 — $22424
Kennel: DQ Williams Kennel [18] — Owner: Patrick Niles — Trainer: Richard Calabro

Dark Brindle F, Apr 27, 1993. Sunburn-Cash N Access

6

10/02 A13	LI	2010 F	37.88	58	7	6	8	8	8¹¹½	38.68	1.70*SAA		Close Qtrs Break	Morella, OurPepperHot, RynsFlyn
09/27 A8	LI	2010 F	37.64	57	1	1	1¹	1³	1³½	37.64	0.70*SAA		Never Headed Mtk	Nita'sDian, PtCMntcrl, StmrllrS
09/23 E15	LI	2010 F	38.21	57	7	2	1³	1⁴	1⁶	38.21	1.70*SAA		Easy Win Drew Off	CharroBlossom, PpsEln, ArdntSn
09/15 E7	LI	2010 F	38.38	57½	7	4	3	3	1²½	38.38	1.30*AA		Driving Wnnr Mdtk	CheckitSaily, OrPpprHt, TrrdZn
09/12 A2	LI	2010 F	38.54	58	5	4	4	4	1½	38.54	0.80*TAA		Blckd Closed Fast	Nita'sDiane, JoeAlbrt, RcktRls
09/08 A4	LI	1650 F	30.54	58	8	7	1²	1⁶	1⁶½	30.54	3.10 AA		Much The Best Mtk	BounceBack, HnrAndGlry, Amlgmn
09/02 S1	LI	1650 F	30.96	58	7	5	7	5	2⁵	31.32	-		Gained Steadily	CheckitSlly, UltrRdnt, EltxRddrv
08/30 S1	LI	1650 F	30.95	58½	5	3	6	6	1nk	30.95	-		Fast In Stretch	GoldenLad, DrrnsfLss*, LZsMrRdcr
06/03 A4	LI	2010 F	38.05	57	4	4	4	3	1⁴½	38.05	1.00*AA		Driving Drew Off	Pa'sPhantom, BoligeeTaco, SeeBS
05/29 A2	LI	2010 F	37.81	57½	2	2	12½	13½	1⁶	37.81	0.70*TAA		Extndng Lead Mtk	Dory'sLmbChp, OrPpprHt, TrrdZn
05/24 A9	LI	2010 F	37.86	57½	2	3	1²½	1⁵	1¹⁰½	37.86	1.10*A		As She Pleased	SpecialPayday, BabySndy, SidGldTp
05/20 A8	LI	2010 F	38.10	56½	3	2	3	6	7¹⁴	39.08	1.20*A		Trouble Thruout	ArdentSon, DakotaCommandr, BlgDk

Yellow

8-1 Pat C Anguish (AA) — 37.50 / 75 — LI 3 1 1 1 0 — AA AA — MH 20 10 7 2 0 — $541
Kennel: Pat Collins Kennel [59] — Owner: Patrick Collins — Trainer: Rebecca Chamberlain

Brindle M, Jan 8, 1993. Torrey Pines-Pat C Alicia

7

10/02 A10	LI	2010 F	37.50	74	1	1	1¹	1²	1⁴	37.50	0.80*SAA		Late Control Mdtk	SR'sSeville, NitasDn, StmrllrS
09/27 A11	LI	2010 F	37.63	75½	8	6	7	3	3⁸½	38.30	1.10*SAA		Bmpd Erly Ofstrd	MidState, ABPowerRngr, OrPpprHt7
09/23 E13	LI	2010 F	37.81	74	7	4	3	2	2³½	38.04	1.40*SAA		Wd Erly Clsd Some	JhnMClssAct, StrightTwty, BbySndy
09/20 S11	LI	2010 F	38.05	75	4	1	1²	1⁵	1⁶	38.05	-		Extnding Lead Mtk	PatCCloudburst, PatCMontecrl, 3

Races below at Mile High

09/15 E12	MH	2050 F	39.02	74	3	1	1¹½	1³	1⁴½	39.02	1.90*A		Columbine Champ	PtCCldbrst, KwJckhrts, PtCMntcrl
09/11 A15	MH	2050 F	39.36	74½	4	2	2	13½	1⁶	39.30	1.80 TA		Convincing Md Wd	CNolaChoice, TwltSidlr, KwClbrt
09/07 A10	MH	2050 F	40.06	74½	3	2	3	3	2½	40.10	0.40*TA		Blckd Str Trn Md	ArjoPoncho, Saber, JessiesJem
09/04 A15	MH	2050 F	39.70	74½	2	3	2	2	2¹	39.78	0.90*TA		Drove To Place Md	OshkoshKper, KwJckharts, Saber
08/31 E13	MH	2050 F	39.79	74½	7	3	3	3	2⁴	40.08	0.20*TA		Gallant Chase Md	JessiesJem, KWJckharts, KanssMg
08/22 E5	MH	2050 F	39.20	75½	2	1	1¹	1¹	1²	39.20	0.60*A		Drove Thruout Md	KwJckharts, Saber, PatCLimbo
08/16 E4	MH	2050 F	39.30	75	7	3	2	13½	1⁵½	39.30	0.60*A		Took Control Esc	KwJckharts, PatCLimbo, AlProBots

Green / White

10-1 Rassluss (AA) — 38.08 / 59 — LI 3 2 0 0 0 — AA AA — WO 34 9 9 5 2 — $1360
Kennel: North Shore Kennel [54] — Owner: W.H. O'Donnell — Trainer: James M. O'Donnell

Red F, Apr 1, 1993. Tipp Lad*-Chicopee

8

10/02 A7	LI	2010 F	37.74	60	7	7	3	5	7¹³	38.64	8.50 SAA		Erly Spd Tiring	JohnMClassAct, SeeyBySlng, MdStt
09/27 A7	LI	2010 F	38.13	60	4	4	2	1¹	1hd	38.13	2.90 SAA		Saved Led Far Trn	StarlghtTwty, ChrrBlssm, Dmntn
09/23 E2	LI	2010 F	38.08	60	4	1	1⁵	1⁴	1ns	38.08	4.30 SAA		Just Held On Mdtk	SR'sNorstar, PineDriv, AwsmArl
09/19 S8	LI	2010 F	38.77	59	1	2	1⁵	1³	2³½	39.03	-		Big Lead Overtkn	SkinMist, CheckThisOut, 3

Races below at Wonderland

09/13 E4	WO	2045 F	38.80	60	4	7	3	3	6¹¹½	39.60	1.30*AA		Tiring Inside	Ryan'sFlyin, MooseSholk, SnnsFntsy
09/06 E13	WO	2045 F	38.66	59	7	1	1⁵	1⁴	1½	38.66	1.80 AA		Lng Ld Held Ins	Morella, Forteza, SayNow7
09/02 E4	WO	2045 F	39.12	59	3	2	2	2	3⁷½	39.66	1.10*AA		Follwed Pace Mtk	Morella, Forteza, PJsKelly
08/25 E4	WO	2045 F	39.07	59½	4	2	1¹	1²	2nk	39.10	1.70*TAA		Cght Lt Str Ins	Morella, Yearbook, RJsMaiTai
08/19 L1	WO	2045 F	39.21	59½	6	3	2	2	2³½	39.44	1.00 SAA		Threat To Str Ins	PineDrive, KidCadillc, PsPhntm
08/15 E13	WO	2045 F	38.42	59	4	3	1⁵	1⁴	1²½	38.42	3.50 SAA		Handily Mdtrk	Morella, RovinCalico, Hyjarj
08/11 E2	WO	2045 F	38.62	59½	4	2	1⁴	1⁴	1¹	38.62	1.00 SAA		Held Safe Ld Ins	EdNorton, KidCreol, Thsctsscrmn7

Yellow / Black

Computer: 4-3-6   SUPERFECTA WAGERING ON EVERY LIVE RACE TODAY!

Tricia's Anchor-1996

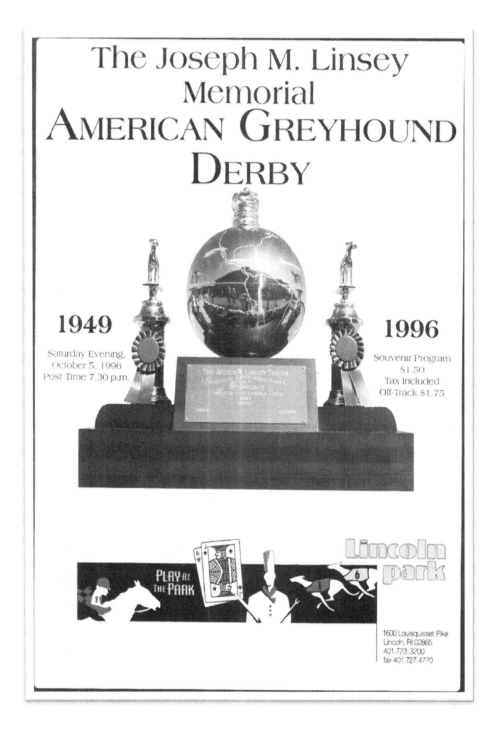

Tricia's Anchor-1996

"THE 1996 $60,000 JOSEPH M. LINSEY MEMORIAL AMERICAN GREYHOUND DERBY"

2010 FEET   **THIRTEENTH RACE**   **GRADE S**

OCEAN COURSE

TRACK RECORD
"Duplantis"
37.25 (9/6/96)

SUPERFECTA, Trifecta, Quiniela, Win, Place & Show Wagering

PP	Event	Trk	Dst	TC	Time	Wt	PP	Off	1/8	Str	Fin	ART	Odds	Grade	Comment	Opponents Finish Order	LI10/05E13
9-5	**Tricias' Anchor (AA)**											37.75	**64**	LI	3 3 0 0 0	Kennel: Michael J. Joseph Kennel [44]	
												AA AA		RT	40 13 8 6 4	Owner: D. Burk or R. Taskey, Jr.	
															$1923	Trainer: Louis Amaral	
	Black F, Jul 4, 1994. King Kev-Spider Woman																
	09/30A10	LI	2010 F	37.88	63½	1	2	1½	1³	14½	37.88	0.80*SAA		Took Control Bks	PacaJoe, CheMarTawny, GreatStff7	
	09/25A15	LI	2010 F	37.75	64	7	1	1½	16½	1⁷	37.75	6.80 SAA		Much The Best Mtk	PioneerPride, JodiDai, BolgLcy	
	09/20E14	LI	2010 F	37.96	63	5	1	2	1½	1³	37.96	4.20 SAA		Drew Clear Mdtrk	AwesomeAriel, PatCAnguish, MoFr	
1	09/16S8	LI	2010 F	38.92	63½	5	4	4	4	3⁹	39.49			No Room Aftr Brk	CharlieDupre, BlgLcy, VctryCll*4	
									Races below at Raynham-Taunton								
	09/12A8	RT	1650 F	31.15	63½	8	2	1²	1³	16½	31.15	2.90 B		Extending Margin	MsShrpMrtn, JAEsyEffrt, NsyGmblr	
	09/06E1	RT	1650 F	31.64	63	6	7	7	6	46½	32.04	1.40*B		Clld 1st Gaining	StarlightJonn, BnjBrrw, PtCHrld	
	09/01E1	RT	1650 F	31.61	63	1	5	5	4	3½	31.65	1.00*B		Crwd 1st Closing	M'sBlueClass, Snell, Abby'sColn	
	08/27A1	RT	1650 F	31.73	64	5	2	4	2	2²½	31.91	1.40*B		Despite Erly Trble	DoltinSped, MsBrthHrt, PtCTckt	
	08/21A4	RT	1980 F	38.23	63½	3	5	4	4	5⁹½	38.89	3.40*A		No Mishaps	Abby'sHowie, PatCSaweya, ChrrBlssm	
									Races below at Wonderland								
Red	08/13E4	WO	2045 F	38.83	64	4	3	3	4	47½	39.36	7.50 SAA		Followed Pace Mtk	BlazingChamp, Scater, FlHfymDn	
8-1	**Paca Joe (AA)**											38.04	**68**	LI	3 1 1 1 0	Kennel: Patrick Collins Kennel [49]	
												AA AA		RT	38 19 6 6 3	Owner: Patricia A. Manning	
															$1275	Trainer: Rebecca Chamberlain	
	Black M, Nov 16, 1993. Tipp Lad*-Blackie Bee																
	09/30A10	LI	2010 F	37.88	68	5	3	2	2	24½	38.19	3.30 SAA		Close Early Mdtrk	TricisAnchr, ChMrTwny, GrtStff7	
	09/25A2	LI	2010 F	38.34	68	3	5	4	3	3½	38.44	1.50*SAA		Gained Grnd Sm Wd	GreatStuff, NodkNxn, CjnGldDst	
	09/20E10	LI	2010 F	38.04	69	8	1	1½	1²	1ⁿˢ	38.04	2.30 SAA		Big Lead Lasted	BlazngIntrg, KwRdRck, ChmrQckkck	
2	09/16S8	LI	2010 F	38.47	68	8	2	1⁸	1⁸	15½	38.47	.		With Ease Mdtrk	BoligeeSandy, MhcnArrw, WtsndTss4	
									Races below at Raynham-Taunton								
	09/08A4	RT	1980 F	37.69	66½	3	8	5	4	5¹²	38.52	2.80 A		Crowded Back Erly	BoligeeLucy, WondrsMgc, ChlsMT	
	09/04A12	RT	1650 F	31.13	68	5	7	5	2	1²½	31.13	1.90 A		Long Drive Mdtrck	Pa'sSadEyes, SkimrMt, KlssRshd	
	08/29A11	RT	1650 F	31.34	68	4	2	7	6	36½	31.74	0.80*A		Despite Trouble	MohawkSmoke, OnePolicy, HtChersh	
	08/24E12	RT	1650 F	30.95	68½	5	3	3	3	2¹	31.02	3.20 A		Driving Hard Mdtk	ChampagnChrs, PsSdEys, HnvrPng	
	08/20A11	RT	1650 F	30.92	68½	3	7	7	5	4⁷	31.41	1.50*A		Broke To Outside	ChampagneChris, M'sStn, PsSdEys	
Blue	08/15E4	RT	1650 F	31.05	68	7	1	1²½	1²	1¹	31.05	2.10 A		Held Safely Mdtk	ChampgnChrs, PDrsyDn, RcklssWnd	
3-1	**SR's Artemus (AA)**											38.01	**71**	LI	3 3 0 0 0	Kennel: Anawan Kennel [50]	
												AA AA		WO	54 13 6 11 7	Owner: Carl A. Petricone	
															$1923	Trainer: Kevin Walker	
	Blue M, Feb 17, 1994. Big Tar-SR's Dolly																
	09/30A5	LI	2010 F	38.21	70	1	1	1²	1²	1½	38.21	0.50*SAA		Never Headed Mtk	BlazngIntrg, ChmrQckkck, OddNtr	
	09/25A7	LI	2010 F	38.01	70½	4	1	13½	13½	14	38.01	2.20*SAA		Led Thruout Ins	CheMarTawny, FLAHftymDn, BlgSndy	
	09/20E2	LI	2010 F	38.21	71	5	2	3	3	1²	38.21	8.20 SAA		Came On Str Mdtrk	Duplantis, MidState, OddNitro	
3	09/16S3	LI	1650 F	30.76	71	7	1	1½	11½	12½	30.76	.		Set Pace Drew Clr	KenKohrGo, BlazingIntrigue, 3	
									Races below at Wonderland								
	09/11E13	WO	1650 F	30.70	71	8	5	3	4	3³½	30.94	5.30 AA		Followed Pace Ins	KiowaKatKy, Invstlt, TMsPwrhll	
	09/04E9	WO	1650 F	30.65	71	4	2	4	7	7⁹½	31.31	3.60*AA		Shuffled 1st Turn	WckStblr, Invstlt, BlssfllyHppy	
	08/30E4	WO	1650 F	30.98	71	1	2	3	3	11½	30.98	0.80*AA		Drove Btween Ldrs	TM'sFllRfnd, BlssfllyHppy, Jbn	
	08/26E12	WO	1650 F	30.37	70	7	3	6	6	512½	31.25	5.50 AA		No Threat Inside	KiowaSissy, NeverStops, Taziluz	
	08/22E12	WO	1650 F	30.97	70½	1	4	3	2	11½	30.97	5.80 AA		Up In Str Inside	KiowaSissy, BlazingLady, Shawnk	
	08/17L2	WO	2045 F	38.64	70	7	3	3	3	36½	39.03	19.70 SAA		Followed Pace Ins	Doyon, CharlieDupre, Morella	
White	08/13E7	WO	2045 F	38.99	70½	2	3	5	4	411½	39.79	7.80 SAA		Followed Pace Ins	PineDrive, BlzngIntrg, MntEpsd	
10-1	**Wake Up Alarm (AA)**							.				37.89	**61**	LI	22 10 6 3 0	Kennel: Brindle Kennel [9]	
												AA M				Owner: Troy D. Stiles	
															$8993	Trainer: Bob Antunes, Sr.	
	Brindle & White F, Nov 1, 1994. FMC's Wake Up-Silver Green																
	09/30A7	LI	2010 F	37.89	60½	4	3	1²	1³	1⁴	37.89	7.70 SAA		Safe Margin Ins	AliskaMaria, PionerPrd, MhcnArrw	
	09/25A14	LI	2010 F	37.85	60½	6	2	1²½	1½	2½	38.13	2.60 SAA		Overtkn Mid-Str	PatCAnguish, KiowaRdRck, SRsSvll7	
	09/20E5	LI	2010 F	37.94	60	8	8	1¹	1½	2½	37.98	4.10 SAA		Rshd Up Cght Late	PopsEiln, Rvngflknght, ChrlDpr	
	09/14E5	LI	2010 F	38.40	60	2	7	2	2	3²½	38.57	2.20 TAA		Chsd Leader Ins	VeeRidge*, OddNitro, SolidGoldTp	
4	09/07A8	LI	1650 F	30.28	60½	1	4	3	3	3²½	30.44	1.50*AA		Gained Grnd Ins	Dr.Sheila, FlorentineGrill, ORck	
	09/02A8	LI	1650 F	30.83	60½	2	4	3	3	2½	30.88	2.20 AA		Closing Late Bid	Dr.Sheila, LotaClout, DrwnsMyth7	
	08/29A8	LI	1650 F	30.32	60	4	2	2	1³	1²½	30.32	2.60 AA		Handily On Inside	DfntBtryl, SntxApch, DrwnsMyth	
	08/24A8	LI	1650 F	30.34	60½	7	2	8	7	7²⁸	32.30	3.90 AA		Trouble Thruout	Darwin'sMyth, BlaznBltz, PnkAngl	
	08/19A8	LI	1650 F	30.46	60	8	6	2	11	13½	30.46	1.70*AA		Long Duel Drw Clr	Dr.Sheila, BillyRayTex, OkClyd	
	08/14A1	LI	1650 F	30.29	60½	2	3	2	2	2¹	30.37	6.60 AA		Second Best Ins	BlazinBlitz, Dr.Sheila, Yrplcrmn	
	08/09A7	LI	1650 F	30.53	61	3	6	5	6	6¹¹	31.29	2.60 AA		Drvng Blkd Fr Trn	HethrAnn, MllgnsWsh, TrcysWsh*	
Green	08/03A10	LI	1650 F	30.76	60½	6	4	8	7	610½	31.48	2.70 AA		Blocked 1st Turn	GarveyLancer, BlznBltz, ChMrJzz	

CONTINUED ON NEXT PAGE

Tricia's Anchor-1996

"THE 1996 $60,000 JOSEPH M. LINSEY MEMORIAL AMERICAN GREYHOUND DERBY"

CONTINUED FROM PREVIOUS PAGE

5 — 10-1 — **Blazing Intrigue (AA)** — AA AA — 63 — LI 3 0 3 0 0 — WO 53 10 10 10 9 — $962

Black F, Mar 16, 1994. HB's Commander-AZ's Eliza

Kennel: Teddy Meadows Kennel [46]
Owner: Charles H. Sabanty
Trainer: Teddy Meadows

PP	Event	Trk	Dst	TC	Time	Wt	PP	Off	1/8	Str	Fin	ART	Odds	Grade	Comment	Opponents Finish Order LI10/05E13
	09/30 A5	LI	2010	F	38.21	63	8	8	3	3	2 ½	38.26	4.10	SAA	Closing Late Ins	SR'sArtemus, ChmrQckkck, OddNtr
	09/25 A3	LI	2010	F	38.11	63	2	5	3	3	2 2½	38.29	1.70*	SAA	Denied Ins Gained	ChmrQckkck, AbbysHw, CldwtrFrlc
	09/20 E10	LI	2010	F	38.04	61½	1	3	2	2	2 ns	38.05	1.80*	SAA	Coming On Bkd Str	PacaJoe, KiowRdRck, ChmrQckkck
	09/16 S3	LI	1650	F	30.76	62½	4	3	3	3	3 8	31.31	-		Raced Inside	SR'sArtemus, KenKohrGo, 3
												Races below at Wonderland				
	09/08 E12	WO	2310	F	44.03	63	4	3	6	5	4 6	44.45	1.30*	SAA	Shffld Back Early	PopsEileen, Turner'sBid, KetVd
	09/01 E4	WO	2310	F	43.89	63	5	1	1 3	1 3	1 3	43.89	2.60	TAA	All The Way Insde	Scatteree, KeotaVeda, PW'sMvng
	08/28 E4	WO	2310	F	44.54	63	7	4	3	2	2 1½	44.64	3.30	TAA	Hard Try Inside	Scatteree, SparkieMarki, HmmMrtn
	08/24 E13	WO	2310	F	43.70	62½	8	4	3	2	2 7	44.19	2.30	TAA	No Room Far Turn	Scatteree, KeotaVeda, PW'sMovng
	08/17 L1	WO	2045	F	38.33	62	1	8	2	2	2 1	38.40	5.50	SAA	Saved 1st Prssng	PioneerPride, SR'sSeville, Olnd
	08/13 E7	WO	2045	F	38.99	63	8	4	7	2	2 3	39.21	3.70	SAA	Svd Esc Trn Clsng	PineDrive, MintEpisd, SRsArtms
Black	08/09 E2	WO	2045	F	38.86	62½	2	2	1 5	1 6	1 6½	38.86	1.50*	SAA	Full Command Ins	Garrunteeya, RbynsChc, ELsDblDr

6 — 5-1 — **Pat C Anguish (AA)** — 37.85 — AA AA — 76 — LI 3 1 1 1 0 — MH 17 7 6 1 3 — $1225

Brindle M, Jan 8, 1993. Torrey Pines-Pat C Alicia

Kennel: Patrick Collins Kennel [49]
Owner: Patrick Collins
Trainer: Rebecca Chamberlain

PP	Event	Trk	Dst	TC	Time	Wt	PP	Off	1/8	Str	Fin	ART	Odds	Grade	Comment	Opponents Finish Order
	09/30 A2	LI	2010	F	38.13	75½	3	1	3	3	2 1	38.20	1.20*	SAA	Gained Grnd Outs	SR'sSeville, KiowaAdrenlin, BCp
	09/25 A14	LI	2010	F	37.85	75	2	1	3	2	1 3½	37.85	0.90*	SAA	Led Str Drw Clear	KiowaRedRck, WkUpAlrm, SRsSvll7
	09/20 E14	LI	2010	F	37.96	76	8	7	6	4	3 3½	38.20	1.80*	SAA	Blocked Thruout	Tricias'Anchor, AwesomeAril, MFr
	09/16 S12	LI	2010	F	38.57	76½	2	1	2	1 2	1 6½	38.57	-		Pulled Away Sm Wd	BeauCoup, MintEpsd, FLAHftymDn4
												Races below at Mile High				
	09/07 E8	MH	2050	F	39.90	75	4	1	2	2	2 4	40.18	0.50*	A	Hard Pursuit Mdtk	OnoFlash, ArjoPoncho, PB'sIndi7
	08/31 E12	MH	2050	F	39.56	74½	7	4	3	1 4	1 6½	39.56	1.40*	SA	Timberline Champ	CarlJo, LrdDempsey, OnoFlash
	08/27 E8	MH	2050	F	39.80	76	6	3	4	3	2 ½	39.84	0.40*	SA	Boxed Str Came On	SeaLegend, PB'sIndia, TawnyTss
	08/23 E5	MH	2050	F	40.27	76	8	3	5	3	2 nk	40.30	0.40*	SA	Gallant Effrt Ins	LrdDempsey, PB'sIndi, OshkshHn
	08/20 E12	MH	2050	F	39.29	74	6	1	2	1 4	1 5½	39.29	0.90*	SA	Outrshd Cme Again	CarlJo, JM'sWldLdy, LkeBadNews
	08/16 E8	MH	2050	F	39.23	76	1	2	1 2	1 4	1 4	39.23	0.80*	SA	Full Command Mdtk	SpclStrike, LkeBadNws, RthsDll
Yellow	08/12 E4	MH	2050	F	39.43	76½	6	3	1 2	1 2	1 1½	39.43	1.80*	TB	Classy Form Mdtrk	LkeBadNews, SpclStrik, TwnyTss

7 — 12-1 — **Che Mar Tawny (AA)** — 37.61 — AA M — 62 — LI 45 11 6 9 5 — RT 2 0 0 0 0 — $15365

White & Brindle F, Mar 8, 1994. Stouke Whisper-Dutch Bouquet

Kennel: Eagle Kennel [33]
Owner: Gerald D. Marten
Trainer: Doug McKenna

PP	Event	Trk	Dst	TC	Time	Wt	PP	Off	1/8	Str	Fin	ART	Odds	Grade	Comment	Opponents Finish Order
	09/30 A10	LI	2010	F	37.88	62	7	5	3	4	3 6½	38.34	9.10	SAA	Even Pace Mdtrk	Tricias'Anchor, PacaJoe, GrtStff7
	09/25 A7	LI	2010	F	38.01	62	8	6	4	4	2 4	38.29	3.80	SAA	Coll Late Drive	SR'sArtemus, FLAHftymDn, BlgSndy
	09/20 E12	LI	2010	F	37.90	62	2	3	3	2	1 3	37.90	9.20	SA	Driving Wnnr Mdtk	KiowaAdrenln, SyBySlng, AlskMr
	09/14 E5	LI	2010	F	38.40	62	5	8	6	6	6 11	39.16	8.10	TA	No Room At Break	VeeRidge*, OddNitro, WakeUpAlrm
	09/11 A13	LI	2010	F	38.35	62½	3	5	6	7	7 11½	39.15	2.50	TA	Shutoff Aftr Brk	BWErin, VeeRidge*, CelticPeanut
	09/06 A7	LI	2010	F	37.48	62	1	5	2	2	2 5½	37.87	1.80	TA	Bmpd Chsd Winner	NodakLadybird, VeeRidg*, BlLmp*
	08/31 E15	LI	2010	F	37.64	62	3	6	5	3	3 7½	38.16	8.80	TA	Closing For Show	Alice'sLdy, RdHllEvnng, AwsmArl
	08/28 A10	LI	2010	F	38.09	62	4	7	4	3	3 6½	38.53	4.40	TA	Gained For Show	TurboScorcher, BlueLmp*, AwsmArl7
	08/23 E7	LI	2010	F	38.28	62	5	7	7	6	5 6½	38.66	5.20	TAA	Raced Inside	Revengeflknght, RdHllEvnng, AwsmArl
	08/17 E13	LI	2010	F	37.93	61½	6	8	5	4	3 3½	38.18	5.20	AA	Steady Drive Mdtk	OkieNadia, CelticPeant, BlLmp*
Green	08/14 A10	LI	2010	F	37.91	62	7	8	8	7	7 10½	38.64	4.70	AA	Taken Wide 1st Tn	DesertIce, CelticPnt, FlyngMst
White	08/09 E15	LI	2010	F	38.25	62	5	5	5	7	6 8½	38.92	3.40	AA	Some Early Speed	GftdChrsty, NdkLdybrd, TrbScrchr

8 — 6-1 — **Pioneer Pride (AA)** — 37.80 — AA AA — 71 — LI 3 1 1 1 0 — WO 24 15 1 1 3 — $1460

Black M, Mar 16, 1994. HB's Commander-AZ's Eliza

Kennel: Teddy Meadows Kennel [46]
Owner: Charles H. Sabanty
Trainer: Teddy Meadows

PP	Event	Trk	Dst	TC	Time	Wt	PP	Off	1/8	Str	Fin	ART	Odds	Grade	Comment	Opponents Finish Order
	09/30 A7	LI	2010	F	37.89	70½	3	1	2	3	3 5½	38.28	1.10*	SAA	Followed Leaders	WakeUpAlarm, AliskaMr, MhcnArrw
	09/25 A15	LI	2010	F	37.75	71	1	2	2	2	2 7	38.24	0.20*	SAA	Led Briefly Ins	Tricias'Anchor, JodiDai, BolgLcy
	09/20 E15	LI	2010	F	37.80	70½	1	2	1 2	1 2	1 4	37.80	0.30*	SAA	Late Control Ins	ChemarPowerkick, BCp, NdkLdybrd
	09/16 S1	LI	1650	F	30.41	71½	1	2	1 1½	3	3 10½	31.14	-		Weakened On Ins	SR'sSeville, MidState, 3
												Races below at Wonderland				
	09/11 E4	WO	2045	F	38.50	71	8	1	1 5	1 7	1 10	38.50	0.10*	AA	Trailblazing Ins	ProudShot, Garrunteeyaa, Doyon
	09/04 E4	WO	2045	F	38.30	71	3	1	1 6	1 2½	1 3	38.30	0.20*	AA	Fast Start Inside	Doyon, Olindo, Garrunteeya
	08/30 L4	WO	2045	F	38.50	71	5	1	1 2	1 6	1 10½	38.50	1.10*	AA	Eight Straight	KiowaSissy, DreamTunes, TurnersBd7
	08/26 E4	WO	2045	F	38.76	71½	7	3	2	1 3	1 5	38.76	0.10*	AA	Ld Rl Bkst Drwout	Adelphi, Turner'sBid, PopsEiln
	08/21 E13	WO	2045	F	38.71	71	5	1	1 8	1 11	1 15½	38.71	0.20*	AA	In A Romp Inside	KeotaClay, MarqueSinatr, PpsEln
Yellow	08/17 L1	WO	2045	F	38.33	71½	8	1	1 5	1 1	1 1	38.33	0.80*	SAA	Derby Champion	BlazingIntrigue, SR'Seville, Olnd
Black	08/13 E11	WO	2045	F	38.38	71	6	1	1 6	1 2	1 2	38.38	0.50*	SAA	Lng Erly Lead Ins	Doyon, Garrunteeya, BadMood

Computer: 8-4-3-7   **THIS IS IT! PLACE YOUR WAGERS EARLY! DERBY POST TIME IS 10:40pm!**

Phoebe Ann-1997

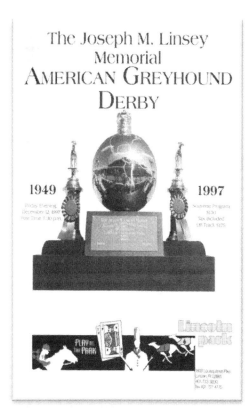

The Joseph M. Linsey
Memorial
AMERICAN GREYHOUND DERBY

1949   1997

◆ PLAY AT THE PARK ◆

Friday Evening   *December 12, 1997*

TWIN TRI FORCEOUT SLATED FOR TONIGHT

SUPERFECTA WAGERING ON ALL LIVE RACES TONIGHT (EXCEPT THE 12TH)

FRED CAIRONE COUNTDOWN RACE 12 TONIGHT 2-DOG MATCH RACE WIN, DD

AMERICAN GREYHOUND DERBY RACE 13 TONIGHT POST TIME 10:35 PM WPS, QUIN, TRI, SUPER

American Greyhound Derby Tonight at Lincoln

The nation's top 3/8ths-mile greyhound racers will gather at Lincoln Park this evening for the 48th running of the Joseph M. Linsey Memorial American Greyhound Derby.

Eight competitors from seven different states will go to post in the nation's oldest greyhound stakes which carries a total purse of $60-thousand.

"Traditionally, 64 greyhounds compete through three rounds of qualifying," said Gary Liberatore, Lincoln's racing director. "Due to the later date on this year's calendar, we decided not to run the risk of having any of the qualifying rounds postponed because of bad weather."

This year's AmDerby is an invitational event. Three of the Derby hopefuls have already experienced the taste of stakes victory.

Slater Shell, a soon to

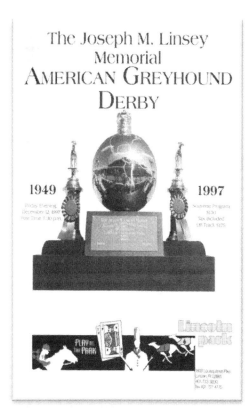

American Greyhound Derby

be two-year old from Gulf Greyhound captured the $25-thousand Texas Fall Derby on November 1. Mile High Greyhound Park will be represented by *Granny* who won the $25-thousand Timberline Stakes this past July. Raynham Greyhound is sending *Cruce* to post. He came out on top in the Blue Ribbon Stakes at Raynham last month.

Here is a look at the remaining field for this year's AmDerby: *Phoebe Ann* from Southland Greyhound Park in Arkansas. This is her first stakes appearance. She is a closer who favors the inside and owns a 67 percent in the money average on her home track.

Florida Carmine from nearby Wonderland Greyhound Park. He was a finalist in the Wonderland Derby four months ago. He is a pacesetting, inside run-

ner with box to wire ability.

Anthem from Connecticut's Plainfield Greyhound Park. She is the only outside invader with experience over Lincoln Park's Ocean Course. She finished off the board in the Lincoln Park Challenge last April.

Ruskyn from Birmingham Race Course in Alabama. This is his first stakes appearance. He has won 18 times at Birmingham this year. Breaks extremely well.

Wake Up Alarm will carry the banner for the home team. She finished 2nd in the Hinsdale (NH) Lottery Sweepstakes Invitational two months ago. *Wake Up Alarm* has late speed along the inside. She has 17 victories at Lincoln Park this year.

Tonight's AmDerby is on the same card as the final round of the Fred Cairone Memorial Countdown. The Countdown is a $10-thousand Lincoln Park in-house stakes of which the final round is a 2-dog match race.

The countdown final (Race #12) is the first half of a late Daily Double with the American Greyhound Derby (Race #13) being the second half.

First race post tonight is 7:30 pm. Post time for the AmDerby is 10:35 pm.

Phoebe Ann-1997

"THE 1997 $60,000 JOSEPH M. LINSEY MEMORIAL AMERICAN GREYHOUND DERBY"

2010 FEET — **THIRTEENTH RACE** — **GRADE S**

OCEAN COURSE

2nd HALF OF THE LATE DOUBLE

SUPERFECTA, Trifecta, Quiniela, Win, Place & Show Wagering

TRACK RECORD
Duplantis
37.25 (09/06/96)

LI12/12E13

8-1 — 1 — Slatex Shell (AA) — AA AA — 59 — LI 0 0 0 0 0 — GG 23 14 2 2 1 — $0

Kennel: George Harlan Kennel [69]
Owner: Bernice Harlan
Trainer: Denise Corey

Brindle F, Mar 17, 1996. Randy Handy-Just Dutch

Event	Trk	Dst	TC	Time	Wt	PP	Off	1/8	Str	Fin	ART	Odds	Grade	Comment	Opponents Finish Order
12/08S2	LI	2010	F	38.45	59½	2	2	1nk	2	2 3¾	38.71	-		Early Bid Mdtrk	ScatillacKing, , 2
Races below at Gulf Greyhound															
12/02E7	GG	1980	F	37.73	59	2	1	1 1	1 1	2 1	37.80	0.80*	TAA	Lost Str Duel Rl	SlatexDigger, AZHotBdn, RnchErn
11/27E7	GG	1980	F	37.07	59	4	4	1 2	1 2	1 4½	37.07	0.90*	TAA	Pulled Away Rail	AZHotBoudin, RaceyJan, RanchErn
11/23E12	GG	1980	F	37.37	59	5	2	1 1	1 2	1hd	37.37	1.30*	TAA	Held On Late Rail	AZHotBoudin, HiHoSlvr, SltxGnr
11/18E12	GG	1980	F	38.35	59	8	2	1 2	1 2	1 1	38.35	0.30*	TAA	Drove Home On Rl	AZHotBoudin, RaceyJan, HiHoSlvr
11/14E9	GG	1980	F	37.28	59	6	1	1 2	1 3	1 3½	37.28	0.90*	TAA	All The Way Rail	RaceyJan, AZHotBoudin, FlyngQsr
11/09E12	GG	1650	F	30.64	58	8	4	6	6	6 8	31.20	1.20*	AA	Hit Twice Inside	GbleCpid, JttaDrthy, BYTxsStr
11/05E2	GG	1980	F	38.04	59	8	2	1 3	1½	4 2	38.20	0.60*	TAA	Outbid Late Rail	AZHotBoudin, SCElgntldy, RacyJn
11/01E8	GG	1980	F	37.13	58	6	1	1 2	1 3	1 4	37.13	0.90*	SAA	Texas Fall Champ	AZHotBoudin, SltxGner, ChnOfFls
10/28E12	GG	1980	F	37.01	58	2	2	1 2	1 2	1 5	37.01	1.10*	SAA	Drove Home On Rl	RadioTrvlr, ChnOfFls, SltxMrsha
Red 10/23E9	GG	1980	F	37.39	58	1	3	1 3	1 4	1 2½	37.39	1.10*	SAA	Coasted Home Rail	RpdoBron, GhostMyst, MrPnsve

2-1 — 2 — Wake Up Alarm (AA) — 37.50 — AA M — 61 — LI 65 18 16 10 9 — HI 1 0 1 0 0 — $47652

Kennel: Brindle Kennel [9]
Owner: Troy D. Stiles
Trainer: Bob Antunes, Sr.

Brindle & White F, Nov 1, 1994. FMC's Wake Up-Silver Green

Event	Trk	Dst	TC	Time	Wt	PP	Off	1/8	Str	Fin	ART	Odds	Grade	Comment	Opponents Finish Order
12/06E2	LI	2010	F	37.83	61	5	5	2	2	1 1	37.83	4.40	AA	Drove Thru On Ins	DrysDwnTwn, PWsMcOnlr, MrchOn*
12/03A2	LI	2010	F	37.60	61	5	4	5	6	6 8½	38.19	3.00	AA	Crwd Bumped Erly	FlyingOrck, MrchOn*, DrysDwnTwn
11/28E2	LI	2010	F	37.67	60½	1	1	1 2	1 1½	1½	37.67	1.60*	AA	Undr Prssure Ins	FlyngOrck, PWsMcOnlr, DrysDwnTwn
11/24A4	LI	2010	F	38.10	61	4	5	4	4	3 7	38.59	2.40	AA	Followed Leaders	FlyngOrck, DrysDwnTwn, PWsMcOnlr
11/19A8	LI	2010	F	38.38	60½	6	5	2	2	2ns	38.39	3.80	AA	Pressing Late Ins	PWsMcOnlr, DrysDwnTwn, ChMrRdr
11/14E8	LI	2010	S	38.71	60	4	6	3	1½	2 1	38.77	3.70	AA	Led Into Str Cght	FlyngOrck, RnchObdh, PWsMcOnlr
11/08A2	LI	2010	F	37.95	60½	8	4	2	2	2 2½	38.11	3.20	AA	Chsd Winner Ins	FlyngOrck, DrysDwnTwn, TrntthLdr
11/01A10	LI	2010	F	37.79	60	1	6	2	2	4 10½	38.51	0.80*	AA	No Excuses	FlyingOreck, TurntotheLeader, ChMrRdr
Races below at Hinsdale															
10/26A10	HI	1980	F	37.27	61	3	2	2	2	2½	37.31	3.60	SA	Hard Try Rail	CeeBarSnow, FlyingOreck, BlazngLdy
Races below at Lincoln															
Blue 10/20A2	LI	2010	F	38.17	60½	5	1	1 4	1 3	1 2½	38.17	2.00*	TAA	Wire To Wire Ins	OkieRicki, CheMarRdr, PWsMcOnlr

10-1 — 3 — Phoebe Ann (AA) — AA AA — 71 — LI 0 0 0 0 0 — SL 57 12 15 11 5 — $0

Kennel: Robert Thorne Kennel [65]
Owner: Randle Kennel, Inc.
Trainer: John Thorne

Black F, Aug 17, 1995. Great Son-Skitch

Event	Trk	Dst	TC	Time	Wt	PP	Off	1/8	Str	Fin	ART	Odds	Grade	Comment	Opponents Finish Order
12/08S1	LI	2010	F	38.07	71	5	2	1 5	1 8	1 11	38.07	-		With Ease Mdtrk	Pa'sMissy, , 2
12/03S1	LI	1650	F	30.89	70½	7	4	2	2	2nk	30.92	-		Coming On Fast	Pa'sMaggieMa, AgntMttHlm, TmmysGl4
Races below at Southland															
11/24E13	SL	1980	F	37.19	71	1	4	5	6	5 8½	37.79	0.30*	A	Blocked Esc Tn Rl	KCGreg, LashngLori, KarenRice
11/18E13	SL	1980	F	37.36	70½	8	1	6	5	4 4	37.63	0.80*	A	Bmpd 1st Drove Rl	RoyalDuke, TskHnySack, LshngLr
11/14E8	SL	1980	F	36.86	71	5	3	3	2	1hd	36.86	2.40*	A	In Final Strides	JollyRyan, Kishka, BoxWrap
11/10E10	SL	1980	F	37.17	70½	5	1	7	6	5 6	37.60	1.80*	A	Bmpd & Blcd Early	KarenRice, JtStJry, OshkshEntc
11/06E14	SL	1980	F	36.90	70	1	3	1 2	1 5	1 5	36.90	0.90*	A	Quick Trip Inside	RoyalDuke, HeyGottaGo, VanlSnw
11/01E14	SL	1980	F	37.29	70	1	4	2	1hd	1 3	37.29	1.10*	A	Took Cntrl Fr Trn	JollyRyan, EarthAngel, SeaLgnd
10/25E12	SL	1980	F	36.92	69	4	3	4	1 1½	1 6½	36.92	2.20	B	Flying In Str Ins	FzzysBlkmr, TskHnySack, BoxWrp7
10/22A15	SL	1748	F	32.65	70½	5	7	6	4	2 2	32.78	0.50*	B	Threat Dspte Bmp	RWRstcWear, TBLghtning, MsWrfld
White 10/18A11	SL	1748	F	32.80	70½	3	7	7	6	4 2½	32.98	1.10*	B	Threat Dspt Block	Barometer, JasonOlvr, MLFnDrmr

7-2 — 4 — Granny (AA) — AA AA — 63 — LI 0 0 0 0 0 — MH 24 8 5 4 2 — $0

Kennel: Robert Feathers Kennel [68]
Owner: Floyd L. Gibson, Sr.
Trainer: James Christmas

Red Brindle F, Dec 17, 1994. Trojan Episode-Miss Athena

Event	Trk	Dst	TC	Time	Wt	PP	Off	1/8	Str	Fin	ART	Odds	Grade	Comment	Opponents Finish Order
12/08S5	LI	2010	F	38.45	63½	6	1	1 3	1 5	1 5	38.45	-		Handily On Inside	Grandirishribbon, , 2
Races below at Mile High															
11/26A12	MH	2050	F	40.01	62	1	1	1 4	1 5	1 6½	40.01	1.00*	AA	In Sherp Form Ins	PblcAblty, MG'sPocoGs, FrstGrb
11/20A15	MH	2050	F	40.24	62½	7	5	5	7	6 14	41.25	7.00	AA	Some Early Trble	OshkoshHowi, OvrThSpd, SHTnLnUp
11/17A12	MH	2050	F	40.18	62½	4	2	1 4	1 1½	2 1	40.24	4.50	AA	Beaten Late Ins	CjnChlngr, OvrThSpeed, PblcAblty
11/10A12	MH	2050	F	39.51	63½	6	2	2	6	7 7	40.00	4.30	TAA	Losing Ground Ins	CjnChlngr, Snidely, OvrThSpeed
11/06A12	MH	2050	F	39.20	63½	5	2	3	6	7 14	40.17	4.50	TAA	Steady Fade Ins	OvrTheSpeed, OshkoshHw, RthssDll
11/03A12	MH	2050	F	39.77	63	3	1	1 3	2	2 1	39.85	6.30	TAA	Hard Try Inside	SanTanGsto, OvrThSpeed, OgalEgng
10/30A8	MH	2050	F	40.29	63½	7	2	1 3	2	4 12	41.17	3.80	TAA	Early Pacesetter	SanTanLnUp, OvrTheSpd, OshkshHw
10/22A4	MH	2050	F	39.42	63	2	1	1 1	1 1½	2½	39.47	4.90	AA	Beat Out Late Ins	OvrThSped, RCsGrbthd, SnTnLnUp7
10/18E12	MH	2050	F	39.21	63	2	1	1 4	1 3	1½	39.21	5.00	TAA	Losing Lead Ins	RC'sGrblhd, OvrThSpeed, ArjPentr
Green 10/15A8	MH	2050	F	38.94	63	4	1	2	2	3 7	39.44	4.60	AA	Lost Place Late	OvrThSpeed, RC'sGrblhd, ForestGr

CONTINUED ON NEXT PAGE

Phoebe Ann-1997

"THE 1997 $60,000 JOSEPH M. LINSEY MEMORIAL AMERICAN GREYHOUND DERBY"

CONTINUED FROM PREVIOUS PAGE

PP	Event	Trk	Dst	TC	Time	Wt	PP	Off	1/8	Str	Fin	ART	Odds	Grade	Comment	Opponents Finish Order	Li12/12E13

6-1 Cruce (AA) — 5

74   AA AA   LI 0 0 0 0 0   RT 42 20 11 7 1 $0

Kennel: North Shore Kennel [47] — Owner: W. E. Cryer — Trainer: Bill Malboeuf

Red Brindle M, Oct 15, 1994. Ari-Expert Clown

Date	Trk	Dst	TC	Time	Wt	PP	Off	1/8	Str	Fin	ART	Odds	Grade	Comment	Opponents
12/08S8	LI	2010	F	38.61	74	3	2	2	1nk	11½	38.61	-		Frcd Pace Up Ins	SnifNWessum, , 2

Races below at Raynham-Taunton

11/30E4	RT	1980	F	38.75	74	8	8	6	2	24	39.02	0.50*A		Crwd Crtn Cls Mtk	FreqntChncs, Stndrd, MystryTrn
11/26A4	RT	1980	F	38.00	74½	7	7	6	3	37	38.50	0.60*A		Just Missed Place	KelsosMrtn, SystmOnDck, PnkshH
11/22A4	RT	1980	F	38.53	74½	4	4	7	3	26½	38.90	1.20*A		Crwd Twc Up Place	CajnBsArrw, MsClftn, AljPrsctr
11/14E4	RT	1980	M	38.98	74	8	8	3	11½	13	38.98	1.00*A		Avoid Trbl Easy	GreatStuff, HandmdwnRs, KlssMldn
11/08E12	RT	1980	M	38.34	72½	6	7	6	2	12	38.34	2.20*SA		Blue Ribbon Champ	Digicom, ZealousZoom, Arbitrtn
11/05A4	RT	1980	F	38.15	74	6	7	5	11	11½	38.15	4.40 SA		Muscled Thru Jam	CajunBo'sArrw, Dgcm, KlssIncgnt
11/01E2	RT	1980	M	38.76	74	4	7	7	7	616	39.87	1.20*SA		Bumpd & Crwd Erly	E'sMissy, ModoFord, DawnsChmpn
10/29A12	RT	1980	F	38.25	74	2	3	11	13½	16½	38.25	1.10*SA		Kept Extending Mt	StarlghtAstr, KlssIngnt, MdFrd
10/22A11	RT	1980	F	38.68	74	4	5	4	2	1ns	38.68	1.30*A		Up For It All Lt	GreatStff, SystmOnDck, RnchFndng
Black 10/17A4	RT	1980	F	38.19	74	7	8	5	3	21½	38.30	2.40 A		Trying Hard Mdtrk	BillySuCn, RnchFndng, KlssMrtn

4-1 Ruskvyn (AA) — 6

69   AA AA   LI 0 0 0 0 0   BM 59 18 12 9 5 $0

Kennel: Derby Henry Kennel [67] — Owner: Darren Henry — Trainer: Darren Henry

Black M, Apr 20, 1995. Iruska Bear-Vyna Lou

| 12/08S4 | LI | 2010 | F | 38.95 | 68½ | 5 | 1 | 120 | 120 | 125 | 38.95 | - | | Never Challenged | TM'sHonorRoll, , 2 |

Races below at Birmingham

11/26E13	BM	2030	F	39.73	69	8	1	4	3	2nk	39.76	0.70*A		Coming Home Strng	MyCrzyLfe, PtCBrzn, JNJStnsGrl
11/22E15	BM	2030	F	39.14	69	3	1	13	17	18½	39.14	0.20*A		Never A Doubt	MyCrzyLfe, FnlBogi, JNJStnsGrl
11/19E13	BM	2030	F	39.53	69	8	1	2	15	110	39.53	0.20*A		As Expected Mdtk	JNJHngLoos, FnlBogi, MyCrzyLfe
11/14E15	BM	2030	F	39.11	67½	2	1	2	15	15½	39.11	0.90*A		Going Away	MyCrzyLfe, FnlBogi, DnsEndora
11/08E15	BM	2030	F	39.44	68½	3	4	3	2	24	39.73	0.70*A		Late Speed Mdtk	JNJStnsGrl, XQHrlyMrgn, JNJhngLs
11/05E13	BM	2030	F	39.10	68	4	1	11	13	17	39.10	0.80*A		Took No Prisoners	NDDandy, PrftMrgn, DnsEndora
11/01E15	BM	2030	M	39.01	68½	5	1	12	15	16½	39.01	0.80*A		Dominated Field	XQHrlyBrty, DnsEndora, FnlBogi
10/29E13	BM	2030	F	38.97	68½	5	1	18	17	111	38.97	2.40*A		In Clss Of Hs Own	CvrSister, BeautiflPt, TomLang
10/25E15	BM	2030	F	39.14	68½	1	1	11	13	13½	39.14	5.60 A		All The Way Rail	XQHrlyBrly, JNJStnsGrl, RGsSplr
Yellow 10/21E13	BM	1650	M	31.23	68½	3	2	6	6	58	31.81	2.80 A		Broke Well Faded	BrdgOut, JD'sCrtfied, PushPuli

10-1 Florida Carmine (AA) — 7

69   AA AA   LI 0 0 0 0 0   WO 62 20 7 12 5 $0

Kennel: Halftime Kennel Inc. [66] — Owner: C. Callahan or M. Silvestro — Trainer: Mike Silvestro, Jr.

Brindle M, Mar 25, 1995. Standingapplause-Bring Joy

| 12/08S3 | LI | 2010 | F | 38.36 | 69 | 3 | 1 | 2 | 2 | 211 | 39.13 | - | | Sm Erly Spd Ins | AlviesStreaker, , 2 |

Races below at Wonderland

11/30E12	WO	2045	M	39.70	68½	5	1	13	11	11½	39.70	7.60 SAA		Gamely Inside	Modem, BlazingIntrigue, AllbiLiz
11/26E9	WO	2045	F	38.75	68	2	1	13	2	36½	39.19	2.40*SAA		Pacesetter Ins	Zillenna, RascalGirl, BlazngIntrg
11/20E4	WO	2045	F	39.36	68½	2	1	14	13	14	39.36	0.70*AA		Handily No Muzzle	FameNGlory, KiowBtDr, JffNwhll
11/16E9	WO	2045	F	39.18	68½	7	4	4	4	56½	39.63	1.40*TAA		Even Effort	Reb'sCarol, BlazingChamp, Lizalot
11/09E4	WO	2045	M	39.41	69	6	6	2	2	26½	39.78	1.10*TAA		Next Best Inside	BlazingIntrg, ExprtGz, CCMksBst
11/05E4	WO	2045	F	39.23	69	2	1	14	11¾	11½	39.23	2.40 AA		Undr Prssre Ins	BlazingIntrigue, CCMiksBst, CssB
11/01E4	WO	2045	M	40.67	68½	1	3	2	11	12½	40.67	1.40*TAA		Led Far Tn, Outs	MohawkRed, BlazingChmp, AmndBlk
10/26E13	WO	2045	F	39.27	68	6	1	12	11	11	39.27	2.10 AA		Gamely Inside	LadyLike, ExpressLane, JeffNewhall
10/21E4	WO	2045	F	38.93	68	6	1	13	13	13½	38.93	10.10 AA		All The Way Ins	Modem, ExpertGaze, GlowingGem
Green White 10/14E4	WO	2045	F	38.90	69	8	2	6	7	612½	39.79	15.50 SAA		No Threat	SR'sArtemus, Without, BlazingIntrg

12-1 Anthem (AA) — 8

61   AA AA   LI 1 0 0 0 0   PL 51 20 8 6 7 $0

Kennel: Prime Time Kennel [70] — Owner: Philip M. Pruett — Trainer: Roger Scharlack

Black F, Mar 5, 1995. Tanqueray Kid-Play Me Only

| 12/08S7 | LI | 2010 | F | 38.88 | 61 | 1 | 2 | 2 | 2 | 2ns | 38.89 | - | | Pressing Late Ins | TryToTakeIt, , 2 |

Races below at Plainfield

12/03E12	PL	2040	F	38.85	61½	4	8	8	8	8	OOP	1.00*A		Fell 1st Turn	ScatillcCndy, KlssWshfl, IsindRvw*
11/28E1	PL	2040	F	38.67	61	6	6	4	2	1¾	38.67	1.10*TA		From Way Back	Kelso'sRampart, JuelIndy, JusoDrcy
11/23A12	PL	2040	F	38.59	61	3	4	4	14	15	38.59	0.40*TA		Drove Through	Kelso'sWishful, JusoDarcy, JulIndy
11/17A8	PL	2040	F	39.31	61	2	6	6	3	43½	39.56	1.80*A		Good Effort	Dr.B'sCarlos, TX'sMoSrprs, BlgSnflwr
11/12E9	PL	2040	F	39.02	60½	5	8	5	2	1½	39.02	1.90*A		Late Inside Drive	BolgSnflwr, GrdyGs, SctllcCndy
11/07E10	PL	2040	F	39.14	61½	5	3	4	3	22	39.28	2.50 TA		Overcm Erly Trbl	DSJamNSam, ScrewyLouie, JulIndy
11/01E12	PL	2040	M	39.55	61	2	2	2	13	13½	39.55	0.40*TA		Best In Stretch	TallTailwind, BamGdy, Gtmymjwrkn
10/25A8	PL	2040	M	40.20	62	1	2	11½	18	18½	40.20	3.40 A		Quickly On Top	DSJamNSam, DestinysDn, DstnysDncr
10/18A5	PL	2040	F	39.40	62	5	6	6	4	47	39.89	5.00 TA		Almost Showed	DestinysDn, DstnysDncr, CstlExprss
Yellow Black 10/12A10	PL	2040	F	39.09	61½	3	7	2	2	13½	39.09	2.20 TA		Won Final Strides	CoastlExpress, DSJmNSm, BBsOzrk

Computer: 3-2-1-8   THIS IS IT! PLACE YOUR WAGERS EARLY, DON'T BE SHUT OUT!

Granny-1998

Granny-1998

**"THE 1998 $60,000 JOSEPH M. LINSEY
MEMORIAL AMERICAN GREYHOUND DERBY"**

2010 FEET

OCEAN COURSE

THIRTEENTH RACE

SUPERFECTA, Trifecta, Quiniela, Win, Place & Show Wagering

GRADE S
TRACK RECORD
Duplantis
37.25 (09/06/96)

PP	Event	Trk	Dst	TC	Time	Wt	PP	Off	1/8	Str	Fin	ART	Odds	Grade	Comment	Opponents Finish Order	L110/03E13

8-5 Kelsos Kingpin (AA) — 73 — LI 0 0 0 0 0 — AA AA — MU 14 11 0 1 2 — $0
Kennel: John Kelly Kennel [43]
Owner: John W. Kelly
Trainer: Maurice Henvey

Fawn M, Jun 12, 1996. Trojan Episode-Kelso's Magnolia

| 09/28s2 | LI | 2010 | F | 37.84 | 74 | 5 | 1 | 1 10 | 1 15 | 1 23¾ | 37.84 | · | | Won With Ease Ins | ZephyrCoveKid, , 2 |

Races below at Multnomah

09/19E13	MU	1650	F	30.57	73	1	3	1 4	1 6	1 5¾	30.57	0.30*A		Drawing Away Ins	GoldJstc, DrvngRnge, S'sEpcLdrs
09/16E14	MU	1650	F	30.88	72½	3	4	5	4	4 5¾	31.28	0.10*A		Jammed Early Ins	EPsIntrndr, MhcnWWPrk, DrvngRng
09/11E3	MU	1650	F	30.31	72½	8	1	1 5	1 6	1 12	30.31	0.50*A		All Alone Inside	GoAnthony, EFsIntrndr, AftThStrm
09/06A0	MU	1650	F	30.37	73	5	2	1 ns	1 2	1 10	30.37	0.50*A		Going Away Inside	MkngDrms, FrgvNGrgt, MhcnWWP
08/29s2	MU	1650	F	30.61	74	4	4	1 4	1 5	1 6¾	30.61	·		Drew Out Mdtrk	OstrsKd, NanaSuhr, Baleyvll
08/22E9	MU	2010	F	38.82	74	3	2	3	3	4 2¾	38.98	0.40*SA		In Hot Pursuit	EF'sHrsyrsgn, VlsRdhtL, TmpRcktfr
08/19E11	MU	2010	F	38.48	73½	1	1	1 6	1 8	1 4	38.46	0.40*SA		Never In Doubt	TmpRcktfr, FrmLstToLd, EFsHrsyrsn7
08/15E8	MU	2010	F	38.40	73½	4	1	1 3	1 4	1 2¾	38.40	0.70*SA		Never Headed Ins	FrmLstToLd, VlsRdhtL, Schprtydg
08/08E6	MU	2010	F	38.31	74	4	2	1 3	1 7	1 8¾	38.31	0.40*SA		All Alone Inside	SystmKlyGl, DoWhop, FrmLstToLd
08/05E10	MU	2010	F	38.40	74	4	1	1 8	1 8	1 5¾	38.40	0.80*SA		All The Way Ins	TmpRcktfr, SystmSybl, SystmKtyGl

Red / 1

10-1 Billy Sue Canoe (AA) — 55 — LI 0 0 0 0 0 — AA AA — RT 43 22 6 5 3 — $0
Kennel: Fortunato & Sarney Kennel [42]
Owner: C. Sarney or A. Fortunato
Trainer: Jim Fortunato

Fawn F, Jun 9, 1995. Johnny Canoe-Beekas Regisgrad

| 09/28s4 | LI | 2010 | F | 38.23 | 55½ | 4 | 1 | 1 7 | 1 8 | 1 9¾ | 38.23 | · | | Full Command Mtk | Kerryhill Tipi*, , 2 |

Races below at Raynham-Taunton

09/12A4	RT	1980	F	38.66	55½	6	6	5	4	6 4¾	38.97	1.90*A		No Mishaps Outs	BadVicky, RiverwoodCigar, HllVck
09/06E12	RT	1980	F	38.47	55	8	6	2	3	2 ns	38.48	2.40*SA		Needed 1 More Stp	KwRaptorRed, RivrwdCgr, HllVck
09/02A11	RT	1980	F	38.28	54	6	3	2	2	3 3	38.49	0.40*SA		Surrendered Place	RiverwodCgr, KlssVvn, KwRptrRd7
08/29E7	RT	1980	F	38.43	54½	7	3	1 2¾	1 4	1 6	38.43	1.60*SA		Running Away Ins	Arbitration, THDaisyMa, DrfldJy
08/26A2	RT	1980	F	38.43	56	4	2	3	3	2 3	38.65	0.60*SA		Grabbed Plce Late	HllVck, TMCsSnddllr, ChrstSnydr
08/21E4	RT	1980	F	38.82	55	8	5	2	1 4	1 4	38.82	0.40*A		Breezing Midtrack	KelssTlsmn, THDsyM, KlssKtchnr
08/15A4	RT	1980	F	38.35	55½	7	1	1 3	1 3	1 3	38.35	0.80*A		Quick Control Mtk	RstrMmbs, KlssKtchnr, MtthwsMrg
08/08A4	RT	1980	F	38.51	55½	5	1	1 1	1 6	1 4¾	38.51	1.80*A		Never Looked Back	Kelso'sChrsma, HeyBgGn, BdVcky
08/02E4	RT	1980	F	38.67	55	4	5	3	1 ns	1 ¾	38.67	1.40*A		Drew Clear Late	Kelso'sChrsm, LckyGs, KlssKtchnr
07/29A4	RT	1960	F	38.54	55½	2	6	7	5	3 4¾	38.84	0.80*A		Crwd Erly Driving	RvrwdCgr, KlssVvn, StrightChck

Blue / 2

10-1 Granny (AA) — 63 — LI 0 0 0 0 0 — AA AA — MH 16 8 3 0 0 — $0
Kennel: Robert Feathers Kennel [45]
Owner: Floyd L. Gibson, Sr.
Trainer: Doris Souza

Red Brindle F, Dec 17, 1994. Trojan Episode-Miss Athena

| 09/28s6 | LI | 2010 | F | 38.19 | 63½ | 6 | 2 | 2 | 1 2 | 1 5¾ | 38.19 | · | | Pulling Away Ins | SCMylce, , 2 |

Races below at Mile High

09/18E12	MH	2050	F	39.16	62½	3	2	8	8	8	OOP	1.80*AA		Fell Early	RedneckDan, BeamsChub, OvrThSpeed
09/14A12	MH	2050	F	39.56	63	5	2	3	3	2 ¾	39.61	4.60 TAA		Hard Try Inside	HpnsSylv, RedneckDan, OvrThSpd
09/09A4	MH	2050	F	39.54	63½	8	1	2	1 4	1 7¾	39.54	0.40*A		Back On Top Ins	HRSandBrwn, Unwoven, TP'sHghHps
09/01A7	MH	2050	F	39.15	63½	6	1	6	8	7 22	40.74	1.60*AA		Offstrd Erly Ins	OvrThSpeed, HyPlnsLane, RdnckDn
08/27E7	MH	2050	F	39.50	63½	2	2	8	8	8 12	40.37	0.60*TAA		Early Trouble Rl	OvrThSpeed, RedneckDn, HyPlnsLn
08/24A7	MH	2050	F	39.71	64	8	6	6	6	6 12	40.55	0.40*AA		Blckd Ent Esc Trn	LRRedIrene, HyPlnsLn, OvrThSpd

Races below at Wonderland

08/15L1	WO	2045	F	38.10	63½	1	2	1 1	1 3	1 3¾	38.10	1.60*SAA		Derby Champ	GrysBtsyRss, GreysFreckles, Dornslfe
08/10E10	WO	2045	F	38.45	64	8	1	1 6	1 6	1 5¾	38.46	5.70 SAA		Handily Inside	JamscaBert, Gwyhead, TM'sDaisy
08/06E10	WO	2045	F	38.51	64	5	3	1 1	1 5	1 4	38.51	1.70*SAA		Drew Out Inside	Zabel, SR'sPding, Marietta7

White / 3

12-1 Phoebe Ann (AA) — 71 — LI 0 0 0 0 0 — AA AA — SL 26 7 10 3 4 — $0
Kennel: Robert Thorne Kennel [40]
Owner: Randle Kennel, Inc.
Trainer: Gerard Ryan

Black F, Aug 17, 1995. Great Son-Skitch

| 09/28s7 | LI | 2010 | F | 39.01 | 71 | 1 | 2 | 2 | 2 | 2 3¾ | 39.25 | · | | Couldn't Close Rl | SomeRooster, , 2 |
| 09/23s3 | LI | 1650 | F | 30.60 | 70 | 2 | 3 | 3 | 3 | 3 11¾ | 31.42 | · | | No Real Threat | OkieHowie, Sneezed, KiowaOnly4 |

Races below at Wonderland

08/10E4	WO	2045	F	38.89	72	6	3	3	4	4 6¾	39.33	3.50 SAA		Followed Pace Ins	GreysFreckles, KodiakKm, Enytt7
09/06E12	WO	2045	F	38.98	71	8	4	4	2	2 2	39.09	2.60 SAA		Chased Winner Ins	Gwynedd, GreysBtsyRss, RbjBndt7
08/01L2	WO	2045	F	38.53	70	4	5	3	2	2 4¾	38.85	1.80*SAA		In Pursuit Inside	GlowingGem*, AmndBlk, SRsPddng
07/27E11	WO	2045	F	38.34	72	6	5	6	6	6 16¾	38.49	2.80 SAA		Carried Wd 1st Tn	FloridaSharp, OmegTrnd, JmcBrt
07/23s3	WO	2045	F	39.43	71	3	2	1 3	1 5	1 3	39.43	·		Handily Inside	Granny, Arbitration, MatthewsMirg4
07/16s3	WO	1650	F	31.08	71	8	4	2	2	2 2	31.22	·		Next Best Mdtrk	BarneyGreen, Kyza, SlegeOfEnnis5

Races below at Southland

| 07/09E5 | SL | 1748 | F | 32.68 | 71 | 7 | 7 | 5 | 3 | 1 2 | 32.68 | 2.30 A | | From Far Back Ins | JtStScrm, FzzysMrcry, PsWhtShdw |
| 07/03E15 | SL | 1980 | F | 36.96 | 70½ | 5 | 1 | 2 | 2 | 2 1 | 37.03 | 2.60 TA | | Catching Wnnr Ins | GrysRndzvs, SanTenPkr, BrtsBrg |

Green / 4

CONTINUED ON NEXT PAGE

Granny-1998

"THE 1998 $60,000 JOSEPH M. LINSEY MEMORIAL AMERICAN GREYHOUND DERBY"

CONTINUED FROM PREVIOUS PAGE

PP	Event	Trk	Dst	TC	Time	Wt	PP	Off	1/8	Str	Fin	ART	Odds	Grade	Comment	Opponents Finish Order	LI10/03E13

8-1 Greys Freckles (AA) — 61 LI 0 0 0 0 0 / AA AA WO 16 8 2 3 3 $0
Kennel: A-Line Kennel, Inc. [44]
Owner: Edward G. Le Roux, Jr.
Trainer: Richard Arno

White & Red Brindle F, Dec 6, 1995. Fortress*-Greys Juliana

5 / Black

Date	Trk	Dst	TC	Time	Wt	PP	Off	1/8	Str	Fin	ART	Odds	Grade	Comment	Opponents Finish Order
09/28 E1	LI	2010	F	38.04	61½	1	1	1	12½	14	16½	38.04	·		Late Command Ins	RedHillSilence, , 2
								Races below at Wonderland								
09/24 E12	WO	2045	F	38.70	60	3	5	4	2	25	39.05	0.60*AA		Next Best Inside	Dornsife, NXSMerryWidow, JoannP
09/19 E8	WO	2045	F	38.73	60½	7	1	16	18	111	38.73	1.50*AA		Unblemished Ins	Centerpivot, FiveStrBeaty, BthMN
09/13 E4	WO	2045	F	39.18	60½	4	1	14	15	14	39.18	1.50*AA		Full Command Ins	FiveStrBeauty, Gwyndd, BrthrsFr
09/09 E4	WO	2045	F	38.90	62	8	3	1½	11	11½	38.90	2.30 AA		Under Prssr Ins	AmandaBlake, Cntrpvt, FvStrbty
09/05 E4	WO	2045	F	38.99	60½	5	8	5	5	43	39.19	1.90*AA		Saved 1st Turn	AmandaBlake, TM'sPhonCll, Cntrpvt
08/31 E4	WO	2045	F	39.14	61	5	8	5	4	42½	39.31	3.10 AA		No Room Early	Gwyendd, CajunCreole, AmandaBlake
08/27 E4	WO	2045	F	39.23	60	3	2	4	2	1ns	39.23	1.00*AA		With Rush Inside	Lybrant, AmandaBlake, CajunCrel
08/23 E4	WO	2045	F	39.39	60	8	3	7	3	36	39.73	0.90*AA		Hld Wd Erly Clsd	AmandaBlake, TM'sPhonCll, Enytt
08/15 L1	WO	2045	F	38.10	60½	5	1	2	2	33½	38.35	8.40 SAA		Good Effort Ins	Granny, GreysBtsyRss, Dornsife
08/10 E4	WO	2045	F	38.89	61	4	6	4	2	11½	38.89	1.10*SAA		Str Drv Midtrack	KodiakKim, Enyatta, PhoebeAnn7

5-1 Monsoon Man (AA) — 37.52 67 LI 9 5 2 2 0 / AA A WO 2 0 0 0 1 $13119
Kennel: Regall Sports [10]
Owner: Jim or Karolyn Van Winkle
Trainer: Carlos Barbosa

Red Fawn M, Nov 16, 1995. He's My Man-RV Snowlady

6 / Yellow

Date	Trk	Dst	TC	Time	Wt	PP	Off	1/8	Str	Fin	ART	Odds	Grade	Comment	Opponents Finish Order
09/25 E2	LI	2010	F	37.51	67	4	1	12½	11½	2½	37.56	1.60*SAA		Couldn't Last Ins	TG'sScoobyDoo, SHKMeatLf, KwOx7
09/19 E12	LI	2010	F	37.91	67	2	4	2	4	32	38.06	0.80*SAA		Never Far Back	FlyingTeton, KiowaOx, JetTime*
09/16 A12	LI	2010	F	37.53	67	5	2	1¼	12½	12	37.53	1.30*SAA		Held Safe Margin	GreysSickLz, Sprklnhry, JAKyChn
09/11 E4	LI	2010	F	37.90	67	6	1	14	14	12	37.90	1.40*SAA		Took Control Erly	GreysSlickLz, Ghsty, Sprklnhry
09/05 E9	LI	2010	F	37.80	66½	2	1	11½	12	11½	37.80	1.70*SAA		Led Box To Wire	KiowaBetDunbar, AdmrlNlly, Dymrk
08/29 E15	LI	2010	F	37.92	67½	2	5	2	2	2½	37.96	2.60 TAA		Led Late Str Ins	Sparkleinhery, JAKyChn, DsylfyD
08/26 A1	LI	2010	F	37.46	68½	3	7	3	3	36½	37.90	1.80*TAA		Saved Grnd Evenly	JAKeyChain, TXsMSrprs, DsylfyD
08/21 A15	LI	2010	F	37.52	67½	3	1	11½	12½	14½	37.52	0.90*TAA		Late Command Ins	AdmirlNlly, Sprklnhry, FlyngTtn
08/15 E10	LI	2010	F	37.92	67½	7	5	2	2	11½	37.92	4.00 TA		Erly Gain Str Drv	NodakRiches, WikiWkTm, SzzlngS
08/12 S2	LI	1650	F	30.84	67	1	2	12	12½	14½	30.84	·		Won Handily Mdtk	WinterCher*, CrtnFrml*, ErnDgls7
								Races below at Wonderland								
08/01 E4	WO	2045	F	39.36	66	1	5	3	7	718	40.49	9.60 SA		Some Wide Turns	FloridaSharp, Enyatta, Dornsife

3-1 Run Vickie Star (AA) — 58 LI 0 0 0 0 0 / AA AA FL 24 17 1 2 1 $0
Kennel: G & R Kennel [46]
Owner: Billy K. Adams
Trainer: Mike Holguin

Red F, Dec 29, 1995. Twilite Drive-Okie Janice

7 / Green White

Date	Trk	Dst	TC	Time	Wt	PP	Off	1/8	Str	Fin	ART	Odds	Grade	Comment	Opponents Finish Order
09/28 S5	LI	2010	F	38.31	57½	2	2	14½	16	116	38.31	·		Extnding Lead Mtk	Largerdebnollate, , 2
								Races below at Flagler								
09/22 E12	FL	1940	F	37.87	58	4	7	7	5	36½	37.95	1.90*A		Knocked Bck Drvng	DLBsHmPrd, Mnshnhlltr, BstAprch
09/16 E12	FL	1940	F	37.93	57	3	4	3	3	11½	37.93	1.10*A		Str Charge Mdtk	CrLoteTune, AbtSylvstr, RazrS!sh
09/11 E9	FL	1940	F	37.03	58	1	1	13	14	112	37.03	0.80*A		Opened Up Str Ins	Jhda'sDsre, Dr'sBgRd, OLAwsmSd
09/06 E9	FL	1940	F	37.63	59	6	7	4	3	1hd	37.63	0.90*A		Up Last Stride Wd	Jhda'sDsre, FthfulDlck, RtRyRl
09/02 E12	FL	1940	F	37.60	59	6	4	6	5	56½	38.05	2.50 SA		Pinched Bck Up Sm	Cd'sLnn, AbtSylvstr, KbsStrbrt
08/29 E12	FL	1940	F	37.71	58	3	7	7	4	1½	37.71	0.50*SA		Closed Hard Mdtrk	BowMask, Okio, OlAwesomeSd
08/25 E9	FL	1940	F	36.94	58	1	2	13	16	16½	36.94	0.70*A		Opened It Up Str	MarborsObl, OldeAlllo, SoonerRd
08/22 E12	FL	1940	F	37.75	58	6	7	3	3	11½	37.75	0.70*A		Long Drive Inside	OLAwesomSd, RmblngSndy, CrLtTn
08/17 E12	FL	1940	F	37.22	57	2	2	12	14	110	37.22	1.50*A		Dominated Str Ins	KowHfln, AbtSylvstr, RvrwdActn
08/13 E12	FL	1940	F	37.30	58	5	2	2	12	14½	37.30	1.20*A		Took Ld Fr Turn	Jhda'sDsre, Jke'sSmart, RekoTekr

6-1 Wigwam Hoss (AA) — 75 LI 0 0 0 0 0 / AA AA PH 26 19 1 2 1 $0
Kennel: Keeter's Kennel [41]
Owner: Keeter's Kennel
Trainer: Ted Chotain

Dark Brindle M, Apr 6, 1995. Wigwam Wag-Riley's Marymary

8 / Yellow Black

Date	Trk	Dst	TC	Time	Wt	PP	Off	1/8	Str	Fin	ART	Odds	Grade	Comment	Opponents Finish Order
09/28 S3	LI	2010	F	38.35	75½	3	2	2	2	21½	38.47	·		Some Late Gain RI	HeatRacer, , 2
09/23 S1	LI	2010	F	37.69	75	1	3	17	110	110	37.69	·		Nvr Challenged RI	Roger'sGrace, YoRckn, HJSBdBlt4
								Races below at Wichita								
09/07 E9	WT	1650	F	30.40	75	2	4	4	3	23	30.60	2.30 SA		Determined To Plc	KwaChipew, WWTmTrvlr, SnTnChnc
09/02 E18	WT	1650	F	30.78	75	1	1	2	2	2ns	30.79	1.40*SA		One Step Away Ins	SystmBlckg, SnTanTeql, SgdBgRd
08/29 E15	WT	1650	F	30.68	75	1	3	2	2	21	30.74	1.10*SA		Hot Pursuit Rail	LRChakaZku, RN'sSpdstr, KoleCor7
08/26 E18	WT	1650	F	30.98	75	6	2	3	12	16½	30.98	1.70*SA		Away In Stretch	IrekExclbr, RD'sRandle, SnTnChnc
08/21 E12	WT	1650	F	30.68	75	5	2	2	12	13½	30.68	8.90 A		Strong Finish Ins	CrystlBrmd, MyBtsBnghm, Rlytrgn
08/15 E16	WT	1650	F	31.33	74½	8	7	8	6	54	31.62	2.50*A		Traffic Bckstr RI	WWOfNRning, SpBlckJack, CliQck
08/09 E1	WT	1650	F	30.72	74	7	4	3	3	36½	31.38			Clipped Early Ins	KwChpw, MyBtsBnghm, ItsHghVltg4
								Races below at Phoenix								
08/03 S8	PH	1650	F	30.83	75½	8	6	2	2	11½	30.83			Drove To Win Ins	WigwamZion, OlLoyFrct, WDsRbnhds

Computer: 6-1-8-5   **SUPERFECTA WAGERING ON EVERY LIVE RACE TODAY!**

Deuce's Wild-1999

American Greyhound Derby boasts very talented lineup

50th running brings best racers together

The lineup of greyhound racing talent assembled for tonight's 50th running of the Joseph M. Linsey Memorial American Greyhound Derby is nothing short of outstanding.

The field features six invitees from across the country — many of them already champions in their own right. They are joined by two qualifiers from host track Lincoln Park, who likely could hold their own at any other track, too.

The task of assembling the best racing talent available for this event fell to our Director of Racing Gary Liberatore. And he has done us proud.

Here is the field:

PA's Bella — Representing Raynham-Taunton Greyhound Park in Massachusetts, she recently won the 1999 Wonderland Derby. She had won 20 of her prior 32 races at Raynham prior to the Wonderland Derby.

NR's Fast Eddie — Representing Phoenix Greyhound Park in Arizona, he was the runnerup in the Wonderland Derby after going undefeated in qualifying and running the second fastest time in the 65-year history of the Revere, Mass., track. He is this year's Kennel Championship winner at Phoenix where he reeled off 13 wins in a recent 18-race stretch.

San Tan Bloomer — Representing Southland Greyhound Park in Arkansas, she won the Razorback Classic and Paul Hartwell Juvenile Stake there and also last fall's Abilene Park Stake and the National Greyhound Association Stake at the NGA track in Kansas with a record sprint time.

Owner Robert Feathers poses with Granny after her victory in last year's American Greyhound Derby. Granny earned All-American honors for 1998.

Impossible Dream — Representing the Jacksonville Greyhound Park in Florida, this talented youngster was a finalist in the Mayor's Cup and Duvall Silver Cup there and a semifinalist in the Orange Park Derby. He posted a 13-race winning streak at the 3-8ths distance at Jacksonville.

CJ Pepto Geno — Representing Multnomah Greyhound Park in Oregon, he won this year's Multnomah Derby and holds the track sprint record. He also was a finalist in this year's Hollywood World Classic.

Deuce's Wild — Running for the Regall Sports Kennel, he was the top qualifier in the in-house stake to determine Lincoln Park's two representatives in the derby. He was victorious in three of the four rounds while improving his career record to 12-8-3-3 in 29 trips to the starting box.

Lightning Snow — Running for the Nanci Caswell Kennel at Lincoln, she was the only other greyhound to post more than one victory in the four-round qualifying stake. Her half-length win in the fourth round moved her into a tie for the second qualifying berth. The deadlock was resolved by a coin toss.

Mark McGwire — Representing Mile High, he earned a derby invite by winning last week's Timberline Stakes at that Colorado track. Just over two years old, he is the youngest entry in the field and has won nine of his 20 career starts including the Great Expectations Championship sprint stake at Mile High.

We're looking forward to a great race for the $50,000 first prize. Best of luck to all.

Deuce's Wild-1999

"THE 1999 $100,000 JOSEPH M. LINSEY MEMORIAL AMERICAN GREYHOUND DERBY"

2010 FEET — **THIRTEENTH RACE** — **GRADE S**

OCEAN COURSE

SUPERFECTA, Trifecta, Quiniela, Win, Place & Show Wagering

TRACK RECORD
Duplantis
37.25 (09/06/96)

LI09/11E13

6-1 — **1** — Red

NR's Fast Eddie (AA)

AA AA 72 — LI 0 0 0 0 0 — PH 18 13 1 3 1 — $0

Kennel: Charlie Sample, Jr. Kennel [43]
Owner: Nadine E. Riggar
Trainer: Henry Chin

Red M, Sep 3, 1996. RD's Banker-Jael

Event	Trk	Dst TC	Time	Wt	PP	Off	1/8	Str	Fin	ART	Odds	Grade	Comment	Opponents Finish Order
09/06 S3	LI	2010 F	38.70	72½	3	1	1 6	1 6	1 6	38.70	.		Quick Command Ins	TSGates, , 2
Races below at Wonderland														
08/31 E8	WO	2045 F	38.74	72	3	1	2	3	3 6½	39.19	0.50*	A	Erly Leadr Ins	ProperStatesman, TM'sSuperEg, Snr
08/24 E4	WO	2045 F	38.23	72	5	1	1 2½	1 1½	1 1½	38.23	0.40*	A	All The Way Ins	TM'sShowBzz, YKntPcn, PrprSttsmn
08/20 E8	WO	2045 F	38.25	72	8	1	1 3	1 4	1 4½	38.25	0.30*	A	Quick Control Ins	TM'sSuperEg, Mllry, PrprSttsmn
08/14 E12	WO	2045 F	38.15	71	1	2	2	2	2 6	38.56	0.40*	SA	Best Of Rest Ins	Pa'sBella, TM'sShowBuzz, Mellry
08/09 E11	WO	2045 F	37.92	71	7	1	1 4	1 3	1 2½	37.92	0.80*	SA	All The Way Ins	Teeara, Athleta, Pa'sBella
08/05 E14	WO	2045 F	38.27	72	5	1	1 3	1 3	1 6	38.27	0.40*	SA	As Expected Ins	Ceecom, EasterDoggy, Magnitude
07/31 E4	WO	2045 F	38.47	72	2	2	1 1	1 4	1 8½	38.47	0.60*	SA	Drew Clear Inside	FloridaSharp, YoAndrea, Famuls 7
07/26 E10	WO	2045 F	38.57	73	1	1	1 5	1 4	1 4½	38.57	0.90*	SA	Fast Start Inside	KiowaRoss, Magnitude, Ceecom
07/22 S3	WO	2045 F	38.95	72	7	1	1 6	1 16	1 21½	38.95	.		Speed To Spare	Kelmmadee, Arno'sDedrv, CTWHsPlns 4

12-1 — **2** — Blue

Impossible Dream (AA)

AA AA 70 — LI 0 0 0 0 0 — JA 28 17 5 4 0 — $0

Kennel: Magic City Kennel [42]
Owner: J. Ametrano or B. Caldwell
Trainer: Randy Finegan

Black M, Jul 10, 1997. Santa Fe Rufus-Poco Mercedes

Event	Trk	Dst TC	Time	Wt	PP	Off	1/8	Str	Fin	ART	Odds	Grade	Comment	Opponents Finish Order
09/06 S1	LI	2010 F	38.70	70	5	2	1 1½	2	2 ½	38.75	.		Set Pace Overtkn	BoominBuella, , 2
Races below at Jacksonville														
08/25 E14	JA	1980 F	38.04	71	4	4	3	3	3 6	38.38	0.90*	A	Showed Inside	EdnaEilene, HhLghtsOt, RapdoRisqe
08/20 E14	JA	1980 F	37.96	70	1	1	2	1 1	1 2½	37.96	0.80*	TA	Six In A Row	OatsMattox, FlynByTim, RapdoRisqe
08/14 E14	JA	1980 F	37.69	70	5	4	1 1	1 3	1 3½	37.69	0.60*	A	Cntnued To Imprss	OatsMattox, VlsHghlnd, RvJoyRd
08/11 E9	JA	1980 F	37.41	69	3	1	1 3	1 3	1 6½	37.41	0.40*	A	Jax Meet Bst Time	VlsHghland, Prplpleter, OncBrt
08/06 E14	JA	1980 F	37.67	69½	1	1	1 3	1 4	1 6	37.67	0.50*	A	Smoking Time	TskKmFlase, ArtieAlves, RnwyFrtne
08/02 E9	JA	1980 F	38.33	69½	6	2	1 hd	1 1	1 2½	38.33	1.20*	A	Cleared Late Mdtk	BlckBlkBab, DrysMntn, RnwyFrtn
07/28 E9	JA	1980 F	37.76	70	3	2	1 ½	1 4	1 5½	37.76	0.70*	A	Flying Midtrack	BavarreMan, ArtieAlvs, FlyngByTm
07/23 E9	JA	1650 F	30.97	69½	2	5	6	6	6 4½	31.29	3.20	SA	Bumped 1st Turn	MnhatanHel, ColsonBlue, KwCocktl
07/17 E7	JA	1650 F	30.80	70	8	1	3	2	2 1½	30.89	0.80*	SA	Moved In Bmpd 1st	TskHpnTens, ColsonBlue, RapdRR
07/14 E11	JA	1650 F	31.21	70	5	7	3	3	2 ns	31.22	1.60*	SA	Trouble Game Bid	RapdoRaeRae, MybleWlkr, GntlHnd

---

9-2 — **3** — White

Pa's Bella (AA)

AA AA 65 — LI 0 0 0 0 0 — RT 39 22 6 4 5 — $0

Kennel: George Benjamin Kennel [41]
Owner: George Benjamin
Trainer: Glenn Atkinson

Red F, Mar 11, 1997. P's Raising Cain-Pacific Episode

Event	Trk	Dst TC	Time	Wt	PP	Off	1/8	Str	Fin	ART	Odds	Grade	Comment	Opponents Finish Order
09/06 S2	LI	2010 F	38.63	64½	6	2	2	1 2	1 4½	38.63	.		Led Bks Drw Clear	GiveMeAtry, , 2
Races below at Raynham-Taunton														
08/28 E12	RT	1650 F	31.35	64½	1	3	2	2	1 ns	31.35	0.30*	A	Just Up Midtrack	PatCCourier, RaymarNatl, MsVlLk
08/23 A11	RT	1650 F	31.19	64½	8	2	1 2	1 2½	1 7½	31.19	0.50*	A	As Expected Mdtrk	PtCCrr, DGsFrtSmth, JcsLnsprrw
Races below at Wonderland														
08/14 E12	WO	2045 F	38.15	64	8	1	1 6	1 5	1 6	38.15	5.40	SA	Derby Champ	NR'sFastEddie, TM'sShowBuzz, Mellery
08/09 E11	WO	2045 F	37.92	66	2	3	4	5	4 13	38.84	2.40	SA	Follwd Pace Mtk	NR'sFastEddie, Teeara, Athleta
08/05 E8	WO	2045 F	38.90	64	7	7	2	1 2½	1 ½	38.90	1.90*	SA	Bkstr Drive Ins	Abeñakee, GreysFreckles, Haddie
07/31 E8	WO	2045 F	38.78	64½	1	3	1 3	1 8	1 8½	38.78	0.50*	SA	All Alone Ins	TM'sShowBuzz, SR'sSabrin, FlMyWrth
07/25 E7	WO	2045 F	39.01	65	2	3	1 1½	1 1	1 ½	39.01	1.20*	SA	Under Prssr Ins	Zahara, Oswayo, Haddie
Races below at Raynham-Taunton														
07/17 A4	RT	1980 F	38.32	65	1	4	1 1	1 2	1 1½	38.32	1.20*	A	All The Way Mdtrk	KwRaptorRd, ChckChck, KlssMchy

---

10-1 — **4** — Green

Mark McGwire (AA)

AA AA 75 — LI 0 0 0 0 0 — MH 20 9 4 2 3 — $0

Kennel: Greg Cruz Kennel [45]
Owner: Michael A. Lasky
Trainer: Greg Cruz

Light Fawn M, Aug 24, 1997. Blazing Desire-Cold Shot Babe

Event	Trk	Dst TC	Time	Wt	PP	Off	1/8	Str	Fin	ART	Odds	Grade	Comment	Opponents Finish Order
09/08 S1	LI	1650 F	30.74	74½	1	1	1 3½	1 9	1 14½	30.74	.		Extnding Lead Ins	EpardHomer, , 2
Races below at Mile High														
09/04 E12	MH	2050 F	39.52	74½	4	2	2	1 6	1 6½	39.52	4.50	SAA	Timberline Champ	Bearability, RednckDn, SystmTpt
08/31 E12	MH	2050 F	39.40	74	4	3	2	2	2 2½	39.57	0.20*	SAA	Good Try Inside	Bearblty, Sprtfthwst, SystmFrtyn
08/27 E15	MH	2050 F	39.41	74½	1	3	2	1 ½	1 3	39.41	2.00	SAA	Hard Earned Win	SystemTapatio, PGTfStrm, CBChttr
08/24 E12	MH	2050 F	39.66	74	2	2	1 4	1 4	1 4	39.66	0.80*	SAA	Maintained Ld Ins	GazeAway, LKPrncsGm, GrysCrsRd
08/19 E13	MH	2050 F	39.55	74	7	4	4	4	4 3½	39.81	10.20	TAA	Trbld Esc Trn Ins	SystemTapat, AgrblGrl, RdnckDn
08/14 E6	MH	1699 F	32.16	74	7	4	4	4	3 1½	32.27	3.00	AA	Dead Heat Shw Ins	Wrongdoing, FrtnVnt, JSCblptDn 7
08/11 A7	MH	1699 F	32.10	75½	1	1	7	7	6 15	33.19	0.40*	AA	Trbl 1st Trn Ins	BemsBarfly, FrStarters, CdlcTst
08/05 E15	MH	1699 F	31.78	74½	4	1	2	2	1 1½	31.78	2.00	AA	Determined Win In	CBConMn, MghtyAphrt, GrndDmntr
07/31 E13	MH	1699 F	31.59	74	8	5	5	4	4 8½	32.06	9.00	SAA	Bumped 1st Tn Ins	BdTThtBon, EM'sBleBy, Unbrshbl
07/27 E15	MH	1699 F	32.34	73½	8	1	2	3	2 1½	32.44	14.80	SAA	Good Effort Ins	BdTThtBon, MrlynMansn, PikesNWO

CONTINUED ON NEXT PAGE

Deuce's Wild-1999

CONTINUED FROM PREVIOUS PAGE

PP	Event	Trk	Dst	TC	Time	Wt	PP	Off	1/8	Str	Fin	ART	Odds	Grade	Comment	Opponents Finish Order	LI09/11E13

7-2 San Tan Bloomer (AA) 70

LI 0 0 0 0 0 — AA AA — SL 32 16 8 0 2 — $0

Kennel: Allen Kennel [40]
Owner: Janet R. Allen
Trainer: Francis Rowe

Fawn F, Feb 18, 1997. My Broadway Joe-San Tan Brassy

09/06S4	LI	2010 F	38.34	70	5 2 1¹⁰ 1¹² 1¹⁶½	38.34	·		Extnding Lead Ins	PenroseKylie, , 2
08/30S1	LI	2010 F	38.57	70	1 1 1⁶ 1⁶ 1⁶	38.57	·		Quick Command Mtk	Blalock, , 2

Races below at Wonderland

07/31A9	WO	2045 F	38.80	70	6 6 6 5 5²¹	40.27	0.80*SA	Bumped 1st Turn	GreysFreckles, YKnotPcn, ArtsCrl
07/26E8	WO	2045 F	38.72	70	8 4 2 2 3²	38.87	0.70*SA	In Pursuit Sm Wd	BlackEntrprs, Athlt, GrysFrckls
07/22S2	WO	1650 F	30.57	70	7 3 1⁴ 1³ 1¹½	30.57	·	Rushed To Lead Md	SeanMan, JBBeckyBeGood, 3

Races below at Southland

07/08E11	SL	1749 F	32.48	69½	5 4 3 3 2ⁿˢ	32.49	1.90*A	Flying In Str Mtk	ChsngFaith, Rc'sTlchr, Dalianc
07/03E11	SL	1980 F	38.75	69	1 4 2 12½ 16½	36.75	1.00*SA	1999 Rzrback Chmp	Cyp, BltzenBanj, ProperPark
06/29E11	SL	1980 F	37.36	70	1 6 2 1³ 14½	37.36	0.90*SA	Incrsng Lead Mdtk	ProperPark, TmSVolcan, FrscCsc
06/24E11	SL	1980 F	37.17	69½	5 4 3 2 2⁴	37.44	0.50*SA	Vied For Ld Fr Tn	TmSVolcano, BascIntent, Jolon
06/19E11	SL	1980 F	37.20	69½	1 4 2 1³ 1⁴	37.20	0.50*SA	Held Safe Mrgn Md	MiTatleTal, StelaBlair, GunMtl

Black **5**

8-1 CJ Pepto Geno (AA) 78

LI 0 0 0 0 0 — AA AA — MU 26 12 2 7 2 — $0

Kennel: Wayne Ward Kennel [44]
Owner: R & F Kennel or W. Ward
Trainer: Jeff Wilcox

Red Brindle M, Dec 25, 1996. CJ Pepto Bahama-Hi Shine

| 09/06S5 | LI | 1650 F | 30.67 | 77 | 2 2 1¹ 1⁷ 1¹³½ | 30.67 | · | Pulling Away Ins | NodakNinety, , 2 |

Races below at Multnomah

08/21E11	MU	2010 F	38.33	77½	5 8 5 2 1²⅜	38.33	5.70 SA	'99 M.G.P. Champ	NbrskRbl, Feelings, KlssKngpn
08/14E11	MU	2010 F	38.18	78½	7 7 7 5 6¹³	39.10	7.00 SA	Coll Escp Trn Mtk	KlssKngpn, JimboScty, NbrskRbl
08/11E11	MU	2010 F	38.67	77½	4 5 6 4 5²½	38.85	3.00 SA	Raced Hard Rail	Feelings, YkonExprss, JmboScoty
08/07E8	MU	2010 F	38.16	78	3 6 4 3 2³⅛	38.40	1.20 SA	Drvng Thruout Ins	KlssKngpn, SystmArHry, IrskErnrps7
08/04E8	MU	2010 F	38.44	78½	3 7 6 3 1²½	38.44	1.00*SA	Driving Far Turn	TonysHarpo, NbrskaRse, GodStpng
07/29E8	MU	2010 F	38.42	77½	3 6 6 3 3⁶	38.84	1.00*TA	Closed Late Ins	Instagone, AstiEthel, DoWhop
07/24E7	MU	2010 F	38.23	78	6 7 6 1² 14½	38.23	0.70*TA	Easily Best Ins	LngshtLuk, SystmAnglr, WtchThsOn
07/21E14	MU	2010 F	38.82	77½	2 8 7 4 4³⅜	39.08	0.60*A	Closed Late Mdtk	TonysMafio, SarnSyren, SySltyMm
07/17E5	MU	2010 F	37.94	77	5 6 3 1⁶ 1⁶	37.94	0.80*TA	Outclassed Fld Rl	SarnSyren, GdStpng, SystmArStv
07/14E5	MU	1650 F	30.80	77½	7 8 8 8 8	OOP	0.90*A	Fell Escape Turn	JtStJmes, JDB'sThsby, MsBgUnser

Yellow **6**

0-1 Lightning Snow (AA) 57

38.00 — LI 31 7 4 5 3 — AA M — LI 4 0 0 0 1 — $14093

Kennel: Nanci Caswell Kennel [3]
Owner: Nanci Lee Caswell
Trainer: Tommy Lee Jones

White F, Jun 23, 1997. Chick's Racey-Dusty Cannon

09/04E7	LI	2010 F	38.06	57	8 1 1² 1² 1½	38.06	9.30 SAA	Box To Wire Mdtk	JustUpAhead, KiowOx, PppsThlgnd7
09/01A7	LI	2010 F	38.06	58	4 1 1½ 3 4⁷½	38.59	5.40 SAA	Erly Bid Weakend	Deuce'sWild, PlayrsEdg, OkSwfty
08/27E6	LI	2010 F	38.00	57	6 1 3 6 6⁴¾	38.33	8.10 SAA	Erly Spd Weakend	CameAgain, JustUpAhed, TmpMystr
08/21E12	LI	2010 F	38.85	57	7 2 1³ 1½ 1½	38.85	12.60 SA	Held Undr Prssure	KiowaOx, JAKeyChain, EpardBell
08/18L2	LI	2010 F	38.00	57	4 2 11½ 11½ 1⅜	38.00	2.20*BB	Game Pace Held On	DsylfyD, Wgglsththng, BckWhtT
08/13E7	LI	2010 F	38.00	57	4 1 1⁴ 2 24¾	38.32	6.60 BB	Set Pace Overtkn	P'sSkidBy, Kadeestattltl, Ghsty7
08/07A2	LI	2010 F	38.58	58	7 1 1½ 1² 1¹½	38.58	7.40 B	Prssured Hld Firm	MagicNadine, CJLAnn, AlngcmBnn
07/31A15	LI	2010 F	38.77	58	5 2 4 4 3²½	38.96	5.00 B	Made Up Grnd Mdtk	EprdHmr, AlngcmBnn, NrthrnDlght
07/24A2	LI	2010 F	38.43	58	1 1 1³ 1⁴ 13½	38.43	3.20 C	Took Control Erly	ABRaider, ClodsRllBy, HyTnsDxn
07/19A7	LI	2010 F	38.31	58	6 2 7 6 5¹¹	39.07	3.60 C	Bumped Crtn Turn	MeonRange*, GreysMoonBm, MgcNdn
07/12A15	LI	2010 F	38.09	58	4 2 3 2 3⁷	38.59	4.40 C	Close Early Mdtk	RoyRoostr, IndnRngd, GrysSlckPt
07/07A9	LI	2010 F	38.61	57	4 7 3 3 3⁶½	39.06	5.20 C	Gd Effort Mdtrk	WiseTraveler*, TXsMSrprs, MnRng*

Green White **7**

8-5 Deuce's Wild (AA) 74

37.70 — LI 28 12 7 3 3 — AA M — WS 1 0 1 0 0 — $21221

Kennel: Regall Sports [10]
Owner: Charles or Judith Moore
Trainer: Richard Calabro

White & Brindle M, Jul 16, 1997. Molotov-Pooky's Rowdy

09/04E4	LI	2010 F	37.80	74½	1 2 2 1⁶ 1⁸½	37.80	0.80*SAA	Easily Best Sm Wd	PowerCrrnt, JAKyChn, FlyngAnds
09/01A7	LI	2010 F	38.06	73	2 4 3 12½ 1⁷	38.06	1.80*SAA	Btwn Ldrs Drw Off	PlayrsEdg, OkSwfty, LghtnngSnw
08/27E12	LI	2010 F	37.94	74	8 4 1⁶ 1⁶ 1¹	37.94	0.60*SAA	Long Lead Lasted	BelloAnnie, Sparkleinhery, OkHw
08/21E9	LI	2010 F	38.47	74½	6 5 6 3 2½	38.51	2.60*SAA	In & Out Driving	BelloAnnie, PppsThlgnd, WkWkMrc
08/18A6	LI	2010 F	37.70	75	3 8 4 2 1¹	37.70	1.40*TA	Driving Wnnr Outs	LesMantle, OkieHowie, RnchObdh
08/14A4	LI	1650 F	30.19	74½	1 5 7 6 46½	30.57	2.70 SAA	Little Gain Mtk	RietasSpdr, GrysWnnbg, BBsPlygrl
08/09A4	LI	1650 F	30.27	75	6 8 8 5 4⁶½	30.64	4.40 AA	Outrun To Turn	EpardMax, JCMegaBrat, RioSantana
08/04L4	LI	1650 F	30.46	74½	2 8 8 6 410½	31.19	4.90 AA	Blocked 1st Turn	EpardMax, RioSantana, CntryCrsn
07/28A4	LI	1650 F	30.68	74	7 5 8 5 3⁶	31.02	3.40 AA	Despite Trouble	Garciaparra, TXsBgJyT, AllATwttr
07/21A4	LI	1650 F	30.79	74	6 8 5 5 2⁶	31.13	3.40 AA	Late Drive Mdtrk	FlyingOak, JuniorQuick, CameAgn
07/14L4	LI	1650 F	30.84	73½	1 2 1 14½ 1⁷	30.84	1.00*AA	Extending Margin	RanchoWakita, Roger'sMd, MnsnMn
07/09A4	LI	1650 F	30.31	74	2 4 4 4 3⁵¼	30.69	3.60 AA	Gd Effort Mdtrk	FlyingAndes, PlayersEdge, WoldlL

Yellow Black **8**

Selections: 8-3-5-1   SUPERFECTA WAGERING ON EVERY LIVE RACE TODAY!

Nr's Fast Eddie-2000

Nr's Fast Eddie-2000

RACE 13 S 2010 — Lincoln, Saturday, September 16, 2000, Evening, Race 13 — **2010 S RACE 13**

"THE 51st ANNUAL JOSEPH M. LINSEY MEMORIAL AMERICAN GREYHOUND DERBY"

Superfecta, Trifecta, Quiniela, Win, Place, Show Wagering

Track Record: DUPLANTIS, 37.25, 9/6/96

---

1 (Red) — 10-1 — **DEUCE'S WILD** — 37.70 AA M — 74 — LI 42 8 10 5 9 / LI 41 16 7 8 6 / $ 113638.60

White & Brindle, M, 07/16/97, Molotov-Pooky's Rowdy

Kennel: Regall Sports[10] — Owner: Charles or Judith Moore — Trainer: Richard Calabro

Event	Trk	Dst	TC	Time	WT	PP	Off	1/8	Str	Fin	ART	Odds	Grade	Comment	
09/11/00S02	LI	2010	F	38.02	74	8	2	15	15	11½	38.02			Lng Erly Lead Mtk	Kadeestattletale Clets 3
08/25/00A09	LI	2010	F	37.89	75	3	1	11	1½	34½	38.23	2.20*	TAA	Overtkn Ent Str	SystemPitaPie RaceyCatch Mellry
08/19/00A04	LI	1650	F	30.22	75½	7	8	7	8	712½	31.10	3.50	AA	Slow Start Coll	Lo Pllknot KKGinger BigRedMagic
08/12/00E04	LI	1650	F	30.45	75	3	7	7	8	610	31.16	4.40	AA	Blkd 1st Shutoff	EpardFish OncoFirbll Lo Pllknot
08/09/00A06	LI	1650	F	31.03	75½	4	8	4	3	1hd	31.03	3.90	AA	Closed With Rush	Wreckford Ceecom KKGinger
08/04/00E01	LI	1650	F	30.37	75½	6	6	4	4	42½	30.57	6.00	AA	Gained Some Mdtk	Galena BowsNWows TXsDynamic
07/31/00A04	LI	1650	S	30.39	75	3	8	7	4	24	30.69	9.00	AA	Steady Gain Outs	GntlMmory* FlyingShllK BowsNWws

2 (Blue) — 6-1 — **FLYING PENSKE** — 73 — LI 0 0 0 0 0 / BR 18 9 3 0 2 / $

Black, M, 09/20/97, Oshkosh Racey-She's A Natural

Kennel: Haynes Kennel[44] — Owner: H. Hal Gill — Trainer: Jason Haynes

Event	Trk	Dst	TC	Time	WT	PP	Off	1/8	Str	Fin	ART	Odds	Grade	Comment	
09/11/00S03	LI	2010	F	37.47	74	4	2	14	16	17½	37.47			Extnding Lead Mtk	SystemPitaDan TNTMagicMae 3
09/02/00E11	SE	1650	F	30.66	72	8	8	7	7	2½	30.70	2.00*	SA	Closing Fast Wide	FlyingShllK JolsVirgin DGsJhnBy
08/30/00E04	SE	1650	F	30.19	72½	5	4	5	5	410	30.90	2.00	SA	Showed Next Step	KiowaCalahn EltxSygdby DGsJhnBy
08/26/00E06	SE	1650	F	30.57	73	1	4	7	5	33	30.78	1.40*	SA	Despite Trbl 1st Trn	SLsSnowDigger Bebe JohnMHolly7
08/22/00E03	SE	1650	F	30.09	72	1	1	2	2	17	30.09	2.70	SA	Strong Str Bid Mdtk	AbenakiSpring KadeesKwl PrssPss7
08/18/00E10	SE	1650	F	30.13	72½	6	1	5	5	512	30.86	0.60*	SA	Trouble In Spots	HerclesSamsn JNBBsyWrkr PrssPss
08/12/00E12	WO	2045	F	38.53	73	7	4	3	5	55	38.89	1.90	SA	Forward Fctr Sm Wd	GreysFreBird NRsFstEddi BilliVn

3 (White) — 10-1 — **WALIGA** — 62 — LI 0 0 0 0 0 / RT 40 19 7 5 2 / $

Red, F, 11/25/96, Trojan Episode-Oriental Bandit

Kennel: Fortunato & Sarney Kennel[41] — Owner: C. Sarney or A. Fortunato — Trainer: Jim Fortunato

Event	Trk	Dst	TC	Time	WT	PP	Off	1/8	Str	Fin	ART	Odds	Grade	Comment	
09/11/00S01	LI	2010	F	37.91	62½	4	1	16	15	11½	37.91			Quick Control Ins	Closer ElNsNickoftime 3
09/04/00S02	LI	2010	F	38.11	62	4	1	15	11	35	38.48			Overtkn On Ins	ChasmosChansy BacToe 3
08/20/00A07	RT	1980	F	38.77	62	7	2	15	12	32½	38.96	3.50	A	Blew Big Lead	CarolinCotton KlsosHtTpc UTJckr
08/16/00A07	RT	1980	F	38.30	62½	8	2	1ns	12	12	38.30	2.40	A	Held Margin Inside	UTooJocker PasMaltese KlssRshmr
08/10/00A13	RT	1980	F	39.05	62½	5	6	4	4	611½	39.84	1.70*	A	Lacked Room Break	KwAggie PasMarcs DollaBrte
07/31/00A04	RT	1980	M	38.64	62½	1	2	2	13½	17½	38.64	0.80*	A	Pulling Away Inside	CarolinCottn KlssHtTpc DgsHghFv
07/23/00A13	RT	1980	F	38.83	62½	1	1	2	2	35	39.19	0.40*	A	Clear Show Rail	RiverwoodCigr KlssCrmpt HnhsFxy

4 (Green) — 4-1 — **NR'S FAST EDDIE** — 73 — LI 0 0 0 0 0 / WO 9 5 2 1 0 / $

Red, M, 09/03/96, RD's Banker Boy-Jael

Kennel: On Line Racing Kennel[45] — Owner: Nadine E. Riggar — Trainer: Richard Arno

Event	Trk	Dst	TC	Time	WT	PP	Off	1/8	Str	Fin	ART	Odds	Grade	Comment	
09/11/00S05	LI	2010	F	38.17	73	4	1	11½	11½	11	38.17			Withstd Challenge	BacToe OnecoTornado 3
09/06/00E07	WO	2045	F	38.77	73	5	1	15	15	17	38.77	0.60*	TA	Full Command Inside	SeanMan HasslerEpisode MdwsSpcy
08/31/00E04	WO	2045	F	38.88	72	2	1	14	13	11½	38.88	0.40*	TA	All The Way Mdtrk	ReadyToDefrost BarbieBlack Hddi
08/26/00E04	WO	2045	F	38.72	72½	6	1	15	17	110½	38.72	0.50*	A	Very Fast Eddie	Certainty TMsGallntSon YKnotRcn
08/19/00E04	WO	2045	F	38.52	73	1	3	12	12	2½	38.56	1.80	A	Caught Late Str Ins	GreysFreeBird Haddi ProprSttsmn
08/12/00E12	WO	2045	F	38.53	71½	4	1	12	11	22	38.68	4.40	SA	Caught Mid-str Ins	GreysFreeBird BillieVan Eloozhn
08/07/00E10	WO	2045	F	38.57	72	7	1	14	14	14	38.57	3.50	SA	Maintained Margn Ins	Song HasslerEpisode Eloozhn7

5 (Black) — 12-1 — **CAIRO TORCH** — 75 — LI 0 0 0 0 0 / MH 19 10 2 1 2 / $

Red Fawn, M, 05/05/98, Molotov-Sunbeam Surfer

Kennel: Linda Blanch Kennel[42] — Owner: Linda Blanch or Steven Licata — Trainer: Neil Newton

Event	Trk	Dst	TC	Time	WT	PP	Off	1/8	Str	Fin	ART	Odds	Grade	Comment	
09/11/00S07	LI	2010	F	38.25	76	1	3	2	2	25½	38.65			Chsd Winner Ins	Zahara GreysShowDown 3
09/01/00E13	MH	2050	F	39.87	75	3	1	3	4	59½	40.54	1.40*	SAA	Much Trouble Thruout	EMsRIDeal LLAshley EJsLaraD
08/25/00E13	MH	2050	F	39.21	76	4	3	5	4	46	39.63	0.20*	AA	Early Trouble Inside	Rdrvrcmver SpceCinamn EJsLaraD7
08/22/00E11	MH	2050	F	39.23	75	7	2	15	16	16½	39.23	0.80*	AA	As Expected Inside	EJsLaraD LrPrnaYama EMsRIDeal
08/18/00A06	MH	2050	F	39.20	76	5	4	13	18	18½	39.20	2.70	AA	In Sharp Form Inside	LLAshley EJsLaraD ByndTheLmt
08/12/00E12	MH	2050	F	38.91	75	1	5	2	18	110	38.91	0.80*	SAA	Timberline Champ	EJInsigr ValeyBonet ByndTheLmt
08/08/00E13	MH	2050	F	39.28	75	5	1	8	5	58	39.84	0.80*	SAA	No Trouble Inside	USSVnota WWEZkesMtch JSUnoRler

6 (Yellow) — 2-1 — **GREYS FREE BIRD** — 64 — LI 0 0 0 0 0 / SP 40 15 5 5 5 / $

Red Brindle, F, 10/16/97, Fortress*-Greys Julianna

Kennel: Greymeadow Kennel[40] — Owner: Joseph M. Frenette — Trainer: Mick Darci

Event	Trk	Dst	TC	Time	WT	PP	Off	1/8	Str	Fin	ART	Odds	Grade	Comment	
09/11/00S04	LI	2010	F	37.72	63	2	1	14½	12	1ns	37.72			Just Lasted Mdtk	SystemPitaRita CJLeeAnn 3
09/04/00S01	LI	2010	F	37.51	63½	7	2	17	18	19	37.51			With Ease Inside	Sandesey OkieDenver 3
08/19/00E04	WO	2045	F	38.52	64	8	8	3	2	1½	38.52	1.10*	A	Str Drive Some Wide	NRsFastEddie Haddie ProprSttsmn
08/12/00E12	WO	2045	F	38.53	64½	2	2	2	2	12	38.53	7.30	SA	Derby Champion	NRsFastEddie BillieVan Eloozhn
08/07/00E08	WO	2045	F	38.48	64	7	5	2	15	19½	38.48	1.80*	SA	Led Rl Bkst Drew Out	KiowaNash Ioda BbWonderMan
08/03/00E10	WO	2045	F	39.05	65	7	6	5	4	26½	39.51	1.10*	SA	Drove To Place Outs	KiowaNash MrgAnthny RchsPrncsss7
07/29/00E10	WO	2045	F	38.36	64	3	4	4	2	13½	38.36	2.70	SA	Driving On Outside	MeadowsTahiti KiowaNash Pzzle

7 (Grn/Wht) — 7-2 — **RC'S DIANES BEST** — 63 — LI 0 0 0 0 0 / PH 22 17 1 1 0 / $

Fawn Brindle, F, 03/01/98, Real Shy-Packin Zip

Kennel: Gray Kennel[43] — Owner: Clayton J. Sword — Trainer: Mary Gray

Event	Trk	Dst	TC	Time	WT	PP	Off	1/8	Str	Fin	ART	Odds	Grade	Comment	
09/11/00S06	LI	2010	F	38.39	63	2	1	13	14½	17½	38.39			Pulled Away Ins	TMsDerbyGy RoosterMccombs 3
09/02/00E08	PH	2055	F	38.90	63	4	2	13	15	18	38.90	0.20*	TA	Far Superior Inside	TaosBisbee RDsAthens PlsStreak
08/28/00E12	PH	2055	F	38.88	63½	4	1	17	18	111	38.89	0.05*	TA	All Alone Inside	NRsDstryr RDsAthens Dlltimit
08/21/00E10	PH	2055	F	38.66	63½	1	1	14½	15	17½	38.66	0.60*	A	Eleven In A Row	CldwtrCesn TaosBisbee CarlsVnGo
08/11/00E12	PH	2055	F	39.64	63	5	2	2	2	13½	39.64	0.80*	TA	Dspt Trbl Early Ins	CldwtrCesn AsTearsGBy JSKtcanBt
08/02/00E10	PH	2055	F	39.12	62	4	4	16	15	13	39.12	0.80*	TA	As Expected Inside	Credos CldwtrCame BlarSimons
07/28/00E08	PH	2055	F	39.05	62	3	5	11	12½	14	39.05	0.30*	A	Quick Control Inside	Evrlstngb CldwtrCame TaosBisbee

8 (Yel/Blk) — 8-1 — **ELOOZHUN** — 37.40 AA A — 81 — LI 35 18 6 3 2 / WO 7 2 2 0 3 / $ 55581.32

Brindle, M, 10/26/97, Rong Jones-Hilara

Kennel: North Shore Kennel[17] — Owner: Linda Jane Kelly — Trainer: Graydon Robtoy

Event	Trk	Dst	TC	Time	WT	PP	Off	1/8	Str	Fin	ART	Odds	Grade	Comment	
09/09/00E15	LI	2010	F	38.07	80½	8	5	2	12½	11½	38.07	3.30	AA	Erly Gain Led Bks	OncoPrsnickty SSSgrBby JAThDnld
09/04/00A08	LI	2010	F	37.94	81	3	3	2	11½	2½	37.98	1.80*	AA	Ovrtkn Near Wire	SystmPitPi BohminGmbo KUPsOxygn
08/30/00A09	LI	2010	F	38.36	80½	4	2	2	2	22	38.52	0.80*	AA	Always A Threat	BohminGmbo KUPsOxygn CJDllyDodg
08/25/00A15	LI	2010	F	37.79	80	7	7	2	2	15½	37.79	2.80	AA	Strong Finish Mtk	BigAnnWalker OkieCoopr NitsJssi
08/12/00E12	WO	2045	F	38.53	80½	5	5	4	3	44½	38.84	12.50	SA	Followed Pace Sm Wd	GreysFreeBird NRsFastEddi BllVn
08/07/00E10	WO	2045	F	38.57	82	4	6	4	3	48½	39.17	0.80*	SA	Followed Pace Sm Wd	NRsFastEddie Song HasslerEpisod7
08/03/00E05	WO	2045	F	39.16	82	5	3	1½	13	21	39.23	0.90*	SA	Caught Str Late Ins	CoachsAndy IBeIngTBrb RnchVintn

SELECTIONS: 6-7-4-2 — **The Joseph M. Linsey Memorial American Greyhound Derby**

Redmoon Clyde-2001

LINCOLN PARK PROUDLY HOSTS TONIGHT'S 52nd RUNNING OF THE JOSEPH M. LINSEY MEMORIAL AMERICAN GREYHOUND DERBY

The 52nd edition of the American Greyhound Derby will be run here tonight for a purse of $60,000.

The Joseph M. Linsey Memorial Trophy, which honors the founder of the race, and $30,000 are the rewards for the winning interests.

This is the 16th consecutive year that the race will be run at Lincoln Park. It is an invitational event again this year, matching two of our top distance greyhounds and six invitees from other tracks throughout the country.

Representing Lincoln Park are Lil Too Sweet from the D.Q. Williams Kennel and JA Rockin Cindi from the J.A. Fortune Kennel, who was selected this week to replace injured Wichita standout Ed P's Linda.

Lil Too Sweet is the Lincoln Park win leader this year with 26 victories in 45 starts and 14 wins in her last 16.

JA Rockin Cindi is a solid top-grade router with nine wins and eight seconds in her 45 starts here this year.

The 2001 American Greyhound Derby invitees are:

• D.Q. Williams' Florida ace Redmoon Clyde, the winner of the Hollywoodian in Florida.

• North Shore Kennel's Medlyr, who had 20 wins at Wonderland through mid-August.

• Douglas Kennels' Fanatic Jasmine, the winner of the Firecracker Stake at Wheeling Downs.

• Hermitage Kennel's Multnomah Derby champion and 3/8ths-mile track record holder System Pita Rita.

• Garden State Kennel's Mesa Frankie X, winner of this year's Raynham Derby.

• Patrick Collins Kennel's Superman Fast, the upset winner of the recent Timberline Stake at Mile High.

We wish all of the entrants the best of luck.

Lincoln Park also extends a special Rhode Island and U.S.A. welcome to Ricky Mullins and Donna Habel from England, the winners of an American Greyhound Derby trip sponsored by our parent company, Wembley, PLC.

Redmoon Clyde-2001

RACE 13 GRADE S 2010 — Saturday, September 15, 2001, Evening — **GRADE S 2010 RACE 13**

" THE 52ND $60,000 JOSEPH M. LINSEY MEMORIAL AMERICAN GREYHOUND DERBY "
Superfecta, Trifecta, Quiniela, Win, Place, & Show Wagering

Track Record: ZATZALL, 37.06, 7/7/01

PP 1 (Red) — 6-5 — LIL TOO SWEET (AA) — 37.21 AA M — 56 — LI 45 26 8 9 1 / LI 16 7 2 1 1
Brindle, F, Mar 11, 1999, Chick's Racey-Run For My Money — $ 71426.22
Kennel: DQ Williams Kennel[18] — Owner: David Joel Garnett — Trainer: Louis Amaral

Event	Trk	Dst	TC	Time	WT	PP	Off	1/8	Str	Fin	ART	Odds	Grade	Comment	
09/08E11	LI	2010	F	38.57	56	8	3	3	3	1hd	38.57	0.40*	AA	In & Out Driving	JARockinCind,CrystlBHt,Hpfl
09/03A14	LI	2010	F	38.67	57	7	1	11½	11	12½	38.67	1.10*	AA	Never Headed Mdtk	MCPsTrcky,CrystalBHot,Ztzll
08/29A6	LI	2010	F	37.98	57	8	1	1½	11½	11½	37.98	0.60*	AA	Pressured Held Firm	DKLdyNRd,HtshtSlsmn,PrmAtlntc
08/22L4	LI	2010	F	37.21	57	8	3	2	2	11	37.21	0.20*	AA	Extended To Win	GNCKngDn,SystmKHHd,JARcknCnd
08/17E9	LI	2010	F	37.93	56	8	2	12½	12½	12½	37.93	0.60*	AA	Held Firm Lead Mtk	JARcknCnd,MCPsTrcky,TrcMyTrck
08/11E15	LI	2010	F	37.20	56	8	4	3	3	37	37.68	0.20*	AA	Evenly For Show	JARcknCnd,SvltfrLtr,DKLdyNRd
08/06A15	LI	2010	F	38.00	56½	6	1	13½	14½	16	38.00	0.80*	AA	Breezing Along Mdtk	DKLdyNRd,SvltfrLtr,JARcknCnd

PP 2 (Blue) — 25-1 — JA ROCKIN CINDI (AA) — 37.20 AA M — 59 — LI 45 9 8 7 8 / LI 19 5 1 2 2
Fawn, F, Jan 02, 1999, P's Skidway-JA Black Lace — $ 32098.59
Kennel: JA Fortune Kennel[24] — Owner: Avanell Conger — Trainer: Jim Fortunato

Event	Trk	Dst	TC	Time	WT	PP	Off	1/8	Str	Fin	ART	Odds	Grade	Comment	
09/08E11	LI	2010	F	38.57	58½	4	5	4	4	2hd	38.59	8.20	AA	Coming On Late Mtk	LilTooSwet,CrystlBHot,Hopfl
09/03A14	LI	2010	F	38.67	58	6	5	8	8	69½	39.34	9.00	AA	Crowded Crtn Turn	LilTSwt,MCPsTrcky,CrystlBHt
08/29A1	LI	2010	F	37.89	58½	8	4	3	2	1ns	37.89	4.20	AA	Closed With Rush	SaveltforLatr,Kein,ElvsWikr
08/22L4	LI	2010	F	37.21	58	3	4	3	3	48	37.78	4.50	AA	Some Early Speed	LilToSwt,GNCKngDn,SystmKHHd
08/17E9	LI	2010	F	37.93	58	5	1	3	3	22½	38.09	6.10	AA	Closed Gap In Str	LilTSwt,MCPsTrcky,TrcMyTrck
08/11E15	LI	2010	F	37.20	58	1	2	13	13	15½	37.20	8.00	AA	All The Way Mdtrk	SvltforLtr,LilTSwt,DKLdyNRd
08/06A15	LI	2010	F	38.00	58	8	2	4	4	47	38.50	6.20	AA	No Mishaps	LilToSwt,DKLdyNRd,SvltfrLtr

PP 3 (White) — 4-1 — MESA FRANKIE X (AA) — 72 — LI 0 0 0 0 0 / RT 34 19 2 3 2
Brindle, M, Mar 27, 1999, Rocksteady Eddie-Mesa Holly — $
Kennel: Garden State Kennel[47] — Owner: Elizabeth Kelly — Trainer: Charles Newcome

Event	Trk	Dst	TC	Time	WT	PP	Off	1/8	Str	Fin	ART	Odds	Grade	Comment	
09/10S2	LI	2010	F	38.84	72	8	3	2	2	2ns	38.85	---		In & Out Closing	PinstripesPower,Medlyr,3
09/03A15	RT	1980	F	38.19	72	7	4	5	6	514½	39.21	0.60*	A	Bumped Twice Early	KlssPloAlt,AnglTdwll,KwErly
08/28A4	RT	1980	F	38.02	72	7	1	15	18½	17½	38.02	0.40*	A	Away Early Mdtrck	KlsosPloAlto,KwAgg,RnchDsgn
08/21S1	RT	1650	F	30.88	73	2	1	1hd	1½	15	30.88	---		Box To Wire Inside	RcyPlin,PinOkPnt,CtwMtrFiry
07/25E11	MU	2010	F	38.68	72	5	6	5	5	33	38.90	2.30	A	Late Speed Mdtrk	RstlssBob,PrmrChmp,PsCstCst
07/18S3	MU	1650	F	30.43	73	4	1	14	16	110	30.43	---		Going Away Inside	SpdLight,PsCostCst,CnnsThNm6
06/29E13	RT	1980	F	38.07	71	6	3	2	16	18½	38.07	1.30*	A	Took Over, Extended	DnnGsppn,McDnWbstr,JsssPffy

PP 4 (Green) — 8-1 — SYSTEM PITA RITA (AA) — 58 — LI 0 0 0 0 0 / MU 13 7 1 1 0
Brindle, F, Sep 22, 1998, System Carl-Pistachio — $
Kennel: System Kennel[45] — Owner: Hermitage Kennels Inc. — Trainer: Michael Bushey

Event	Trk	Dst	TC	Time	WT	PP	Off	1/8	Str	Fin	ART	Odds	Grade	Comment	
09/10S1	LI	2010	F	38.28	59	7	2	2	2	316	39.41	---		Close Early Tired	RedmoonClyde,FlashyDonny,3
08/25E11	MU	2010	F	37.58	58	5	1	11	1hd	1½	37.58	2.90	SA	Drby Chmp, Trck Rcrd	CBrGrdon,KiowWttRos,RstlsBb
08/18E11	MU	2010	F	38.49	58½	1	3	3	2	11½	38.49	1.30*	SA	Steady Drive Inside	VillagJill,Thrstr,CBrGordon
08/15E8	MU	2010	F	38.59	59½	3	4	2	3	24½	38.89	0.50*	SA	Late Speed Inside	SystmPtAnn,IrskFlx,SystmHrrcn
08/11E11	MU	2010	F	38.10	58	5	1	14	14	12½	38.10	0.50*	SA	Never Headed Ins	JnMri,SWTriplBLm,SystmMrSmk
08/08E11	MU	2010	F	37.99	58½	3	5	5	6	322	39.57	0.70*	A	Bmpd Aftr Break Rl	CBrGrdn,SWTrplBlm,SystmMrSmk
07/26E9	MU	2010	F	38.01	59	8	1	13	12	13	38.01	0.80*	TA	Easily Best Rl Str	SWTrplBlm,TwstrBndt,SystmEdEscp

PP 5 (Black) — 15-1 — SUPERMAN FAST (AA) — 76 — LI 0 0 0 0 0 / MH 9 2 2 1 1
White Brindle, M, May 01, 1999, Blazing Desire-Molley West — $
Kennel: Pat Collins Kennel[46] — Owner: Michael A. Lasky — Trainer: John Venuto

Event	Trk	Dst	TC	Time	WT	PP	Off	1/8	Str	Fin	ART	Odds	Grade	Comment	
09/10S3	LI	2010	F	38.52	76	7	2	11½	2	23½	38.78	---		Led To Far Trn Ins	FanaticJsmin,TNTWishingStr,3
09/01E13	MH	2050	F	39.44	75	6	1	2	12	11½	39.44	11.40	SAA	Timberline Champion	ByndThStrs,GSSnshn,ClvrCrbn
08/28E8	MH	2050	F	39.39	75½	5	5	4	2	24½	39.71	3.00	SAA	Placed Despite Trbl	GSSnshin,ByndWhtvr,SltxEmpr
08/24E6	MH	2050	F	39.41	75	8	3	11	13	17½	39.41	4.80	SAA	Pulling Away Md	ByndThLmt,RDMerit,LLAcqitl
08/21E4	MH	2050	F	40.20	75	5	2	4	5	53½	40.44	11.70	SAA	Trouble Twice Md	LLMgstrt,ClvrCrbn,WWKowGsto
08/14E13	MH	2050	F	39.36	76½	7	2	2	3	48	39.93	17.10	AA	Couldn't Gain Md	ByndThrts,PksEclps,PdchFrdy
08/09E13	MH	2050	F	39.87	76	2	7	3	3	311	40.69	7.10	AA	Distant Show Mid	PksEclips,ByndThLmt,CroTrch

PP 6 (Yellow) — 12-1 — FANATIC JASMINE (AA) — 59 — LI 0 0 0 0 0 / WD 44 20 10 6 5
Red, F, Feb 12, 1999, Trojan Episode-Airdale — $
Kennel: Douglas Kennel[43] — Owner: Francis J. Bogus — Trainer: Kenneth Bryant

Event	Trk	Dst	TC	Time	WT	PP	Off	1/8	Str	Fin	ART	Odds	Grade	Comment	
09/10S3	LI	2010	F	38.52	59	1	3	2	12	13½	38.52	---		Drawing Clear Mdtk	SpermanFast,TNTWishingStar,3
09/01E10	WD	2284	F	44.11	59½	6	5	5	5	42½	44.29	4.50	SAA	Impoved Some	KiowTmLyd,KwRsMst,DCsHmyDrv
08/29E11	WD	2284	F	44.45	59½	2	8	8	7	53	44.67	2.10*	SAA	Some Late Speed	KiowSki,DCsHldDriv,KiwRsMst
08/25E11	WD	2284	F	43.61	60	1	5	7	5	38½	44.19	1.10*	SAA	Midtrack Gain	JNBChgwtr,KiwRsMst,DvsAldrn
08/22E9	WD	2284	F	43.72	59½	6	6	5	3	14	43.72	2.00	SAA	Driving Thruout	KiowSki,CrigMSMlly,DvsAldrn
08/15A15	WD	2033	F	39.63	60	7	8	8	7	2ns	39.64	0.80*	AA	From Last, Missed	BohminOriol,BigDlly,SgldBrn
08/10E15	WD	2033	F	39.04	59½	1	8	6	3	14½	39.04	0.50*	AA	Drove From Last	BohminAbsrd,JCsMikl,SgldBrn

PP 7 (Grn/Wht) — 20-1 — MEDLYR (AA) — 70 — LI 0 0 0 0 0 / WO 41 20 7 6 4
Red, M, Jul 31, 1998, Real Economy-Makenz — $
Kennel: North Shore (Wonderland)[42] — Owner: W. H. O'Donnell — Trainer: Brian Gaskill

Event	Trk	Dst	TC	Time	WT	PP	Off	1/8	Str	Fin	ART	Odds	Grade	Comment	
09/10S2	LI	2010	F	38.84	70	2	1	3	3	34½	39.17	---		Blckd Ent Front Str	PinstripesPower,MesaFrnkiX,3
08/19E12	WO	2045	F	39.19	70	8	1	1½	5	69	39.83	1.10*	A	Early Leader Faded	TMsLckyTop,JimboRevn,EprdTp
08/14E4	WO	2045	F	39.43	69	3	2	13	4	2½	39.48	1.30*	A	Wide Fr Tn Almst Bk	BabyTata,EpardTap,TMsTara
08/10E4	WO	2045	F	39.35	70	6	3	4	4	410½	40.08	1.60*	A	Raced Inside	EpardTap,BabyTata,TMsTara
08/06E4	WO	2045	F	39.26	70	7	1	12	11	1½	39.26	1.40*	A	Held On Some Wide	TMsShowBzz,EprdTp,MystcWnkn
08/01E4	WO	2045	F	39.46	69½	1	3	3	3	37	39.95	1.60*	A	Followed Pace Inside	CrzyBbbls,BlzngTrblt,MCTnyS
07/27E4	WO	2045	F	39.20	69	4	1	12	12	11	39.20	1.50*	A	Fast Start Some Wide	BigDaddysGm,JimboRvn,EprdTp7

PP 8 (Yel/Blk) — 9-5 — REDMOON CLYDE (AA) — 73 — LI 0 0 0 0 0 / FL 13 6 1 3 0
Black, M, Mar 29, 1999, Rapido Rambo-Redmoon Ruby — $
Kennel: DQ Williams (Flagler)[41] — Owner: Sharon L. Williams — Trainer: Bill Scott

Event	Trk	Dst	TC	Time	WT	PP	Off	1/8	Str	Fin	ART	Odds	Grade	Comment	
09/10S1	LI	2010	F	38.28	73	1	1	12½	17	113½	38.28	---		Extending Lead Ins	FlashyDonny,SystemPitaRita,3
08/08E7	FL	1940	F	37.20	72	5	3	6	4	32½	37.36	1.20*	A	Hustled Bk Again Rl	CretvWhiz,GrmrStg,CnchSrprs
08/01E12	FL	1940	F	37.29	72½	8	3	2	11	11½	37.29	2.00*	A	Drove Home Rail	SlBrandy,CretvWhiz,RlThWrld
07/26E10	FL	1940	F	37.20	73	6	2	2	2	14	37.20	2.40	A	Drove Backstr Inside	CretveWhiz,Viggo,OtlawRico
07/22E7	FL	1940	F	37.19	72	3	1	12	13	12½	37.19	2.00	A	Leader Thruout Ins	Viggo,CretvWhiz,OtlawRico
07/18E12	FL	1940	F	37.13	72	6	3	5	4	35½	37.52	1.40*	A	Shuffled Clsng Late	INwlmtlkn,WhtFlsh,SwtAsCnch
07/12E10	FL	1940	F	37.51	71	7	2	2	2	11½	37.51	3.70	A	Won Str Battle Ins	EddyGarmae,LadyChnl,Chllngr7

SELECTIONS: 1-8-6-3 The 52nd $60,000 Joseph M. Linsey Memorial American Greyhound Derby!

Kiowa Sweet Joe-2002

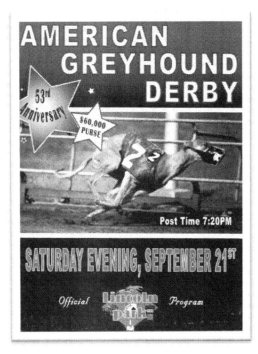

Performance profiles of the starters in 53rd American Greyhound Derby

BABY TATA — Representing Wonderland. He won this year's $30,000 Hollywoodian stake in Florida and was the winner of the 2001 Hollywood Inaugural at that Florida track. He raced to a Revere Course victory in Wonderland's 2001 Night of Stars feature race. Trainer Richard Arno of the On-Line Kennel says of Baby Tata: "He always seems to be an underdog, but he explodes like Superman in stake finals."

GABLE VERMILION — Based at the Gulf Greyhound Park in Texas, this June 2000 female is the youngest entry in the field. She won the $125,000 Great Greyhound Race last month at Seabrook and has shown speed in sprints and routes with six sub-30 second wins at 5/16ths and two sub-37 second scores at 3/8ths. Jim Ebbs. director of racing at Gulf, says: "I'm very impressed with her at 3/8ths of-a-mile."

JJ's JUST GABBY — The winner of this year's $75,000 Multnomah Derby at that Oregon track, he also has had success elsewhere, breaking in at Wichita and climbing to Grade A at Hollywood. Owner Jeff Kessler, a former jockey, considered withdrawing Gabby after a disappointing fourth-place effort in the first round of the Multnomah Derby, but trainer Jeff Wilcox persevered and got a win in the big stake.

KIOWA SWEET JOE — This well-traveled invitee, owned by Flying Eagles Kennel, carries the banner of the Derby Lane track in St. Petersburg, Fla., although he has been racing recently at Wheeling Downs. He won the St. Petersburg Derby in June, holding off 2001 Greyhound All-American Talentedmrripley in the process as a 14-1 longshot. Littermates to this pup include '01 All-American Kiowa Sweet Trey.

NAME ME WHAT — Earned his invitation to the 53rd American Greyhound Derby by winning the $45,000 Labor Day Classic at Wheeling Downs in West Virginia. He has won only 4 of 30 starts this year, but he seems to be at his best when it counts the most. Name Me What is owned by Sharon Williams, the wife of D.Q. Williams, who shipped Redmoon Clyde here from his Flagler kennel to win the race in 2001.

RAN D RASCAL — Comes in from Mile High in Colorado with the reputation as that track's top distance performer. Her racing record this year shows 12 victories and 17 in-the-money finishes in 19 starts through August. Her front-running style had carried her to 8 wins in her 10 starts prior to Aug. 31. Rascal is owned by Lois Roth and races for the Pat Collins Kennel at Mile High. The trainer is John Venuto.

VICKY'S WAY — This fast female won the Raynham-Taunton Sprint Championship this spring. She had been in the money in 19 of 21 starts this year, mostly in sprints, but also had won her only three outings at 3/8ths of-a-mile, including a 2002 track-best clocking of 37.39 seconds less than two weeks ago on Sept. 5. Owned by Nicholas Vento and trained by Doris Marie Rae, she races for the new Patriot Kennel at R-T.

WIZZARD WALKER — The Lincoln Park nominee. This lightly raced pup climbed to Grade AA as a sprinter with 9 wins in 22 starts through early June. He was given time before the $125,000 Great Greyhound Race at Seabrook, where he ran fourth in the final. The Tutalo-Richard Kennel runner was moved to the Ocean Course distance upon returning to Lincoln and notched two front-running wins to earn this berth.

Kiowa Sweet Joe-2002

"THE 53ʳᵈ ANNUAL $60,000 JOSEPH M. LINSEY MEMORIAL AMERICAN GREYHOUND DERBY"

RACE 13 GRADE S 2010 feet · Thirteenth Race · 09/21/02 · Evening · **2010 feet GRADE S RACE 13**

Superfecta, Trifecta, Quiniela, Win, Place, & Show Wagering

Track Record: ZATZALL, 37.02, 3/30/02

PP	Event	Trk	Dst	TC	Time	WT	PP	Off	1/8	Str	Fin	ART	Odds	Grade	Comment

6-1 NAME ME WHAT 71

LI 0 0 0 0 / WD 30 4 8 6 3
Brindle, M, Sep 24, 1999, Oswald Cobblepot-Fastest Doll
Kennel: Majestic Kennel[40]0%
Owner: Sharon L. Williams
Trainer: Natalie Cole

09/16 S2	LI	2010F	38.50	70	2	2	2	11	1½	38.50	---		Ran Down Leader Ins	ChicksSpeed VickysWay Dzndza3
08/31 E11	WD	2033F	38.48	71	5	4	2	2	1ns	38.48	11.10	SAA	Labor Day Champ	RraPenta SanTanClipper ClirDoln
08/28 E7	WD	2033F	38.27	70½	4	4	4	3	23½	38.52	10.30	SAA	Gained To Place	FreerideJana BDsPotomac FPJsmin
08/24 E13	WD	2033F	38.46	70½	1	3	2	2	27	38.94	7.80	SAA	Tiring Held Place	RedWitch DCsEscrow OkieBev
08/21 E13	WD	2033F	38.33	71½	1	3	3	2	25½	38.70	12.10	SAA	Nice Effort Midtrack	ClairDolan SnTnClippr PnrosClir
08/16 E15	WD	2033F	38.58	71	6	5	5	6	78½	39.17	9.90	AA	Weakened Midtrack	WesCooley ClairDoln SkiddyInvdr
08/11 A15	WD	2033F	38.01	71½	2	2	2	3	36½	38.45	5.70	AA	Steady Bid Inside	ClairDoln KrftyMichll KiowSwtJo7
08/07 A16	WD	2033F	38.83	71	5	1	2	1ns	1½	38.83	8.80	A	Was Determined	FlightAttndnt IrskPr KiowTrrTm
08/02 E11	WD	2033F	38.59	71½	2	2	3	2	36½	39.06	15.40	A	Steady Effort	WWNickOfTime OHappyDy BDsPotomac
07/27 A16	WD	2033F	38.36	71½	1	3	3	4	35	38.70	7.60	A	Game Effort Inside	DZLaidBack OHappyDay BDsPotomac
07/21 A7	WD	2033F	38.11	72	6	8	8	8	818	39.37	10.30	AA	Blocked Back Break	ItsDrthVdr WsCooly OshkoshIIIsv
07/15 S2	WD	1643F	30.02	73½	7	6	3	4	315	31.06	---		Good Effort Midtrack	RivrsWst BrooklynGl MotlyComBck

Red

5-1 VICKY'S WAY 61

LI 0 0 0 0 / RT 21 14 3 2 2
White & Brindle, F, Oct 31, 1999, Oswald Cobblepot-Frequent Chances
Kennel: Patriot Kennel[43]0%
Owner: Nicholas J. Vento
Trainer: Doris Marie Rae

09/16 S2	LI	2010F	38.50	61½	8	3	12	2	33½	38.76	---		Caught Far Trn Mdtk	NameMeWhat ChicksSpeed Dzndza3
09/05 E12	RT	1980F	37.39	61	7	1	14	15	17½	37.39	.60·A		Never Looked Back	Bellamy FortnateFreda GrndSlmmr7
08/28 A13	RT	1980F	37.95	60½	8	3	15½	15½	16	37.95	.70·A		All Alone Outside	GrndSlmmr DcoJoclyon CmmndoBbby
08/20 A12	RT	1650F	30.97	60½	8	3	2	15	19½	30.97	.50·A		Left'em Behind Outs	DsCoolZima JGBdboy KlsosGirlyct
08/16 E13	RT	1650F	30.99	60½	5	3	2	11	15½	30.99	.50·A		Powered By Outside	DrfldChmp CrolinFr MsContssAmy7
08/11 A4	RT	1650F	30.57	62½	3	1	12½	14	18	30.57	.90·A		Drew Away In Stretch	SplendidMarie MsMargaret Earl
08/06 A12	RT	1650F	31.24	62	7	6	2	2	22	31.39	.50·A		Lost Race Duel Outs	KlsosGirlyct MsChrchll CrolnFr
08/01 A4	RT	1650F	30.60	62	3	4	1hd	19	112	30.60	.70·A		Much The Best Outs	DgsNabls SolThief MsMargaret
07/26 A4	RT	1650F	30.78	61½	8	3	19	19	110½	30.78	.70·A		Breezing Outside	FGsRockford BrinksIronhed Bllmy
07/20 A14	RT	1650F	31.45	61½	8	2	11	110	113	31.45	.30·A		In A Romp Outside	EtherealHntr MsMrgrt MolotovBby
07/14 E4	RT	1650F	30.99	61	7	5	4	4	44	31.27	.50·A		Wide Entering Str	Mongoose MsPrincssAnn DrmysGirl
07/09 S1	RT	1650F	30.87	62	7	1	1½	14	14½	30.87	---		Handily Outside	Bisby TKSDimnionmoon SystmCGBob6

Blue

3-1 WIZZARD WALKER 70

37.73 AA M
LI 25 10 2 1 3 / SE 6 2 2 1 1
$ 19017.15
White & Black, M, Mar 05, 2000, P's Raising Cain-Mag Walker
Kennel: Tutalo - Richard Kennel[21]13%
Owner: Charles O. Malone
Trainer: Ken Richard

09/11 A9	LI	2010F	38.57	69	4	5	8	8	824½	40.29	0.50·AA		Jammed Erly Offstrd	VegasNights RmboForAWin Endrcht
09/06 E9	LI	2010F	37.75	71	3	2	19	15	1nk	37.75	1.40·AA		Big Lead Just Held	Hopefl KiowaYrSgar JJsStinger
08/31 E13	LI	2010F	37.73	69	5	7	14½	15½	14½	37.73	3.50·AA		Drew Out Early Ins	KiowaYrSgar Kandarr LotsWinndin
08/24 E11	SE	1650F	29.68	70	6	3	7	4	415½	30.76	11.00·SA		Tangled Up 1st Turn	GableVermilion WWJmbor GblGnsis
08/21 A9	SE	1650F	30.06	71	2	3	11	12½	15	30.06	2.60·SA		Ducked In Drew Out	GablGnsis WitnssTick CriglOCddy7
08/17 E8	SE	1650F	30.07	70	3	7	3	3	25	30.42	1.80·SA		Fine Race Placed	GableGenesis ABarRockIt Ushala7
08/13 A4	SE	1650F	30.41	71	6	6	5	4	33½	30.65	1.20·SA		Stumble Break Closed	KKGoGetIt GableJdges Mr.Troble6
08/09 E4	SE	1650F	30.39	70	8	8	5	2	2nk	30.42	2.50·SA		Closing Fast Placed	GblOrlns MohicanMndM OhkChrdnny
08/03 A14	SE	1650F	30.25	70½	7	7	2	13	19	30.25	0.70·A		Accelerated Bckstr	PsBddyLea ABrRockIt MinakiBell
07/29 S1	LI	1650F	30.48	71	1	5	3	2	11	30.48	---		Saved Came On Str	EAsltzboy ICUShowTim FlyngOlymp6
07/26 S2	LI	1650F	30.60	70½	4	6	2	13	14	30.60	---		Handily On Inside	FlyingGrtzky RoylTroon EAsRdRvr6
06/01 E3	LI	1650F	30.22	69	3	8	5	3	2hd	30.24	3.30·AA		Driving Just Missed	SnazzySn EAsltzaboy GarthRaider

White

9-5 GABLE VERMILION 66

LI 0 0 0 0 / GG 18 12 0 2 0
Red, F, Jun 23, 2000, Gable Dodge-Seegold Panache
Kennel: Gable Kennel[44]0%
Owner: Harlyn Or Janna Goebel
Trainer: Kim Hawkins

09/16 S1	LI	2010F	38.00	66	1	2	12	18	110	38.00	---		With Authority Mdtrk	PasCaptGeorg RnDRscl NitsSlyEly3
09/02 A12	GG	1650F	30.36	65½	8	4	6	5	59	30.98	.80·SAA		Bumped Both Turns	BeDiscrete Glfstream SnTnBrwsky
08/29 S1	GG	1650F	30.14	65½	1	1	12	13	11½	30.14	---		Quick Control	GableOrleans GblRvltion Gbljdgs6
08/24 S1	SE	1650F	29.68	66	8	4	12	15	18½	29.68	1.90·SA		02 Great Race Champ	WWJamboree GableGnsis WizrdWlkr
08/21 A11	SE	1650F	30.27	66	7	6	7	5	514	31.25	.50·SA		Blocked Wd 1st Turn	GableOrlns RomoloMstWin EprdEdg7
08/17 E9	SE	1650F	30.09	65	4	2	11½	1½	11½	30.09	.50·SA		Withstood Challenge	EAsltzaboy WitnessTick PsBddyLe7
08/13 A13	SE	1650F	30.05	65½	5	4	12	13	13½	30.05	.30·SA		Brisk Pace Inside	YoponTracy MomoniHy RomlsMstWn
08/09 E2	SE	1650F	29.86	66	4	3	13½	13½	14½	29.86	.80·SA		Sizzling Trip Inside	IcBckdrft EAsltzboy DGsRghtnbby
08/04 A14	SE	1650F	30.16	65	1	4	13	14½	110	30.10	.50·A		Sailed The Rail	EAsltzaboy LRsHeracles Zareba
08/01 S1	SE	1650F	30.55	66	7	3	2	2	21	30.61	---		Raced Hard Placed	MohicanMAndM GableGnsis MrTrobl5
07/19 E13	GG	1650F	29.91	65	2	1	12	13	18	29.91	.50·AA		Dominated Field	SpsStormRidr GblOrlns SnTnOswld
07/11 E10	GG	1650F	30.10	65½	3	4	1½	14	16	30.10	.30·AA		Best By Far	SanTanCobblr MoonDoggy SkkrVlor7

Green

This Race Is Continued On Next Page

Kiowa Sweet Joe-2002

"THE 53rd ANNUAL $60,000 JOSEPH M. LINSEY MEMORIAL AMERICAN GREYHOUND DERBY"

RACE 13 GRADE S 2010 feet   Thirteenth Race - 09/21/02 - Evening   **2010 feet GRADE S RACE 13**

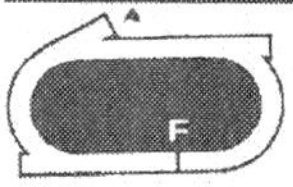

This Race Is Continued From Previous Page

Track Record: ZATZALL, 37.02, 3/30/02

PP	Event	Trk	Dst	TC	Time	WT	PP	Off	1/8	Str	Fin	ART	Odds	Grade	Comment	

10-1 BABY TATA 70 LI 0 0 0 0 0 / WO 12 5 1 0 3   Kennel: On-Line Racing Kennel[45]0%
Owner: William J. Chamness
Trainer: Richard Arno

Brindle, M, Feb 02, 1999, Fantastic Memory-Small Town Allie

																$
5	09/16S3	LI	2010F	38.59	70½	7	4	3	3	2⁴	38.88	---		Off Slow Clsd Rail	JJsSlick JJsJstGabby GrtHrmony*4
	09/10E8	WO	2045F	38.64	70	2	4	3	2	2½	38.69	1.70	TA	Almost Up Inside	Campbell NachoKindaGy Drydor
	09/04E13	WO	1650F	30.30	70	8	3	2	1³	15½	30.30	2.00	A	Going Away Some Wide	Relic KLBaxterBlack UTooDish
	08/31E13	WO	1650F	30.88	71	8	6	6	4	4³	31.09	3.30	A	Bumped 1st Closed	Tada TMsVeryFewDo OccltRomeo
	08/25E12	WO	1650F	30.91	70	7	8	6	4	1ns	30.91	3.10	A	Dead Heat Win	Tada Relic BleBerry
	08/21E5	WO	1650F	30.90	69½	7	5	2	1⁵	19½	30.90	3.20	B	Going Away Mdtrk	ABarQeenBl Tryton TMsKissMiss
	08/16S3	WO	1650F	30.79	70	1	6	5	4	34½	31.09	---		Blckd Far Tn Closed	SRsHonorRs MllrdFilmr VysAnnE7
	08/12S2	WO	1650F	31.10	70	5	8	5	4	45½	31.50	---		Blocked 1st Closed	SRsWoody VaysAnnieE FollowMyLd
	07/13E7	WO	2045F	38.94	70	2	6	6	7	74½	39.26	2.00	TB	Wide 1st Turn	NachoKindaGy KLRedDog Relic
	07/09E4	WO	2045M	40.20	70	5	8	7	6	6⁹	40.84	1.00*	TA	Bumped 1st Turn	FzzysBigHorn WhosHere Aleeya
	07/04E4	WO	2045F	38.63	69	8	8	4	4	45½	39.03	1.00*	TA	Followed Pace Inside	NachoKindaGy Aleeya ABarPorm
Black	06/30E14	WO	1650F	30.58	69	1	6	6	6	67½	31.12	1.30*	A	Blocked 1st Turn	Konsidamee UTooFerd FzzysCogar

12-1 KIOWA SWEET JOE 73 LI 0 0 0 0 0 / WD 5 1 1 0 1   Kennel: ZEZ Kennel[46]0%
Owner: Flying Eagles Kennel
Trainer: Kim Sine

Dark Brindle, M, Jan 07, 2000, Oswald Cobblepot-TM's Sweet Dream

6	09/16S4	LI	2010F	37.85	72½	2	3	3	2	22½	38.02	---		Saved Bks Clsd Gap	PrimcoDodge KlsosSplpn CJRoostr4
	09/05E15	WD	2033F	38.42	73	7	5	5	8	812	39.27	10.30	AA	Dropped Back	RraPenta GreysScooter KraftySly
	08/28E11	WD	2033F	38.49	73	6	4	4	5	2⁹	39.13	6.00	SAA	Big Late Move	ClairDolan KnockotAnn AbitQstor
	08/24E2	WD	2033F	38.84	73	2	3	2	2	1¹	38.84	3.50	SAA	Closed For Win	SeekersValkerie OkieMcki Plldim7
	08/21E7	WD	2033F	38.81	73	1	5	5	6	6⁴	39.09	1.60*	SAA	No Rally Outside	SssHillry KiowaJilJim DCsHldDrv
	08/11A15	WD	2033F	38.01	72½	7	6	6	5	48½	38.61	5.90	AA	Little Gain	ClairDolan KraftyMitchll NmMWht7
	08/05S2	WD	1643F	30.70	73½	7	6	6	5	3⁴	30.98	---		On The Move Inside	IrskTylor OLsContZro OshkshMrtn
	07/27E15	TS	2030F	38.91	72	4	2	3	3	2²	39.03	4.00	AA	Again To Place Ins	VnllStr KnickrBockr DrinknCrwn
	07/22S5	TS	2030F	30.98	72	7	6	4	2	2 1½	30.98	---		Took Win Late	ShataRandy PrimScotmn ImJstADog7
	06/29E10	SP	1980F	37.64	72	6	8	1½	1½	1¹	37.64	14.20	SA	2002 Derby Champion	Tlntdmrriply PrpdlSmilr BgtHtWv
	06/26E6	SP	1980F	37.65	72	4	7	6	5	410	38.40	2.20	SA	Steady Gain Outside	PerpetlSmilr BttrcpLk TimWrpZck
Yellow	06/22E6	SP	1980F	37.83	72½	7	7	2	1³	1⁴	37.83	5.30	SA	Avoided Early Trbl	JNBDrango RwrdGrn BootScootinGl

10-1 JJ'S JUST GABBY 81 LI 0 0 0 0 0 / MU 12 2 3 3 2   Kennel: Wayne Ward Kennel[42]0%
Owner: Jeff Kessler
Trainer: Jeff Wilcox

Red, M, Jan 29, 2000, Greys Statesman-JJ's Webecruisin

															$	
7	09/16S3	LI	2010F	38.59	80½	1	3	1⁴	1²	35½	38.98	---		Leader To Mid-str	JJsSlick BabyTata GreatHarmony*4
	08/31S2	MU	1650F	30.77	80½	2	5	3	3	1¹½	30.77	---		Drvng Fnsh Wd Bkstr	MommasBoy BadmoonThndr OnThTown5
	08/24E11	MU	2010F	38.53	80½	2	3	1⁵	15	1nk	38.53	12.00	SA	2002 Mgp Derby Champ	PikesEclipse BFHarvey MolsRspct
	08/17E13	MU	2010F	38.69	81½	3	6	1³	13	1³	38.69	4.70	SA	Handily Best Mdtrk	RoleModel KiowaMariamari BFCpck
	08/14E9	MU	2010F	38.30	81	5	5	3	3	3³	38.53	7.10	SA	Evenly Midtrack	KiowMrimri Doblivnmgic NnDMolly
	08/10E13	MU	2010F	38.51	81	2	5	3	2	2²	38.66	6.00	SA	Fine Effort Midtrack	BFCarmaleta HotWird SystmPitRit7
	08/07E5	MU	2010F	38.58	81	1	3	3	3	44½	38.89	1.40	SA	Evenly Midtrack	Doyabelievinlv BFCrmlt NnDMolly6
	08/02E9	MU	1650F	30.79	81	7	7	5	5	2³	30.98	5.50	A	Dspt Erly Trbl Mdtrk	DynamicEve JRsRacer CFDReece
	07/27E7	MU	1650F	31.10	81	4	7	8	8	6⁸	31.64	10.80	A	No Room Esc Tn Rail	CrlyCannon BigBoyDnnis MommsBoy
	07/21A11	MU	1650F	30.36	81	4	8	3	3	3⁶	30.76	7.80	A	Fine Effort Inside	BstinctAggie DynamicEve CynnFrn
	07/13E11	MU	2010F	38.35	81½	7	6	4	4	5⁷	38.86	6.10	A	Even Effort Inside	MolsRespect PikesEclipse BFCpck
Grn/Wht	07/06E14	MU	2010F	38.04	80½	6	6	4	3	3⁹	38.65	3.10	A	Fine Effort Inside	BFHarvey PikesEclipse FoxyDsign7

8-1 RAN D RASCAL 59 LI 0 0 0 0 0 / MH 19 12 3 2 0   Kennel: Patrick Collins Kennel[41]0%
Owner: Lois C. Roth
Trainer: John Venuto

Black, F, Dec 26, 1998, Pat C Anguish-Cara's Penny

8	09/16S1	LI	2010F	38.00	59	3	1	2	2	310½	38.73	---		Led Briefly Inside	GblVrmilion PsCptGorg NtsSlyEly3
	08/31E2	MH	2050F	39.56	59	2	2	1⁵	12½	1¹	39.56	.40*	AA	Driving Start Held	WWsFastDyln RdDingo RLMsExprsso
	08/27E14	MH	2050F	39.67	59	5	2	7	7	730	41.80	1.60*	AA	Trouble Early Inside	EMsMagnm RLMsExpresso RedDingo
	08/22E14	MH	2050F	39.10	60	5	1	1³	11	1¹	39.10	1.40*	AA	Four In A Row!	RLMsExpresso EMsMagnm TSFlyBy
	08/16E14	MH	2050F	39.78	58	1	2	1⁴	12	1½	39.78	1.00*	AA	She's In Top Form!	EMsMagnm RLMsExpresso DcoHrricn
	08/10E12	MH	2050F	39.13	58	6	1	1⁵	12½	11½	39.13	.90*	AA	Continues Domination	EMsMagnm TSFlyBy RLMsExpresso
	08/07E14	MH	2050F	39.12	59	6	1	1⁴	13	1³	39.12	1.50*	AA	Full Of Run Inside	WWsFastDyln RLMsExprsso EMsMgnm
	07/31E14	MH	2050F	39.07	59	4	3	3	2	25½	39.45	.60*	AA	Chased Winner Inside	RLMsExprss CGSlthnkcn ByndThGlry
	07/27E14	MH	2050F	39.04	58	4	2	1⁶	110	1⁹	39.04	.30*	AA	Dominated Inside	RdDingo WWPixiStck CGSWhnpgsfly7
	07/24E14	MH	2050F	39.28	59½	3	1	1³	14	13½	39.28	1.10*	AA	As She Pleased Ins	ByondThGlry WWsFstDyln WWPxStck
	07/19E14	MH	2050F	39.08	58	1	1	1⁴	17	1⁷	39.08	1.40*	AA	Uncontested Inside	ByndThGlry ThrsdyFlwr WWsFstDyln
Yel/Blk	07/13E12	MH	2050F	39.28	58	8	7	7	4	3⁴	39.58	1.60*	AA	Held Wd Erly Showed	WWsFastDylan PiksKboom KiowAgnt

SELECTIONS: 4-3-1-2

Sale N Pelletier-2003

In 2003 a stakes event was held at Lincoln Park and it was limited to in house kennel entries only. The winner was designated as the American Greyhound Derby champ for that year

2004

No Derby Run

Inspecda Deck-2005

The American Greyhound Derby will be run for 55th time tonight

Certain things about the Joseph M. Linsey Memorial American Greyhound Derby are fact.

It has always been regarded as one of the most prestigious stake races in the sport wherever and whenever it has been run.

And the race is sure to generate great interest and draw top greyhounds, whether it be an open stake or an in-house competition here at its new home at Lincoln Park.

This time around is no exception.

The race is back on the Lincoln Park calendar as an open stake this year after an absence of one year and the field of eight finalists that will chase the $60,000 purse in tonight's 55th running of the event is as strong as any ever assembled.

The call for race entries attracted a total of 56 greyhounds, with 16 shipping in from outside tracks to challenge the always-strong Lincoln forces for supremacy over the 670-yard distance.

The first two rounds of qualifying were run on Sept. 23 and Sept. 28.

The field was trimmed to 32 for the third and final round this past Monday afternoon, Oct. 3. The top eight greyhounds based on total points scored in the three rounds advanced to the final that will be run as Race 13 tonight.

So balanced was the original field that only one greyhound managed to register more than one qualifying victory.

That honor belonged to Inspecda Deck, who does his racing for the Andrew Sarras Kennel at Raynham-Taunton Greyhound Park. He went two steps better than all the rest by winning in all three rounds.

The finalists include five Lincoln Park-based greyhounds representing five different kennels, and two other invaders in addition to the talented Inspecda Deck.

The American Greyhound Derby has been named for the late Joseph M. Linsey since 1990 and has been run in his memory since 1995.

The first owner of Lincoln Park founded the race as a $25,000 stake at his former Taunton track in 1949 and it was run at Taunton every year thereafter through 1981 except 1975.

Raynham hosted the race from 1982 to 1985.

Lincoln Park has been the home of the Derby since 1986 and the race was last run in 2003.

The field for the 55th American Greyhound Derby, listed with qualifying points::

Inspecda Deck (68 points) – This impressive son of Flying Penske-Bellerose showed his early speed in the first two rounds and his versatility by winning from off the pace in the third round. He has won six straight races since falling in the final of the Taunton Derby in August.

Compton (38 points) – This Regall Sports Kennel entry adjusted well to the route distance of the Derby and clinched a berth in the final with a solid second-place effort in round three.

I'm So Special (38 points) – The March 2003 youngster gave the Tutalo-Richard Kennel a spot in the final by rallying to finish fourth in her third-round heat after an earlier win and second.

OHK Royal Flush (38 points) – The July '04 daughter of 1999 Derby winner Deuce's Wild, representing Frederick's Kennel, looks to be part of the early speed contingent in the final.

Merry Mile (36 points) – The late-running Pat Dalton Kennel entry joined Inspecda Deck as the only other finalist to get a win in the third qualifying round.

Rooftop Gizmo (34 points) – This one made the trip from Wheeling Island in West Virginia to join the Lincoln-based Kerry Hills Kennel and gave a consistent performance in qualifying.

Tipsy Character (34 points) – Represents the Steve Merlock Kennel at Raynham-Taunton where he won the Taunton Derby in August. His good early speed should make him a factor.

TNT Queen (33 points) – She survived a troubled seventh-place finish in the third round to claim the last spot in the final for the Melvin Langford kennel after two solid performances.

Inspecda Deck-2005

55th American Greyhound Derby

The $60,000 Joseph M. Linsey Memorial
American Greyhound Derby

RACE 13   GRADE S   670 yards   Thirteenth Race · 10/08/05 · Evening   **670 yards   GRADE S   RACE 13**

Superfecta, Trifecta, Quiniela, Win, Place, & Show Wagering

Track Record: Rysta, 36.81, 09/06/03

PP	Event	Trk	Dst	TC	Time	WT	PP	Off	1/8	Str	Fin	ART	Odds	Grade	Comment	

7-2 ROOFTOP GIZMO 37.72 AA AA **76** LI 3 1 0 1 1 WD 36 12 3 6 5 Kennel: Kerry Hills Kennel[11]11% Owner: Gary L. Weber Trainer: Gerard Ryan

Red Brindle, M, Jun 26, 2002, Craigie Whistler-Rich's Princesss $ 2523.16

10/03A4	LI	670	F	37.89	76	2	6	5	5	4⁵	38.24	9.90	SAA	Blocked Crtn Turn	MerryMile* Compton CJGramCrackr
09/28A9	LI	670	F	37.72	75	6	5	3	2	1³	37.72	6.00	SAA	Stretch Win Mdtrk	Nevah CrystalHonda ListdBilding
09/23E9	LI	670	F	37.73	76	2	4	5	5	3⁶	38.16	3.50	SAA	Str Gain For Show	TntQeen ContryLore SnshinGlory*
09/17S4	LI	670	F	37.69	76½	6	3	3	3	3³½	37.94	---		Closed Some Mdtrk	GrandpasPrincess Blackjckgmblr 3
09/12S3	LI	550	F	31.14	76	8	4	3	2	2¹	31.20	---		Gaining In Str Mdtrk	NimbyTpJan Regallsleta RglIMdy6
09/05A7	WD	678	F	38.27	75	6	2	7	5	4⁸½	38.86	1.10*	AA	Improved Mdtk	PrmaBrs PenrsSw EsTmbr
08/29A9	WD	678	L	38.18	75½	7	3	1nk	14	14	38.18	4.90	AA	Easy Win Today	ContryL KliwaCnd LzykTry
08/19A7	WD	678	F	37.79	75	4	4	4	5	4¹⁰	38.50	0.80*	AA	Varied Some Insd Run	Cmplete ContryL JagSaw
08/12A7	WD	678	F	37.95	76	3	6	8	5	5⁶½	38.41	2.70*	AA	Slight Late Gain Ins	ContryL RnsSpe KayVCrt
08/05A7	WD	678	F	37.66	76	2	2	1½	13	1⁷	37.66	1.70*	AA	On Path To Glory	ContryL IrskaHa KiwaCnd
07/31A11	WD	678	F	37.99	75½	6	6	6	4	3³	38.20	1.70*	AA	Steady Drive Mdtk	RnsSpe USTyme FzzysLe

1 Red

4-1 TIPSY CHARACTER 37.47 AA AA **68** LI 3 1 0 1 1 RT 28 11 5 3 3 Kennel: Steve Merlock Kennel[55]25% Owner: Leonard V. Wood Trainer: Paul Briggs

Red, M, Aug 03, 2001, Giles Blues-Tipsy Sue $ 2210.60

10/03A2	LI	670	F	37.89	68	2	2	3	3	3⁴½	38.22	1.30*	SAA	Dspt Early Trouble	CrystlHnd SnshnGlry* AllChrgdUp
09/28A2	LI	670	F	37.47	69	1	1	1²	12	1²	37.47	7.20	SAA	Box To Wire Inside	GlddScrt* KyVSwtKy Blckjckgmblr
09/23E2	LI	670	F	37.55	67½	8	5	4	4	4⁶½	38.00	2.70	SAA	Bmpd Ent Front Str	Compton OHKRoyalFlsh NimbyTpJan
09/17S2	LI	670	F	38.00	69	2	1	15	11½	31½	38.12	---		Long Lead Cght Ins	AntRedmoon Kiowamysticmarie 3
09/12S1	LI	670	F	39.18	67½	1	3	2	2	3⁴	39.47	---		Good Effort Inside	RainsAComing KenyaDenise Cardoz4
09/05A2	RT	660	F	38.20	68½	1	1	13	15	1³	38.20	0.50*	A	Box To Wire Inside	MsPbody LsrgiddGirl KlsosOckfx
08/27E7	RT	660	F	37.96	69	6	1	811	8	8	OOP	2.50	A	Judgesok 9/1	InspcdDck KlsosDrkvdr MovnBcksd
08/20E9	RT	660	F	37.82	67	4	1	14	12½	11½	37.82	1.90*	SA	Taunton Derby Champ	MovinBcksid Townsnd KlsosNictnt
08/14A7	RT	660	F	37.86	68	5	1	16	16	1⁷	37.86	4.30	SA	Total Control Inside	Unstopblkovck KissTmln EthrlFrc
08/10A6	RT	660	F	38.41	68½	7	3	2	14½	16	38.41	2.70	SA	Drawing Away	EthersalForce RNRRspons HotGirl6
08/06E6	RT	660	F	37.89	67½	7	1	13	15½	1⁸	37.89	8.50	SB	Away Early Midtrack	KlsosDrkvdr Sriosfirpwr NckNTck

2 Blue

12-1 MERRY MILE* 37.89 AA BB **60** LI 19 4 3 5 2 Kennel: Pat Dalton Kennel[5]16% Owner: Pat Dalton Trainer: David O'Keeffe

Blue, F, Sep 23, 2002, Pacific Mile-Mantle Glory $ 8723.33

10/03A4	LI	670	F	37.89	61	6	8	7	3	11½	37.89	35.20	SA	Last Erly Long Drive	Compton CJGrmCrckr RooftopGizmo
09/28A1	LI	670	F	37.61	60½	7	8	4	3	33½	37.86	5.50	SA	Good Effort Inside	OHKRylFlsh CJGrmCrckr PjsDtchmn
09/23E4	LI	670	F	37.25	60	1	8	6	4	3⁴	37.52	9.90	SA	Gradual Gain Wd	KyVSwtKy ImSoSpcil FirstEdition
09/17A4	LI	670	F	37.57	60½	3	8	6	5	4²	37.71	11.40	A	Slow Start Gaining	TntMlbMy CJGrmCrckr CrystlBGntr
09/10E9	LI	670	F	38.29	61½	6	8	5	4	3²½	38.47	3.90	A	Steady Advance Mdtk	OHKRoyalFlsh Enga RcsVera
09/05A9	LI	670	F	38.11	60½	7	8	7	2	1hd	38.11	9.50	TBB	Outran The Field Wd	PondThRock CJChrriWinks ImSSpcl
08/29A15	LI	670	F	37.90	58½	4	8	6	4	33½	38.13	4.00	TBB	Closed Well Mdtrk	CJNillaWaffer ClrLkStr* Prrform
08/26A4	LI	670	F	37.73	60	7	8	8	7	6⁹½	38.40	5.10	TA	Bmpd Ent Front Str	Lazaine HighSierra OHKRoyalFlsh
08/19E6	LI	670	F	38.73	59½	8	8	7	5	6⁵½	39.12	2.10*	A	Off Slow Blkd Turn	Enga MissDateable Lazaine
08/13L9	LI	670	F	37.95	59½	6	8	6	4	4⁶½	38.42	4.90	TA	Very Slow Start	KayVSweetKy AllChrgdUp TntMlbMy
08/06E16	LI	670	F	38.33	60	6	8	3	13	15	38.44	2.70*	TBB	Extended Lead Mdtk	OHKRoyalFlsh Enga Lazaine
08/01A15	LI	670	F	38.07	60	4	8	6	4	35½	38.44	4.50	BB	Off Slow Clsd Well	Enga PjsMaywest CarolsCandy

3 White

8-1 COMPTON 37.53 AA M **75** LI 40 9 3 11 7 Kennel: Regall Sports[10]11% Owner: Bernie Collette Trainer: Richard Calabro

Red, M, Jan 18, 2003, Be My Bubba-Silver Motion $ 18265.99

10/03A4	LI	670	F	37.89	74	3	5	4	4	2¹½	38.00	7.70	SAA	In & Out Closing	MrryMil* CJGrmCrckr RooftopGizm
09/28A13	LI	670	F	37.68	75½	2	6	4	5	4⁷	38.17	3.50	SAA	Factor Thruout Mdtrk	InspecdaDck ContryLor AntRdmoon7
09/23E2	LI	670	F	37.55	75½	7	2	2	2	1nk	37.55	8.10	SA	Saved Erly Driving	OHKRoylFlsh NmbyTpJn TpsyChrctr
09/17A13	LI	550	F	30.44	74	2	3	7	6	3²	30.57	11.10	A	Late Speed Mdtrk	LeagBoss* OncoLcozd CobblpotBrt
09/12A13	LI	550	F	30.15	74½	8	7	5	5	44½	30.47	5.10	A	Bmpd Gained Ground	BeachHotel Nylajo SnsandsTr BI
09/07A9	LI	550	F	30.37	75	6	3	5	5	4⁶	30.79	7.70	A	Crwd After Break	FlyingDict DngrSignl* DrvnByARd
09/02E11	LI	550	F	30.20	75½	4	8	7	5	34½	30.50	7.70	A	Slow Start Stdy Gain	PaindaPaind FightingHngr JnsBsh
08/27A15	LI	550	F	30.60	75½	5	7	7	4	1¹½	30.60	6.30	BB	Came A Long Way Mtk	GillsCrystal ToABoil ManaSomTim
08/20A9	LI	550	F	30.38	75½	8	8	8	6	4³	30.60	8.10	BB	Steady Advance Ins	RCSOneFinDy SkyMjor ColdBHosfly
08/13L4	LI	670	F	38.42	75½	7	5	6	6	5⁸	38.98	2.60	TA	Crwd Erly Bumped	ClosInspctn Ttllyltln PSRdmnClr
08/08L2	LI	670	F	38.55	75	1	7	7	6	33½	38.79	3.30	TA	Bmpd Late Gain Ins	RcsVera CJNillaWffr Totllyltln
08/03A13	LI	670	F	39.03	74	8	8	5	5	6²½	39.19	3.30	TA	Raced Inside	CrystalBGntr DwnDrmr FlyingSlvo

4 Green

This Race Is Continued On Next Page

Inspecda Deck-2005

55th American Greyhound Derby

The $60,000 Joseph M. Linsey Memorial
American Greyhound Derby

| RACE 13 | GRADE S | 670 yards | Thirteenth Race · 10/08/05 · Evening | 670 yards | GRADE S | RACE 13 |

This Race Is Continued From Previous Page

Track Record: Rysta, 36.81, 09/06/03

6-1 OHK ROYAL FLUSH — 37.61 AA M — 51 — LI 32 7 4 3 1 / LI 48 5 10 5 3
Kennel: Frederick's Kennel[13]11%
Owner: Michael W. Strodtman
Trainer: Mike Cimini
Dark Brindle, F, Jul 04, 2002, Deuce's Wild-Snowflake — $ 13681.01

5 Black

Event	Trk	Dst	TC	Time	WT	PP	Off	1/8	Str	Fin	ART	Odds	Grade	Comments	
10/03A9	LI	670	F	37.72	51	4	2	4	4	49½	38.40	6.20	SAA	Even Pace Mdtrk	InspecdaDeck GildedSecrt* RcsVr
09/28A1	LI	670	F	37.61	51½	1	1	1²	12½	11½	37.61	4.30	SAA	Box To Wire Midtrk	CJGramCrackr MrryMil* PjsDtchmn
09/23E2	LI	670	F	37.55	52½	4	1	16	12½	2nk	37.58	18.00	SAA	Long Lead Overtkn	Compton NimbyTpJan TipsyCharctr
09/17A6	LI	670	F	37.25	51½	1	1	7	8	814½	38.27	8.80	AA	Faded Back Early	KayVSweetKay Lazaine GilddScrt*
09/10E9	LI	670	F	38.29	52½	1	2	2	2	12½	38.29	5.20	A	Driving Drew Clear	Enga MerryMile* RcsVera
09/05A2	LI	670	F	38.23	51	1	4	6	6	610	38.94	4.50	A	Shutoff Crtn Turn	BabyShrimp RcsVera FlyingSalvo
08/31A9	LI	670	F	38.49	52	6	5	3	5	55½	38.89	4.20	TA	Even Pace Inside	GlddScrt* SnshnGlry* CrystlBGntr
08/26A4	LI	670	F	37.73	52½	2	1	1¹	2	35½	38.13	10.00	TA	Caught Far Trn Ins	Lazaine HighSierra RedmoonNina
08/19A15	LI	670	F	38.21	51	4	1	2	1½	2ns	38.22	6.20	TA	Led Into Str Nipped	FlyingSlvo SnshinGlry* BbyShrmp
08/13L2	LI	670	F	38.46	50	7	6	5	7	715½	39.54	4.40	A	Much Early Trouble	GildedSecret* RcsVer FlyingSlvo
08/06E15	LI	670	F	38.33	50½	3	2	2	2	25	38.68	8.10	TA	Good Effort Mdtrk	MerryMile* Enga Lazaine
07/29A11	LI	670	F	38.62	50	5	1	8	8	8	OOP	9.90	TA	Judged Ok 8-3	Excheqer SkllyGirl BackTalker

10-1 I'M SO SPECIAL — 37.66 AA M — 65 — LI 21 6 3 2 / LI 3 0 1 2 0
Kennel: Tutalo - Richard Kennel[21]13%
Owner: Donna Barr
Trainer: Ken Richard
Blue Brindle, F, Mar 02, 2003, Bean Brewer-Chicago Hope — $ 11833.59

6 Yellow

Event	Trk	Dst	TC	Time	WT	PP	Off	1/8	Str	Fin	ART	Odds	Grade	Comments	
10/03A12	LI	670	F	38.14	64½	7	7	5	5	42½	38.33	7.70	SA	Erly Trbl Late Gain	SkyMajor CrystlBGntr AntRdmoon7
09/28A4	LI	670	F	37.66	64	2	7	3	2	1nk	37.66	5.50	SBB	Stretch Win Mdtrk	Enga SkyMajor CJNillaWaffer
09/23E4	LI	670	F	37.25	66	3	6	4	3	22½	37.41	15.50	SBB	Steady Drive Mdtrk	KayVSwtKy MrryMil* FirstEdition
09/17A4	LI	670	F	37.57	63	2	5	7	7	77	38.06	11.10	A	Trbl Ent Front Str	TntMlbMy CJGrmCrckr CrystlBGntr
09/10E9	LI	670	F	38.29	63½	3	6	4	5	66½	38.73	15.60	A	Some Early Speed	OHKRoyalFlsh Enga MerryMile*
09/05A9	LI	670	F	38.11	64	5	5	4	4	48	38.67	9.20	TA	Coll Wide Front Str	MrryMil* PondThRock CJChrriWnks
08/31A4	LI	670	F	38.32	65	3	6	8	8	811½	39.13	11.00	TAA	Blckd Erly Shutoff	Lazaine HighSierra BabyShrimp
08/26A9	LI	670	F	37.78	66	8	8	5	5	512½	38.64	16.40	AA	No Real Threat	KayVSweetKy AllChrgdUp KyVSwtPt
08/19S1	LI	550	F	30.38	65½	8	5	5	5	45	30.72	---		No Mishaps	BohemianLito NitasOtlaw Nasgoen5
08/12S1	LI	550	F	30.75	66½	4	6	6	6	68	31.32	---		Slight Factor	BJsExpress PinkMoonGhost TntQen7
07/04S1	LI	550	F	29.90	64½	4	6	6	6	622½	31.48	---		Never Prominent	LetsMakeMsic OnecoToken JnesBsh6
03/28A6	LI	670	S	38.85	65½	8	8	8	8	8	OOP	2.30	SAA	Pulled Up Bkstrch	GreatTitn GilddScrt* AllChrgdUp

10-1 TNT QUEEN — 37.73 A M — 63 — LI 26 3 6 1 3 / LI 7 1 1 0 3
Kennel: Melvin Langford Ent. Inc.[12]12%
Owner: Tom Taplin Or Corinne Callahan
Trainer: Mike Roderick
Black, F, Jun 16, 2003, Iruska Zederiah-Lovey's Pick — $ 9846.53

7 Grn/Wht

Event	Trk	Dst	TC	Time	WT	PP	Off	1/8	Str	Fin	ART	Odds	Grade	Comments	
10/03A7	LI	670	F	37.89	64	4	4	8	8	713½	38.83	4.60	SA	Bmpd Ent Front Str	CrystlHnd SnshnGlry* TpsyChrctr
09/28A11	LI	670	F	37.81	63	5	5	5	3	2ns	37.82	8.00	SA	Coming Fast Mdtrk	TakeAWalk ClearLakeStr* RCsBrin7
09/23E9	LI	670	F	37.73	62	8	8	3	1²	16	37.73	3.10	SBB	Extending Lead Mdtk	ContryLor RooftopGzm SnshnGlry*
09/17A7	LI	550	F	30.12	63½	5	7	8	8	77½	30.63	7.20	BB	Bmpd 1st Frcd Wd	ScenicSpot* SobRbcc TotllyItlin
09/10A15	LI	670	F	37.93	62½	7	8	5	2	2ns	37.94	5.40	BB	Catching Winner Mdtk	Nevah CarolsCandy ClearLakeStr*
09/02E9	LI	550	F	30.48	63½	6	7	7	7	54½	30.79	8.20	BB	Wide Turn & Bkstr	ColdBXbeliever Nhvhdr KpsNorstr
08/27E9	LI	550	F	30.01	63	1	4	6	6	412	30.86	3.70	BB	Crwd Bmpd Far Trn	FlyingBckford ReglIGilligan Nrtt
08/22A11	LI	550	F	30.63	63½	4	5	4	4	23½	30.89	17.80	BB	Stretch Gain Mdtrk	BbsWhileUCn BrindlGhost BNSAIrt
08/17A12	LI	550	F	30.67	63½	1	7	7	6	51½	30.79	1.40	BB	Trbl Twice Str Gain	LivingDesire ManaSomTime TFPckr7
08/12S1	LI	550	F	30.75	64	3	5	5	5	32	30.89	---		Late Speed Mdtrk	BJsExprss PinkMoonGhost TlsMcLn7
08/08S1	LI	550	F	30.07	64	5	4	5	5	313	30.98	---		Crwd Wide 1st Trn	CrystalHond BrnStormr* ModrnDy*6
05/30A2	LI	550	F	30.36	63½	7	8	6	8	716	31.48	5.40	BB	Crowded On Turns	DangerSignl* SjsGto DrivnByARod

2-1 INSPECDA DECK — 37.42 AA AA — 78 — LI 3 3 0 0 0 / RT 39 14 10 2 4
Kennel: Andrew Sarras Kennel[54]40%
Owner: Andrew Sarras Kennel
Trainer: Andrew Sarras
White & Fawn, M, Dec 25, 2002, Flying Penske-Bellerose — $ 4711.08

8 Yel/Blk

Event	Trk	Dst	TC	Time	WT	PP	Off	1/8	Str	Fin	ART	Odds	Grade	Comments	
10/03A9	LI	670	F	37.72	76½	5	4	2	13	15½	37.72	1.90*	SAA	Bks Drive Drew Away	GildedSecret* RcsVr OHKRoylFlsh
09/28A13	LI	670	F	37.68	77½	7	4	11	15	15½	37.68	1.20*	SAA	Extending Lead Ins	ContryLore AntRedmoon Compton7
09/23E6	LI	670	F	37.42	78	4	2	12½	14	14½	37.42	2.20	SAA	Took Command In Bks	JJsBecca KayVSweetPete HighSirr
09/17S6	LI	670	F	37.94	78	4	1	13	11½	2nk	37.97	---		Almost Lasted Ins	ForeverNanc OtOfLine 3
09/09E14	RT	660	F	38.36	78	7	3	2	13	15½	38.36	1.30*	A	Drawing Away Inside	Unstopblkovck MotorcyclAnni Bdd
09/03A2	RT	660	F	37.59	79½	1	1	13	14	14	37.59	1.00*	A	Quick Trip Inside	MovinBcksid KlsosDrkvdr PtCVLcn
08/27E7	RT	660	F	37.96	77½	1	2	13½	13	1hd	37.96	2.20*	A	Enough Left Midtrack	KlsosDrkvdr MvnBcksd EmrldSnclr
08/20E9	RT	660	F	37.82	77½	3	5	8fl	8	8	.	2.20	SA	Judgesok 8/24	TipsyChrctr Movinbcksd Townsnd
08/14A2	RT	660	F	38.23	78½	6	1	2	11	14½	38.23	3.10	SA	Pulled Away Inside	EmrldSinclr KlssRstl AtscctBrst
08/10A4	RT	660	F	38.14	78	5	1	2	13	13	38.14	1.10	SA	In Control Inside	Synilla FastCisco RiverwoodOprh

SELECTIONS: 8-1-6-2   The $60,000 Joseph M. Linsey Memorial American Greyhound Derby

143

Will Ferrell-2006

PLAY AT THE PARK

WHAT'S DOING AT LINCOLN...

SIMULCAST HOURS SUNDAYS, MONDAYS, WEDNESDAYS, THURS-DAYS:
NOON TO 7:30 PM

FRIDAYS & SATURDAYS: NOON TO MIDNIGHT

NO RACING OR SIMULCASTS ON TUESDAYS
***
56TH AMERICAN GREYHOUND DERBY CHAMPIONSHIP: TONIGHT'S 13TH RACE
***
$10,000 RUN WITH THE GREYHOUNDS PROMOTION FINAL DRAWINGS AND EVENT TONIGHT
***
CHURCHILL DOWNS FREE TIP SHEETS FROM AMERICA'S HANDICAPPER TOBY CALLET NOV. 1st - 25th
***
NIGHT OF STARS XVIII GREYHOUND RACING SIMULCAST ON NOV. 11 17 RACES AT 17 TRACKS STARTING AT 7:30 PM FREE PROGRAMS

TODAY'S SCHEDULE

LAUREL 12:10
FINGER LAKES 12:15
LINCOLN 12:20
CALDER 12:25
AQUEDUCT 12:30
FREEHOLD (H) 12:30
RAYNHAM 12:30
CHURCHILL 12:40
FLAGLER 1:00
WOODBINE (T) 1:10
TURF PARADISE 2:25
GULF 2:30
HAWTHORNE 4:00
MILE HIGH 5:00
HOOSIER (T) 6:10
MOUNTAINEER 7:00
CHARLES TOWN 7:15
LINCOLN 7:20
MEADOWLANDS (T) 7:30
RAYNHAM 7:30
WOODBINE (H) 7:40
ORANGE PARK 7:45
HOLLY DOGS 7:45
SOUTHLAND 8:30
TUCSON 9:20
HOLLYWOOD (T) 10:05
BAY MEADOWS 10:20

EIGHT OF THE COUNTRY'S FASTEST AND FINEST GREYHOUNDS WILL COMPETE TONIGHT IN THE 56TH AMERICAN GREYHOUND DERBY

THE FIELD IS SET...

WILL FERREL, 52 pts.– Rounding out qualification sharing the top total of 52 points was Lincoln's own Will Ferrell He is owned by Driven Racing Inc. and will be racing for Fortune Kennel.

SUN SAND AND SEA, 52 pts.– Also from Lincoln and racing for Frederick's Kennel this top earner also attained a high of 52 points. Sun Sand and Sea is owned by Donald J. Grissom.

PHENOMENAL DREAM, 44 pts.– From Tampa this greyhound earned a total of 44 points while racing for Battle Kennel. Owned by J. Ametrano, R. Finegan & B. Caldwell Phenomenal Dream is one of two littermates to run in the AmDerby on Friday.

EXTRUDING DREAM, 40 pts.– Phenomenal Dream's littermate and all around speedster, Extruding Dream collected 40 points. He too races for Battle Kennel and is owned by J. Ametrano, R. Finegan & B. Caldwell.

COLD B CALMDOWN, 40 pts.– Also coming out with 40 points this greyhound races for Frederick's Kennel and is owned by Georgia Medis & Pameula Bullard

NO MORE LOVING, 40 pts. - DQ

Williams Kennel was shown some love by this 40 point earning greyhound. No More Loving is owned by Sharon L. Williams

DRIVEN LEE, 32 pts.- Kerry Hills Kennel racer Driven Lee showed his home track, Lincoln Park, he'd been taking notes around the Ocean Course a time or two.

ARHOOLIE, 32 pts.– Another Battle Kennel greyhound will try for a chance to hold the AmDerby title, Friday Night. Arhoolie is owned by Raymond Thurber.

Greyhounds will take to the 670-yard Ocean Course this Friday Evening, November 10th. The American Greyhound Derby Champion will be known after one of these top eight greyhounds crosses the finish line first in the 13th-Race.

The event is named for the late Joseph M. Linsey who was the first owner of this facility - then called Lincoln Greyhound Park. Mr. Linsey founded the American Greyhound Derby at his former Taunton, MA track in 1949. Lincoln Park has hosted the race since 1986.

THE $10,000 RUN WITH THE GREYHOUNDS PROMOTION FINAL DRAWINGS AND EVENT TO TAKE PLACE TONIGHT

PLEASE LISTEN FOR ANNOUNCEMENT AND/OR WATCH IN-HOUSE CH. 3 TO SEE IF YOUR NAME HAS BEEN CHOSEN. WINNER WILL HAVE 15 MINUTES TO REPORT TO THE PROGRAM STAND.

OFFICIAL ENTRY FORM AS WELL AS RULES AND REGULATIONS IS ON THE LEFT HAND PAGE OF THIS PROGRAM AND WILL CONTINUE TO RUN UNTIL AMDERBY NIGHT, NOVEMBER 10TH.

Visit our web site at www.lincolnparkri.com

Will Ferrell-2006

The 2006 Joseph M. Linsey Memorial American Greyhound Derby

RACE 13 GRADE S 670 yards — **Thirteenth Race - 11/10/06 - Evening** — **670 yards GRADE S RACE 13**

2nd Half Of The Derby Double

Superfecta, Trifecta, Quiniela, Win, Place, & Show Wagering

Track Record: Rysta, 36.81, 09/06/03

1 (Red) — 8-1 **DRIVEN LEE** 37.11 AA M **59** LI 22 7 6 3 1

Black, F, Oct 04, 2004, Brett Lee-Fast Melody $ 10939.47

Kennel: Kerry Hills Kennel[11]11%
Owner: Kerry Hills Kennel
Trainer: Gerard Ryan

Event	Trk	Dst	TC	Time	WT	PP	Off	1/8	Str	Fin	ART	Odds	Grade	Comment	
11/04 A4	LI	670	F	37.56	59	5	2	2	2	2 1½	37.68	5.40	SAA	In Pursuit Next Best	PhenomenlDrm SkllyGirl GninForc
10/30 A15	LI	670	F	38.18	58½	7	4	2	2	2 2	38.33	3.10	SAA	Always Close Inside	FlyingCndykiss GrysBnnngtn Twtr
10/25 A12	LI	670	F	38.61	59½	2	5	5	5	3 5¼	39.01	0.80•	SAA	Stretch Gain Mdtrk	WillFrrll NitsWtrgrl AllChrgdUp
10/16 A6	LI	670	F	38.20	58½	4	4	6	5	7 9	38.84	4.40	TAA	Trouble Front Str	NnlsRvng GtGrysPinto BbsDislpwr
10/11 A6	LI	670	F	38.36	58½	8	4	4	2	2 hd	38.38	3.50	AA	Good Effort Inside	SnSndAndS ContryJmbor WillFrrll
10/06 E4	LI	670	F	37.64	59½	7	8	8	8	8 9	38.26	6.20	TAA	Shutoff After Break	ContryJmbor DrvnByPsd SnSndAndS
09/30 E9	LI	670	F	37.48	59	2	1	1 3½	1 2½	1 2½	37.48	3.40	SAA	Led Wire To Wire	ContryJmbor DrvnByPsd GtGrysPnt
09/20 A9	LI	670	F	37.28	58½	4	5	5	5	4 7½	37.82	5.90	SAA	Factor Thruout Ins	GtGrysPinto CntryJmbr GlddScrt*
09/15 E13	LI	670	F	37.11	59	2	1	1 3	1 3½	1 1½	37.11	2.30•	TA	Quickly On Top Mdtk	Voyal Vagelmplse Jawan
08/30 A13	LI	550	F	30.11	60	4	5	5	8 FL	8	OOP	4.50	A	Judged Ok 9-6	MsRosyRainbow JrmysWy MissSwtbl
08/25 E2	LI	550	F	30.15	58½	7	1	4	3	3 2	30.30	1.80•	A	Made Up Ground Str	BohemianJolie BitOfBe MissSwtbl
08/19 A4	LI	550	F	30.03	60	5	8	3	3	2 1½	30.14	2.80•	A	Gaining In Str Mdtk	DottisDrm BohminJoli CTWUltrsnc

2 (Blue) — 2-1 **SUN SAND AND SEA** 37.57 AA J **66** LI 34 11 8 2 4 / SP 17 5 2 2 3

White & Brindle, F, Jan 19, 2004, Kiowa Sweet Trey-Greys Witch Hunt $ 21677.38

Kennel: Frederick's Kennel[13]13%
Owner: Donald J. Grissom
Trainer: Mike Cimini

Event	Trk	Dst	TC	Time	WT	PP	Off	1/8	Str	Fin	ART	Odds	Grade	Comment	
11/04 L2	LI	670	F	37.64	67	8	7	3	3	2 3½	37.87	1.00•	SAA	Good Effort Outside	NoMorLovng CntryJmbr KpsCrlysmn
10/30 A12	LI	670	F	37.74	67	8	5	2	1 2½	1 6½	37.74	1.50•	SAA	Pulling Away Sm Wd	Arhoolie BbsDislpowr AllChrgdUp
10/25 A6	LI	670	F	38.07	66½	3	3	2	1 2	1 2½	38.07	2.50	SAA	Edged Clear Outside	PhnomnlDrm NnlsRvng GtGrysPinto
10/21 A4	LI	670	F	38.24	66½	7	7	5	4	4 4	38.53	1.50•	AA	Some Stretch Gain	ContryJambor VrdMontin NnlsRvng
10/11 A6	LI	670	F	38.36	66½	6	7	5	3	1 hd	38.36	3.30	AA	Erly Trbl Great Win	DrivenLee ContryJmbor WillFrrll
10/06 E4	LI	670	F	37.64	66½	8	6	5	4	3 3	37.86	1.50•	TAA	Steady Gain Sm Wd	ContryJmbor DrivnByPsd WllFrrll
09/30 E11	LI	670	F	37.78	66	5	6	4	2	1 4½	37.78	1.50•	TAA	Going Away In Str	Vglmpls AllChrgdUp KpsCrlysimon
09/25 A4	LI	670	F	37.23	66	3	3	3	2	2 3½	37.47	4.40	SAA	Gave Chase Sm Wd	SkllyGirl DrivnByPosd GtGrysPnt
09/20 A2	LI	670	F	37.57	65	3	6	3	1 3	1 7	37.57	2.00•	TA	Led Far Turn Inside	BbsDieselpowr Vglmpls SkllyGirl
09/15 E2	LI	670	F	37.55	66	3	5	5	4	2 4	37.83	1.50•	TA	Steady Gain Outside	DrivnByPosd TxsMistrT ICUDisyDk
09/08 E4	LI	670	F	37.49	66½	4	6	2	2	2 ns	37.50	2.60•	TA	Late Bid Almost Up	AllChargedUp HiKayler Voyal
09/02 A4	LI	670	F	37.90	65	7	5	3	2	2 3½	38.13	2.50•	TA	Gave Chase Mdtrk	KpsCrlysimon Compton BbsFlwrpwr

3 (White) — 7-2 **WILL FERRELL** 37.15 AA J **67** LI 52 18 4 3 9

Brindle, M, May 03, 2004, Craigie Whistler-Thanks Nanc $ 29036.32

Kennel: JA Fortune Kennel[24]12%
Owner: Driven Racing Inc.
Trainer: Dick Child

Event	Trk	Dst	TC	Time	WT	PP	Off	1/8	Str	Fin	ART	Odds	Grade	Comment	
11/04 A9	LI	670	F	37.75	66	5	4	3	2	2 4	38.03	2.50	SAA	Good Effort Mdtrk	CldBClmdwn NtsWtrgrl FlyngCndykss
10/30 A9	LI	670	F	37.76	66	4	4	2	2	1 1	37.76	3.70	SAA	Ran Down Leader Str	HiGene ColdBCalmdown SwtDimonds
10/25 A12	LI	670	F	38.61	67½	8	7	1 2	1 2½	1 4½	38.61	3.50	SAA	Rushed Drew Off Str	NitasWatrgirl DrivnL AllChrgdUp
10/21 A9	LI	670	F	37.94	67	7	2	1 4½	1 7	1 8½	37.94	2.10•	TA	Won With Ease Mdtk	RCKissing TxsMstrT FlyngCndykss
10/16 A4	LI	670	F	37.99	67½	4	3	4	4	4 4½	38.30	1.30•	A	Steady Pace Mdtrk	GninForc KpsCrlysimn CldBClmdwn
10/11 A6	LI	670	F	38.36	68	3	3	3	5	4 3	38.56	10.10	AA	Evenly Some Wide	SnSandAndSea DrivnL ContryJmbor
10/06 E4	LI	670	F	37.64	66½	5	3	2	3	4 4	37.92	13.80	TAA	Gave Chase Mdtrk	ContryJmbor DrvnByPsd SnSndAndS
09/30 E11	LI	670	F	37.78	66½	7	5	5	5	5 9	38.42	3.90	TAA	Coll Ent Front Str	SnSandAndSea Vglmpls AllChrgdUp
09/25 A9	LI	670	F	37.64	66	1	3	1 ½	2	1 1½	37.64	2.00	TA	Long Duel Came Back	ICUDisyDk MnBlckJck PSRdmoonClr
09/20 A2	LI	670	F	37.57	66½	7	5	8	8	7 13½	38.53	2.90	TA	Slight Bump 1st Turn	SnSandAndSe BbsDislpowr Vglmpls
09/08 E9	LI	670	F	37.81	66	6	5	4	4	4 6½	38.26	2.70	TA	Even Pace Mdtrk	GildedScrt* SkllyGirl ICUDisyDk
09/02 A12	LI	670	F	37.66	67	2	6	8	8	8 19½	39.04	14.40	SAA	Erly Trbl Offstrided	NoMorLvng CntryJmbr GrysBnnngtn

4 (Green) — 10-1 **ARHOOLIE** 37.61 AA M **65** LI 35 8 6 6 3 / SP 4 0 0 0 0

Black, F, Feb 01, 2004, Stan's Boy Flyer-Designing $ 16957.41

Kennel: Battle Kennel[2]11%
Owner: Raymond C. Thurber
Trainer: Graydon Robtoy

Event	Trk	Dst	TC	Time	WT	PP	Off	1/8	Str	Fin	ART	Odds	Grade	Comment	
11/04 L2	LI	670	F	37.64	65½	1	3	7	8	8 13	38.56	4.40	SAA	Erly Trbl Wide Turn	NoMorLoving SnSndAndS CntryJmbr
10/30 A12	LI	670	F	37.74	65	2	4	3	2	2 6½	38.20	2.60	SAA	Close Until Stretch	SnSndAndS BbsDislpwr AllChrgdUp
10/25 A4	LI	670	F	38.45	64½	8	1	1 5	1 5	1 ½	38.45	1.50•	SAA	Wire To Wire Outside	BBImprssionist Hmcd GrysBnnngtn
10/21 L2	LI	670	F	37.61	65	6	3	1 5	1 5	1 2	37.61	5.00	TAA	Quickly In Front Wd	HiKylr GtGrysPinto ColdBClmdown
10/16 A13	LI	550	F	30.32	66½	2	8	7	2	2 6½	30.76	16.60	AA	Bkstr Drive Sm Wide	PASOsirs GoodbyGmdrop BohminRdx
10/13 A9	LI	550	F	29.83	64½	3	3	6	5	5 6½	30.27	13.00	AA	Slight Factor	FlyingBckford Savalas VrdMontin7
10/06 A11	LI	550	F	30.21	65	6	8	7	6	6 8	30.78	2.80	AA	Bmpd 1st Frcd Out	Hayvril VerdMontin RdclodChrlot
09/29 E9	LI	550	F	30.67	64	7	8	4	2	1 ns	30.67	6.20	AA	Driving Up On Outs	Savalas VerdeMontin LilTintTlks
09/23 A9	LI	550	F	30.08	63½	5	4	5	4	3 5	30.44	15.70	AA	Steady Advance Wd	PASOsirs JNBAtomicBomb Savalas
09/16 E9	LI	550	F	30.14	65	8	6	6	5	4 4	30.42	11.10	AA	Wide 1st Clsd Some	BBsQickDrw IC LilDbb LlTintTlks
09/11 A9	LI	550	F	30.35	65	5	8	7	5	1 ns	30.35	1.40•	A	Outran The Field Wd	SmoothSeagrms Svls Rgllprofssor7
09/06 A13	LI	550	F	29.95	64	6	6	3	3	2 ns	29.96	3.50	A	Outnodded Midtrk	KiowRmRnnr GtRdyMlody GdbyGmdrp

SELECTIONS: 2-7-3-6 — **2006 American Greyhound Derby Final Post Time 10:08 PM**

Will Ferrell-2006

The 2006 Joseph M. Linsey Memorial American Greyhound Derby

RACE 13 GRADE S 670 yards	Thirteenth Race - 11/10/06 - Evening	670 yards GRADE S RACE 13

2nd Half Of The Derby Double
Superfecta, Trifecta, Quiniela, Win, Place, & Show Wagering

Track Record: Rysta, 36.81, 09/06/03

PP	Event	Trk	Dst	TC	Time	WT	PP	Off	1/8	Scr	Fin	ART	Odds	Grade	Comments	
10-1	**COLD B CALMDOWN**										37.52 AA M	**79**	LI 46 7 6 8 4 / LI 21 2 8 1 1			Kennel: Frederick's Kennel[13]13%
	Brindle, M, Dec 19, 2003, Flying Penske-Coldwater Marana												$ 16138.93			Owner: Georgia Medis Or Pameula Bullard / Trainer: Mike Cimini
5	11/04A9	LI	670	F	37.75	78	8	2	2		12½ 14	37.75	18.50	SA	Led Far Trn Drewout	WilFrrll NtsWtrgrl FlyingCndykss
	10/30A9	LI	670	F	37.76	78	2	6	3		3 3⁷½	38.30	4.40	SA	Good Effort Inside	WillFerrell HiGene SweetDimonds
	10/25A9	LI	670	F	38.19	79	7	6	3		2 24¾	38.52	10.40	SA	Chased Winner	NoMorLoving DrvnByPsd ShmlssDrm
	10/21L2	LI	670	F	37.61	78½	1	2	4		3 43	37.83	2.20	TA	Steady Effort	Arhoolie HiKayler GetGreysPinto
	10/16A4	LI	670	F	37.99	77½	1	4	3		3 32¾	38.17	8.80	A	Never Far Back Ins	GninForc KpsCrlysimon WillFrrll
	10/11A9	LI	670	F	38.06	79½	7	5	3		3 34	38.33	6.60	TA	Good Effort Inside	NenalsReveng GtGrysPinto HiKylr
	10/06E6	LI	670	F	37.52	79½	5	2	12		12½ 13	37.52	18.80	TBB	Handily On Inside	AllChrgdUp KpsCrlysimn TxsMstrT
	09/30E4	LI	670	F	37.52	79	5	6	6		7 716	38.65	8.30	TBB	Coll Ent Front Str	GeninForc MnBlckJck Pictrmprfct
	09/22S1	LI	550	F	30.73	79	4	4	3		15 111½	30.73	---		Extending Lead Ins	LawcareAviator Pctl OrinocoFlow5
	09/18S1	LI	550	F	30.40	80½	4	6	5		5 54¾	30.72	---		Crowded 1st Turn	DkKoval WildAbotTeddy SantaMari6
	09/15S2	LI	550	F	30.64	72	1	5	4		5 511	31.40	---		Saved Blkd Far Trn	DiamondsShin WikiBddyBoy Cohsst5
Black	09/11S1	LI	550	F	30.37	80	7	7	6		7 718¾	31.66	---		No Factor	FlyingJtFl GrysRoylhonr DptyDst7
5-1	**EXTRUDING DREAM**										37.53 AA AA	**71**	LI 3 2 0 0 0 / TP 8 2 2 1 1			Kennel: Battle Kennel[2]11%
	Black, M, Feb 23, 2004, Impossible Dream-Iwatthattrophy												$ 1357.84			Owner: Ametrano, Finegan, Or Caldwell / Trainer: Graydon Robtoy
6	11/04A9	LI	670	F	37.75	71	3	5	8		8 814	38.72	1.00*	SAA	Blkd Erly Offstrided	ColdBClmdown WilFrrll NtsWtrgrl
	10/30A6	LI	670	F	37.53	71	3	1	16		15 14½	37.53	2.10	SAA	Wire To Wire Mdtrk	ContryJambore VrdMontin Homicid
	10/25A15	LI	670	F	38.39	70	4	1	11½	11	11	38.39	2.60	SAA	Held Under Pressure	RCKissing ContryJmbor TxsMistrT
	10/21S3	LI	670	F	38.36	71	5	2	1½		2 26	38.78	---		Early Bid Frcd Pace	SkllyGirl IndigoNight 3
	10/16S1	LI	670	F	38.09	70½	4	2	2		2 31½	38.20	---		Threat Thruout Mdtk	Homicide PhenomenlDrm ShmlssDrm7
	10/09S2	LI	550	F	30.23	71	7	2	3		3 37½	30.77	---		Good Effort Mdtrk	ShmlssDrm SprCCoco BBsStoolfool
	09/29E11	TP	660	F	37.99	71	5	2	11	14	1 1½	37.99	5.20	TA	Coasted Home Midtrck	GrysHnt Phenmen FlyingAw
	09/25E11	TP	660	F	38.12	71½	8	4	2		2 21	38.21	1.00*	TA	Reeling In Leader In	KaasPcc TrbPens KyVKeyl
	09/18E11	TP	660	F	38.31	71	5	5	4		3 36	38.73	2.10*	TA	Held Safe Show In	KassPcc Phenmen ClickCl
	09/11E11	TP	660	F	38.61	71	8	6	2		2 2ns	38.62	0.90*	TA	A Nose Too Short Ins	Phenmen OshkshP GreysMd
	09/05E13	TP	660	F	37.87	70½	3	1	18	18	1 18	37.87	0.70*	B	Much The Best Inside	BaKanss FlyingM JhnWayn
Yellow	08/31E11	TP	660	F	38.21	69½	3	8	5		4 48	38.75	1.30*	TA	Gain To Stretch Ins	TrbPens GreysMd EvasveD
4-1	**PHENOMENAL DREAM**										37.56 AA AA	**73**	LI 3 1 2 0 0 / TP 19 4 4 5 3			Kennel: Battle Kennel[2]11%
	Black, M, Feb 23, 2004, Impossible Dream-Iwantthattrophy												$ 678.92			Owner: Ametrano, Finegan, Or Caldwell / Trainer: Graydon Robtoy
7	11/04A4	LI	670	F	37.56	72½	3	1	12		11½ 11½	37.56	3.20	SAA	Box To Wire Rail	DrivenLee SkllyGirl GenineForce
	10/30A2	LI	670	F	37.91	73	7	1	11		2 21½	38.02	1.20*	SAA	Led Early Next Best	KpsCarlysimon GilddScrt* HiKylr7
	10/25A6	LI	670	F	38.07	72½	2	1	12		2 22½	38.23	2.20*	SAA	Rail Overtkn In Bks	SnSandAndS NnlsRvng GtGrysPinto
	10/21S2	LI	670	F	38.06	72½	2	1	15	16	16	38.06	---		Full Command Inside	InspecdaDeck Centexldol 3
	10/16S1	LI	670	F	38.09	72	1	1	11		1½ 2½	38.14	---		Set Game Pace Rail	Homicide ExtrdingDrem ShmlssDrm7
	10/09S1	LI	550	F	30.41	73	8	4	11½	11	1 11	30.41	---		Held Firm Lead Ins	LovSickBls BBsPitipot ShnMyStyl5
	09/29E11	TP	660	F	37.99	72	8	1	2		3 38	38.53	9.30	TA	Quick Start Shwd Ins	Extrdng GrysHnt FlyingAw
	09/25E11	TP	660	F	38.12	71½	1	2	3		3 34	38.38	3.50	TA	Held Safe Show Rail	KaasPcc Extrdag KyVKeyL
	09/21E9	TP	660	F	37.78	71	8	4	2		3 412	38.66	7.30	TA	Crowded Far Trn Rail	GrysHnt KaasPcc LmrgeAg
	09/14E6	TP	660	F	38.42	72	7	1	8		8 8	OOP	4.30	TA	Clipped Early Fell	LmrgeAg OshkshP GrysHnt
	09/11E11	TP	660	F	38.61	72½	5	1	12	11	1ns	38.61	4.60	TA	Shrinking Lead Mid	Extrdng OshkshP GreysMd
Grn/Wht	09/06E7	TP	550	F	30.44	73	3	7	5		4 413	31.35	4.80	A	Trying Hard Inside	KaiasSn GrysStr Jnblncm
12-1	**NO MORE LOVING**										37.31 AA M	**68**	LI 52 10 6 7 5 / LI 13 3 3 3 3			Kennel: DQ Williams Kennel[18]15%
	White & Black, M, Jun 17, 2004, Flying Penske-Gather Em Up												$ 22284.33			Owner: Sharon L. Williams / Trainer: Marcie Edwards
8	11/04L2	LI	670	F	37.64	67	5	2	11½	12½	13½	37.64	11.10	SAA	Drew Clear On Ins	SnSndAndS CntryJmbr KpsCrlysmn
	10/30A6	LI	670	F	37.53	69	7	3	8		8 818	38.80	5.70	SAA	Erly Trbl Crwd Back	ExtrdingDrm ContryJmbor VrdMntn
	10/25A9	LI	670	F	38.19	67½	4	1	13		14 14½	38.19	5.30	SA	Led Thruout Mdtrk	ColdBClmdwn DrvnByPsd ShmlssDrm
	10/21L9	LI	550	F	30.71	67	6	7	8		8 810½	31.46	5.50	A	Drppd Back 1st Trn	IC LilDebbie JeremysWay PTLLeon
	10/14L9	LI	550	F	30.62	69½	6	1	2		3 2nk	30.65	4.40	A	Closing Late Bid	DarrlHmond MdowStrm* GitrChrli
	10/07L4	LI	550	F	30.74	69	8	6	8		8 810½	31.46	2.20*	A	Erly Spd Trbl Turn	Boytroy MeadowStrem* LwcrAvitor
	10/02A4	LI	550	F	29.75	68	4	1	3		3 35	30.09	8.60	A	Good Effort Inside	Jarva DrivenByBrdy HolidyVochr*
	09/25A13	LI	550	F	30.76	68½	5	2	6		7 67	31.24	2.10*	A	Some Early Speed	OwlSally* AnswrToChvs BBsFinwin
	09/20A9	LI	670	F	37.28	67	7	6	6		6 68½	37.88	6.00	SAA	Close Qrtrs Early	GtGrysPinto CntryJmbr GlddScrt*
	09/15E6	LI	670	F	37.70	68	4	1	7		7 715½	38.77	7.00	SAA	Shutoff Crtn Turn	GrysBnngtn GtGrysPnt KpsCrlysmn
	09/08E13	LI	670	F	37.31	68	2	2	6		6 612	38.15	4.80	SAA	Erly Trbl Knckd Back	ContryJmbr GrysBnngtn NnlsRvng
Yel/Blk	09/02A12	LI	670	F	37.66	68	6	1	13		13 14½	37.66	7.60	SAA	Wire To Wire Inside	CntryJmbr GrysBnngtn BbsDslpwr

SELECTIONS: 2-7-3-6   2006 American Greyhound Derby Final   Post Time 10:08 PM

BNS Jimbo Di-2007

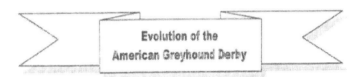

Evolution of the
American Greyhound Derby

1949 - The American Greyhound Derby was the first open greyhound race in the world. It carried the largest purse in the world - $25,000, -$15,000 to the winner. Taunton Dog Track was the host track. Managing Director Joseph M. Linsey was the originator. First year was run as a sprint stake over the 525-yard Dighton Course (1575 feet) There were only two elimination rounds. The first round had eight heats with the first two finishers in each heat staying in the competition. The second round had two heats with the first four greyhounds in each continuing to the final. The lure was an outside lure. The Official Program was 15 cents. There were two greyhounds entered from England, 1 from Ireland and 1 from Canada. There was only Win, Place, Show and Daily Double wagering. Winning times were recorded in tenths of a second. The winner was crowned World Champion. This "World Champion" label until 1969. The Grading System as we know it didn't exist.

1950 – For the first time in Greyhound history, the American Greyhound Derby was aired nationally by NBC on "Watch the World" program Sunday September 10th at 5:00 pm. The distance was changed to the 675- yard (1925 feet) Bristol Course. The lure was moved to the inside. The qualifying was increased to three elimination rounds. In each round the first four finishers qualified for the next round eventually eliminating the field to the final eight

1951 – The Point System was introduced to the three rounds of qualifying. 8 points for first, 7 for second, 6 for third all the way down to 1 for eight. A new Grading System (the Welsh System) was introduced going from 1 for greyhounds with the most ability down to 5 for those with the least. Mixed grades were designated as 4-5 or 1-2 for example, while stakes races such as the American Derby were designated as Grade S.

1952 – The American Greyhound Derby was tabbed the " Race of Champions" and continued to get entries from overseas. Captain R.H. Joliffe, a close and dear friend of Mr. Linsey, acted as the overseas racing manager procuring the best greyhounds from Ireland and Europe. Joliffe worked for Linsey on the Derby until he passed away in the late 70s. The Scoring System changed slightly. The points ranged from 7 for the winner to 0 points for 8th.

1954 – The Scoring System changed to 24 pts, 12 pts, 8 pts, 6 pts, 3 pts, 2 pts, 1 pt, 0 pts.

1958 – The price of a racing program went to 25 cents. The Grading System was again changed. A, B, C, D, E were used instead of numerals.

1962 – For the 14th American Greyhound Derby the distance was changed to a true 1980- ft, 3/8th -mile course.

1963 – The flip-flop starting box was first used. The final won by Thermal was marred by heavy fog. Only a portion of the front stretch was visible. Mr. Linsey in response from many letters received from patrons as far away as New York and Maine as well as the owners and trainers of the finalists. Initiated a Challenge Cup, rematching 7 of the 8 finalists. No record of the winner was found but the late Bill L'Italien, the Taunton Dog Racing Director at the time, who hadn't missed a derby through 1986 yet Believed that the winner was Bustleton who finished second in the actual Derby.

1964 – First year that a foreign greyhound made the finals and the first year that a foreign greyhound won. Canadian Hi There was the Derby winner . Time was measured by 1/100ths of a second.

1967 – The Grading System was changed to AA, A, BB, B, C, D.

1975 – The Derby was cancelled for that year.

1977 – The purse was raised to $35,000.

1981 – This was the last year to be run at Taunton Dog Track, Taunton, Ma.

1982 - The American Greyhound Derby was moved to Raynham Park during the Taunton Meet.

1949   2007
The Joseph M. Linsey Memorial
58th American Greyhound Derby
Twin River
Lincoln, Rhode Island

1984 - The Purse was raised to $50,000.

1985 - Last year to be run at Raynham Park.

1986 - First year to be run at Lincoln Greyhound Park. The distance was changed to 2010 feet.

1987 - The Derby was telecast (live) in a special one-half hour show on NESN.

1990 - Officially named "Joseph M. Linsey's American Greyhound Derby" in honor of Greyhound Hall of Fame inductee Joseph M. Linsey, a true pioneer in the sport of Greyhound Racing.

1992 - The Purse was raised to $60,000.

1994 - The Derby was beamed to a nationwide simulcast network.

1995 - Renamed " The Joseph M. Linsey Memorial following the passing of the events founder on 11-29-94 at the age of 95.

1997 - The race was changed to an invitational event.

1999 - in honor of the race's 50th Anniversary, the purse was $100,000.

2005 - The American Greyhound Derby became an open event again.

BNS Jimbo Di-2007

The $100,000 Joseph M. Linsey Memorial Greyhound Derby

RACE 13 GRADE S 670 yards | **Thirteenth Race - 09/29/07 - Evening** | **670 yards GRADE S RACE 13**

Adopt A Greyhound! Please Contact June Bazar At 401.749.1649
Trifecta, Quiniela, Win, Place, & Show Wagering

PP	Event	Trk	Dst	TC	Time	WT	PP	Off	1/8	Str	Fin	ART	Odds	Grade	Comment	Track Record: Rysta, 36.81, 09/06/03
4-1	**NO MORE LOVING**										37.31 AA M	70	LI / LI		35 12 6 3 1 / 62 11 7 11 6	Kennel: DQ Williams Kennel[18]16% Owner: Sharon L. Williams
	White & Black, M, Jun 17, 2004, Flying Penske-Gather Em Up														$ 22017.94	Trainer: Graydon Robtoy
	09/24A11	LI	670	F	**37.50**	70	4	1	1 1½	1 1½	1 3	37.50	1.20	SAA	Game Pace Drw Clear	SpeedSign* Zadero MakinChilli
	09/19A9	LI	670	F	**37.62**	70	2	1	4	5	5 8½	38.21	1.60•	SAA	Rshd Up Early Threat	DrivenLe GtGrysPinto DkotsConni
	09/14E2	LI	670	F	**37.89**	70½	4	1	1 1	1½	1 1	37.89	0.70•	SAA	Withstood Challenge	SolKetchp BoheminClyso GrysRIDI7
	09/08E11	LI	670	F	**37.74**	69	5	1	7	6	5 6½	38.18	4.60	SAA	Shuffled Back Early	MkinChilli TKSwtEnding PTLFling
1	09/03A9	LI	670	F	**37.48**	70	7	6	7	5	6 12	38.32	2.30•	SAA	No Rng Room Early	WhytllGG GrysBnnington StrzSprm
	08/29A9	LI	670	F	**37.76**	70½	4	2	1 2	1 2	1 2½	37.76	3.30	SAA	Quickly On Top Ins	ContryJmbor ICUMrvlUs BnsJimboD
	08/25A6	LI	670	F	**37.85**	71	5	8	7	8	8 14½	38.87	4.30	SAA	Off Slowly Blocked	TKRocketMan JsJob NitasMrJake
	08/20A6	LI	670	F	**37.93**	71	4	1	1 2½	1 1	1 1½	37.93	5.00	SAA	Never Headed Inside	GetGrysPinto GrysBnnington Myln
	08/15A12	LI	670	F	**38.18**	70	3	3	8	8	7 14½	39.19	3.80	AA	Trouble Thruout	BnsJimboDi NitsMrJk ContryJmbor
	08/10E6	LI	670	F	**38.33**	70	2	1	1 1	1 2	1 4½	38.33	3.20	SAA	Took Control In Str	ContryJmbor WillFrrll GtGrysPnt
	08/04A9	LI	670	F	**38.10**	69½	8	2	4	3	3 6½	38.56	2.70•	SAA	Good Effort Mdtrk	BBImprssnst BcTrprJ GrysBnnngtn
Red	07/28E9	LI	670	F	**38.63**	71	2	1	1 4½	1 4½	1 5½	38.63	8.10	AA	Led Wire To Wire	BcTrooprJ NtsWldBll GrysBnnngtn
12-1	**BNS JIMBO DI**										37.20 AA M	60	LI / LI		41 8 7 4 6 / 46 10 12 5 4	Kennel: Brindle Kennel[9]13% Owner: Patricia Stover Or Brindle Kennel
	Black, F, Mar 09, 2003, Jimbo Scotty-Ps Nosey Posey														$ 15690.78	Trainer: Joe Souza
	09/24A4	LI	670	F	**37.52**	59½	1	1	2	2	1½	37.52	7.90	SA	Led Erly Came Again	TKRocktMn BNSBbyGirl ExpnsivPrl
	09/19A6	LI	670	F	**37.64**	60	4	1	2	2	2 5½	38.03	7.90	SA	Next Best Midtrack	SlashNCash Gwist FlyinBridgport7
	09/14E9	LI	670	F	**37.69**	60	6	1	1 3½	2	2 4	37.96	13.60	SA	Caught Far Trn Mdtk	SpeedSign* Hellion GetGrysPinto
	09/08E9	LI	670	F	**37.33**	60	6	2	5	6	6 9	37.96	8.20	SA	Followed Pace	WhytellGeeG MgicPnnyAnt VgImpls
2	08/29A9	LI	670	F	**37.76**	60½	3	4	3	4	4 9½	38.43	37.70	SAA	Some Early Speed	NoMorLoving CntryJmbr ICUMrvlUs
	08/25A6	LI	670	F	**37.85**	60	4	2	4	4	5 10½	38.58	11.10	SAA	Cls Qtrs Aftr Break	TKRocketMan JsJob NitasMrJake
	08/20A6	LI	670	F	**37.93**	59	6	4	3	4	5 11	38.70	8.10	SAA	Early Speed Mdtrk	NoMorLvng GtGrysPnt GrysBnnngtn
	08/15A12	LI	670	F	**38.18**	59	1	1	1 1½	1 2	1 4	38.18	5.10	AA	Late Command Mdtrk	NitasMrJk ContryJmbor WillFrrll
	08/10E12	LI	670	F	**38.63**	61	6	1	1 2½	1 2½	1 2½	38.63	6.60	TA	Led Box To Wire	SobAftonRls NitsWtrgirl MknChll
	08/04A15	LI	670	F	**38.42**	59½	8	2	2	2	1 ns	38.42	2.40•	TBB	Up Last Stride Ins	ColdBCalmdown Voyal KpsMstang
	07/28E4	LI	670	F	**38.95**	61	2	1	4	4	3 7	39.43	3.50	TBB	Str Gain For Show	GetGreysPinto ExpensivePrl Myln
Blue	07/23A2	LI	670	F	**38.19**	60½	1	1	1 2	2	2 2½	38.37	2.50	TBB	Caught Far Trn Mdtk	BcTrooperJoe KpsMstng ICUMrvlUs
7-2	**SLASH N CASH**										37.64 AA J	73	LI		33 11 3 1 4	Kennel: DQ Williams Kennel[18]16% Owner: Sharon L. Williams
	Brindle, M, Sep 20, 2005, Craigie Whistler-Big Girl Starlet														$ 14952.33	Trainer: Graydon Robtoy
	09/24A9	LI	670	F	**37.81**	73½	8	3	1 2½	1 1	2 1	37.87	1.40•	SAA	Caught Late Mdtrk	Hellion Voyal ColdBCalmdown
	09/19A6	LI	670	F	**37.64**	73	5	2	1 3	1 5½	1 5½	37.64	2.00	SAA	Held Safe Lead Mdtrk	BnsJimboDi Gwist FlyinBridgport7
	09/14E11	LI	670	F	**37.77**	74½	6	1	1 3½	1 2	1 3½	37.77	3.40	SAA	Quickly In Front Mtk	BcTrooprJo SntsPlygirl KUPsFnny
	09/08E15	LI	670	F	**37.75**	72½	3	3	3	3	4 5½	38.12	1.80•	SAA	Collided Crtn Trn	BWGTaxAdit KUPsFanny Zadero
3	09/03A13	LI	670	F	**37.28**	72½	7	6	6	5	5 12½	38.16	3.20	SAA	Rough Trip Early	GtGrysPnt MgcPnnyAnt SntsPlygrl
	08/29A4	LI	670	F	**37.91**	74	1	3	1 2	1 2½	1 1	37.91	2.50•	TAA	Set Pace Led Mdtrk	GtGrysPinto WillFrrll BcTrooprJ
	08/25A4	LI	670	F	**37.68**	73½	8	3	2	2	1 1	37.68	2.70•	TAA	Ran Down Leader Str	GetGreysPinto Attyood WillFrrll
	08/20A4	LI	670	F	**37.96**	73½	7	5	1 5	1 5	1 5	37.96	5.70	TA	Quickly In Command	MissNancy OrDvilWomn ExpnsivPrl
	08/15A9	LI	670	F	**38.19**	74	5	3	1 nk	3	4 7	38.69	7.10	SA	Early Bid Mdtrk	DrivenByScotty Zadro ExpnsivPrl
	08/10E4	LI	550	F	**30.61**	73½	4	6	8	8	7 13½	31.57	3.20	A	Trbl 1st Frcd Wide	StarzKiss CoolNikita SperCJrico
	08/04A13	LI	550	F	**30.44**	73	3	7	3	3	2 ns	30.45	6.40	A	Late Bid Just Missed	Leverett Broadmoor CTWSwetbbylv
White	07/30A13	LI	550	F	**30.32**	74	6	8	7	6	7 17½	31.55	2.30	SA	Crwd Bmpd 1st Turn	CTWWIIDfind FlyngLymn OncGldTch
10-1	**SPEED SIGN***										37.69 AA M	81	LI		41 7 9 6 4	Kennel: Pat Dalton Kennel[5]11% Owner: Pat Dalton
	Black, M, May 15, 2005, Larkhill Jo-Glass Orchid														$ 14722.53	Trainer: David O'Keeffe
	09/24A11	LI	670	F	**37.50**	80	1	3	2	2	2 3	37.71	1.10•	SAA	Blckd Pressing Ins	NoMoreLoving Zadero MakinChilli
	09/19A2	LI	670	F	**37.79**	80½	7	8	7	6	6 11	38.55	3.50	SAA	Blocked On Break	DrvnBySctty ExpnsvPrl CntryJmbr
	09/14E9	LI	670	F	**37.69**	80½	3	7	2	1 2	1 4	37.69	7.00	SA	Drew Away Late Rail	BnsJimboDi Hellion GetGrysPinto
	09/08E4	LI	670	F	**37.78**	81	3	2	2	1 3	2 1	37.85	6.10	SA	Caught Late Inside	BeatiflBride ValidHalyHll JsJob
4	09/03A4	LI	670	F	**37.65**	81	7	8	6	7	7 15	38.69	3.20	TA	Blckd After Break	BNSBlldozer StarzStn OrDvilWomn
	08/29A6	LI	670	F	**38.25**	81	5	6	4	2	2 2	38.38	8.40	TA	Closing In Str Ins	FlyingWhoopin ExpensivePrl Zdro
	08/25A9	LI	670	F	**37.76**	81½	6	8	7	5	5 9	38.40	7.90	TA	No Mishaps Inside	ICUMarvelUs RebelRacer Zadero
	08/18E9	LI	550	F	**31.25**	80	8	8	8	5	4 2	31.38	2.40	A	Slow Start Gained	RCPooh SnsandsHoney JSRedPlse
	08/15A14	LI	550	F	**30.64**	81	6	8	7	4	3 6	31.07	3.50	A	From Far Back Mdtk	ImperiolisWay Hmar GrysStrLilly
	08/10A13	LI	550	F	**30.95**	81½	7	8	8	3	2 1½	31.07	3.20	A	Last Erly Clsd Well	SolBsta BoheminSwill FlyingSndi
	08/03E4	LI	550	F	**31.01**	81	2	8	6	5	4 6	31.42	3.50	A	Some Stretch Gain	FrmSpirit BohminSwll Jstkcknthm
Green	07/28E13	LI	550	F	**31.14**	81	4	8	7	7	6 10	31.83	6.20	AA	Lacked Early Speed	SolRoghshod VageImplse Atatyood

BNS Jimbo Di-2007

The $100,000 Joseph M. Linsey Memorial Greyhound Derby

RACE 13 GRADE S 670 yards — **Thirteenth Race · 09/29/07 · Evening** — **670 yards GRADE S RACE 13**

This Race Is Continued From Previous Page

Track Record: Rysta, 36.81, 09/06/03

---

5 — 8-1 — **DRIVEN LEE** — Black

37.11 AA M — 59 — LI 25 4 3 1 4 / LI 23 7 6 3 1

Black, F, Oct 04, 2004, Brett Lee-Fast Melody — $ 7534.65

Kennel: Kerry Hills Kennel[11]12% — Owner: Kerry Hills Kennel — Trainer: Steve Haenel

Event	Trk	Dst	TC	Time	WT	PP	Off	1/8	Str	Fin	ART	Odds	Grade	Comment	
09/24A2	LI	670	F	**37.21**	60	1	1	1 5½	1 4	1 2½	37.21	1.70•	SA	Wire To Wire Mdtrk	BeatiflBrid ICUMrvlUs SnSndAndS
09/19A9	LI	670	F	**37.62**	60	7	2	1 1½	1 2	1 1½	37.62	8.40	SBB	Held Safe Lead Mdtrk	GetGreysPinto DkotsConni Hllion
09/14E15	LI	670	F	**37.58**	60½	5	5	5	5	6 11	38.35	2.40	SBB	No Real Threat	JsJob ExpensivePearl DkGlnnJons7
09/08E6	LI	670	F	**37.63**	60½	6	3	2	2	2 2½	37.79	6.70	SBB	In Pursuit Mdtrk	WillFerrell Hellion ICUMarvelUs
09/03S3	LI	550	F	**30.27**	60	2	2	3	3	2 5	30.63	---		Saved Erly Str Gain	SnSndAndS JSExplodingRoo SlJrdn5
08/31S3	LI	550	F	**30.89**	59½	7	1	6	5	2 5	31.24	---		Late Speed Mdtrk	AndreannasWay TippBeazer NSLail6
07/30A8	LI	550	F	**30.74**	59½	2	8	8	8	7 5	31.10	11.10	A	Blckd After Break	BohemianJolie Elfyn NitasLacy
07/25A12	LI	550	F	**30.38**	58½	8	4	3	4	4 2½	30.54	4.90	A	Steady Effort Mdtrk	BNSBabyGirl StarzKiss RcTooTall
07/20E13	LI	550	F	**30.73**	58½	3	3	7	6	4 9½	31.40	10.00	A	Blckd 1st Collided	DoorPrize JsEclipse CKarlC
07/14E9	LI	550	F	**30.49**	59	3	1	6	6	6 16½	31.63	27.00	AA	Trbl 1st Offstrided	Happenz NitasMrJake PASOsirs
07/07E4	LI	550	F	**30.25**	60	3	8	8 FL	8	8	OOP	17.90	AA	Judged Ok 7-11	OnecoFaxPas TippViolet Jetwave
07/02A9	LI	550	F	**30.76**	60	2	3	5	4	4 5½	31.16	5.00	AA	Some Stretch Gain	FlyingLyman NitasMrJk TippViolt

---

6 — 10-1 — **VOYAL** — Yellow

37.37 AA J — 59 — LI 47 9 7 4 4 / LI 47 5 8 8 9

White & Fawn, F, Oct 12, 2003, Taziluz-Sastee — $ 16865.05

Kennel: Kerry Hills Kennel[11]12% — Owner: Daniel P. Ryan — Trainer: Steve Haenel

Event	Trk	Dst	TC	Time	WT	PP	Off	1/8	Str	Fin	ART	Odds	Grade	Comment	
09/24A9	LI	670	F	**37.81**	60	1	1	5	4	3 2½	37.97	3.50	SA	Crwd Steady Gain	Hellion SlashNCash ColdBClmdown
09/19A6	LI	670	F	**37.64**	60½	1	4	6	6	5 11½	38.44	1.60•	SA	Blkd On Rail Early	SlashNCash BnsJimboDi Gwist7
09/14E4	LI	670	F	**37.76**	59½	5	1	2	2	1 2	37.76	32.90	SBB	Driving Up On Ins	TKRocktMn SnSndAndS BBImprssnst
09/08E2	LI	670	F	**37.46**	59½	8	5	2	2	2 4	37.73	16.80	SBB	Closed Gap Mdtrk	BNSBbyGirl ExpnsivPrl SnSndAndS
09/01E15	LI	670	F	**38.37**	60	3	8	5	5	5 2	38.52	5.00	TBB	Some Stretch Gain	PTLFling Zizabel DkGlennJones
08/29A6	LI	670	F	**38.25**	59	4	8	7	7	5 5½	38.62	14.80	TBB	Blckd After Break	FlyingWhoopin SpdSgn* ExpnsvPrl
08/25A11	LI	670	F	**37.51**	60	1	4	3	1 2	1 4	37.51	3.60	TB	Driving Drew Off Mtk	CJLckyRip RCHighPckts Cnyhrmyft
08/20A2	LI	670	F	**37.91**	60½	5	2	8	7	4 5½	38.31	14.90	TB	Erly Trbl Offstrided	BWGTaxInvader Zadero KpsMstang
08/15A9	LI	670	F	**38.19**	60	6	6	7	7	7 9½	38.87	25.60	SBB	Blckd After Break	DrivenByScotty Zadro ExpnsivPrl
08/10E9	LI	670	F	**38.51**	58½	7	8	8	6	5 11	39.28	8.70	BB	Trouble Aftr Break	ExpnsivPrl DrvnBySctty OrDvlWmn
08/04A15	LI	670	F	**38.42**	59½	1	4	4	4	3 2½	38.59	4.50	TBB	Made Up Ground Str	BnsJimboDi ColdBClmdwn KpsMstng
07/28E4	LI	670	F	**38.95**	59	4	3	8	8	8 13½	39.89	4.80	TBB	Erly Trbl Knckd Back	GtGrysPinto ExpnsivPrl BnsJimbD

---

7 — 6-1 — **BEAUTIFUL BRIDE** — Grn/Wht

37.69 AA M — 59 — LI 42 11 5 12 7 / LI 0 2 2 2 0

Red Brindle, F, Feb 19, 2005, P's Raising Cain-Whistler's Bride — $ 24067.25

Kennel: Kerry Hills Kennel[11]12% — Owner: Daniel P. Ryan — Trainer: Steve Haenel

Event	Trk	Dst	TC	Time	WT	PP	Off	1/8	Str	Fin	ART	Odds	Grade	Comment	
09/24A2	LI	670	F	**37.21**	60	3	4	8	3	2 2½	37.37	3.30	SAA	Ins & Outs Clsd Well	DrivenLee ICUMarvelUs SnSndAndS
09/19A13	LI	670	F	**37.47**	60	5	6	5	4	3 9	38.10	3.50	SAA	Steady Gain For Show	TKRocketMan WhytellGeeGee JsJob
09/14E13	LI	670	F	**37.69**	60	5	6	3	2	2 ns	37.70	1.60•	SAA	Pressing In Str Wide	ColdBClmdown MkinChilli RgllRbi
09/08E4	LI	670	F	**37.78**	60	8	8	6	3	1 1	37.78	1.90•	SAA	Fast In Str Outside	SpeedSign* ValidHaleyHall JsJob
09/03S1	LI	670	F	**37.80**	60½	1	1	1 3	1 8	1 11½	37.80	---		Alone & Extending	StarzTamatha WillyFixIt 3
08/31S2	LI	550	F	**30.80**	60	2	3	5	3	1 hd	30.80	---		Last Erly Long Drive	BoonsCochmik DoorPrz GrysRlnrgy5
07/28E9	LI	670	F	**38.63**	60	7	8	8	6	5 16	39.76	7.20	AA	Blkd Erly Raced Wd	NoMorLoving BcTrooprJ NtsWldBll
07/23A9	LI	670	F	**38.22**	59½	5	6	6	5	4 1½	38.33	4.70	SAA	Stretch Gain Wide	WillFrrll NoMorLvng GrysBnnngtn7
07/18A12	LI	670	F	**38.18**	59½	3	5	7	3	3 4½	38.48	3.50	SAA	Good Effort Midtrack	NoMorLvng BBImprssnst BNSBlldzr
07/13E6	LI	670	F	**37.90**	60	5	7	6	4	3 6½	38.36	3.20	SAA	Str Gain For Show	GrysBnnington NMrLvng GtGrysPnt
07/07A11	LI	670	F	**37.53**	60½	2	6	4	4	3 8	38.08	1.10•	TAA	Despite Trouble	GrysBnnngtn BBImprssnst GtGrysPnt
07/02A6	LI	670	F	**38.72**	60	5	6	6	5	3 nk	38.75	5.10	SAA	Coll Coming On Outs	BBImprssnst GrysBnnngtn CntryJmbr

---

8 — 2-1 — **TK ROCKET MAN** — Yel/Blk

37.38 AA J — 65 — LI 34 12 7 4 6 / WS 6 0 2 3 1

Black, M, Jul 14, 2005, Dodgem By Design-Iruska Giggle — $ 20548.98

Kennel: Tutalo - Richard Kennel[21]13% — Owner: Finn, Bradley, Miller, Tutalo — Trainer: Ken Richard

Event	Trk	Dst	TC	Time	WT	PP	Off	1/8	Str	Fin	ART	Odds	Grade	Comment	
09/24A4	LI	670	F	**37.52**	66	2	3	1 1	1 1½	2 ½	37.57	1.40•	SAA	Overtkn Near Wire	BnsJimboDi BNSBbyGirl ExpnsvPrl
09/19A13	LI	670	F	**37.47**	66	4	1	1 10	1 8	1 7	37.47	4.00	SAA	Much The Best Mdtrk	WhytellGeeGee BeatiflBrid JsJob
09/14E4	LI	670	F	**37.76**	65½	7	3	1 6½	1 3½	2 2	37.91	1.70•	SAA	Long Lead Overtkn	Voyal SnSandAndS BBImprssionist
09/08E13	LI	670	F	**37.38**	65½	3	1	1 8	1 9	1 9	37.38	3.60	SAA	Never A Doubt Mdtk	BcTrooperJo GrysRIDI BNSBlldozr
09/01A9	LI	550	F	**30.65**	66	7	7	4	3	3 2½	30.81	4.60	AA	Blckd Erly Clsd Gap	Trackrecordtrent Mcdff OncoFxPs
08/25A6	LI	670	F	**37.85**	66½	8	4	1 5½	1 6	1 1	37.85	2.40•	SAA	Sprinted Away Early	JsJob NitasMrJake GrysBnnington
08/17A4	LI	550	F	**30.88**	65½	4	6	4	4	4 5½	31.25	1.80•	AA	Shutoff 1st Collided	SolRoghshod PASOsirs BBsDickDrw
08/11A12	LI	550	F	**30.40**	65½	2	2	4	3	3 3½	30.63	0.30•	AA	Blckd Twice Driving	JsEclipse HiKervin Doesfblosboy
08/04E9	LI	550	F	**31.40**	66	3	2	2	2	2 1½	31.51	1.60•	SAA	Trbl 1st In Pursuit	FlyngGdLck FlyngLymn CTWWllDfnd
07/30A4	LI	550	F	**30.60**	64½	3	2	2	1 1	1 3	30.60	2.00	SAA	Arnd Leader Drew Clr	Baton Dosfblosboy Trckrcordtrnt
07/25A4	LI	550	F	**30.42**	66	5	1	1 1	1 4	1 5	30.42	3.70	SAA	Pulling Away Sm Wd	Dsfblsby RgllDddlr Trckrcrdtrnt
07/21A2	LI	550	F	**30.20**	65½	8	6	1 1	1 5	1 6½	30.20	2.20	SAA	Command In Bkstrch	FlyingLyman JnsMony BTRCptinJck

SELECTIONS: 3-8-1 — **THE 2007 AMERICAN GREYHOUND DERBY**

Magic Penny Ante-2008

Magic Penny Ante captures $115,000 American Derby

September 25, 2008

By STAN PAWLOSKI, Times Leader Wire Editor

It was a magical night for the Haber Kennel racing family.

Magic Penny Ante made sure of that.

The much-traveled Penny Ante finally won the big one as the Wheeling invader shot to the front early and never looked back in capturing the $115,000 American Derby at Twin River (formerly Lincoln) last weekend. She raced out of the Kerry Hills Kennel.

No More Loving (DQ Williams Kennel) took runnerup honors while favorite Lovely Sonia (DQ Williams Kennel) recovered from a slow start to grab third.

Completing the final field were Bad Influencecat (Pat Dalton Kennel), fourth; Flying Mancini (EP's Kennel), fifth; Rossmore Althia (Kerry Hills Kennel), sixth; BWG Tax Audit (Kerry Hills Kennel), seventh; and Chasen Tail (DQ Williams Kennel), eighth.

Mitchell Haber of Florida was ecstatic with Penny Ante's stake victory.

"I have to be the happiest guy in the world. We are so proud of her," Haber said. "We sent her up to Wheeling from Tri-state in July to prep her for the American Derby. Everything worked out perfect."

Magic Penny Ante-2008

RACE 13 GRADE S 670 yards	Thirteenth Race · 09/20/08 · Evening	670 yards GRADE S RACE 13

The 2008 Joseph M. Linsey Memorial $115,000 American Greyhound Derby
Superfecta, Trifecta, Quiniela, Win, Place, & Show Wagering

PP	Event	Trk	Dst	TC	Time	WT	PP	Off	1/8	Str	Fin	ART	Odds	Grade	Comment	Track Record: Rysta, 36.81, 09/06/03

8-1 BAD INFLUENCECAT — 37.93 AA M **70** — LI 17 5 2 4 3
Kennel: Pat Dalton Kennel[5]11%
Owner: John Dalton
Trainer: David O'Keeffe
Brindle, M, Jun 02, 2006, Pacific Mile-Make Me Crazy — $6768.79

Event	Trk	Dst	TC	Time	WT	PP	Off	1/8	Str	Fin	ART	Odds	Grade	Comment	
09/15A15	LI	670	F	36.90	70	3	5	4	4	47½	37.42	99.00	SAA	Steady Effort Mdtrk	LovlySoni FlyingMncn MgcPnnyAnt
09/10A2	LI	670	F	37.93	68½	4	5	3	2	12	37.93	24.00	SA	Bmpd Kept Driving	URockMyWorld RssmrAlth VnOnThRn
09/06A12	LI	670	F	37.59	70	7	5	12	1½	32½	37.75	9.40	SA	Outfinished Mdtrk	BWGTaxAdit NoMoreLoving NSLaila7
09/01L9	LI	670	F	37.74	69	4	2	3	3	45	38.08	13.60	SA	Steady Effort Mdtrk	FlyingMncini WWsAtlntic AHsCorl
08/23E15	LI	670	F	38.18	69	3	5	2	2	1nk	38.18	5.50	TBB	Driving Up Near Wire	RdeAwakning OncoFxPs SmoothCiro
08/20A15	LI	670	F	37.58	71½	2	8	4	3	33½	37.83	6.40	TBB	Good Effort Mdtrk	MkinChilli HrdLovingWomn AHsCrl
08/16A2	LI	670	F	37.62	71	7	6	3	3	56½	38.06	3.20	TBB	Early Speed Mdtrk	NSLaila HardLovingWoman AHsCorl
08/11A8	LI	550	F	30.16	71	6	7	7	5	36	30.58	4.10	BB	Coll 1st Stdy Gain	ContryPosy StrzDonld BohminOtlw
08/08A11	LI	550	F	30.28	71½	4	6	5	3	33	30.48	13.60	BB	Gained Steadily	FavorSeeker DlsMjor RooftopCili
08/01A14	LI	550	F	30.22	71	5	7	7	5	29½	30.87	7.70	BB	Dspt Trouble Mdtrk	SierraWay PalsSargnt LovrBoyJon7
07/26A1	LI	550	F	30.10	71	4	8	3	3	1½	30.10	5.70	B	Driving Up Nr Wire	ChmrTigry DkotsRmbo FlyngPrncss
07/19A1	LI	550	F	30.32	70	5	8	5	3	2½	30.37	9.80	B	Coming On Late Mdtk	BDsHarper JoInn Sibbeston

1 Red

3-1 ROSSMORE ALTHIA — 37.03 AA M **62** — LI 18 7 2 3 1
Kennel: Kerry Hills Kennel[11]12%
Owner: Kerry Hills Kennel
Trainer: Steve Haenel
Red, F, Oct 02, 2006, Dodgem By Design-Oneco Mariacalas — $8304.81

Event	Trk	Dst	TC	Time	WT	PP	Off	1/8	Str	Fin	ART	Odds	Grade	Comment	
09/15A2	LI	670	F	37.21	62	4	1	11½	11	11	37.21	1.00·	SAA	Held Gamely Inside	BrnJohn ContryLk FlyingNorthprt6
09/10A2	LI	670	F	37.93	60½	1	2	2	3	32½	38.09	1.30·	SAA	Led Erly Gave Chase	BdInflncct URockMyWrld VnOnThRn
09/06A15	LI	670	F	37.41	62	3	1	3	3	2½	37.50	5.20	SAA	Made Up Ground Str	LovlySoni WWsAtlntic StrzCynthi
09/01A4	LI	670	F	37.66	61	6	1	12	12	13½	37.66	8.40	SA	Never Headed Inside	SnsandSpphir URockMyWorld IcLdy
08/27A4	LI	670	F	38.06	61½	6	4	7	5	412	38.89	2.50·	TA	Trbl Twice Early	TKHotRod KpsCrlysimon MkinChill
08/18A9	LI	550	F	29.95	61½	7	4	8	7	68½	30.56	11.10	AA	Blocked 1st Turn	RossmrPlyby Lthlcnvctn RmrdEzWn
08/15S1	LI	550	F	30.69	61½	2	4	3	3	23½	30.94	---		Gave Chase Mdtrk	GreysRoyalOak TippViolt RCBigBn7
08/01A15	LI	670	F	37.20	61	4	5	7	7	714	38.18	11.70	AA	Crowded After Break	LovelySoni ContryRodo DKStvMson
07/25E2	LI	670	F	37.03	61	1	1	12	11½	11½	37.03	1.90·	SA	Box To Wire Inside	SlashNCash AHsCoral OkgoBreakot
07/18E12	LI	670	F	37.48	61	6	7	8	8	819	38.82	4.00	SA	No Factor	LovelySonia MeBoss ContryRodeo
07/12A2	LI	670	F	37.40	61	3	1	15	15	17½	37.40	5.10	TBB	Never In Doubt Mdtk	RgllBowFlx OkgBrkt FlyngNrthprt
07/05E15	LI	670	F	38.19	61	7	6	7	7	718½	39.49	5.20	TBB	No Room Shutoff	WhtATroopr ICUWldThng MsUnrlyOr

2 Blue

12-1 BWG TAX AUDIT — 37.39 AA M **57** — LI 42 7 5 10 3 / LI 64 10 7 8 16
Kennel: Kerry Hills Kennel[11]12%
Owner: Big Water Greyhounds
Trainer: Steve Haenel
Red, F, Apr 15, 2005, Dodgem By Design-Ifb Slam N Natle — $16065.36

Event	Trk	Dst	TC	Time	WT	PP	Off	1/8	Str	Fin	ART	Odds	Grade	Comment	
09/15A12	LI	670	F	37.08	58½	7	6	7	6	616½	38.25	5.10	SAA	Coll Ent Front Str	NoMoreLoving BNSBea WWsAtlantic
09/10A15	LI	670	F	37.45	57	4	1	7	8	69½	38.12	13.30	SAA	Erly Spd Bmpd Turn	FlyingNorthport LovlySoni BNSB
09/06A12	LI	670	F	37.59	58	6	2	2	2	12	37.59	5.20	SAA	Led Erly Came Again	NoMoreLoving BadInflncct NSLil7
09/01A9	LI	670	F	37.63	57	1	1	15	18	18	37.63	5.00	SAA	All The Way Mdtrk	RogeCorleone StrtCrdit AnglTrri
08/22A6	LI	670	F	37.91	58	3	4	8	8	820	39.32	3.00	TAA	Jammed Erly Stumbld	FlyingNorthprt CntryLk VnOnThRn
08/16A9	LI	670	F	37.39	56½	2	1	13	15	16½	37.39	10.10	TA	Easy Win Drew Away	MeBoss RogeCorleone BernJohn
08/11A2	LI	670	F	38.37	57½	8	6	6	6	59	39.01	3.40	TA	Bumped Crtn Turn	DrivenLee AHsCorl HrdLovingWomn
08/06A15	LI	670	F	37.71	58½	4	6	5	4	57	38.19	14.40	SA	Crowded Crtn Turn	SobeOkiePolie SlashNCash Baton
08/01A4	LI	670	F	37.47	58	2	1	12	18	112½	37.47	3.70	TBB	Alone & Extending	WhenInRom KpsCrlysimon KpsMstng
07/26L4	LI	670	F	37.62	56½	2	2	2	11½	11½	37.62	3.40·	TB	Led Far Turn Mdtrk	KpsMstng ICUWildThng AljDntBlnk
07/19E15	LI	670	F	38.62	57½	8	2	6	5	35	38.98	1.80·	B	Wd Erly Stdy Gain	WhnInRom SmoothCiro RcsJbbinJms
07/16A2	LI	670	F	38.13	57	2	4	5	4	32½	38.29	4.50	TB	Closed Gap Mdtrk	IcLdy AljoDontBlink HrdLovngWmn

3 White

9-5 LOVELY SONIA — 36.90 AA M **61** — LI 42 24 7 1 3 / LI 13 5 1 2 0
Kennel: DQ Williams Kennel[18]16%
Owner: DQ Williams Kennel
Trainer: Graydon Robtoy
Red, F, Apr 12, 2006, Teamster-Let's Run To Win — $39510.20

Event	Trk	Dst	TC	Time	WT	PP	Off	1/8	Str	Fin	ART	Odds	Grade	Comment	
09/15A15	LI	670	F	36.90	61½	2	1	12	13½	16	36.90	0.80·	SAA	Quick Pace Extending	FlyngMncn MgcPnnyAnt BdInflncct
09/10A15	LI	670	F	37.45	61	2	3	12	12	21	37.52	0.50·	SAA	Set Pace Caught Late	FlyingNorthport BNSB WWsAtlntic
09/06A15	LI	670	F	37.41	62	1	2	12	13	11½	37.41	0.40·	SAA	Best Again Inside	RossmreAlth WWsAtlntc StrzCynth
09/01L4	LI	670	F	37.48	60½	2	1	11	11½	11½	37.48	0.50·	SAA	Withstood Challenge	MagicPennyAnte BNSBe ContryRodo
08/27A12	LI	670	F	37.88	61	2	1	11½	15½	16½	37.88	0.90·	SAA	Quick Start Drw Away	VaneOnTheRn NSLaila ExpensivPrl
08/22A15	LI	670	F	37.89	61½	6	2	2	2	12	37.89	0.80·	SAA	Determined Drive Mtk	BNSBea OkgoStinger ContryRodeo
08/16L9	LI	670	F	37.47	61	3	1	15	18	17½	37.47	1.60·	TAA	Never A Doubt Inside	DrivenLee BNSBea HaysBravo
08/09E12	LI	670	F	37.47	61	7	2	11	14	16	37.47	0.50·	SAA	Took Command In Bks	ChMrOlton FlyingNorthprt RgCrln6
08/01A15	LI	670	F	37.20	61½	1	1	14	14	14	37.20	1.10·	AA	Wire To Wire Inside	ContryRodeo DKStvMson RogCorlon
07/25E9	LI	670	F	37.52	61½	7	4	5	5	54	37.79	1.10·	SAA	Slight Bump Early	ContryRodeo NSLaila SobeOkiPoli
07/18E12	LI	670	F	37.48	61	3	1	16	18	17½	37.48	1.30·	SAA	Won With Ease Ins	MeBoss ContryRodeo ICUMarvelUs
07/12L9	LI	670	F	37.64	61	7	2	16	15	14	37.64	1.10·	SAA	Sprinted Away Early	ContryRodeo NSLaila MeBoss

4 Green

SELECTIONS: 4-7-2-5	2nd Half Of The Derby Double, 3rd Leg Of The Derby Pick 3	RHODY: 4-7-2-1

Magic Penny Ante-2008

RACE 13 GRADE S 670 yards | **Thirteenth Race - 09/20/08 - Evening** | **670 yards GRADE S RACE 13**

The 2008 Joseph M. Linsey Memorial $115, 000 American Greyhound Derby
Superfecta, Trifecta, Quiniela, Win, Place, & Show Wagering

Track Record: Rysta, 36.81, 09/06/03

5 — NO MORE LOVING (10-1, Black)

37.08 AA M **71** | LI 45 12 7 7 3 | LI 42 12 6 4 1 | $ 19579.74

White & Black, M, Jun 17, 2004, Flying Penske-Gather Em Up

Kennel: DQ Williams Kennel[18]16%
Owner: Sharon L. Williams
Trainer: Graydon Robtoy

Event	Trk	Dst	TC	Time	WT	PP	Off	1/8	Str	Fin	ART	Odds	Grade	Comment	
09/15 A12	LI	670	F	37.08	71	6	2	1 4½	1 5	1 7¾	37.08	5.60	SAA	Full Command Inside	BNSBea WWsAtlantic ChasenTail
09/10 A9	LI	670	F	37.83	71½	3	3	6	6	3 ½	37.87	3.70	SAA	Gaining In Str Mdtk	StarzSprm KpsCrlysimon AnglTrri
09/06 A12	LI	670	F	37.59	71	5	1	4	4	2 2	37.74	8.00	SAA	Made Up Ground Str	BWGTaxAdit BadInflencecat NSLil7
09/01 A9	LI	670	F	37.63	70	8	2	6	6	6 17½	38.86	2.20	SAA	Erly Spd Knckd Back	BWGTaxAdit RogeCorlon StrtCrdit
08/27 A9	LI	670	F	38.04	71	3	5	5	5	3 9	38.67	3.30	SAA	Bmpd Gd Effort Ins	AHsCorl URockMyWorld ContryRodo
08/20 A9	LI	550	F	30.04	72½	1	2	8	7	7 11½	30.83	1.10•	AA	Close Qtrs 1st Trn	BllymcFlight* BDsHvn RooftopEnc
08/15 A9	LI	550	F	30.05	71	4	8	4	4	2 7	30.55	2.20•	AA	Beneftd Gained Place	RossmrPlyby StrzMgrn Lthlcnvctn
08/08 A14	LI	550	F	29.88	71	4	1	1 2	1 3	1 5	29.88	3.80	AA	Easy Win On Inside	YnkdoodlDg UcmHldntght StrzMgrn
08/02 L4	LI	550	F	30.10	72	1	1	1 3½	1 3	1 3½	30.10	0.40•	A	Wire To Wire Inside	SnsandSapphire MDJet StrzCnShin
07/28 A9	LI	550	F	30.27	71½	5	5	8	7	7 9	30.89	6.40	AA	Crwd Bmpd 1st Trn	RlphSlmmr UcmHldntght Lthlcnvctn
07/19 E9	LI	550	F	30.76	72½	6	4	7	6	5 8½	31.35	6.80	SAA	Faded Back Early	TalkProsper Hmara BDsHerby
07/14 A12	LI	550	F	30.31	72	7	6	8	8	8 10½	31.04	7.40	SAA	Slight Bump Turn	Hmara DKSteveMason TalkProsper

6 — FLYING MANCINI (6-1, Yellow)

37.74 AA AA **60** | LI 4 1 2 0 0 | WD 1 0 0 0 0 | $ 1816.65

Red Brindle, F, Oct 03, 2006, Kiowa Sweet Trey-Gable Acadia

Kennel: EP's Kennel LLC.[16]12%
Owner: Vince Berland
Trainer: Doris Benedetti

Event	Trk	Dst	TC	Time	WT	PP	Off	1/8	Str	Fin	ART	Odds	Grade	Comment	
09/15 A15	LI	670	F	36.90	61	1	2	2	2	2 6	37.33	4.40	SAA	Erly Thrt Next Best	LovlySoni MgcPnnyAnt BdInflncct
09/10 A4	LI	670	F	38.07	60	4	8	7	7	6 10½	38.81	3.90	SAA	Rough Trip Early	MagicPennyAnt BrnJohn ChMrDlton
09/06 A4	LI	670	F	37.60	61	3	3	2	1 1½	2 1	37.66	1.30•	SAA	Overtkn Late Inside	ChasenTail MeBoss LittleCpcake
09/01 L9	LI	670	F	37.74	58½	3	3	1 5	1 4	1 ns	37.74	2.80•	SAA	Sprinted Away Early	WWsAtlantic AHsCoral BdInflncct
08/27 S1	LI	670	F	37.97	58½	3	3	2	2	2 3	38.17	---		Gave Chase On Inside	StreetCredit BigfootsBst 3
08/16 A18	WD	548	F	30.11	59	3	6	7	6	5 10½	30.83	1.80	A	Little Change, Mdtk	KyVArrington BrtsEminnc JckSlck
08/11 S1	WD	548	F	30.37	59½	8	5	1 ½	2	1 2½	30.37	--- •		Refused To Lose	MakinBakin Shadowy JdJohnBoy
07/19 E10	WS	550	F	29.82	60	6	2	1 1	1 3	1 12	29.82	2.20	SA	Ks Bred Sprint Champ	OddSimca IDReqired DtchViking
07/14 A7	WS	550	F	29.82	59½	5	1	1 6	1 8	1 9	29.82	1.40•	SA	Grabbed Lead 1st,mid	KSBdgirlGinny SntnSwtTry IDRqrd7
07/10 A10	WS	550	F	30.30	60½	5	6	5	4	4 3½	30.55	1.00•	SA	Blocked Esc Gain,mid	SantanSweetTry DtchViking BHsKL
07/07 A10	WS	550	F	30.19	60½	8	5	1 2	1 3	1 6½	30.19	1.60•	SA	Dominated Field Mid	Clemency IDReqired DtchViking

7 — MAGIC PENNY ANTE (5-1, Grn/Wht)

37.34 AA AA **62** | LI 4 2 1 1 0 | LI 5 1 2 0 0 | $ 3023.67

Black, F, Aug 10, 2005, Ben Awhile-Snookered

Kennel: Kerry Hills Kennel[11]12%
Owner: Haber Kennels. INC.
Trainer: Steve Haenel

Event	Trk	Dst	TC	Time	WT	PP	Off	1/8	Str	Fin	ART	Odds	Grade	Comment	
09/15 A15	LI	670	F	36.90	63	4	3	3	3	3 6½	37.37	3.70	SAA	Saved Ground In Bks	LovlySoni FlyingMncn BdInflncct
09/10 A4	LI	670	F	38.07	61	7	5	2	2	1 ns	38.07	1.90•	SAA	Ran Down Leader Mdtk	BernJohn CheMarDalton NSLaila
09/06 A2	LI	670	F	37.34	62	3	2	1 7	1 8	1 8	37.34	0.60•	SAA	Never In Doubt Mdtk	KpsCrlysimon TKHotRod MkinChill7
09/01 L4	LI	670	F	37.48	61	4	2	2	2	2 1½	37.59	9.20	SAA	Tried Hard Next Best	LovelySonia BNSBea ContryRodeo
08/27 S2	LI	670	F	38.26	62½	6	2	2	2	2 2	38.41	---		In Pursuit Mdtrck	StarzSpreme AngelTerri 3
08/17 A15	WD	678	F	37.92	62	4	1	1 2	1 2	2 2½	38.08	4.10	AA	Long Lead- Caught	TkQickStrike BraskaKato Creednc
08/13 A13	WD	678	F	37.88	62	4	2	3	3	7 7	38.38	4.80	AA	No Stretch Speed	McsStdyddi TkQckStrk WwsBmbBlst
08/09 A13	WD	678	F	38.38	62	8	5	4	3	3 10	39.07	1.30•	AA	Advanced For Show	KyVKpWt WwsBombBlst GrysMystcrs
08/03 A13	WD	678	F	37.93	62	1	1	1 2	1 ½	1 ½	37.93	0.50•	AA	Held Advantage	KiowaPowerPk KyVKpWt FtkOvrhlin
07/30 A13	WD	678	F	37.96	61½	1	2	1 4	1 5	1 3	37.96	0.80•	AA	Easy Striding, Ins	BowWorkrond FlyingWhling MrlSns
07/25 S1	WD	548	F	29.89	63	5	3	1 3	1 4	1 11	29.89	---		Pulled Far Away	MariaGalante MrlElctr PrimcoMys7
09/24 A4	LI	670	F	37.52	61½	8	6	7	8	8 12½	38.40	3.20	SAA	Bmpd Wd Aftr Break	BnsJimboDi TKRocktMn BNSBbyGirl

8 — CHASEN TAIL (6-1, Yel/Blk)

37.28 AA BB **76** | LI 42 10 3 6 8 | MG 32 21 3 2 2 | $ 19066.81

Red, M, Feb 26, 2005, Golddust Memory-Talk N Doing

Kennel: DQ Williams Kennel[18]16%
Owner: DQ Williams Kennel
Trainer: Graydon Robtoy

Event	Trk	Dst	TC	Time	WT	PP	Off	1/8	Str	Fin	ART	Odds	Grade	Comment	
09/15 A12	LI	670	F	37.08	75½	4	5	5	4	4 10½	37.81	2.90•	SAA	Blocked Aftr Break	NoMoreLoving BNSBea WWsAtlantic
09/10 A9	LI	670	F	37.83	76½	8	7	4	4	8 5	38.17	2.30•	SAA	Shutoff Ent Stretch	StrzSprm KpsCrlysimon NoMorLvng
09/06 A4	LI	670	F	37.60	76	1	1	3	2	1 1	37.60	1.50	SAA	Ran Down Leader Outs	FlyingMancini MeBoss LittleCpck
09/01 L2	LI	670	F	37.45	75	1	1	1 6	1 8	1 9	37.45	1.90•	SA	Never In Doubt Mdtk	ContryLke SpeedSign* MeBoss
08/22 E12	LI	550	F	30.30	77	2	4	5	6	6 11½	31.09	11.10	AA	Bumped Ent Bkstrch	OncoGldTch RCKIntmdtr WWsAtlntc
08/16 E4	LI	550	F	30.15	76½	3	6	5	5	5 8	30.72	5.00	AA	Bumped 1st Turn	RCKIntimidator MDJet FloFelt
08/11 L2	LI	550	F	30.09	76	1	1	1 2	1 1½	1 1½	30.09	1.50•	A	Never Headed Mdtrk	DakotasSlim SesHomeFr SvMyMints
08/08 A9	LI	550	F	29.83	76½	8	7	5	4	4 5½	30.20	4.10	A	Blckd Early Evenly	PrimcoMck RossmorSofi DkotsSlim
08/01 E12	LI	550	F	30.75	75	6	3	3	3	2 3	30.97	10.50	A	Stretch Gain Mdtrk	HysBrvo RgllDiddlr RooftopWrght
07/26 L9	LI	550	F	29.92	75	1	6	8	8	8 15	30.96	1.80•	AA	Crwd 1st Collided	OaklandBelle RogeLcaBrsi BigEgo
07/18 E12	LI	670	F	37.48	76	5	6	5	7	7 17½	38.71	4.40	SAA	No Real Threat	LovelySonia MeBoss ContryRodeo
07/12 L9	LI	670	F	37.64	73	6	7	5	5	6 10½	38.39	45.90	SAA	Wide Early Evenly	LovelySonia ContryRodeo NSLaila

SELECTIONS: 4-7-2-5 | **2nd Half Of The Derby Double, 3rd Leg Of The Derby Pick 3** | **RHODY: 4-7-2-1**

The Mardi Gras Years
(2012-????)

???-2012

The American Greyhound Derby will return in the winter of 2012 to be run at its new home the **Mardi Gras Racetrack and Casino** in Hallandale Beach, Florida. Make your plans to see this classic event live as the *"Run for the Orchids"* will be staged for the first time ever in the state of Florida.

Mardi Gras Racetrack And Casino the New Home of

The American Greyhound Derby

Made in the USA
Lexington, KY
11 December 2011